Intervention
and
Detachment

ALSO BY G. EDWARD WHITE

The Eastern Establishment and the Western Experience (1968)
The American Judicial Tradition (1976) (Expanded Ed., 1988)
Patterns of American Legal Thought (1978)
Tort Law in America: An Intellectual History (1980)
Earl Warren: A Public Life (1982)
The Marshall Court and Cultural Change (1988)
Justice Oliver Wendell Holmes: Law and the Inner Self (1993)

INTERVENTION AND DETACHMENT

Essays in Legal History and Jurisprudence

G. EDWARD WHITE

New York   Oxford
OXFORD UNIVERSITY PRESS
1994

Oxford University Press

Oxford   New York   Toronto
Delhi   Bombay   Calcutta   Madras   Karachi
Kuala Lumpur   Singapore   Hong Kong   Tokyo
Nairobi   Dar es Salaam   Cape Town
Melbourne   Auckland   Madrid

and associated companies in
Berlin   Ibadan

Copyright © 1994 by Oxford University Press, Inc.

Published by Oxford University Press, Inc.
200 Madison Avenue, New York, New York 10016

Oxford is a registered trademark of Oxford University Press

Library of Congress Cataloging-in-Publication Data
White, G. Edward.
Intervention and detachment :
essays in legal history and jurisprudence /
G. Edward White.
p.   cm.   Includes index.
ISBN 0-19-508495-0 (cloth)
ISBN 0-19-508496-9 (pbk.)
1. Jurisprudence—United States—History.
2. Law—United States—History.
I. Title.   KF379.W54   1994
349.73—dc20   [347.3]   93-14629

2 4 6 8 9 7 5 3 1

Printed in the United States of America
on acid-free paper

For
Frances McCafferty White
Alexandra White-Ritchie

Preface

The essays in this book appeared between 1979 and 1988, and consequently this volume represents something of a sequel to my 1978 collection of essays, *Patterns of American Legal Thought,* although its emphasis is quite different.

As was the case with the *Patterns* collection, this volume seeks to provide scholars and students who lack easy access to law journals with a reference for research and classroom use. It also seeks to gather in one place discussions of several substantive and methodological issues that are of current interest for students of American legal history and jurisprudence. While my treatment of those issues necessarily reflects one person's perspective, I have included references to other relevant scholarship in the notes to the essays. My hope is that as a consequence this volume might function for some students as an introduction to the fields of American legal history and jurisprudence. It also provides material for more specialized discussion of the substantive and methodological topics it addresses.

I am indebted to several people for the appearance of this book. The first group I decline to single out by name lest they inadvertently be identified with the views expressed in the volume: the numerous members of non-law school faculties who have encouraged me to make my law journal essays more accessible to people in colleges and universities without law libraries. There are few things more encouraging to this author than to receive unsolicited communications from people who have not only read his work but apparently profited from it. In addition, Kimberly Willoughby of the class of 1994 at Virginia Law School deserves considerable credit for her editorial assistance, which included giving me a sense of which of my recent essays might (and might not) appeal to students. Thanks also to William Rolleston-Daines for his help in readying the book for production and for preparing the index.

The dedication singles out two members of my family who share my interest in books and ideas. It is a pleasure to recognize Alexandra White-Ritchie on the occasion of her marriage and Frances White in her ninetieth year. The two share an ability to put others' concerns before their own and a capacity to extract fun from life. In order not to distract from their recognition, I will spare readers the usual account of the comings and goings of other humans and animals in the White family, an update of which the insatiable reader can find in *Justice Oliver*

Wendell Holmes: Law and the Inner Self, which recently appeared from the same publisher.

Previous versions of the essays in this volume appeared in the *Arkansas Law Review,* the *Capitol University Law Review,* the *Harvard Law Review,* the *Hofstra Law Review, Judicature,* the *Law and History Review,* the *Michigan Law Review,* the *Southwestern Law Journal,* the *Stanford Law Review,* the *Suffolk Law Review,* the *Texas Law Review,* and the *William and Mary Law Review.* Some minor differences in footnoting style that reflect the tastes of these separate reviews have been retained in this collection.

Charlottesville, Va.   G.E.W.
July 1993

Contents

Introduction, 3

PART I DOING HISTORY: METHODOLOGY

Truth and Interpretation in Legal History, 17

The Text, Interpretation, and Critical Standards, 35

The Art of Revising History: Revisiting the Marshall Court, 50

PART II DOING HISTORY: PRACTICE

The Integrity of Holmes' Jurisprudence, 75

Looking at Holmes in the Mirror, 106

Revisiting the New Deal Legal Generation, 132

Felix Frankfurter, the Old Boy Network, and the New Deal: The Placement of Elite Lawyers in Public Service in the 1930s, 149

Recapturing New Deal Lawyers, 175

PART III JUDICIAL REVIEW

Reflections on the Role of the Supreme Court: The Contemporary Debate and the "Lessons" of History, 207

Judicial Activism and the Identity of the Legal Profession, 222

Chief Justice Marshall, Justice Holmes, and the Discourse of
Constitutional Adjudication, 238

PART IV THE POLITICS OF JURISPRUDENCE

The Inevitability of Critical Legal Studies, 255

From Realism to Critical Legal Studies: A Truncated Intellectual History, 274

Conclusion, 299

Index, 303

Intervention
and
Detachment

Introduction

The most obvious difference between the essays in this volume and those in my 1978 collection, *Patterns of American Legal Thought,* is that the earlier essays are, for the most part, unreflective about their methodological orientation. In introductory portions of *Patterns of Legal Thought* I commented on the implicit methodological perspective exhibited by some essays, but that was after the fact: in writing the essays themselves I was more concerned with "doing" history than with exploring the implications of a given historiographical perspective.

The latter concern has been a central theme of the essays in this volume. Indeed the organizing theme of the volume, as its title suggests, has been an inquiry into the process by which a person whose scholarship concerns the past "intervenes" in the debates with which he or she comes to be engaged in the present. In looking over the essays collected here I have concluded that my form of intervention in contemporary debates has been to marshal evidence that suggests those debates can be viewed with "detachment."

Let me say more precisely what I mean by the terms intervention and detachment. The theory of historical writing that I hold, which is set forth in detail in some of the essays in this volume, posits that a historian's decison to study a particular segment of the past is never accidental: it is, at one level, a product of presentist concerns. Not only are the historian's choices of historical subject matter affected by the way he or she relates to contemporary culture, the historian's interpretations of the subjects chosen are likewise affected. The act of examining the past is thus a form of intervention, in which the historian brings a contemporary perspective to bear on the subjects of a past time, and necessarily casts those subjects in a different light.

Here the first of the professional quandries inherent in writing history surfaces. There is a well-established difference between history and fiction. There is an equally well-established, if perhaps less clear-cut, difference between history and polemics. If historical scholarship is primarily motivated by presentist concerns, how does the historian prevent those concerns from overwhelming historical subject matter? Or, put another way, why should it matter if they did? While generations of historians have wrestled with those questions, their answers have been remarkably similar: when the concerns of the present overwhelm the materials of the past, history ceases to exist.

Thus along with the impulse to intervene a historian struggles with another impulse, the impulse to achieve detachment. In this initial meaning of the term, detachment refers to a distancing of the historian from the presentist concerns that impelled him or her to seek out a particular subject from the past for study. As a professional goal, detachment in this sense requires that distancing: it requires an immersion by the historian in the mores and thought patterns of an alien culture. Only with this sort of detachment from one's subject, the historical profession assumes, is one able to produce history, as distinct from fiction or polemics. The production of historical scholarship thus is assumed to require a certain suspension of belief on the part of the historian, rendered in the conventional phrase of "taking the past on its own terms."

Detachment in the sense in which I have used it above is a widely held canon of historical scholarship, so widely held that the impulses to intervene that accompany it are often not discussed as part of a description of the process of historical scholarship. I am seeking to suggest in this volume that the two impulses need to be paired more openly and the complex relationship between them better understood. I am arguing that the search for detachment invariably takes place in the face of interventionist impulses; that those impulses are more important in generating historical scholarship than has been recognized; and that complete detachment, in the form of the historical profession's traditional canon of "objectivity," is an impossibility. One of the purposes of this collection of essays is thus to explore the tension between intervention and detachment as I have thus far defined those terms.

There is, however, a second level at which intervention and detachment operate in the process of historical scholarship. History is not written in a vacuum: it is written to be read by others, and, one hopes, to influence others. It is written to intervene in contemporary life. This dimension of historical scholarship is widely sensed, but rarely stated categorically, for reasons I will subsequently discuss. Consider the phenomenon of varying treatment, over time, of certain historical subjects. Until the 1950s the history of black Americans was largely "invisible" within the corpus of mainstream scholarship; beginning in the 1960s came a ground swell of monographs on individuals and subjects related to the heritage of Afro-Americans. A similar "invisibility" existed for women as historical subjects until the 1970s; a comparable explosion of "women's history" has occurred since that decade. The 1990s version of this phenomenon is the history of homosexual sexual preferences in the United States. In the last decade it has come to be regarded as "interesting" and "relevant" to discuss such preferences in studies of the lives of historical figures; very recently signs have appeared that point to a "discovery" and rewriting of the history of sexual preferences themselves. Each of these "waves" of historical scholarship can be linked to the emergence, in presentist culture, of issues directly affecting the subjects under historical consideration. In this sense the "rediscovery" of previously "invisible" subjects becomes a form of legitimating the stature of those subjects in the present, a form of intervention.

The intervention just described might seem at first to be quite different from that previously discussed in connection with a historian's original motivation to pursue given historical subjects. In its first sense intervention seems highly personal; in its second sense directed at influencing others. Yet the two interventionist impulses are, of course, intimately connected. Just as one goes to the past looking, at one level, to "find" something, one communicates one's findings back to the present because one wants them to be treated as important and authoritative. It is difficult to separate the impulse to "rediscover" a "lost" historical subject, which the present has invested with a heightened significance, for the impulse to communicate one's "discovery" so the subject can be taken as having gained stature from now having a "history."

At this point a second professional quandry for the historian surfaces. Just as historians are socialized not to allow their interpretations of past subjects to so overwhelm those subjects as to strip them of their sense of place, historians are socialized not to let presentist concerns "distort" their rendering of the past. Interpretations that are too congenial with presentist perspectives are treated as reifications: polemics or fiction rather than "history." Such interpretations smack of "bias" and "presentism" and offend the canon of objectivity. Detachment is also valued here: detachment in the sense of distance not only from the past but from the present. The former version of detachment is what gives a historian "perspective"; the latter form bestows legitimacy.

But the second version of detachment appears to run squarely up against intervention, or at least turn intervention into an ironic stance. As an example, consider my two essays, included in this volume, on the Critical Legal Studies movement. Let us assume something that was not the case, that I was motivated to write those essays because of my enthusiasm for Critical Legal Studies as a jurisprudential perspective. I wanted to "discover" the origins and development of Critical thought; I wanted to supply the movement with a "history" in order to give it legitimacy. I wanted, in short, to intervene.

Assume further that the course of my research took me in the same direction revealed by my essays: I found that Critical Legal Studies was in a "tradition" of twentieth-century jurisprudential "reform movements," bearing a relationship to Sociological Jurisprudence, Realism, and the Law and Society movement. While such a "history" served to legitimate Critical Legal Studies, it also arguably served to undermine the movement's claims to be a truly revolutionary phenomenon. In addition, when one learns that all the previous reform movements ended by being absorbed into "mainstream" legal thought and over time losing their reformist thrust and perhaps even their identity, the "history" tends to deflate and constrain the contemporary ambitions of the Critical Legal Studies movement.

One could argue that those findings about Critical Legal Studies were a product of "detachment," a perspective on the earlier reform movements generated by distance and a certain indifference to the "fate" of those movements. But if that detachment were carried over into the present, the results would be inconsistent, in this hypothetical scenario, with my original motivation to intervene. I would have started on the project seeking to legitimate Critical Legal Studies as a movement of great jurisprudential promise and ended up implicitly predicting its future demise.

This is the point where the historian's impulses toward intervention and detachment clash most openly. To choose to reframe the "history" of Critical Legal Studies—so as to show, for example, that Critical thought has sufficient power and uniqueness to resist being co-opted by mainstream ideologies—would violate the prerequisite of detachment, resulting in fiction or polemics being produced instead of history. To carry over the "detached" posture of the investigator of past subjects into the political universe of the present, however, would be to offer a response to current participants in that universe that appears profoundly unsatisfying. When one holds current enthusiasms with great passion it is hardly energizing to be told they will all wash out in time. There is little solace in being told at the same time that the ideologies of the enemy will likewise wash out. Detachment, at some level, is not very compatible with intervention, or generates the kind of interventions that enthusiasts don't welcome.

Nonetheless I maintain in this volume that this tradeoff between intervention and detachment constitutes the central challenge of historical scholarship. The challenge, my essays suggest, takes place on two levels. One is the level of epistemology, where the historian tries to fashion a stance that rejects objectivity as illusory and at the same time distinguishes between history and fiction or polemics. The other is the level of politics, where I argue that the only stance the historian can properly offer is that of detachment, which is a form of intervention. In my own work I have sought out subjects I have been engaged with, and I have tried to rewrite the "history" of such subjects. At the same time I have sought out subjects for which, from the onset of my work, I could maintain a certain form of detachment. I have found that if I were not too passionately involved in the present implications of my subjects, or with them as personalities, that I could add to the perspective I achieve from cultural distance a certain perspective from ideological or psychological distance. I do not offer this as a formula for others, but I do think that in the end the historian's impulse to intervene must not overwhelm detachment.

Perhaps the most precise way in which I can describe the relationship between intervention and detachment in historical scholarship is as a paradox. The historian begins his or her inquiries by caring passionately about what happened in some portion of the past. But that engagement, if the historian's intervention in scholarship about that subject is to be effective, must be sublimated in a larger stance of detachment. Sublimated, but not overwhelmed: the paradox is that the most effective interventions are those that retain elements of the historian's initial passion. Thus if the role of detachment is properly understood, the historian may come to learn that such a stance can precipitate the birth of creative, influential scholarship.

The groups of essays collected in this book explore various features of the above paradox. The first group deals with the paradox at its most abstract levels, exploring the roles of "truth" and "interpretation" in legal history; the "text," "interpretations" of texts, and "critical standards" for scholarly performance; and the nature and process of historical "revisionism." All three essays start from the same methodological "place," a professional universe in which the substantive orientations of the historian and of "communities" that evaluate scholarship are assumed to be significant influences on the kind of scholarship that is produced and the kind of scholarship regarded as meritorious. The question raised by this assumption is whether anything is left of conventional scholarly evaluation: how can one tell "good" work from other work? The essays suggest that despite the importance of interpretive communities in shaping the reception of historical works, there remains a kernel of source material—variously termed the "text" or the historical "record"—that resists being overwhelmed by interpretations. The complex interaction between "text" or "record," the intepretations advanced by individual scholars, and the scholarly communities that receive those interpretations, these essays argue, takes us to the center of the processes of historical and historiographical evaluation.

The next group of essays deals more concretely, and less self-consciously, with particular historical topics. Two general subjects are the focus of the second set of essays: the career of Justice Oliver Wendell Holmes and the generation of elite lawyers who entered private practice and public service at the time of the New Deal. The choice of subjects reflects projects I have been recently working on, my just-completed book, *Justice Oliver Wendell Holmes: Law and the Inner Self,* and a book in progress, *Law and the New Deal: A Cultural History.* Readers may be primarily interested in the essays as substantive historical contributions. They nonetheless reflect my growing interest over the past years in the relationship between the perspectives of historians and their choice of subjects. The Holmes essays, when compared with earlier work,[1] reveal my changing attitude toward Holmes as well as my interest in emphasizing different features of his life and career at different periods. The three New Deal essays, written closer together in time, illustrate my sense that by the late 1980s it was possible to achieve detachment on the New Deal, and thus to write about its actors not as heroes or villains but as actors in a distinctive culture, a culture that I argue was the first generation to exhibit a fully developed modernist sensibility. A characterization of the New Dealers as modernists raised for me the question whether our newly acquired detachment from them is a signal that the starting epistemological assumptions of contemporary scholarship are now "postmodernist."[2] That question is addressed in the Harvard essay.

The next section consists of essays on judicial review, written over a ten-year period. At first blush the connection between judicial review and the themes previously identified as central to this volume might not seem apparent, and, moreover, my views on judicial review have themselves changed with time. The basic argument of the essays, however, remains constant, and it is an argument premised on the decisive role of history in shaping judicial decisionmaking.

Debates about the role of judicial review in American culture, I believe, have centered around the problem of deriving constraints on decisionmaking by judges. Premodern jurisprudence derived constraints from the nature of law itself. Judging was assumed to be merely an exercise in "law finding," in which the judge simply located and declared the authoritative legal rules and principles that governed a particular case. While the exercise was assumed to require a degree of professional expertise, it was not assumed to be an exercise in creativity. As John Marshall said in *Osborn v. Bank of the United States,* the will of the law was not synonymous with the will of the judge.[3] Since the "will of the law" was authoritative and discernible, judges were constrained by its presence.

As this conception of the nature of law was abandoned in the early twentieth century, jurisprudential theory faced the question of how to constrain judicial decisionmaking in a universe in which judges were regarded as creative and ideological actors. One option could have been to simply acquiesce in the fact of judicial lawmaking, but this option has never been regarded as permissible. The assumption that some constraints on judges are necessary has been a product of the place of the judiciary in the American system of government. That system is premised on democratic theories of sovereignty, but the judicial branch of government has been regarded as "undemocratic" in the sense of not being politically accountable for its decisions. Modern jurisprudence has fastened on the "countermajoritarian difficulty" as the central puzzle for theories of judicial review.

My essays suggest that theories of judicial review that seek to derive constraints on judges from the assumptions of majoritarian democracy misunderstand the nature of those constraints. Such theories assume that the Constitution is primarily a majoritarian document, that the legislative process reflects majoritarian values, and that, in the absence of majoritarian constraints, judging would become an exercise in the naked wielding of power. I argue that those assumptions are misplaced. The historic role for judges in American constitutionalism, I believe, has been "countermajoritarian": the judicial branch was initially conceived as a brake against the demagogic passions that the Framers associated with legislatures and felt threatened the existence of a republic. History suggests that the "countermajoritarian" status of the judiciary was not a "difficulty," but a necessity.

In the universe of modern jurisprudence, however, one could argue that the "countermajoritarian" status of the judiciary necessarily leads to unconstrained decisionmaking by judges, since the set of contraints on judges that the Framers derived from the nature of law have been deemed illusory. My view is that at one level this argument is sound, and at another level it is incomplete. Judicial decisionmaking is necessarily creative and ideological, like other forms of decisionmaking by governmental officials. Nonetheless, constraints on the decisionmaking process of judges exist.

The constraints on judges are not a product of the nature of law or the structure of American institutions, but of expectations about the process of judicial decisonmaking and the tacit role of the public in that process. While judges are for the most part not elected officials, they are expected to be accountable for their decisions. In other branches of government accountability is centered in the political process itself: disappointed or alienated constituents can react to unpopular decisions by voting the decisionmakers out of office. The accountability of the judiciary is centered in the tacit requirement that judges offer published justifications for the results they reach. Not only are the results publicized, the reasoning on which those results are based is offered to the public in the form of opinions.

It is often assumed that the public has no recourse, on being presented with judicial opinions, other than to acquiesce to them. Such an assumption misunderstands the relationship between courts and the public at large. Many judicial decisions require the input of the public to enforce the rules a court declares: an alienated or unpersuaded public can undermine the enforcement process. When the Supreme Court declared, in *Brown v. Board of Education*,[4] that segregation in the public schools was unconstitutional, a number of communities declined to integrate their schools, and continued to do so for the next fifteen years. The eventual formal desegregation of all public schools in the United States came about not simply because the Supreme Court had said it was legally necessary, but because over time the Court's principal justification for eradicating racial seg-regation—that it violated the moral principle that people should not be treated differently on the basis of so arbitrary a characteristic as skin color—was accepted by a majority of Americans. The Court's decision in *Brown,* then, was inseperable from its reasoning process. Only when the Court's reasoning took root was the decision legitimated.

If one recognizes the obligation of judges to ground their decisions on pub-lished justifications, and the ability of the public to "approve" or "disapprove" of those justifications over time, the theory that judges are unconstrained deci-sionmakers because they are not politically accountable seems misplaced. Judges are in fact accountable to the public, just not in the same manner as other branches of government. Because judges are accountable, they are constrained. The con-straints on judges center on the acceptability of the reasons they offer as justifica-tions for the results they reach.

In this view of the process of judicial decisionmaking history, in the sense of the changes in public attitudes produced by time and changes in the larger culture, is the principal source of constraints on judges. Judges are tacitly "bound" to conform their decisions, and their justifications for those decisions, to the "ap-proved" rhetorical arguments of their time and place. When judges exceed the tacit boundaries of "approved" justifications, their decisions do not secure legiti-macy, and are consequently not invested with the authoritative status of "law." Judging, in my view, is thus not a process in which actors holding power impose their views on the public at large; it is a process in which there is an implicit colloquy between judges and the public as to the appropriateness of given judicial decisions and the reasons used to justify those decisions.

Examples of this implicit colloquy playing itself out over time are readily available. Consider the explicit delegitimation of two prior constitutional law deci-sions of the Supreme Court, *Dred Scott v. Sandford*[5] and *Plessy v. Ferguson,*[6] because of the racist assumptions on which those decisions were based. Consider further the tacit delegitimation of a decision such as *Hoyt v. Florida,*[7] in which the Warren Court unanimously upheld a Florida statute excluding women from jury service on the ground that such civic participation was not compatible with the domestic orientation of the female sex, as being grounded on sexist assump-tions now regarded as illegitimate.

Finally, consider the status of *Bowers v. Hardwick,*[8] in which the Burger Court concluded that a state could criminalize consensual adult homosexual conduct sim-ply because the idea of homosexual liaisons was "offensive." That decision, which assumes that homophobia itself is a legitimate ground for criminalizing such conduct, rests on continued public respect for that assumption. Should the assumption that the state may prevent consenting adults from engaging in sexual activity merely because the particular form of the liaison is regarded as "unnatural" to a majority of the public be abandoned, *Bowers* would then appear to be a case resting on one of two equally unacceptable propostions. The first would be that any "unnatural" sexual activity among consenting adults could be prohibited by the state, a proposition that most Americans would regard as sanctioning unacceptable intrusions into the privacy of individuals. The second would be that the right to engage in consensual intimate conduct can be exercised only by persons of a heterosexual persuasion, a proposition for which there seems no justification other than homophobia. In short, should homophobic assumptions become, in the future, as comparably delegitimated as racist or sexist assumptions, the *Bowers* decison would likely be abandoned. The process by which *Dred Scott, Plessy,* and *Hoyt* were delegitimated was ultimately a historical process; the future delegitimation of *Bowers* will likewise be a function of history.

It may be little solace to contemporary opponents of judicial "activism" that in the end all judges are required to conform their justifications to those that the public regards as legitimate. The process, as I have conceived it, concededly allows a fair amount of breathing space for judges to impose their ideological premises on the rest of us, at least in the short run. But in my view the set of constraints I have outlined is all we can fairly expect if we are to retain a governmental system in which judicial review is taken seriously as a countermajoritarian governmental function. We could change the rules and allow Congress to become the final interpreter of the Constitution, or we could pretend that judges only find the law in the nineteenth-century sense. The first solution would radically affect the status of individual rights in America, and it is a little late to revive the second. Those discomfited by the short-range interpretive freedom of judges should take some solace in the suggestion that in the long run American culture gets the judicial decisions that, collectively, it "wants."

The lenses of history can also be turned on the academy: scholarship is no less time bound than judicial opinions or lay politics. Yet the role of scholarship in the twentieth century has been significantly affected by a quite different assumption about its function. As knowledge became secularized in the latter portion of the nineteenth century, and as educational institutions became an index of social mobility, the role of the scholar as "expert" was created, with expertise taking on overtones of neutrality, impartiality, and elite status. Within specialized fields expertise came to be associated with criteria that deemphasized the ideological orientation of the scholar and emphasized criteria, such as "merit," objectivity, and professional training, that suggested that scholarship was largely a neutral exercise. In history this emphasis manifested itself in the canon of objectivity; in legal scholarship it was reflected in an analogous canon, that of analytical reasoning. By the 1950s "approved" conceptions of scholarly work were firmly in place in both disciplines, emphasizing modest, specialized work in which the ideological orientation of the scholar was firmly suppressed.

In the field of law this "approved" conception of scholarship was pervasively and firmly established, so that as late as the close of the 1960s the standard scholarly offering from law professors was a narrowly conceived, "closely reasoned" article free from the taint of any "extralegal" analysis, whether that analysis came from another academic discipline or the larger culture in which legal issues were set. Beginning in the 1970s this "approved" conception of scholarship began to lose stature, and by this writing it has completely collapsed as a scholarly orthodoxy. So complete has been the collapse in fact, that the very sort of scholarship that was taken to be the approved norm for law professors in the 1950s and 1960s now bears a burden of being thought prosaic and insignificant.

An important causal factor in the collapse of the orthodox model of legal scholarship in the past decade has been the emergence of the Critical Legal Studies movement.[9] Together with the Law and Economics movement, Critical Legal Studies has expanded the boundaries of "approved" legal scholarship, emphasizing interdisciplinary approaches and de-emphasizing—one could say ridiculing—conventional analytics. The motivation of many Critical scholars was not so much to establish interdisciplinary research as legitimate as to identify conventional analytics with an ideology—which Critical scholars called liberalism—that suppressed its internal contradictions in order to perpetuate the status quo. "Trashing" of "liberal" scholarship was the first device by which Critical scholars sought to establish their "voice" in scholarly discourse.

My own relationship with the Critical Legal Studies movement in its early stages was complex. Initally some Critical scholars, who had become convinced that a form of intellectual history was an important scholarly project of the movement, reacted against my version of intellectual legal history, describing it as "idealist," by which they meant either insufficiently mindful of the manipulative character of legal rhetoric or insufficiently attentive to the role of materialist forces as causal agents in history.[10] I found this reaction puzzling, as I viewed my work as treating ideas as products of the historical culture in which they were set, including the academic milieu in which they originated, and in that sense significantly limited in their universality or in their power. At the same time I did not find myself particularly sympathetic to the political goals of Critical scholars, regarding myself as far less troubled than they about the elitist character of academic life and of life in general. On the other hand I was heartily supportive of the Critical scholars' attention to the relationship between law and ideas, both in history and contemporary culture, and found their interdisciplinary orientation far more congenial and sophisticated than that of the Law and Economics movement in its early stages.

The result was that I came to take Critical Legal Studies more seriously than some of the other scholars whose works had been singled out for criticism by Critical theorists, and began to give some attention to the origins and nature of the movement itself. The two essays on Critical Legal Studies reflect that interest. Both were written in the mid 1980s, when the polemical influence of Critical Legal Studies was at its height, when a "backlash" in the academy against Critical theorists had not yet emerged, and when many "mainstream" academics remained mystified and troubled about the purposes and goals of Critical Legal Studies.

The essays consider Critical Legal Studies from two vantage points. The Stanford essay sees the Critical Legal Studies movement as another in a successive series of "reform" movements in twentieth-century legal education, and suggests that one of the characteristics of such movements has been to be "absorbed and converted" by legal orthodoxy. Although part of my purpose in characterizing Critical Legal Studies in such terms was to deflate what I felt were the movement's pretensions in claiming to be a radically new intellectual force, the years after the appearance of the essay have to an extent vindicated my prediction. The methodological self-consciousness and interdisciplinary ambition of Critical Legal Studies have become characteristic of legal scholarship generally, and at the same time a mild form of the Critical theorists' assertion that all scholarship is ultimately politics has come to affect appointments and tenure decisions at several law faculties. At the same time Critical Legal Studies, as a movement for radical change within legal education and the legal profession, has had more difficulties gaining a foothold than its early practitioners hoped.

The *Southwestern Law Journal* essay attempted to explain the origins of Critical Legal Studies. In several essays by Critical theorists in the Stanford symposium in which my essay appeared I noticed that the Realist movement of the 1920s and 1930s was claimed as an ancestor of Critical Legal Studies, and I had commented on the "absorption" of Realism into mainstream legal thought after World War II. I wondered whether the lineal descent from Realism to Critical Legal Studies was as straightforward as some Critical theorists suggested, and why Critical theorists would want to claim the Realists as ancestors. The result was the Southwestern essay, in which I identified the Law and Society movement of the 1950s and 1960s as an intellectual "link" between the Realists and the Critical theorists.

In the course of writing the two essays I reflected on the contemporary impact of Critical Legal Studies. I found that I had come to believe, by the mid 1980s, that despite the severe reaction that many legal academics had to the offerings of Critical theorists, and despite the very marginal impact of Critical Legal Studies on other segments of the legal profession, that the emergence of Critical Legal Studies had profoundly changed the culture of elite legal education in America. At this writing I remain convinced in that belief, but I confess it is a little hard to say exactly why, and I am sure that many Critical theorists would find such a conclusion ironically sanguine, given their sense that they remain marginal figures in the academy.

Perhaps the readiest explanation is one that treats the Critical Legal Studies movement as a cultural phenomenon rather than a causative agent. Critical Legal Studies appeared at the time when a class of literature that can be characterized as "postmodernist" had begun to take hold within academic life. In this literature, represented by works as diverse as the *Annaliste* histories, the works of Jacques Derrida, and Thomas Kuhn's *The Structure of Scientific Revolutions,* the significance of cultural and subcultural "mentalities" that placed important limitations on the discourse of ideas was emphasized. The literature can be called "postmodern" in that rather than unequivocally embracing the "new" values and attitudes of the present and seeking to transform the past and future in accordance with those values, it stepped back and observed the process of "modernization" while at the same time being attracted to some of its goals.[11] Modernization itself became seen as a stage in cultural history, a transient, time-bound phenomenon. All human experience, in fact, was regarded as contingent in that respect. This meant, for the Critical theorists, that orthodoxy could be radically transformed, but it also meant that the transformation itself would be a transient one.

In some fashion the epistemological insights of Critical Legal Studies and other "postmodern" scholarship have taken hold in contemporary academic life to an extent far surpassing the political insights of Critical theorists. Thus the contingent nature of belief and belief systems has become an energizing force in contemporary scholarship, but not necessarily one in contemporary politics. This accounts, I believe, for the proliferation of scholarly perspectives and the great difficulty in formulating "universal" standards for meritocratic performance that characterizes contemporary legal academics. It also accounts for the odd success of Critical Legal Studies in an area—definitions of what sorts of scholarship contemporary academics find stimulating, or, more broadly, definitions of what contemporary academics seek to give a priority in their professional lives—that probably was not among the areas singled out for "transformation" in the early history of the Critical Legal Studies movement.

In the essays on Critical Legal Studies, as in the other groups of essays, I have sought to intervene in a contemporary issue of scholarship or politics with a view toward generating detachment. But in each of the groups of essays the detachment ultimately generated has revealed itself to be of an ironic cast. The "distance" that a historical inquiry generates ultimately serves to reinforce the degree to which all historical actors, including contemporary ones, are trapped within the boundaries of their culture and thus never fully "detached." Nor can the motivation precipitating historical inquiries be fairly described as detached; nor can the methodological techinques employed in those inquiries; nor can the historiographical conclusions. Detachment is generated only by the recognition of the futility of humans transcending the times and places with which they are associated. That sort of detachment could, hypothetically, lead to feelings of powerlessness and inertia, but it can equally lead in another direction. Since time and culture invariably change, history can never precisely repeat itself: its "lessons" can never fully be mastered. If that is so, it follows not so much that everything is up for grabs, but rather that everything and anything is worth learning about.

NOTES

1. See, e.g., G. Edward White, "The Rise and Fall of Justice Holmes," 39 *U. Chi. L. Rev.* 51 (1971).

2. For present purposes, the following definitions of "modernism" and "postmodernism" should suffice. Modernism is the epistemological stance that assumes the collapse of universal ideological precepts (such as religion) capable of organizing and explaining experience, and seeks to ground meaning in experience itself, "experience" being taken as situational and varied, but nonetheless "real." Postmodernism takes modernist logic one step further, assuming that even experience can be ideologically constructed, and thus universal principles and "reality" are equally problematic.

3. 9 Wheat. 738, 866 (1824).

4. 347 U.S. 483 (1954).

5. 19 How. 393 (1857).

6. 163 U.S. 537 (1896).

7. 368 U.S. 57 (1961).

8. 478 U.S. 186 (1986).

9. The principal identifying characteristic of the Critical Legal Studies movement has been its governing assumption that "law" and "politics" are indistinguishable entities, and thus any effort to separate the two, or to present legal rules or policies as neutral or apolitical in their formation or content, is flawed. For a fuller discussion, see the essays in "Critical Legal Studies Symposium," 36 *Stan. L. Rev.* 1 (1984).

10. See, e.g., Jay Feinman, "The Role of Ideas in Legal History," 78 *Mich. L. Rev.* 722 (1980).

11. In this sense most of the essays in this book are examples of "postmodern" literature, and their appearance is evidence of the growing methodological self-consciousness of scholars since the late 1970s.

PART I

Doing History: Methodology

Truth and Interpretation in Legal History*

In the past few years I have published two books[1] that have generated several responses from commentators in scholarly journals. This essay has been generated by those responses, and by the kind invitation of the editors of this volume. Since the essay responds to commentary principally through an effort to clarify my views on methodology in legal history, I want briefly to dispose of some less indirect reactions to commentators. Some of the commentary has been principally appreciative,[2] and I want to acknowledge the pleasure that an author takes in discovering that someone has read, enjoyed, and perhaps even profited from his work. Other commentary has infused appreciative comments with searching criticism;[3] it is this set of responses that has provoked me to respond. Yet another set of commentators has criticized my work without, seemingly, making the effort to understand my scholarly purposes or to ensure that their criticisms were fairly stated or fully supportable.[4] I have noted the names of this set of commentators—a Revolution or a Day of Judgment may yet come, and the information may be useful—but this essay is hardly for them.

The purpose of this essay is to distinguish my approach toward historical scholarship from two other approaches. One approach rests on the premise that historical scholarship is a search for objective truth; this is most clearly articulated in the work of general historians but shared by some contemporary legal historians.[5] The other approach rests on the premise that historical scholarship should be informed by the philosophical perspectives of Marxism.[6] While I shall spend some time criticizing these two approaches, I shall expend the bulk of my efforts in attempting to set forth, in preliminary form, the basis of my own position.

This essay consists of four sections. Section I discusses the nature of historical explanation, devoting some attention to the roles of "truth," interpretation, and detachment in historical scholarship; Section II continues that discussion by exploring the meaning and the purpose of what I call "interpretive detachment" in the writing of history. Section III considers the theoretical assumptions of Marxist legal historians from the point of view developed in preceding sections. Section

*79 Mich. L. Rev. 594 (1981)

IV, taking into account some issues that remain problematic or troublesome, restates my approach.

I The Nature of Historical Explanation

A work of historical scholarship can communicate at four levels. On a first level of communication, which is commonly taken to be the most significant, the work seeks to contribute to or to recast existing scholarly wisdom through a proposed interpretation of a particular series of events. I call this level the level of historical narrative. At a second level, the work seeks to subsume this proposed interpretation within a particular perspective on the subject of history itself. I call this the level of historiography. At a third level, the work argues for the general primacy of that historiographical perspective as a way of interpreting reality: I call this level the level of metahistory. And at a fourth level, if the basic assumptions and perspectives of the second and third levels are adopted, the work suggests that certain normative implications for contemporary policymaking follow. I call this level the level of metapolitics.

Not all historical scholarship, of course, explicitly communicates on each of these four levels, and some does not even address the kinds of issues that one associates with the levels of metahistory and metapolitics. Increasingly, however, scholarship in legal history has communicated on several of these levels, and the more visible legal history scholarship of the last decade can be read as conveying messages on all four levels of communication. Lawrence Friedman's *A History of American Law*[7] provides an example.

When I reviewed Friedman's *History* in 1973, I suggested that with its publication the field of American legal history may have "come of age."[8] By "coming of age" I meant principally that Friedman's work might provoke others to examine source materials in the field and to provide alternative scholarly explanations of past events where they thought Friedman's were deficient, thereby causing scholarship in American legal history to proliferate and mature. I also intended, almost as an afterthought, a second meaning that seems to have been more prophetic: that Freidman had created a new type of work, one that expanded the boundaries of American legal history as a field of scholarly interest. In addition to covering a wide variety of historical themes and topics, Friedman propounded a theory of relationship between law and society in America. He suggested that, at any point in its history, American law has reflected the "push and pull" of elite groups that seek to fashion it to further their current interests;[9] he also suggested, less overtly, that such a process has continued into the present; he could also fairly be read as suggesting that this process contains elements of injustice that should be exposed and modified.

Friedman, in short, communicated on all the levels I have previously identified. His *History* first proposed that changes in legal doctrine are principally brought about by changes in the distribution of economic and political power in society: that theme was the organizing principle of his historical narrative. He next argued for the general significance of viewing law in American history as an "instrument" or "tool" of "the people in power," [10] and thereby communicated his historiographical perspective. He then argued further for the primacy of a general view of the history of American society that attributed great significance to the current self-interest of elite pressure groups, thereby communicating on the level of metahistory. Finally, Friedman argued that, as contemporary Americans, we ought to be concerned about the implications of that general view, and that the methodological perspective he was employing in *A History of American Law* had distinctive implications as a contemporary political statement. By making this last argument, Friedman communicated on the level of metapolitics and suggested a close relationship between theories of history and theories of contemporary affairs.

The multileveled communication of works such as Freidman's *History* invites us to reconsider the nature of historical explanation, and to ask what distinguishes historical scholarship from contemporary theorizing. I begin that reconsideration by noting the existence of an enduring professional constraint upon historical writing that I shall call the "canon of detachment." This canon has two distinct aspects. What I call "interpretive detachment" is the suspension of prejudgment toward the historical evidence that one is examining. Interpretative detachment focuses tangentially on the first, but principally on the second and third levels of communication in historical scholarship. Interpretive detachment seeks to insure that the organizing interpretive principle of a historical narrative—the feature that defines the work's historiographical perspective—will be selected solely by reference to the criterion of plausibility, with plausibility determined by the "internal logic," the "contemporary fit," and the "current common sense" of the interpretation. [11] Interpretative detachment assumes that while it may well be impossible for a historian to choose an organizing interpretation that ignores his metahistorical and metapolitical perspectives, the plausibility of his chosen interpretation may not rest solely on the purported validity of those perspectives.

The second aspect of the canon is what I call "truth detachment," and its focus is primarily on the levels of historical narrative and historiography. Truth detachment assumes that the organizing interpretive principle on which a historical narrative rests must be capable of being refuted through reference to the evidence on which the interpretative principle rests: that is, the principle must contain the seeds of its own falsification. I shall have more to say about both these aspects of the canon of detachment shortly; here I merely seek to define them.

One of the striking features of the canon of detachment in historical interpretation is that it has endured, albeit represented imprecisely in terms such as "objectivity" or "neutrality," despite significant changes in professional research techniques. Qualitative and quantitative analyses of historical data have gone in and out of fashion, and ideas and events have risen and fallen in their stature as causative agents. But a professional judgment has persisted that a historian should produce plausible and falsifiable interpretations of the subject matter that forms the basis of his narrative. An obvious conclusion to be drawn from the persistence of the canon of detachment is that "bias," either at the level of historical narrative or at the levels of historiography and metahistory, is regarded an "unprofessional" quality in a historian.

I want to probe the basis of that apparent judgment about bias in historical scholarship by discussing the canon of detachment in more detail. But at this early stage it is worth noting that adherence to the canon of detachment cannot be said to be the sole prerequisite for "successful" historical scholarship. Another prerequisite seems equally necessary to "success": the criterion of engagement. The engagement criterion, like the canon of detachment, can be seen as containing two distinguishable features. Engagement first refers to the scholar's immersion in his subject. This feature of the criterion, while vital in generating narratives that give a charged meaning to historical subject matter and thereby create a vicarious appeal for readers, is less significant for my purposes. I am principally concerned with the feature of engagement that refers to the professional reader's immersion in the organizing interpretive principle of an historical narrative.

Engagement in this second sense becomes a synonym for the process of stimulating further scholarly inquiry. When a professional reader becomes engaged by an historical explanation, he may be motivated to pursue related inquiries. When a reader is thus engaged, the explanation can be said to be suggestive. It is suggestive in the sense that it gives a vivid meaning to a narrative about the past, and it is suggestive, when the reader is a professional historian, in that it may stimulate ideas for further study. In a professional context, the principal value of an interpretation that satisfies the criterion of engagement is that it provides examples for future work. I shall return to this feature of engagement at a later point.

Historical explanation can thus be seen as a process where two entities—a canon of detachment and a criterion of engagement—interact, sometimes in complementary and sometimes in opposing ways. Such features of historical explanation as the choice of a topic for research, the extraction of meaning from sources, or the juxtaposition of the experiences of the writer and readers against those of another age, can be seen as techniques by which a historian's engagement with his subject is conveyed. In effective historical writing this quality of engagement is transferred to the reader, who is made to feel that the topic is stimulating and timely, that the sources are rich and fascinating, and that the subject matter merits further exploration. Sometimes the detachment of the scholar adds to this sense of reader engagement by suggesting that all this fascinating "history" is not just the product of a vivid scholarly imagination.

At other times, however, the canon of detachment serves as a reminder that the engagement of a historian may not overwhelm his interpretive stance if his scholarly product is to be deemed "successful." The canon suggests, for example, that if a topic seems chosen for its contemporary attractiveness, and the writer's stance toward the topic reflects a partisan current perspective, readers will become suspicious. It suggests that if a historian habitually extracts one meaning from his sources, or seems to strain their meaning, or seems to use them selectively, readers will begin to reconstruct in their minds an historical "record" that lies beyond the writer's interpretations. It further suggests that if the juxtaposition of past and present experiences seems to lead inexorably to a simplistic "lesson from history," readers will wonder if the lesson is merely a self-fulfilling prophecy. And it suggests, finally, that if all the above reactions on the part of readers produce a sense that a given historian is "biased," that historian's arguments will probably be dismissed, and will not serve as guidelines for future study.

The interplay of engagement and detachment in historical writing is especially important in historical scholarship that communicates at the four levels previously identified. Such scholarship consciously seeks to increase its audience's engagement, and also to expand the meaning of history, by interweaving historical explanation with contemporary political theory, thereby suggesting that "good" history and "good" politics are not easily separable. How can this genre of historical scholarship avoid being regarded as lacking proper detachment?

To address this question is to reconsider the professional function of the historian. Both interpretive detachment and truth detachment rest on certain assumptions about the unique contributions of history as a profession. I want first to consider some assumptions on which truth detachment could be said to rest. One is that laypersons regard historians' interpretations of the past as truth, or at least as approximations of truth. Another is that "true" interpretations of the past are possible because the historical "record" has some objective reality. A third is that a detached stance in the historian fosters a faithful reproduction of the historical record. Each of these assumptions needs qualification. While laypersons may regard history as merely a faithful reproduction of "the record," most historians do not. Most historians view history as the interplay of a "record," which can vary in its content, with scholarly efforts to interpret that record.[12] Indeed, the conception of an historical record as a set of indisputably "true" facts that have a meaning independent of their presence in various historical interpretations is a highly problematic notion. Karl Popper has argued, categorically, that "there can be no history of 'the past as it actually did happen'; there can only be historical interpretations, and none of them final."[13]

If Popper is correct, the value of historians' interpretations of the past lies not so much in their "truth," or faithful reconstruction of an objective record, as in their current suggestiveness and plausibility. If fidelity to truth were the principal goal of historical writing, the concededly continuous process of historical revision would be meaningless: faithful reproductions of history, once found to be true, would be incapable of being revised. Popper thus shifts attention from questions about the objective accuracy of an historical explanation to questions about the success of the explanation as a suggestive and plausible, if temporary, interpretation. For Popper, a successful historical explanation is conscious of its "point of view," thereby avoiding "uncritical bias," is fertile, thereby stimulating others to think about its propositions, and is "topical," thereby helping to "elucidate the problems of the day."[14]

Despite Popper's rejection of the idea of history as synonymous with objective truth, he endorses truth detachment as I have defined it. Popper argues that for a scholarly explanation to be professionally successful, it must be capable of being falsified: its propositions must rest on evidence that contains the seeds of their prospective revision.[15] This is the point where I part company with Popper and find the concept of truth detachment precarious. If one accepts, *arguendo*, Popper's claim that "truth" in history cannot be divorced from interpretation, on what basis can an interpretation be falsifiable? Surely not by a testing of it against "truth." Indeed, Popper himself suggests that the tests for "successful" scholarship (self-consciousness, fertility, topicality) are tests that presuppose some inarticulate professional "common sense" about scholarly interpretation. But interpretations are necessarily different from "what actually happened."

At this point, I believe, one has to choose. One may resurrect the idea of truth in history, and argue that while "what actually happened" is of limited utility until it is interpreted, conformity to the integrity of a finite historical record is a justifiable valuative criterion for "successful" historical scholarship. Or one may reject both truth in history and Popper's notion of falsification, and argue that all the valuative criteria for successful historical scholarship are interpretive criteria, and that therefore the canon of detachment in historical writing is meaningful only in its interpretive aspect.

In the following section I want to develop a justification for the latter choice, and to explore more fully the relationship of my views to those of Popper and Thomas Kuhn. Before so doing, let me summarize the presentation to this point. I have argued that visible and prominent contemporary scholarship, as evidenced by recent work in the field of legal history, communicates on levels—the levels of historiography, metahistory, and metapolitics—that go far beyond the narrow definition of history as "what actually happened in the past," and implicitly cast serious doubts on the intelligibility of that definition. The communication levels that I find striking in contemporary historical scholarship are levels of interpretation, such as the levels of metahistory and metapolitics, that convey distinctly normative contemporary messages. These levels of communication, which are intended, among other things, to increase reader engagement, confront a canon of detachment in historical scholarship. The process of historical explanation can be seen as an interplay between a search for engagement and this canon, whose meaning, I have begun to argue, lies not at the level of fidelity to truth, but at the level of interpretation. I now turn to a further extrapolation of that last argument.

II The Significance of Interpretive Detachment

An example based on one of the hypotheses I advanced in *Tort Law in America* may serve as a useful introduction to some of the distinctions I intend to make in this portion of the essay. In that book I argued that the "modern" negligence standard in American tort law, which conditioned liability on legal fault and defined fault to include "unreasonable" misfeasance as well as nonfeasance, was not solely or even principally a response to industrialization. Let us suppose that my support for this argument rests on two kinds of evidence: evidence of the absence of "modern" negligence cases at a time when industrialization has become a feature of American society, and evidence of the appearance of a distinctive mode of American legal thought—a mode that placed great emphasis on the derivation, articulation, and application of generalized standards for legal conduct—precisely at the time when "modern" negligence cases began to appear in striking numbers.

Now assume that a legal historian, in evaluating the "success" of my argument, discovers numerous "modern" negligence cases decided before the time when I assert that the new mode of thought came into being. The historian claims that these cases suggest that my argument is flawed. What assumptions have been made by my argument and by that claim, and how do those assumptions relate to the roles of truth and interpretation in history?

In resting my argument about modern negligence on "evidence" from the past, and especially in attaching some significance to time demarcations of the past, I seem to be deriving a hypothesis from some finite, discoverable, temporally divisible historical record. But a moment's reflection suggests that this is not quite what I am doing. Instead, I am assuming the established salience of industrialization as a causal factor in the growth of negligence law, and then attempting to show that the salience of that factor can be undermined through the use of currently acceptable research techniques, such as analysis of common-law cases. The critical steps in my argument are not what I "find" in the record about industrialization and a modern negligence standard, but what I assume to be the appropriate frame of reference for pursuing scholarly inquiries.

In discovering the modern negligence cases that I ignored, the critic seems also to be bringing evidence from a finite historical record "to light" and then claiming that my argument is not faithful to the "record." Again, the critic is not quite doing that: the critic is assuming that my "counterhypothesis" (changed ideas about law) is also a salient causal factor, and then employing a currently acceptable research technique (the discovery and analysis of cases and their correlation with time segments) to question that hypothesis. The critic and I, in short, share an assumed technique of scholarly inquiry.

Where do these assumptions about the saliency of hypotheses and the acceptability of research techniques come from? One thing seems clear: they do not come simply from observations of the record of the past. Given the multifaceted quality of American society and the diverse products of the legal profession, mere observation of the past would not seem to compel the assumptions that industrialization invariably helps to explain changes in American law, or that common-law cases are significant manifestations of how American law changes, or that the dates of particular types of cases have any generalizable significance. It appears that assumptions such as these are produced in a much more complex way. I referred earlier to the notion of plausibility in historical scholarship, which I said was determined by the "internal logic," the "contemporary fit," and the "current common sense" of a proposed hypothesis. The factors determining plausibility can also be taken as rough descriptions of the factors that go into determining saliency in a scholarly hypothesis or acceptability in a scholarly research technique.

"Internal logic" is a dangerous phrase to use in this context, because it may connote some finite sense of rationality or truth and thereby resurrect conceptions this essay has sought to place to one side. I am using the phrase in what might be called a "weak" sense. Thomas Kuhn, while agreeing with Karl Popper that history cannot properly be equated with "what actually happened," has argued that Popper's work, taken as a whole, presses one to the conclusion that hypotheses can be "tested" and found "false," that they can thus be labeled "mistakes," and that scholars "learn from [their] mistakes." [16] Kuhn rejects these views, arguing that the "success" or "failure" of scholarly hypotheses is not determined by "exclusively logical criteria" but by the "professionally shared imperatives" of a scholarly community. [17]

I agree with Popper and Kuhn that history is best understood as tentative interpretations of the past, and with Kuhn that no exclusively logical criteria can be supplied to determine whether a given interpretation "rings true." But that is not to say that an interpretation could never be deemed "unsuccessful" because it offended some variety of internal professional logic. An interpretation, for example, that "industrialization" caused the development of an Old English dialect in remote regions of Appalachia, even though such regions were devoid of any of the characteristics conventionally associated with an industrial environment, could, I believe, be rejected on "logical" grounds. The "internal logic" would, however, be "weak" in that it rested on a professional assumption that "industrial characteristics" could be defined and understood. If "logic" is used in this weakened sense, I find it to have some effect not only on the plausibility of historical interpretations but on the saliency of hypotheses and the acceptability of research techniques.

The "internal logic" criterion, however, is less central than the remaining two criteria. The Appalachian dialect example shows how closely "contemporary fit" and internal logic are linked. If a profession takes for granted a working definition of "industrial characteristics," and no such characteristics appear during a time segment in the past, an interpretation of that period that emphasizes the "industrialization" hypothesis has no "contemporary fit." But few hypotheses are as clearly flawed as the Appalachian dialect example; the process of evaluating a hypothesis in light of "contemporary fit" is usually far subtler. In fleshing out the "contemporary fit" criterion one reaches such issues as the relevancy of temporal demarcations, the intelligibility of a "period gestalt" and of "social change," and other familiar puzzles for philosophers of history. I shall merely note here that "contemporary fit" analysis seems to be a central feature of historical criticism.

The Appalachian dialect example also illustrates a link between the criterion of internal logic and the criterion I have called "current common sense." This is the most mysterious, and perhaps most central, of the criteria being discussed. The Appalachian dialect hypothesis would be likely to offend this criterion because the hypothesis seems nonsensical not only when applied to the time period it seeks to illuminate, but also as a general piece of wisdom. A hypothesis focusing on a causal factor that is not present at the time that it is supposed to be "causing" things to happen offends our notions of the meaning of causation. Although it is perhaps possible to redefine some terms so as to avoid this difficulty, that enterprise, in the Appalachian dialect example, does not seem particularly promising. [18] Its lack of promise, however, is not just a function of the absence of evidence about "industrial characteristics." Its lack of promise is also a function of current understandings about how scholars use and reason from evidence.

Here "current common sense" takes on another level of meaning. It does not mean simply the "common sense" of an ordinary rational person; it means in addition the "common sense" of the professional community that is evaluating a work of scholarship. At this point I find the insights of Kuhn most useful. Kuhn has argued that "rhetorically induced and professionally shared imperatives" are the central factors that affect the direction of scholarly research and criticism. These imperatives become "institutionalized," and emerge as "maxims and values" that "explain the outcome of choices that could not have been dictated by logic and experiment alone." [19]

"Current common sense" in a professional community can be said to be a crude encapsulation of this insight of Kuhn's. The concept of current common sense, I have said, is both mysterious and central. It is mysterious because the process by which "professionally shared imperatives" emerge and disappear is not one that seems capable of precise or rigorous analysis. One senses that in one scholarly generation the formulation of "grand theory" is taken to be a serious or even an essential task of scholarship, whereas in another the same task is regarded as counterproductive. One senses that scholarship in given disciplines or professions is conducted within what Kuhn used to call "paradigms" and now calls "disciplinary matrices": [20] contexts based on shared professional assumptions about the scope, direction, and design of research. But one cannot seem to articulate, in any precise fashion, how such "professionally shared imperatives" are created. When one tries, as I have on occasion, one's critics are sometimes provided with a reason for keeping their teeth sharpened.

Although the common-sense criterion may be mysterious, it is also central to an understanding of the nature of historical explanation and of the significance of interpretive detachment in the writing of history. Interpretive detachment, I have suggested, has as its principal purpose the neutralization of bias. Taking interpretive detachment seriously assumes that one also takes bias as a given. Historical explanations are assumed to be personal interpretations of the past that gain legitimacy by persuading other persons that they are provisionally acceptable as a form of professional wisdom. I think that we might agree, as a preliminary matter, that an interpretation that does not sufficiently divest itself of its "personal" or "individualized" features is an interpretation that appears as "biased." But why is bias stigmatized, and what is the relationship between this stigmatization and the current common-sense criterion?

If we believe, with Kuhn, that current common sense is a mysterious but powerful force in the legitimation of scholarly hypotheses, it seems that current common sense bears a close and potentially treacherous relationship to plausibility in scholarly discourse. Plausibility seems to contain, on initial reflection, a component of "rationality," "inner logic," or some such "neutral" or "objective" standard for evaluating scholarship. I have included such a component in my definition of plausibility. But suppose one seeks to build on the insights of Kuhn, and argues that mysterious imperatives control the direction of scholarly research, and that such imperatives are neither irrational nor rational, neither logical nor illogical; they merely exist. Then why could current common sense not be rephrased as "current collective bias"? Why could not the "success" of a work of scholarship be equated with it "fashionability," using that term in its most whimsical sense?

This troublesome logic suggests that communities of scholars may well be receptive to works whose methodology implicitly denies that collective bias and fashionability are the basic determinants of successful scholarship. Put another way, a work whose methodology minimizes the importance of its own individualized origins, a work that appeals to others through arguments other than nakedly biased ones, is also seeking to reassure a professional community of readers that current common sense ultimately means something more than fashionability. Interpretive detachment can perform part of the professional function.

I have earlier argued that the "success" of a work of historical scholarship is not determined solely by its plausibility, but also by its suggestiveness. I have argued further that currently "successful" scholarship in legal history communicates not only on interpretive levels that are analytically descriptive, but on levels that are analytically normative. Finally, I have argued that the suggestiveness of an historical explanation is ultimately linked to its capacity to engage the reader: to succeed in convincing the reader of its promise as a guideline for future study and as a normative message. How can one reconcile these observations with the idea of interpretive detachment?

At this point I want to return to the levels of communication that were set forth earlier. Recall that arguments at the level of historiography make claims for the primacy of a particular interpretation of historical evidence, while arguments at the level of metahistory make claims for the primacy of a theoretical organization of reality. To the extent that historiographic interpretations are overwhelmed by a metahistorical perspective, the biases of the presentation have not been adequately neutralized. An apparent consequence of unneutralized bias is that arguments at the level of metapolitics, which call for taking stock of the contemporary implications of the presentation, may be perceived as unprofessional or even as lacking in "current common sense," and may therefore not sufficiently engage the reader.

One could say at this point that the solution is to exorcise communication at the levels of metahistory and metapolitics from historical writing, and to return to a "truth in history" stance, where a scholar's interpretations are based on their fidelity to an "objective" historical record. But I have sought to show that such a stance misconceives the historian's function and is almost impossible to implement. Historians cannot avoid interpretation, and "successful" interpretations become, through the process of provisional acceptance of their explanations by a professional community, surrogates for truth.

Therefore, it is too simple to believe that "truth in history" is a way out of the dilemma. It is also too simple to believe that an historian can seriously advance historiographic arguments that lead to metahistorical arguments without identifying himself with his metahistorical perspective. Writers of fiction regularly respond to scholarly criticism of their work by categorical statements that they did not "intend" the meaning a critic "found" in their writing. But if their writing can fairly be said to have supported such a meaning, they can hardly cut off inquiry by a denial that it was intended.

There is another option possible. Those who welcome the presence of metahistorical arguments in historical writing but also believe in the value of interpretive detachment can pay sharper attention to the precise relationship in their writing between theories of historical interpretation and theories of metahistory and metapolitics. That relationship can be seen, using the terms of this essay, as a process of engagement, detachment, and reengagement. The writer engages the reader with the suggestiveness of an interpretation, but presents that interpretation in a manner that emphasizes its internal logic, its contemporary fit, and it current common sense. In so doing the writer is seeking, as a preliminary strategy, to detach his interpretation from any grand theory of reality that the interpretation conveys. Then, after the reader has digested and assessed the plausibility of the interpretation, he is led, by the power of interpretation itself, to consider its suggestiveness—to assess the theoretical perspective on which it implicitly rests and the guidelines it provides for future research. In the schema of this essay, metahistorical perspectives must not be permitted to overwhelm historiographic interpretations: historiographic interpretations must be consistent with a number of plausible metahistorical perspectives and must provide suggestive examples for professionals. An interpretation of this kind can be said to be consistent with, but not dependent upon, a view of reality. A reader can reject that view of reality but still consider the interpretation plausible. But if the reader finds the interpretation plausible, and suggestive as well, he will be exposed anew to its theoretical implications, including its normative messages as a current political statement. Once an interpretation conforms to the canon of interpretive detachment at the level of historiography, it qualifies as an interpretation that can yield suggestive and plausible theories of metahistory and metapolitics.

I now want to consider whether Marxist legal historiography attempts historical explanations that can be said to attempt to neutralize bias and thereby take into account the canon of interpretive detachment. That inquiry, of course, places Marxist historical explanations within the general analytic framework of this essay, which offers a theory of historical explanation. A Marxist legal historian could assert that my theory is flawed and therefore my analysis of Marxism is not germane. But at that point the common ground of discussion would be lost. My analysis assumes an inquiry of common concern to historians, regardless of their ideological persuasion, that can be stated as follows. If the professional standing of an historical narrative cannot be based on its fidelity to truth, but must be based on the plausibility and suggestiveness of its organizing interpretations, can a historian advance an interpretation of stature that violates the canon of interpretive detachment?

III Marxist Legal History and the Process of Historical Explanation

Marxism takes a distinctive view of history that is normally labeled "materialist." The materialist view of history can be said to be composed of two elements: a theory of the principal locus of thought and a theory of change. Marxism asserts that thought emanates from "the mode of production of material life." In Karl Marx's words, the mode of production "conditions the social, political, and intellectual life process in general," so that "definite forms of social consciousness," including "a legal . . . superstructure," emanate from "the economic structure of society." [21] Ideas are thus "anchored in . . . the material setting of history"; [22] they do not exist independent of it.

The concept of a mode of production, however, refers to "economic activity" in an expansive sense of that term. "Modes of production" are intended to include the means by which participants in the economic structure of society establish, and justify, their relations in society and their relations with one another. Here Marxism makes the assumption that within any mode of production there will be disharmonies among participants, and that these disharmonies will take the form of class antagonisms arising from "the unequal relations between the superior and inferior class within any mode." [23] The principal unequal relationship is that between the "ruling class" and the "under class," and the chief manifestation of inequality is "the vastly disproportionate access to, or ownership of, wealth that is the prerogative of the ruling class." [24]

Marxists believe that class antagonisms arising from inequalities within a mode of production are the chief source of historical change. The underclasses protest such inequalities and the ruling classes seek to justify them. The result is a complex of responses: "false" ideologies created by the ruling classes to deemphasize their power or to emphasize the common values that they share with the underclasses; shifts in the composition of ruling and underclasses as new means of production come into being; open attempts on the part of the ruling classes to oppress the underclasses. This complex of responses to class antagonisms produces change. History is the progressive record of such change.

The use of the adjective "progressive" in Marxist theories of history is necessary because for Marxists the class struggle, and the consequent changes that it produces, is only a stage of history that will ultimately lead to sharpened class antagonisms, a "dictatorship of the proletariat," and ultimately a classless society. This predictive feature of Marxism has caused its adherents acute practical problems, but my concern here is with Marxist approaches to history, not Marxist prognostications of the future. More specifically, my concern centers upon the materialist treatment of ideas and the motivation of those who articulate them.

Marx once said that "it is not the consciousness of men that determines their being, but, on the contrary, their social being that determines their consciousness." [25] His collaborator Friedrich Engels added that "the ultimate causes of all social changes . . . are to be sought, not in the minds of men . . . but in changes in the mode of production and exchange." [26] Engels noted, on another occasion, that "constitutions established by the victorious class after a successful battle," "judicial forms," and "juristic [and] philosophical theories" were "various elements of the superstructure" whose "basis" was "the economic situation." [27] The clear import of these comments for legal history is that the presence of ratified constitutions, or of established legal doctrines, or of commonly accepted theories of law, is explained by their connection to the existing class struggle within the existing mode of production.

When this theory of the ultimate explanatory source of legal history is combined with the notion of "false" ideology in the ruling class, the legal historian who approaches history from a Marxist perspective seems to adhere to a theory of the causes of legal change whose metahistorical and metapolitical components overwhelm its historiographic component. If the ruling classes invariably seek to further their interests at the expense of the underclasses, but may do so in a variety of "apparent" or "false" ways, any justification that legal institutions advance for their decisions becomes fodder for a Marxist interpretation. If a judge, for example, states that the purpose of a decision barring workers from suing their employers for injuries caused by the negligence of co-workers is to promote the interests of owners of the means of production rather than the interests of workers, his decision can be taken as overt evidence of a ruling class perspective held by courts. If, however, the judge states that the basis of his decision is to encourage workers in an occupation to be more mindful of their safety, his reasoning can be interpreted as a "false" ideology designed to disguise the true purpose of putting the costs of such injuries on workers.[28]

If a judge decides to change an existing rule of law for "the public good" or because "public policy demands" it, a Marxist can treat such rhetoric as "false" and can initiate a search for the "true" impact of the change on the various classes within the mode of production. Alternatively, if a judge decides to follow an existing rule on the grounds of its longstanding acceptance or because settled expectations would be upset if it were changed, a Marxist can equate "settled expectations" with the expectations of the ruling class, and "acceptance" of the rule with furthering the interests of the ruling class or disadvantaging the interests of the underclasses.[29] As the logic of this methodology is played out, any evidence of change in legal history—the establishment or modification of a constitution, the rise and fall of legal doctrines, the shifting theories used to justify on outcome or another—can be seen as emanating from tensions within the mode of production.

In the works of leading Marxist legal historians, law serves as an instrument for establishing or ratifying the hegemony of the ruling class. But it is not necessary to a materialist interpretation of legal history that law be so designated. An occasional judicial decision, piece of legislation, or constitutional provision may be directed at curbing the power of the ruling class, reducing the inequalities between actors in the means of production, or even sharpening awareness of the class struggle. Indeed, given Marxism's progressive view of history, one might expect such instances to occur. Scholarly interpretations of a given legal rule as promoting the interests of one or another set of actors within the class struggle, however, need not depend on the justifications articulated on behalf of the rule. Those justifications may be taken as "true" or discarded as "false" because of assumptions made about the way antagonistic actors within the mode of production behave.

The writing of legal history from a Marxist theoretical perspective therefore appears to face two related problems: the problem of not being able to neutralize its biases, and the problem of convincing other scholars that its contributions can serve as fruitful examples for further work. Such scholarship seems to violate the canon of interpretive detachment, and because it has violated that canon to fail to satisfy the criterion of engagement as well. Perhaps a saving distinction can be made. A Marxist legal historian could argue for the primacy of the model that he advances but concede that there will be instances when the model breaks down.

The model is extremely useful, one could say, in providing a hypothetical set of motivations for participants in the class struggle who make use of law. One can presume that actors will want to use law to ratify or to change their position in the class struggle, or perhaps to make others aware of the internally contradictory nature of ostensibly cooperative social efforts, such as production of goods and services for the marketplace. But that presumption is not conclusive: sometimes the language reveals that actors do not see themselves as motivated by their position in the class struggle or do not even seem aware that it is taking place. At that point the purpose of a Marxist approach to legal history is to supply ''secret'' or ''unconscious'' motivations for actors who cannot avoid participation in the class struggle even though they fail to recognize it.

If this distinction is to be truly saving, it would seem that Marxist interpretations of legal history should acknowledge the potential plausibility of interpretations that deny the primary assumptions of Marxist theory. Marxist interpretations would then pose a different question: Given several historiographical interpretations that satisfy the criteria of internal logic and contemporary fit, does a Marxist interpretation better accord with current common sense?

To pose such a question is to treat interpretations of legal actors' motivations that rely on factors other than the actors' place in the economic structure of society as competitive with the interpretations of Marxism. If several interpretations achieved reader engagement, current common sense could then determine whether, in the main, a Marxist approach to the motivation of legal actors or some equally suggestive alternative approach would be deemed more plausible, and hence ''successful,'' or whether a Marxist approach could be regarded as more plausible in some situations but not in others.

I suspect that some Marxist historians might be inclined to accept this compromise. But when the issue is one of causation in history, the very universality of Marxist theory makes such a compromise precarious. Take the role of ideas as a causative agent in history as an example. If, according to Marxist metahistory, ideas have no independent meaning apart from their material context, how can one take seriously ''competitive'' historical interpretations that suggest that ideas can be unrelated to their material contexts or can even shape the contexts themselves? Such interpretations must seemingly be treated as misguided because they do not account for the difference between ''false'' and ''true'' justifications; their arguments are accordingly based on the ''wrong'' historical evidence. No compromise seems possible here: the theory of ideas as causative agents violates the initial assumptions of Marxist theory.

In sum, when one subjects an internally coherent and self-reinforcing system of belief, such as Marxism, to the tests of effective historical interpretation advanced in this essay, the very qualities that give that system its internal consistency cause it to yield historical interpretations that may ''fail'' in two respects. The comprehensiveness of Marxism as a system of metapolitics is based on the fidelity of its practitioners to assumptions whose primacy is not challenged; since that primacy is never questioned, the interpretations supplied by Marxist historians seemingly provide suggestive guidelines for future research only to those who adopt Marxist metapolitics. Uncompromised Marxist interpretations thus fail to achieve interpretive detachment and to engage non-Marxist professionals.[30]

IV Conclusion: Some Issues for Further Exploration

In attempting to find a middle ground between theories of historical interpretation that rest on the idea of "truth in history" and theories, such as Marxism, that rest on metahistorical and metapolitical assumptions, I have, as is doubtless apparent by now, exhibited a logical vulnerability to both of the approaches I have been criticizing. How can I argue for "detachment" in historical interpretation, an apostle of "truth in history" might ask, and yet deny the intelligibility of an objective historical record? Where does "detachment" come from if not from phenomena external to the interpreter? And how can I concede that ultimately "current common sense" determines the success of historical interpretations, a Marxist might ask, and yet claim that a Marxist interpretation would offend current common sense? What if the great bulk of historians were Marxists?

These hypothetical queries lead me to stress again the complex relationship between interpretive detachment and the unintelligibility of "truth in history." Once one denies that historical interpretations can be tested by recourse to some objective record, the dragon is out of its cave. One can no longer, as an interpreter of the past, claim that one is merely recording the past: it is the act of interpretation that counts, and, as Popper says, interpretations are never final.

What does a member of a professional community whose perceived function is to make the past intelligible and meaningful to persons living in the present do with this insight? One response, of course, is that of the Marxists: since interpretation is history, and since interpretations are necessarily personal and to some extent ideological, Marxists refine their ideological beliefs, make them explicit, and argue for their interpretations. There is a kind of courage in this position, in addition to its apparent logic. Such a response, however, strikes me as quixotic because it misconceives the nature of professional communities in contemporary society. Professional communities, I believe, are united not by ideology, but by tacitly accepted definitions of their professional functions. However one defines the function of a historian, it is not synonymous with the function of an ideologue. Even if one rejects the criteria for "successful" historical scholarship that I have set forth in this essay, I suspect that one would have to substitute criteria that sharply distinguish between the art of historical interpretation and the art of ideological oratory. The principal reason this substitution would be necessary is the collapse of the idea of truth in history. That idea, or some version of it, has been sufficiently powerful and sufficiently long-lived to associate the role of being an historian with the act of suspending intuitive contemporary judgment when examining the past. The reflex of judgment suspension—the avoidance of anachronistic reasoning—is sufficiently ingrained in historians, I believe, to constitute what Kuhn would call a shared professional imperative.

What is the future of this professional imperative, however, if we reject the idea of truth in history and the corresponding idea that the historian can be "objective?" What if a version of Kuhnian logic that ends up with the proposition that one cannot say how or why professional imperatives come and go, that the process is essentially mysterious, is correct? My sense is that Kuhn's logic may be terrifying for historians who have abandoned the idea of truth in history. The "objective" criteria for testing the worth of historical interpretations have been discarded, but no one can say where the remaining "subjective" criteria come from, how long they will last, or even, when pressed, what they are. How does one then know "good" history from "bad" history; where does one find the basis of one's professional judgment?

It is the sense of crisis that this logic engenders that, I suggest, has stimulated the production of historical scholarship that communicates on the four levels I have previously identified. I do not see this "crisis" negatively; such crises are common in, and generally beneficial to, the creative life of a profession, and this crisis has already contributed to the appearance of a number of significant works in American legal history. I also doubt that this crisis will resolve itself through a dramatic change in the roles and functions of members of a profession; I doubt that historians will abandon their strictures against anachronistic reasoning and become ideologues.

Having said all this, I confess that I would like to see whether, on closer inquiry, the criterion of "current common sense," and indeed all of the criteria I have identified with plausible, suggestive, and "successful" historical scholarship, are as mysterious as they seem to be. Their very mysteriousness introduces a fascinating ambiguity to the concept of professionalization. If one is defining oneself as a professional and training others to act as such, but one can only say that the criteria for success in the profession are mysterious in nature and in origin, what is the difference between a profession and a secret society? I have been down this path before in considering what, if anything, it means to "think like a lawyer"; it is a little disconcerting to find the same snarls in the phrase "writing like a historian."

Thus this essay is a prolegomenon in the sense that the criteria that I advance to support my approach are neither precisely stated nor rigorously applied. I have sought only to sketch the general framework of my position, to identify its philosophical assumptions, and to contrast it with other general views. I have not filled in many of the details. Maybe all one can say about successful historical scholarship is that one "knows it when one sees it." But that despairing suggestion ought not to excuse historians from attempting a fuller understanding of the relationship between truth and interpretation in history. The dragon may be out of its cave, but it may not be a dragon after all.

NOTES

1. G. White, Patterns of American Legal Thought (1978); G. White, Tort Law in America (1980). This essay does not consider reviews prompted by G. White, The American Judicial Tradition (1976).

2. *E.g.*, Corrigan, Book Review, 60 B.U. L. Rev. 801 (1980); Fellman, Book Review, 85 Am. Hist. Rev. 1253 (1980); Yarbrough, Book Review, 5 Va. B. Assn. J. 25 (1979).

3. *E.g.*, Feinman, *The Role of Ideas in Legal History,* 78 Mich. L. Rev. 722 (1980); O'Connell, Book Review, 1980 Duke L.J. 1201; Powers, Book Review, 67 J. Am. Hist. 704 (1980); Teachout, Book Review, 67 Va. L. Rev. 817 (1981).

4. *E.g.*, Christie, *The Perils of Writing an Intellectual History of Torts,* 79 Mich. L. Rev. 947 (1981); Fleming, Book Review, 1980 Am. B. Foundation Research J. 614. These names do not exhaust the list, but at this point they head it.

5. *See, e.g.*, O. Handlin, Truth in History (1979); Bridwell, *Theme v. Reality in American Legal History,* 53 Ind. L.J. 449 (1978). Professor Handlin states the premise succinctly: "[T]he world of the elapsed past has its own reality, independent of who attempts to view and describe it, and is thus objective." O. Handlin at 1.

6. *See, e.g.*, Feinman, *supra* note 3, at 730–36; Gabel, *Intention and Structure in Contractual Conditions: Outline of a Method for Critical Legal Theory,* 61 Minn. L. Rev. 601 (1977); Tushnet, *A Marxist Analysis of American Law,* 1 Marxist Perspectives 96 (1978). A less explicit Marxist perspective appears in M. Horwitz, The Transformation of American Law 1780–1860 (1977).

7. L. Friedman, A History of American Law (1973).

8. White, Book Review, 59 Va. L. Rev. 1130 (1973).

9. L. Friedman, *supra* note 7, at 25.

10. *Id.* at 10, 25.

11. "Internal logic," "contemporary fit," and "current common sense" are defined and discussed *infra* at text accompanying notes 16–19.

12. Handlin, for example, juxtaposes his conception of an "objective" record against "the scholar's vision," which he calls "subjective, at least to the extent that his own point of observation and complex lenses of prejudice, interest, and preconception shape what he discerns and therefore what he can portray." O. Handlin, *supra* note 5, at 1.

13. 2 K. Popper, The Open Society and Its Enemies 268 (4th ed. 1962).

14. *Id.*

15. *See* K. Popper, Conjectures and Refutations 215–17, 312–14 (1963); K. Popper, The Logic of Scientific Discovery 31–50 (1959).

16. T. Kuhn, The Essential Tension 270–78 (1977).

17. *Id.* at 288, 292.

18. The Appalachian dialect hypothesis could be made more credible by a redefinition of "dialect." One could argue that industrialization "caused" Appalachian language patterns to take the form of a "dialect" by facilitating greater social intercourse in areas other than Appalachia, and thereby deprovincializing American language patterns. A "dialect" would then be an original provincial language pattern that, given deprovincialization, appeared to be unique. This restatement of the hypothesis would not be patently illogical, although its working definition of historical causation would seem to strain that concept.

19. T. Kuhn, *supra* note 16, at 292.

20. *Compare* T. Kuhn, The Structure of Scientific Revolutions 38–42 (2d ed. 1970) *with* T. Kuhn, *supra* note 16, at 297–319.

21. Marx, *Preface to a Contribution to the Critique of Political Economy, reprinted in* The Marx-Engels Reader 3, 4 (R. Tucker ed. 1978).

22. R. Heilbroner, Marxism For and Against 63 (1980).

23. *Id.* at 68.

24. *Id.*

25. Marx, *supra* note 21, at 4.

26. Engels, *Herr Eugen Dühring's Revolution in Science (Anti-Dühring), reprinted in* A Handbook of Marxism 279 (E. Burns ed. 1935).

27. Letter from Friedrich Engles to Joseph Bloch (Sept. 21–22, 1890), *reprinted in* The Marx-Engels Reader, *supra* note 21, at 760.

28. Morton Horwitz, in The Transformation of American Law, seems aware of this difficulty and attempts to avoid it. He demonstrates that courts made use of a "contractarian" doctrinal framework to "transform" a conception of fellow-servant cases as raising issues of "substantive justice" into a conception of those cases as raising issues of the economic marketplace. M. Horwitz, *supra* note 6, at 209. One reading of Horwitz's interpretation, then, is that the courts merely adopted a different set of "intellectual premises" on which their doctrinal framework rested. *Id.* at 210. For Horwitz, however, "intellectual premises" have a central purpose. He argues that through "contract ideology" the law had "come simply to ratify those forms of inequality that the market system produced." How, then, would Horwitz interpret fellow-servant cases that, during the period "contractarian" analysis was dominant, grounded their decision in the "substantive justice" of safety for workers? It seems that either those decisions do not support Horwitz's interpretation, or the decisions are engaging in "false" rhetoric.

29. One might note here that Horwitz parallels his demonstration of the emerging formalism of American private law in the nineteenth century with a characterization of formalism as representing "the successful culmination of efforts by mercantile and entrepreneurial interests during the preceding half century to transform the law to serve their interests, *leaving them to wish for the first time to 'freeze' legal doctrine . . . " Id.* at 259 (emphasis added). In the conclusion of The Transformation of American Law Horwitz argues explicitly at the levels of metahistory and metapolitics: "[T]he paramount social condition that is necessary for legal formalism to flourish in a society is for the powerful groups in that society to have a great interest in disguising and suppressing the inevitably political and redistributive functions of law." *Id.* at 266.

30. The difference between "uncompromised" and "compromised" Marxist historiography is largely a question of how universal one takes the metahistory of Marxism to be. If the metahistory is taken to be so universal that counterexamples must be incorporated within it, as in the fellow-servant example, then, in the terms of this essay, metapolitics and metahistory have overwhelmed historiography and interpretive detachment has been lost. If counterexamples are taken, however, as fodder for the competitive interpretations that Marxism seeks to dispute, then to some extent a Marxist interpretation seems to recognize that its success depends not exclusively on its "correctness," but also on the "current common sense" of historians.

The Text, Interpretation, and Critical Standards*

I

This essay has as its subjects the nature of scholarly interpretation and the formation of standards for evaluating scholarship. One is hard pressed to summon up subjects that are more important for American academic culture at this juncture in its history. Their importance comes from the juxtaposition of two conflicting perceptions now widely shared by American academics: the perception that the enterprise of scholarship is significantly dependent upon the tacit values and presuppositions of "communities" of scholars, and the perception that very little concordance on values exists among scholarly communities. It is the simultaneous recognition that value judgments may be "all that count," but that no consensus on value judgments exists, which gives issues such as the nature of interpretation and the formation of critical standards their urgency. If we, as scholars, have no objective criteria for determining distinguished scholarship and no basis of agreement for deciding how we can go about formulating such criteria, we are close to conceding that what we do has as much significance as sound and fury. The threat of such a concession would seem to stir even the most resolute academic devotee of idleness.

Twenty years ago Thomas Kuhn argued[1] that even those professional communities (such as physical scientists) whose "normal" mode of research rests on unquestioned empirical assumptions go through periods in which those assumptions are radically questioned and often replaced by other assumptions; and that nothing inherent in empiricism compels the acceptance of one set of assumptions over another. As controversial as Kuhn's argument may originally have been, and may remain to some scholars, his logic seems to be increasingly regarded as compelling.

Kuhnian logic leads one to the proposition that scholarly interpretation cannot be starkly separated from either scholarly evidence or from the "metatheories" (tacit value judgments) on which scholarly interpretations are premised. Such a

*60 Texas L. Rev. 569 (1982).

proposition, while useful at one level, becomes threatening at another level. So long as one has distance from one's subject, Kuhnian logic adds a new dimension to criticism, for as soon as one unravels a scholar's metatheory, and then reexamines the scholar's evidence, one can see how the metatheory was so compatible with certain interpretations of evidence that they were virtually preordained. One's understanding of the concepts of evidence and interpretation takes a quantum leap. But what if one applies Kuhnian logic to one's own work? Here the results appear disquieting.

Distance from one's own metatheory is not always possible. It may even be a permissible gloss on Kuhnian logic to claim that metatheories are themselves culturally determined, and that one can no more achieve distance from one's tacit assumptions than one can achieve distance from being white, male, American, or a father, if one is those things. But the absence of distance from one's metatheory suggests that one cannot help doing the scholarship one does, and that others in the professional community cannot help rewarding or punishing it and other received scholarship. That might all be very well if the community at large could agree upon and articulate its tacit preferences. But where tacit preferences and metatheories are themselves scattered and diverse, the direful end of Kuhnian logic is reached. "We didn't like your book because it raised the wrong questions." "Why were the questions 'wrong' "? "Because our questions are 'right.' " "Why are your questions right?" "Because we believe them to be so, and we can't help following our beliefs."

In order to avoid the possibility that future academic dialogues will need to be borrowed from the language of the Red Queen, the contributors to this Symposium have presented us with some conceptual devices to avoid pressing Kuhnian logic too far. Three such devices potentially prevent us from racing to conclusions that Kuhn himself would repudiate. The devices are the concept of a text, the concept of interpretation, and the concept of critical standards. Each of the essays in the Symposium discusses one or more of these conceptual devices.

The discussion that follows may appear to focus on only some of the contributions to this Symposium, but it draws on the insights of each of the participants. The arguments of Professors Levinson,[2] Fish,[3] and Nelson[4] receive extended attention, but my comments on the relationship between "the text" and its "meaning" have been informed by the essays of Professors Hancher[5] and James White,[6] and those on interpretation by the essay of Professor Graff.[7] It seems to me pointless, in fact, to consider any of the arguments I subsequently advance without the benefit of exposure to each of the articles that precipitated them. I have had the advantage of seeing those articles in draft form; the authors have also had the advantage of not seeing mine.

II

The role played by the concept of a text in the dialogue invited by this Symposium is nicely illustrated by the example from which Stanley Fish draws the title of his recent book, *Is There a Text in This Class?*[8] In Fish's book a student asks an

English professor that question; the professor responds by saying, "Yes, it's the *Norton Anthology of Literature*." Such a response conveys the "normal" meaning of a text: a common source that is agreed upon as the basis of classroom work. But Fish tells us that the student meant the question in another way; her meaning was (to paraphrase): "Do the source materials of this course have a meaning independent of the way in which they are interpreted?"[9] In asking the latter version of the question the student may well have been seeking to ascertain whether she would be given a choice not of sourcebooks but of methods of interpretation.

The second version of the student's question is designed to make Fish's point: appeals to texts need not be seen as appeals to anything finite or definitive. For example, when a teacher or a judge or a club member says, "Our text (or our rule or practice) is such and such," he or she may be attempting to remind others in a "community" that the community tacitly agrees to regard a particular source as a significant piece of data from which discussion may begin or even where, in the views of some, it may ultimately end. ("The Constitution requires"; "the practice of the club is _____.") But if others regard the speaker as really saying, "Our 'text' is the gospel according to me and others who hold my theoretical viewpoint," then the community consensus is not one about the significance of a document. Indeed, the consensus assumes that the document has no importance independent of how it is interpreted. An agreement by a community to regard a source as a legitimate basis from which interpretations can emanate, Fish argues, is not an agreement to regard that source as objectively valid.

One can readily see that if the second meaning of text is accepted, the concept of a text does not end up being much help as a device to resolve interpretive disputes. If, as Fish claims, the only value of a text is what it means to the reader, if meaning is necessarily subjective and personal, and if one person's meaning has no necessary claim to superiority over another's, then a decision to begin with the text is just a decision of administrative convenience. And that is just the point Sanford Levinson seeks to make in his essay on constitutional interpretation. For Levinson, beginning the process of constitutional adjudication with the constitutional text does not advance the process at all because the text is susceptible of so many possible meanings and has been so regularly interpreted in diverse and contradictory ways. One can understand the role of the Constitution in adjudication, Levinson argues, only if one substitutes for the word "text" the phrase "currently dominant theory of the meaning of the text." And Levinson suggests that at present no currently dominant theory of meaning exists, except in the sense that theory of meaning can be equated with political preference.[10]

With Levinson's conversion of Fish's second meaning of text to a principle of constitutional interpretation we may be very near despair, as Justice Holmes was wont to say. But something rather elementary seems to have been forgotten: why does the practice of beginning with a text (in the conventional sense) exist? Why not teach a class on constitutional law without the Constitution, or a course on the Iliad (to borrow one of the illustrations used by James White in his essay) without the Iliad? Fish and Levinson would have a ready answer: it is convenient to designate certain entities as starting places for discussions of meaning. But in saying that, they come perilously close to saying that the entity (Constitution or Iliad) is a source of meaning, or at least a place where the possible superiority of one theory of meaning over another can be demonstrated.

I suspect that one begins with a text, rather than beginning—and ending—with one's glosses on the text, not only because one wants a basis for exegesis but because one senses that one's glossed conclusions are not the end of the matter. It is an obvious fact of academic life that many texts endure longer than their glossators. It is significant that, notwithstanding all the Supreme Court cases that have glossed the Constitution, one still begins the process of constitutional adjudication by asking, "What does the text say?," even if the meaning of the words has changed dramatically over the years. The fact that texts will have different meanings for different people in the same generation, or even radically different meanings to different generations, is no reason to conclude that the concept of meaning entirely subsumes the concept of text.

Indeed, it would seem that on those occasions when meaning seems most radically indeterminate, the role of a text becomes most powerful. If none of us sitting in a room can agree what sexual freedom means, and we begin by positing radically different theories of the concept, sooner or later the discussion becomes so personalized, or so abstract, or so polarized, that it collapses. To save the discussion we need an example, a case, a passage—something against which we can test our observations. Texts serve this function; this may be the reason we agree to begin with texts in the first place. And while we may want to end with a theory of meaning, that theory is literally meaningless without the text. When the student in Fish's example asked her professor, "Is there a text in this class?" and he finally understood that she meant the question in its second sense, the professor gave an answer. His answer was "Yes there is a text in this class; what's more, it has meanings, and I'm going to tell you what they are." [11] His answer assumed that talking about meaning made little sense without a reference point for the discussion.

Thus Fish and Levinson seem not to have distinguished clearly between two uses of texts: as a repository of objective truths and as a basis for giving concrete application to proposed relative truths. It is not necessary to believe that the Constitution embodies certain timeless values, and that its language must be made to conform to those values, for one to claim that constitutional adjudication must at some point refer to the Constitution's text. One need only believe that it is relevant and necessary, in order to clarify the meaning of a designated source, to use the source itself as a basis for extracting the meaning. We see here a kind of epistemological overkill: in order to prevent texts from being a source of objective meanings, Fish and Levinson are attempting to prevent texts from being a source of any meanings.

III

One can see how the two uses of text merge in the professor's response quoted above. By saying the text has "meanings and I'm going to tell you what they are," the response seems to be assuming that the meanings of a text could be discovered and articulated. Here one moves from the concept of a text to the concept of interpretation. Fish and Levinson may not actually be claiming that texts do not really exist, but rather that the meaning of a text cannot be distinguished from the currently persuasive interpretations of that text. That is a distinction worth lingering over.

Assume that a scholar discovers a previously inaccessible set of source materials and publishes the materials, with emendations and an introduction. If the introduction interprets the materials, there may come a point where it is difficult for others to distinguish what makes the materials accessible from what makes them interesting or significant. In the conventional view of interpretation, this point is likely to endure until some other scholar is able to penetrate the materials themselves and use them to challenge the first scholar's interpretation. When the challenge surfaces, it seems that we have one text with two possible meanings.

Fish and Levinson argue that this view of interpretation is misplaced. It is not the accessibility of materials that determines how they will be interpreted; it is the presence of interpretive communities that determines what materials will be made accessible. As Fish puts it, "one doesn't just find a history. . . . The distinction between a 'found' history and an 'invented' one is finally nothing more than a distinction between a persuasive interpretation and one that has failed to convince." [12] While such a response may sound extreme, it appears to have some powerful explanatory value. How else does one account for the emergence of approved subjects for research at various points in history? How else can one explain the rejection and subsequent acceptance of whole disciplines, such as psychology, or entire theories, such as natural selection or relativity? And cannot the marked fragmentation and polarization of certain growth disciplines, such as economics or legal history, be similarly explained as by-products of the subtle pressures of an interpretive community? Moreover, Fish's and Levinson's arguments seem to rest on a proposition of marked common sense, that scholarly evidence in itself is not very interesting without accompanying interpretations of that evidence. [13]

But before we conclude too easily that the argument that interpretive communities shape the directions of scholarly research is simply a grandiose way of articulating the perfectly sensible proposition that evidence, data, and source materials are what one makes of them, we should recall the implications of that argument. For this relativistic approach undermines the concept of the text as an independent entity. How does one assess the value of interpretations if their truly significant feature is not the evidence on which they rest but what they do with that evidence? Moreover, if the source materials of interpretations are themselves tacitly predetermined, an appeal to the approved source materials of an interpretive community to test the validity of interpretations advanced by members of that community is not an appeal to anything. In short, interpretation is all, text is nothing. As Fish puts it, "getting 'back-to-the-text' is not a move one can perform, because the text one gets back to will be the text demanded by some other interpretation." [14] And now, if we hear Levinson chiming in, "Yes, and all interpretations are just personal preferences," we seem, perhaps, closer to despair than ever.

But the argument of Fish and Levinson contains some unresolved internal difficulties. One involves its response to breakthroughs in scholarship (revolutions in the Kuhnian sense). By its insistence that the tacit presuppositions of interpretive communities determine the worth of scholarly source materials as well as the success or failure of current scholarly interpretations, the argument places itself in a dilemma. Either its concept of interpretation is sufficiently deterministic that it inadequately characterizes the presence of breakthroughs, or its concept of an interpretive community is so broad and open-ended as to be virtually meaningless.

Suppose a work appears that fundamentally reorients scholarly inquiry (at least within a discipline). The work is acclaimed not only because it seems to provide plausible and suggestive interpretations of source materials, but also because it seems to have asked the right questions. The work becomes famous within its discipline. It is talked about, dissected, criticized; it stimulates additional work that uses its methodological framework or asks similar questions. On some occasions such a work may even transform the identity of a discipline; scholars in that discipline cease adopting one perspective on research and adopt another.

How can this phenomenon occur—and it has occurred regularly in the history of academic learning—if interpretation is as constrained a process as Fish and Levinson claim? If the selection of fruitful source materials and the success or failure of interpretations is predetermined by the inarticulate values of a community, why should anyone attempt a breakthrough? Indeed, how can one admit the notion of breakthroughs at all if one is a determinist about the nature of scholarly research?

Fish's response to the last point is that while most scholarly activity begins from "shared points of departure," some is more "radically innovative": it "challenges the assumptions within which ordinary practices go on . . . in order to refine [the category of the ordinary] and reshape its configurations." [15] Thus there will be persons who begin work within the community's tacit boundaries, but who find those boundaries confining or disturbing and eventually persuade others that the boundaries need redefinition. The idea of scholarship as persuasion rather than demonstration is, in fact, central to Fish's analysis.

But how does the scholar go about persuading? Obviously it is not enough to simply assert "my research paradigm is better than yours": one has to demonstrate its superiority. Moreover, if the idea of an interpretive community is to be taken seriously, one would expect the demonstration (or persuasion) to occur with respect to source materials that the community approves. In other words, to persuade other scholars who start (in Fish's model) with a commitment to shared points of departure that those points of departure are wrongheaded, one needs to work within the common language of the community. But then what does it mean to talk about "challenging the assumptions within which ordinary practices go on"? The scholar is, in Fish's view, always within the assumptions; he or she cannot persuade others that the assumptions are misguided without using the language and techniques that the assumptions permit.

Thus if the concept of an interpretive community is broadened to allow for the phenomenon of breakthroughs, the concept appears to become so broad as to be unintelligible. It may at first seem illuminating to say, as Fish says in his essay, that if a judge "decided a case on the basis of whether or not the defendant had red hair . . . he would be continuing the direction of an enterprise . . . other than the judicial," [16] but to say that "lunatic fringe" or "off the wall" scholarship is not within the enterprise does not really advance discussion. If an interpretive community includes everyone who even marginally performs the enterprise of intradisciplinary scholarship, how seriously can one take the idea that scholars are truly constrained by the community? One might as well say that one is constrained by living in the Occident. To be sure, one is, but does that mean that one cannot demonstrate that some well-intentioned ideas put forth by Occidentals are worthy of less respect than others? And if one cannot—if any well-intentioned idea put forth is worthy of equal respect at its initial formulation, and persuasion is everything—then the burden seems to me to be on Fish to articulate more fully how the persuasion process works. I fear that if Fish were to attempt such an articulation he would find that his distinction between persuasion and demonstration cannot be usefully maintained.

There is, however, an important distinction lurking here: the distinction between scholarship as ultimately contingent, in the sense that it is shaped by paradigms within a professional community and beliefs within the larger culture, and scholarship as provisionally finite, in the sense that certain works appear, are evaluated, and provide opportunities for concrete disagreements by persons who may share metatheories but differ sharply on issues of a less exalted kind. By missing this distinction Fish and Levinson apparently fail to recognize that one cannot address the question of how scholarship is received by communities without addressing the scholarship that in fact appears. On some occasions new scholarship may be wholly cognizable within the tacit interpretive framework of a community; on other occasions it may not. But on all occasions, the merits of a work of scholarship cannot be determined independently of an assessment of the work itself. Judgments about scholarships cannot be said to be wholly determined; they are susceptible to reevaluation by exposure to the scholarship being judged. Indeed it may be the appearance of seminal scholarship that stimulates the formation of mini-communities ("schools" of thought), rather than the presence of communities that predetermine what scholarship will be seminal.

In making these last comments am I intending to resurrect objectivity in interpretation? [17] I have earlier suggested that one of the purposes of arguments of interpretive indeterminacy is to expose as fiction the idea that the contributions of a work of literature, academic or otherwise, can be objectively or universally valid. But before we take delight in the exposure of another fiction, it is worth asking what is being claimed as fictional. Several possibilities exist. One is the idea that there can be an objectively right answer for any question of interpretation at any time. Another is the idea that an answer that is right is correct for all time. Still another is the idea that human beings can suspend their own subjective beliefs and come to accept an answer as right that they first felt was wrong. And still another is the idea that criteria other than subjective political judgments exist for addressing the question, "How does one determine whether an answer is right?"

Of the four possibilities, I think that Levinson regards all four as fictional, and that Fish regards the former two as fictional and the latter two as problematic. I have no quarrel with Fish or Levinson about the second of the possibilities being fictional. My differences center on the other possibilities, where, again, I think Fish and Levinson have begged some questions.

It is hard to separate objectivity from universality. If both ancient Greece and early nineteenth-century America tolerated the practice of human slavery, those cultures can be said to have tacitly admitted that an answer to the problem of developing a labor force was making some humans the property of others. Slavery was thus a "right" answer for those cultures. It is now a "wrong" answer for us. Does that mean that it was never right? (The same evolutionary argument could be made for democracy or equality.) In short, if one admits that all values are eventually culturally and temporarily determined, must one admit that no answer can ever be truly right? If so, relativism must surely prevail over objectivism, because for every truth one can find, if one searches far and wide enough in the history of human civilization, its negation.

But suppose the first possible meaning of objectivity is a more modest one: what has been demonstrated to be a right answer for a community at a point in time and space. I use "demonstrated" rather than "asserted" or "assumed" advisedly. If every community paradigm has its "puzzles," to use Kuhn's language, there will be questions to which the community urgently seeks answers, and if I am correct that the quest for the answers must take place within the common language of the community, then prospective answers to urgent questions must be shown to be right; the questions would not be urgent if they could be asserted or assumed away. And it is clear that for a time some answers are shown to be right, at least in the sense that they are provisionally accepted and used as a basis for inquiring about other questions. (The theory of relativity is currently taken to have been shown to be right in this sense.)

All objective truth is, in this usage, merely current provisionally accepted truth. But while the usage is modest, it is not identical to no truth at all or to the aggregate of prejudice. This is because when members of an interpretive community are persuaded (or have demonstrated to them) that a question has been answered successfully, they cannot be said to have arrived at a consensus of subjective beliefs. They retain their widely divergent beliefs on most of the rest of life; they merely agree that for a time an answer is right. But that agreement is not insignificant, and it is not untutored. It is, in the case of those persuaded, something like a suspension or rejection of an earlier belief that another answer, or no answer, was right. In this modest sense, then, objectivity does not oppose relativism, it opposes the belief that no answers that do not flow from one's prejudices are ever possible. It opposes a political determinism that leads very rapidly to nihilism.

Levinson, I think, is prepared to embrace nihilism as I describe it; Fish, however, is not. Fish would retain the possibility that humans can accept an answer as right that they first thought was wrong: they have been persuaded. But Fish also wants to retain, along with the idea of persuasion, the claim that reader sensibilities rather than texts determine interpretation. To avoid the apparent contradiction between making the personal beliefs of a reader all that counts in interpretation and his persuasion model, he posits the idea that if one is persuaded to adopt the interpretation of another, when one first thought that interpretation to be wrong, one has changed one's belief structure. As Fish puts it, "the fact that my mind may someday be other than it now is does not alter the fact that it is what it now is."[18] One "cannot be a relativist," Fish claims, "because . . . one believes what one believes, and one does so without reservation."[19] The fact that "one's beliefs . . . are subject to change" has "no real force" since "until a change occurs the interpretation that seems evident to me will continue to seem so."[20]

At this point Fish goes to extreme lengths to avoid any close encounters with nihilism. Instead of conceding the common-sense possibility that one of the major reasons interpretations and even beliefs are regularly subject to change is that they confront evidence that renders them suspect even to their proponents, Fish insists that one either holds beliefs (which dominate the evidence supporting those beliefs) or relinquishes those beliefs for other equally dominating ones. But that description of the process of changing one's mind as a scholar borders on the nonsensical. It forces Fish to make claims like "to live by . . . the position that [one is] forever analyzing beliefs, without ever being committed to any . . . is not a position any of us can occupy."[21] Such a position, however, is not only comprehensible, it has been and continues to be occupied by numerous scholars.

The fact is that one changes one's beliefs and one's scholarly interpretations when they do not seem to comport with or illuminate the world around one. The world may be a confined scholarly world, consisting largely of specialized evidence and interpretations, or it may be the larger culture. Although one's own perceptions necessarily shape one's understanding of the world, experience also shapes one's perceptions, and the normal state of belief may well be one in which people are trying to make sense of their experiences, whether professional or not, and are having difficulty making sense of them.

Why does Fish insist on pretending that changing one's beliefs and interpretations is so unimportant? I suspect it is to avoid the nihilism of the fourth possibility outlined above, that the rightness of a scholarly answer can only be determined by subjective political preferences. By refusing to admit that one can analyze beliefs without being committed to any, or that changing one's mind is a process with real force, Fish avoids the relativist-nihilist dilemma, in which persons who claim that successful scholarship is always a question of politics are asked, "But if I then disagree with your politics, why should I pay any attention to your scholarship?" Fish would have us all being persuaded by each other, but none of us relativists. But if once we hold a belief that we cannot admit the superiority of another belief, how can we be persuaded? Or if we are being persuaded, why are we not making relative comparisons between beliefs? Ultimately Fish avoids the relativist-nihilist dilemma by pretending that it isn't there.

It is curious to observe Fish and Levinson, who acknowledges his debt to Fish, ending up opponents on the questions of whether relativism exists and is a good thing. I do not think they are true opponents, because I think Fish's claim that he and no one else can be a relativist is a pretense. But assuming Fish's position to be genuinely held, neither his nor Levinson's responses to the issues of interpretation and critical standards ultimately lead anywhere. Fish ends up as trapped in his persuasion model as Levinson is in his political preference model. William Nelson, on the other hand, seeks to avoid both traps, and to formulate some criteria for distinguishing minimally competent and outstanding scholarship. The question is whether one ought to encourage Nelson in his effort.

IV

Nelson's essay argues that "new standards of criticism and evaluation are needed"[22] in the field of legal history, and by extrapolation asserts that the issues of the content of critical standards is a highly significant one for academic life as a whole. One could hardly disagree with Nelson's extrapolation. Moreover, he makes some useful points along the way. Nelson correctly surmises that American legal history is currently a strikingly divided field; that the causes of the divisions are "deep and structural"; and that the field will continue to be divided for some time to come.[23] Nelson's principal purpose in writing his essay—to seek to defend the proposition that critical standards need to be taken seriously against a barrage of polemics—is an admirable one. But it should be apparent from the respectful tone of these comments that I don't agree with most of the observations I find central to Nelson's argument. In particular, three distinctions that Nelson seeks to make are incapable of being drawn as sharply as he claims, and the problems with those distinctions plague his effort to advance criteria for judging the worth of scholarly work.

One distinction is that between "plain error of fact" and "differing factual interpretations."[24] Nelson attempts to argue that "factual accuracy" is a threshold criterion for minimum competence in scholarship, but that too often critics confuse errors of facts with alternative interpretations of ambiguous facts. He would restrict factual criticism, in legal history, to plain errors of fact. Nelson concedes, however, that critics will "rarely find plain errors in published scholarly work,"[25] so it is a little hard to see what is accomplished by his restriction.

But even if one holds a different view of the practical effect of Nelson's suggestion, the earlier discussions of text and interpretation have illustrated how difficult it is to draw bright lines between the source materials of scholarship and the use to which those materials are put. It is equally difficult to draw bright lines between fact and interpretation in legal history. I have claimed elsewhere that to the extent objective facts exist in history, their existence is rarely very meaningful until they are placed in some interpretive structure, at which point they cease to be objective.[26] One need not adopt that position, however, to reject Nelson's distinction. What is the point of making factual accuracy an evaluative criterion for scholarship if factual accuracy is either so obvious (and uninteresting), or so problematic?

Moreover, what does it mean to distinguish between an error of fact and a factual interpretation? Such a distinction seems at first glance to presuppose that some interpretations are nonfactual. Nelson, however, is not talking about different types of interpretations; he is talking about the process by which ambiguous facts lend themselves as support to contrary interpretations. But how does one know whether a fact is ambiguous until one has sought to interpret it? If Nelson seeks to deter scholar P, who has spent his or her working life studying a given set of source materials, from criticizing scholar Q's interpretation of those materials because P's and Q's "factual interpretations [are] derived from different perspectives,"[27] his task is a quixotic one.

Nelson does not linger over the "plain error of fact/differing factual perspective" distinction; he may not even regard it as central. His next two distinctions, however, are at the core of his essay. One is a distinction between aesthetic or ideological preferences and critical standards;[28] the other is a distinction between a pluralistic political order, which "treats all ideological choices as equal,"[29] and a consensus of scholars from which evaluative "standards of quality" emanate.[30] Neither distinction survives close analysis.

Nelson apparently feels that while it is legitimate for scholars to allow their aesthetic or ideological preferences to shape their critical responses, the aesthetic and ideological dimensions of criticism should be made explicit. That suggestion reminds me of proposals in the 1930s that judges should search their souls, discover their biases, and state them in their opinions. Even if scholars were able to do so, what would be the point? Suppose someone writes a review of a book by Nelson and says, "Nelson has a very pleasant style. But then I always have liked short, snappy sentences." Does making the aesthetic preference explicit inform the character of the review?

Not only is it difficult to separate ideological and aesthetic preferences from critical reactions, but criticism would probably suffer if the separation could be achieved. Penetrating critiques come when ideology, aesthetics, and conventional techniques of criticism are fused. A critic may be motivated to attack an author for ideological or aesthetic reasons, but the criticism cannot take place wholly at that level in order to be effective. The critic must also ground his or her attack on appeals to a spectrum of practitioners who share a common sense of the discourse of a discipline. Penetrating criticism invariably comes to use this language of professional discourse, but its penetrating qualities come from the superimposition of ideological or aesthetic judgments onto that language. Thus ideological and aesthetic preferences not only cannot disclaimed be in professional criticism, but they should not be disclaimed. Their value is that they inform and add a new dimension to discourse.

Finally, Nelson claims that American political culture is pluralistic, but that interpretive communities of American scholars are consensual. That is, in the larger world all ideological choices are equal, but in the academic world a consensus will (and should) determine that some choices are more equal than others. Nelson seems to be suggesting that one of the reasons for having such consensual determinations is to surmount the disintegrative efforts of pluralism. Again, this distinction seems to assume a sharp separation between ideological judgments and professional discourse. If all ideological choices are equal, how can some professional choices be worth more than others? Only, apparently, because professional choices are somehow not ideological. But then what is the meaning of consensus as Nelson employs the term? It surely cannot be a neutral, objective consensus, for Nelson began his essay by showing how such a consensus, at least within the discipline of American legal history, has broken down decisively.[31] It seems that what Nelson means by consensus is something like what Fish means by interpretive community: shared tacit presuppositions about the nature of scholarly inquiry.

The trouble with that meaning of consensus is that Nelson repeatedly insists that he is not prepared to make distinctions between aesthetic or ideological preferences within the academy and those in the rest of life. But if Nelson is correct, why should there be any fear that communities of scholars will make such distinctions? Nelson seems to be claiming that American academic life either neutralizes one's preferences when one is doing scholarship or enables one to determine that one set of disciplinary preferences is better than another. Yet Nelson also claims that Americans cannot make such a determination in the outside world.

In short, Nelson's approach repeatedly insists on separations—academic life from outside life, facts from interpretations, preferences from standards—that cannot usefully be made. That is why, when Nelson ultimately comes to define the criteria he believes can be used to identify competent or outstanding scholarship, he has to resort to words and phrases like "comprehensibility," "contribution to the growth of knowledge," "unconventionality," and "influence"[32]—words and phrases that beg questions. An essential feature of modern academic life—a major reason symposia like this currently exist—is that scholars have come to realize that the separations Nelson proposes simply do not solve the problems he addresses.

V

The contributions of Nelson's essay, taken together with Fish's and Levinson's, demonstrate the interrelationship among the three themes I am addressing. As Nelson's assumptions become evident, the issues of text, interpretation, and critical standards reveal themselves as of a piece. Each of the themes can be seen as subsidiary to a larger inquiry: how is it that contemporary scholars have become so self-conscious—one might even say nervous—about the meaningfulness of the two basic features of their enterprise, the source material with which they work and the process by which they make sense of that material? How is it that at a time when scholarly life seems liberated from conventional constraints, its practitioners are so unsure about what they ought to be doing and how to judge its worth?

These questions lie at the bottom of the efforts to unravel the relationship between text and context, fact and interpretation, objectivity and subjectivity, professional standards and personal bias that occur throughout this Symposium. How does one begin to explain the presence of these questions at this juncture in the history of American academic life? The safe answer is that one ought not to begin such an explanation; it is likely to result in what one of my critics has attempted to call "ad hoc sociological apercus."[33] But I cannot resist noting that Nelson's effort to distinguish between ideological pluralism and a professional consensus on what constitutes good scholarship has a discernible (and to me revealing) character. It is the distinction of a scholar who seeks to reaffirm the validity of hierarchical professional standards while at the same time suggesting that hierarchical social values are no longer permissible in today's society; all ideological positions deserve equal respect.

There is a vivid modern history behind that position. The period between the end of the Second World War and the present has been one in which class values, in the areas of taste, intellect, and culture, have given way, at least symbolically, to pluralistic values. Homogeneous and hierarchical definitions of what is "best," in fields as disparate as politics and popular music, have been replaced by heterogeneous and pluralistic definitions. But while these trends have been occurring in the larger culture, the trends in academic life have been in the opposite direction. Specialization, advanced training, the development of jargon, and the emergence of academic journals and academic presses have been features of scholarly life since the War. Indeed the position of intellectuals without specialized academic credentials—the Edmund Wilsons and Walter Lippmanns of another era—has become precarious to the point of unrespectability.

Given these trends, the discovery by Kuhn and others that interpretive communities perform a sociological as well as a pristine educational function takes on a certain inevitability; moreover, the trends help explain the excitement and unease that Kuhnian contributions have generated within academic life. But it seems that in a post-Kuhnian world a simple point needs to be remembered: it is profoundly disconcerting to hold starkly separate a commitment to elitism within one's professional life and a commitment to pluralism outside it. The two lives cannot be so facilely separated. The lessons taught by exposure to the mores of hierarchical professional communities spill over into the rest of life; a commitment to pluralism in the larger world spills over into a commitment to pluralism in one's professional concerns. Some individuals may seek, and even achieve, the stark separation I have described; but I suggest that for others the task will reinforce an always present concern that in American culture academic life is somehow marginal.

The basic normative issue here, however, is not whether people should hold apart or fuse their personal and professional lives. It is whether a pluralistic theory of the process of gaining knowledge represents an abdication of what scholarship and education is all about. For me education is not, and cannot be, an interchange between equals. If every person's opinion is valued equally, regardless of ability or training or experience, education is simply not taking place. Academic life has been arranged on the principle that contributions are not valued equally; efforts to replace that principle with parliamentary democracy have resulted in academic freedom of an uninformed and unsettling kind. It is unsound (to use a word Fish deplores) to think that because one is an egalitarian one is therefore unqualified to recognize the unequal quality of educational achievements; it is unsound to think that because one is a pluralist one must view all scholarship as equally meritorious.

To characterize the evaluative standards of academics or other professional elites as radically indeterminate is therefore either to abdicate educational responsibility or to advocate an alternative approach to education that is profoundly misguided. Professional life in American culture, at this time in its history, is dominated by elites. Elite status is not just linked to luck and politics; it is also linked to training and competence. To pretend that training and competence are just euphemisms for luck and politics is as self-deluding as to pretend that there is no text in which to find meaning, or that there are no materials against which interpretations can be judged, or that there are no critical standards except majoritarian aesthetics and ideology. This sort of self-delusion can lead in a variety of negative directions: toward emptiness; toward hypocrisy; toward a withdrawal into one's inner torment; toward unrealistic expectations that braver, happier political communities will emerge. For me such solutions start from the wrong premise. Academic life, like the rest of life, doesn't need to be made over; it is difficult, complicated, and enjoyable enough as it is.

NOTES

1. T. Kuhn, The Structure of Scientific Revolutions (1962). See also Kuhn's second edition (1970) and T. Kuhn, The Essential Tension (1977).

2. Levinson, *Law as Literature,* 60 Texas L. Rev. 373 (1982).

3. Fish, *Working on the Chain Gang: Interpretation in Law and Literature,* 60 Texas L. Rev. 551 (1982); *see also* S. Fish, Is There A Text In This Class? (1980).

4. Nelson, *Standards of Criticism,* 60 Texas L. Rev. 447 (1982).

5. Hancher, *Dead Letters: Poems and Wills,* 60 Texas L. Rev. 507 (1982).

6. J. White, *Law as Language: Reading Law and Reading Literature,* 60 Texas L. Rev. 415 (1982).

7. Graff, *"Keep off the Grass," "Drop Dead," and Other Indeterminacies: A Response to Sanford Levinson,* 60 Texas L. Rev. 405 (1982).

8. S. Fish *supra* note 3.

9. *Id.* at 305. The student's actual words, as reported by Fish, were: "Do we believe in poems and things, or is it just us?" *Id.*

10. Levinson, *supra* note 2, at 374–75 n.7.

11. Fish, *supra* note 3, at 371.

12. Fish, *supra* note 3, at 557, 559.

13. As an example, take the tendency of Supreme Court Justices in the early nineteenth century to engage in a variety of practices—manipulation of the Court's docket; correspondence with lawyers about cases pending before the Court; drafting of bills for congressmen and speeches for Presidents; membership in banks and educational institutions that regularly litigated in the federal circuit courts on which the Justices sat—that would now be regarded as raising serious questions of judicial ethics. Justice Joseph Story was notable, though not unique, among Justices who engaged in such practices. When Story's son published a *Life and Letters* of his father in 1851, he not only did not choose to comment on the practices, he included correspondence that made their existence unequivocally clear. Nor did Albert Beveridge's four volumes on John Marshall and his Court, published in 1919, or Charles Warren's three-volume *A History of the Supreme Court of the United States,* which appeared three years later, find the practices interesting enough to comment upon. Now we are in an age in which the ethics of past judges are of great public interest; the Marshall Court practices might well be worth interpreting. But the evidence of their existence is nothing new.

14. S. Fish, *supra* note 3, at 354.

15. *Id.* at 366.

16. Fish, *supra* note 3, at 556–57.

17. *Cf.* the dispute between Professors Owen Fiss and Paul Brest: Fiss, *Objectivity and*

Interpretation, 34 STAN. L. REV. 739 (1982); Brest, *Interpretation and Interest,* 34 STAN. L. REV. 765 (1982).

18. FISH, *supra* note 3, at 361.
19. *Id.*
20. *Id.*
21. *Id.* at 370.
22. NELSON, *supra* note 4, at 452.
23. *Id.* at 451.
24. *Id.* at 484.
25. *Id.*
26. White, *Truth and Interpretation in Legal History,* 79 MICH. L. REV. 594 (1981).
27. NELSON, *supra* note 4, at 484.
28. *Id.* at 490–91.
29. *Id.* at 481.
30. *Id.* at 492.
31. *Id.* at 452–72.
32. *Id.* at 478–89.
33. Gordon, Book Review, 94 HARV. L. REV. 903, 912 (1981). I say "attempted" because "apercus" (a more telling word) appeared in an earlier draft of the review and was changed to "perceptions" by some zealous editor, who may have thought that the periodical's readership couldn't understand French. As Gordon was kind enough to point out, my having read and criticized his draft can hardly be taken as endorsing his review, except for its widely scattered compliments.

The Art of Revising History:
Revisiting the Marshall Court*

The subject of this essay is the nature and process of historical revisionism. In the course of my presentation I first focus on the meaning of a historical "record" and then advance some generalizations about the process by which that record becomes revised. The generalizations are then tested in an examination of "revisionist" scholarship on the Marshall Court, the history of which I am currently engaged in "rewriting." My central argument in this essay is that the role of revisionism in history has been widely misunderstood, and that a clearer under-standing of what is being revised and how the revising takes place is necessary.

A certain number of terms, such as "revisionist" history, "historiography," "angle of vision," "interpretive structure," and "shared sense" of the materials of history, are used throughout this essay. Although each term is defined and discussed as it arises, the first two terms are sufficiently central as to be worth some preliminary attention. "Revisionist" historical scholarship conventionally refers to that scholarship which seeks to displace an established interpretation of some feature of the past with a fresh interpretation; the new interpretation is said to "revise" professional understanding of a segment of history. The term revision-ist, in the conventional usage, presupposes the possibility that a fair amount of historical scholarship quite consciously accepts and fortifies established interpreta-tions (one might call such scholarship nonrevisionist). Whether that presupposition is sound is one of the inquiries of this essay.

Historiography conventionally refers to the study of scholarly interpretations of history, as distinguished from the history itself. In a subsequent section of this essay I survey the historiography of the Marshall Court and my focus, one could say, is not so much on what happened during the tenure of Chief Justice John Marshall as on the successive explanations that have been offered by historians for what happened. But another inquiry of this essay is whether a sharp distinction between the raw materials of history—the record of what happened—and interpre-tations of those raw materials can be meaningfully advanced. Thus the terms revi-

*16 Suffolk L. Rev. 659 (1982). A previous version of this essay was delivered as the 1982 Donahue Lecture at Suffolk Law School.

sionist history and historiography are first used in their conventional sense, but may require reformulation as the assumptions behind their orthodox usage are probed.

I The Historical "Record"

"[T]here can be no history of 'the past as it actually did happen,'" Karl Popper has written, "There can be only historical interpretations, and none of them final."[1] This deceptively categorical statement contains, on reflection, two seminal insights that form the starting point of my discussion. The first insight is that scholars who work with evidence from the past can never discover "what happened" in an unvarnished sense: the "facts" of history cannot be divorced from the significance attached to those facts by past and present interpretations. If one considers some logical implications of this insight, the traditional conception of a historical "record" appears in need of reconsideration.

The "record" of history has typically been conceived as an entity that exists and can be "discovered" by scholars. Many historians are taught, as graduate students, to test established scholarly interpretations against the record, an exercise not only calculated to teach critical reading of secondary sources but to instill in prospective scholars a faith that objective evidence exists in the historian's world. Much historical scholarship, in fact, seems to presuppose the possibility of an appeal beyond interpretations of the past to the record itself; the existence or non-existence of evidence is treated as a potential corrective to interpretations that ignore or distort that evidence.[2] At first glance this presupposition seems sound. Suppose a historian's interpretation of the causes of a war than began in 1616 places great emphasis on the religious persecutions of a particular sect. If the persecutions can subsequently be shown to have originated no earlier than the 1620s, their candidacy as a principal cause of the 1616 war is considerably undermined.

This example of an appeal to the record of history, however, turns out to be misleading. For current historians, the primary significance of the religious persecutions of the 1620s was not so much that they happened at all but that they ostensibly happened at a given time. By purportedly occurring prior to 1616 they became elements of a scholarly interpretation about the causes of war; by actually occurring later than 1616 they robbed that interpretation of much of its evidence. The meaning of the persecutions, then, was largely an interpretive meaning; their significance was linked to the interpretive framework in which they came to the attention of scholars from another time period.

When I say "primary significance" I do not mean to suggest that historical events are unintelligible without accompanying explanations for their occurrence. But I think that the primary use of the record of history is to confirm or correct existing interpretations of that record, and at some point it becomes hard to separate "fact" from interpretation. Thus I think Popper's assertion that there can be no history of the past as it actually did happen is not a mere flippancy. Truth in history, I have argued elsewhere, cannot easily be divorced from interpretation;

indeed, it may not make much sense to debate whether something actually happened in the past without assessing the significance of what is said to have taken place.[3]

It is, of course, possible to identify "facts" in history whose existence is significant independent of interpretations of why they occurred, and I am certainly not prepared to argue that unless an explanation for why some historical event happened can be provided, the event did not "happen." That there was an atomic bomb dropped on Nagasaki in 1945 we may surmise from tangible evidence in the record. Whether or not we know why the bomb was dropped, it was dropped. It may even be possible to formulate a continuum of historical events ranging from those whose occurrence has the potential to dwarf efforts to interpret them, to those whose occurrence has virtually no interest except as data for interpretations. But the point remains that it is hard to detach the existence of historical events from the meaning subsequent generations attach to their existence.

This brings me to Popper's second insight, that there can be "only" historical interpretations, and none of those interpretations can be considered final. If we think of the historical record as an entity in itself, distinct from any interpretations of it, this statement of Popper's seems problematic, because at some point there must be a "right" answer to the question "what did happen in the past," and once one has found that answer—discovered the record—it would seem there would be nothing more to ask. But if the major significance of historical events is not so much in their existence as in their meaning, then the question "what did happen?" is generally not worth separating from the questions "why did it happen?" and "what, if anything, can we learn from its occurrence?"

If I am right that what actually happened in the past is difficult to separate from the currently perceived significance of what is taken to have happened, one can see how interpretations of history can never be final. Each generation in the history of a civilization can be said to undergo at least a slightly different experience from the previous one. As a generation with a "new" sense of the present comes to approach the past, the perspectives from which it looks at events, personages, or ideas in history—what I will call its "angle of vision"—may well differ from the perspectives of previous generations. The "lessons" one generation draws from history may not be another's; one decade's priorities may be compatible with a reading of the past that differs from earlier readings.

One can readily think of examples illustrating this last point. In the 1960s the historical community "discovered" black history; did that mean that the records of historical actors who happened to be black had just surfaced in that decade? At various points in the twentieth century, Justice Holmes has been treated as a New Deal liberal, a proto-Fascist, a civil libertarian, an anti-civil libertarian, and a Chicago-school economist.[4] Did each new treatment of Holmes rest on new evidence? The American Revolution has been successively portrayed as a domestic power struggle, a triumph of mercantile and landowning interests, a legitimization of mob rule, the culmination of advanced natural rights theory, and a manifestation of the persistence in America of an anachronistic version of republican thought.[5] It may well have been all of those things at the same time.

The changing meaning different generations seem compelled to find in the past forms the basis of historical revisionism. A fascinating feature of revisionism in history is that it appears in the face of professional strictures that deemphasize it. Prospective historians are not encouraged to simply rewrite history according to their current predilections. On the contrary, many are cautioned, as part of their professional socialization, about reading history "backwards," or imposing their own value judgments on the past. They are warned about "presentism," urged to assume the "objective" role of the scholar, and exhorted to seek the truth, regardless of its contemporary implications. Given all this advice, it may seem remarkable that a significant percentage of historical scholarship deals with historiographical issues: historians regularly devote time and effort to reviewing the perspectives previous generations have brought to historical topics. Why should the historiographic perspectives of a work be so apparent, one might ask, if the historian's principal task is to find the truth and present it in an "objective" manner? Moreover, why should there be so much "revising" of the past if seeking and stating the truth is the principal function of the historian?

Historiographic issues inevitably emerge in the writing of history, I believe, because the principal purpose of historical scholarship is to confront the perspectives of previous historians. While the record of history plays a role in these confrontations, it is a role that is to an important extent determined by differences between the contrasting angles of vision of successive generations of historians. Revisionist scholarship in history can be seen, therefore, as not merely an occasional side effect of searches for "what actually happened," but as the normal mode of professional discourse. If I am correct in this suggestion, the conventional definition of historical revisionism may well rest on a misunderstanding of the process by which scholarly works in history become revised. There are some reasons for this apparent misunderstanding that I will subsequently discuss. At this point I want to set forth in more detail my conception of the process of revisionism.

II The Process of Historical Revisionism

If one compares successive scholarly interpretations of a historical topic, one will regularly find that the interpretations are often remarkably similar in their communication of certain information—dates, comments made by contemporary participants in events, physical settings, and so on—but are often dissimilar in their assessment of the significance of the information they take as a given. Moreover, one will rapidly become aware of the fact that while some historical topics are reconsidered far more than others, the reconsideration is not generally dependent on the degree of extant evidence about what is being reconsidered. There are abundant primary sources relating to the political career of Calvin Coolidge, but one is not greeted every Christmas, or even every Christmas in five, with a new Coolidge biography. There is very little reliable information available about the assassinations of Presidents Lincoln and Kennedy; that has not deterred historical investigations of those incidents from proliferating at a staggering pace.

One will also note that in nearly every case where a historian sets out to research a particular topic, previous interpretations of that topic exist, and some of those interpretations have more "standing" in the historical profession than others. The standing of an interpretation, however, cannot be said to rest exclusively on the authenticity of its research and the power of its writing, for, if this were the case, certain interpretations that are widely acknowledged as "classics" of scholarship and literature would have been infrequently revised. Yet it is just such "classics"—Henry Adams's history of the Jefferson and Madison administrations,[6] Frederick Jackson Turner's essays on the American frontier,[7] and Charles Beard's "economic interpretation of the Constitution"[8]—that subsequent historians most frequently address and "revise."

The principal reason that classics of historical scholarship provoke rather than deter revisionism is that their major impact on the community of historians is as interpretations rather than as repositories of information. The information they convey about a historical topic cannot easily be separated from the interpretations given to that information, and the "interpretive structure" of the works cannot be concealed. By the "interpretive structure" of a work of scholarship I mean the way in which the author's angle of vision informs and organizes his[9] use of raw materials. Adams' history of the Jefferson and Madison administrations has been denominated a "classic" because generations of scholars have come to regard the interpretive structure Adams employed in his portrayal of events during those administrations as peculiarly fertile and suggestive.

The realization that works of history necessarily have an interpretive structure leads us back to the earlier discussion of generational perspectives. It appears that the interpretive structures of historical works contain conscious and unconscious elements. A historian may selectively structure his narrative events to produce a particular interpretation, but at the time he may not be fully aware that he and his scholarly peers are coming to fasten increasingly on one set of interpretations as particularly illuminating and stimulating. The tacit choice by scholars to regard some interpretations as stimulating and fruitful, and other as hackneyed and prosaic, seems, at one level, to be unconscious and culturally determined. In a sense, different generations of historians can't help holding different angles of vision. The interpretive structure of a historian from one generation can never fully resemble that of his predecessors or successors.

The juxtaposition of different angles of vision held by different generations of historians provides the principal motivation for revisionist historical scholarship. Adams' history becomes revised because subsequent historians sense that Adams' reaction to the first quarter of the nineteenth century is that of an historian writing in the last years of that century. As Adams' angle of vision reveals itself to scholars who do not share it, Adams' portrait of the Jefferson and Madison administrations comes to be seen by twentieth century scholars as containing "archaic" and uncongenial elements.

Here we come upon a paradox that explains the peculiar vulnerability to revision of "classics" of historical scholarship. "Classics" can be seen as works in which the angle of vision of the historian and the raw materials of his subject are especially congruent, so that the interpretive structure of the work is invested with a striking coherence. It is that coherence which exposes the author's angle of vision and thereby invites subsequent historians, with different angles of vision, to revise the work's interpretations. Professor John Diggins, in a recent effort to resurrect the reputation of Charles Beard,[10] has argued that the strength of Beard's *An Economic Interpretation of the Constitution* came from the relevance of central questions addressed by the Constitution's framers—questions about the proper role of "interests" in society and the relationship of ideas about governance to the presence of "interests"—to the "progressive generation" of the early twentieth century, from whose experience Beard's angle of vision emanated.[11] The congruence of Beard's "progressive" view of history with the framers' view of society, Diggins argues, helped make *An Economic Interpretation of the Constitution* a "classic."[12] At the same time the uncongeniality of Beard's interpretive structure to "neo-Whig" historians of the 1950s and early 1960s resulted in Beard's being "dismissed . . . as well-intentioned but rather simple-mined historian who led astray an entire generation of scholars."[13]

Historical revisionism begins, then, not so much with a sense that a previous work is "wrong" in its recording of reality as that its interpretative structure is uncongenial. That sense, of course, emanates from the contemporary perspective of the revisionist. Arguably the most important step in the process of revisionism is one taken before any primary research is done—it is the realization that an existing interpretation of a subject is "dated." This realization is rarely based on an assessment of the reliability of evidence presented in an existing interpretation; it is normally based on a response to the questions an interpretation asks, its points of emphasis, its theoretical framework—in short, an assessment of its interpretive structure. Put another way, the most important step in the process of revisionism is the confrontation of dissimilar angles of vision. And the significance of angles of vision, for the theory of historiography being advanced here, is not that they exist but that they cannot be avoided; that they mirror the distinctiveness of a historian's perspective on the past whether or not the historian chooses to make them overt.

At this point a brief summary seems appropriate. I began with the argument that the historical record is difficult to distinguish from interpretations of that record and in many instances may have relatively little scholarly value independent of those interpretations. This argument led me to focus on the interpretative structure of works of historical scholarship, which, I argued, constitutes their most significant dimension. I then discussed, using "classics" of historical literature as illustrations, the relationship between the interpretive structure of a work and its angle of vision, and then went on to claim that historical revisionism is the inevitable product of the interaction of the different angles of vision of different generations of historians.

One will note that I use the word "inevitable" to describe the process of revisionism, and that I earlier suggested that angles of vision cannot be avoided. The determinism in that language is deliberate. To paraphrase Holmes, historical scholarship is a continuous series of "can't helps"; to paraphrase him again, confronting the works of previous historians is not so much a duty as a necessity.[14]

But so deterministic a view of historical scholarship, it may be said, does not help us explain why some works of history fare better than others, a phenomenon

I earlier took as a given. If all works of history eventually become revised, and if revisionism is bound to take place regardless of the coherence of a given work, how can one distinguish "good" from "bad" historical writing? In particular, if, in historical scholarship, interpretation is far more important and more interesting than the raw materials of the record, but at the same time the interpretive structure of a work is to an important extent inevitable, how does one formulate any criteria for assessing the worth of a historical work that are not themselves products of a peculiar generational angle of vision?

There is both a long and a short response to these queries. I have elsewhere attempted a preliminary version of the longer response;[15] here I shall content myself with the short one. The formulation of criteria for assessing the worth of a piece of scholarship cannot easily be divorced from the "merits" of the work itself. Different generations of scholars will have different definitions of what constitutes meritorious work, but those definitions will be affected by the work that appears. Thus, in one sense, a volume of historical scholarship is frozen in time, and will inevitably be revised; in another sense that volume helps define "good" and "bad" scholarship not only within its own time frame but elsewhere.

As a brief illustrative example, consider the works of three "progressive" historians who all produced "classics" of scholarship between 1910 and 1930: Turner, Beard, and Vernon Parrington.[16] By the 1950s and 1960s, changed perspectives in the community historians had resulted in the revision of Turner, Beard, and Parrington's major works; by 1968 Richard Hofstadter had written a volume on the three men that can fairly be called "post-revisionist," at least in the conventional sense of revisionism.[17] Hofstadter was not principally concerned with revising or repudiating the insights of Turner, Beard, and Parrington; he was concerned with understanding the interpretative structure of their works. His stance was that of the historiographer and the historian of ideas.

One might be tempted to conclude from this example that the current scholarly "fashions"—enthusiasms and disaffections—of historians are all that determine what a generation regards as "good" history. At one level, the level of generational "can't helps," I am prepared to argue that that conclusion is accurate. But at another level it is highly misleading. Turner, Beard, and Parrington did not merely reflect the approved modes of historical discourse between 1910 and 1930; they helped set the terms of that discourse. The "frontier thesis" as an explanation for American character captured the imagination of early twentieth-century historians in part because Turner advanced it, originally in an essay in 1893.[18] According to Diggins, Beard's "economic" interpretation "dramatically broke the spell of conventional political history."[19] Parrington's *Main Currents in American Thought,* which assumed that the writings of novelists, essayists, scholars, and statesmen were, despite their different genres, all fruitful sources for the historian of ideas, revitalized intellectual and literary history and anticipated the emergence, in the 1940s of the American Studies movement.[20]

The leap from recognizing the possibility of generational intellectual blinders to concluding that stature in a work of historical scholarship is simply a product of professional fashion is thus too facile a leap. Yet it is equally facile to assume the existence of universalistic criteria for determining the stature of historical works. The question of what constitutes "meritorious" scholarship in history, as in other disciplines, is as complex a question as the question of what caused a historical event to occur. But one need not explore the question of how "meritorious" scholarship qualifies for that designation, though it is surely worth independent exploration, to advance the general theory being proposed in this essay. The theory's postulate is that historical revisionism is essentially an interpretative process set in motion by factors deep within the generational context in which a work of scholarship is constructed, and that therefore nearly all historical writing is revisionist. That some revisionist works are taken to have more stature than others does not affect that claim, it merely raises additional questions. The conventional view that only some historical works can claim to be revisionist, and the implication of that view that revisionist works are superior to nonrevisionist works, therefore seem misplaced.

III Revisionism and Historiography

Let us recall, by way of introduction to this portion of the essay, the conventional definition of historiography previously set forth. Historiography has been conventionally defined, I noted, as the study of how history is written: one of the self-appointed tasks of historiographers is to compare and contrast the different perspectives of successive historical studies of the same topic. In the language of this essay, historiography can be seen as an effort to explore the effects of different angles of vision on the interpretive structures of various historical works, especially works whose interpretive structure is especially coherent and therefore peculiarly intelligible.

A query surfaces at this point. If nearly all historical writing is revisionist, and if the interpretive structure of a historical work dominates the raw materials from the "record" that the work uses, then the only truly interesting questions to ask about historical scholarship may be questions at the level of historiography. That query ostensibly confronts the general theory of this essay with a difficulty. If historiography is so basic to an understanding of the process by which historical scholarship is created, why do comparatively few historians devote themselves to historiography, at least as more than a preliminary excursus to their historical narratives? One response, of course, is that many historians have not appreciated the significance of historiography, as they have perhaps not appreciated the significance of revisionism. But I am not prepared to make that response. There appears to be a widely, and I think rightly, shared assumption among historians that a historiographic focus on the past, even when employed by skillful practitioners, needs to be supplemented by foci that penetrate closer to the materials in the historian's interpretive structure.

Beard's *An Economic Interpretation of the Constitution* again furnishes an example. With distance and a different angle of vision, a historian can easily see the value-laden dimensions of Beard's interpretive structure. Linguistic clues to Beard's "progressive" angle of vision abound in his "classic" history of the framers' motivations; it is easy to see how, at one level, Beard found in his raw materials what he expected, and perhaps needed, to find. The problem is that such an analysis is too easy. Beard's work is not a classic because Beard was a "progressive"; it is a classic, as Professor Diggins has pointed out, because the social issues that were central to Beard and other scholars of the progressive generation were also central to the generation of the framers, although the different generations gave radically different responses to those issues.[21] The dialectic of Beard's inquiries and his responses produced a work that took the framers both on their terms and on Beard's terms; a work that achieved a congruence of material and angle of vision.

To explain Beard's interpretation as that of a "progressive," then, is not very interesting or useful unless one further explains why a "progressive" angle of vision was particularly illuminating to the historical topic it addressed. To make that further explanation one needs a working understanding of the topic itself. Surface varieties of historiography only take us so far; they need to be supplemented by investigations of the body of material that is being filtered through a given historian's historiographic perspective.

It now appears that the general theory of this essay has doubled back on itself. The significance of raw materials in the historical record, I have argued, is difficult to assess independently of an assessment of the interpretative structure in which those materials are presented. Yet historical scholarship whose exclusive focus is on the history of angles of vision—"surface" historiography—is inadequate, I have claimed, unless one understands the materials being viewed as well as the viewpoint. But how does one understand those materials except through the interpretive structures of individual historians? I have suggested that current fashion may not be all that counts in historical scholarship, but what about current patterns of "interpretation," which may just be another version of fashion?

Here an analogy to my earlier discussion of stature in historical scholarship presents itself. Just as fashion can be said to be established by a work of scholarship as much as it can be said to reflect a response to a work of scholarship, the interpretive structure of a historian's product can be said to help define professional understanding of the "raw materials" that form the basis of his interpretation. Over time, continued reading of interpretations, supplemented by research in and teaching of the "raw materials" themselves, produces what is casually termed "expertise" with respect to selected historical topics, but is perhaps better described as a nascent interpretive structure. The reaction of one historian (the "critic") to another's (the "author's") published work can be described as the interaction of two interpretive structures, both of which contain a sense of the raw materials being interpreted. Such interactions can produce varieties of responses in the critic, ranging from a wholesale abandonment of the critic's interpretive structure for that of the author's, to a wholesale retention of the critic's interpretive structure, with consequent "dismissal" of the author's. Classics of historical scholarship tend to be works that at some phase of their existence caused numerous critics to adopt the interpretive structure of their authors; "forgotten" works are on the other end of the continuum; most works lie somewhere in between.

Historiography is thus an ingredient of the general theory of this essay, but not the whole recipe. The "record" of history, interpretations of that record, the angles of vision producing those interpretations of that record, and the contexts in which distinctive angles of vision appear are both separable and inseparable entities. One needs to understand the distinctiveness of such entities; one also needs to understand the process through which they interact with one another. I am calling that process the art of revisionism.

I have thus far spent no time on the term "art." That term is best approached, given the level of abstractness to which this essay has now ascended (or descended), through some concrete historiographic examples. My purpose in undertaking the following survey of previous writings on the Marshall Court is twofold: to illustrate some of the general observations made in the first two portions of this essay and to provide arguments for my conclusion that historical revisionism is best described as an art form. The examples given are somewhat more detailed than previous examples because they have also served, for a prospective "revisionist," as entry points to the materials of his prospective revision.

IV Visits and Revisits to the Marshall Court

A historiographical survey of works on the same topic not only uncovers changes in angles of vision, but also reveals certain continuities in the presentation of material and its interpretation. In addition, it reveals certain common assumptions about the topic itself. Let us characterize those continuities and common assumptions as constituting the "shared sense" of the topic under consideration. This "shared sense" seems to persist over time and to link different interpretive structures; it serves as an assumed frame of reference for investigations of the topic.

In the case of the Marshall Court the shared sense of historians can be encapsulated in four talismanic labels: it was a "nationalistic," "Federalist," "property-conscious," and "Chief Justice-dominated" Court. The origins of those labels, their shifting emphasis, and the complexities they conceal can be discerned from a brief review of the Court's historiography.

The first notable assessment of Chief Justice John Marshall and his Court by a noncontemporary came from Oliver Wendell Holmes, then Chief Justice of the Massachusetts Supreme Judicial Court, in 1901.[22] Holmes spoke on "Marshall Day," the centennial of Marshall's confirmation as the third Chief Justice of the United States. "Marshall Day" was celebrated all over the country; hundreds of testimonials were delivered, nearly all of them laudatory.[23] Holmes' remarks, also intended to be commemorative, were noteworthy because they were much less fulsome in their praise of Marshall than most of the other tributes. Holmes identified Marshall as possessing only "a strong intellect, a good style, personal ascendancy in his court, courage, justice, and the convictions of his party."[24] This assessment might seem reverent enough, but in the midst of the filiopietistic superlatives commemorators issued on "Marshall Day," it suggested, at least to Theodore Roosevelt, who was offended by Holmes' remarks, a certain grudging spirit.[25]

For our purposes, however, Holmes' assessment serves as the most interesting manifestation of the shared sense of the Marshall Court existing at the dawn of the twentieth century. Other commentators had stressed the "nationalistic" and "patriotic" features of the Marshall Court, often to the point of treating the Marshall decades as the first years of the Court's existence, although thirteen years had preceded Marshall's appointment. Holmes did not pursue the "nationalism" theme, but he seems to have assumed that the Marshall Court was "nationalistic." He also identified Marshall with the Federalist Party, thus raising the question of how a member of that party could dominate a Court that was composed, for the great bulk of Marshall's tenure, of five Republicans and only two Federalists. Finally, Holmes assumed that Marshall had achieved "personal ascendancy" in his Court. A conception of the Marshall Court as dominated by its Chief Justice had been fostered by contemporaries of Marshall, such as Thomas Jefferson and Justice William Johnson;[26] Holmes simply asserted Marshall's dominance as a given.

Interwoven with the "shared sense" of Marshall and his Court were Holmes's distinctive critical observations. Holmes argued, for example, that if Marshall was a "great man," he was "great" in part because he was "there" at a felicitous moment in history for "greatness."[27] In this argument a shared sense of Marshall was interwoven with Holmes' deterministic view of historical change. The result, to more conventional early twentieth-century minds such as that of Roosevelt, was to strip Marshall of some of his majesty. Roosevelt believed that "great men" made history; no such theory was contained in Holmes' angle of vision. In this sense Holmes was representative of the leading edge of academic opinion at the turn of the century and unrepresentative of more orthodox views.[28]

Between 1916 and 1919 the first and only "classic" of Marshall Court scholarship appeared—Albert Beveridge's four volume *The Life of John Marshall*.[29] Written by a U.S. Senator who was not a professionally trained historian, Beveridge's biography was so well received that even Parrington, who deplored Beveridge's "old Federalist prejudices," conceded that Beveridge's account was "able," "carefully documented," and "readable."[30] Yet Beveridge's account did not alter the image of Marshall and his Court presented in Holmes' brief remarks; it merely added details designed to reinforce that image. In Beveridge's pages Marshall consistently appeared as an "adamantine Federalist conservative,"[31] whose "influence over his associates was unparalleled,"[32] and whose "one and only great conception" was "American Nationalism."[33]

The image of Marshall presented by Holmes and Beveridge was perpetuated by Charles Warren in his multivolumed history of the Supreme Court of the United States, which first appeared in 1922.[34] Warren, who called Beveridge's life of Marshall "masterly,"[35] saw Marshall as preeminent among a line of judges whose "decisions . . . steadily enhanced the power of the National Government,"[36] as a figure of "overmastering mind and influence" on his Court;[37] and as a Federalist who "possessed a highly conservative nature and mental attitude."[38] The central jurisprudential theme of Warren's history was the role of the federal judiciary in "maintaining National supremacy," a role which, he argued, originated with Marshall.[39]

While Beveridge and Warren retained Holmes's emphasis on the labels "nationalist," "Federalist," and "Chief Justice-dominated" to characterize the Marshall Court, neither scholar retained Holmes' deterministic view of Marshall's role in history. For both Beveridge and Warren, Marshall's personal presence, intellectual acumen, and political convictions made a significant difference in the character of the Marshall Court. Indeed Beveridge's biography took on the stature of a classic, in part, because Beveridge believed that Marshall made a difference. The intellectual universe of Albert Beveridge was a universe in which the "great man" biography was still acceptable, a powerful "activist" Supreme Court was established, "nationalism" was a popular theme, and Federalism had moved from the status of a discredited political ideology to the status of a romanticized ancestral memory.[40] The interpretive structure of Beveridge's work, caricatured by Parrington as "old Federalist," appeared to be peculiarly congruent with Beveridge's topic.

With Parrington's mixed characterization of Beveridge came the first popular twentieth-century alteration of the Marshall Court's image.[41] In *Main Currents in American Thought,* published in 1927, Parrington retained the established labels for Marshall and his Court but also added a new label. Marshall, for Parrington, was still "the last of the old school of Federalists," still a "masterful, tenacious" Chief Justice who "manipulat[ed] his fellow judges like putty," and still dedicated to preserving "the sovereignty of the federal state" against "Jeffersonian and Jacksonian assaults upon the outworks of nationalism."[42] But Marshall was also "the first of the new [Federalists]" who were committed to "the new philosophy of capitalistic exploitation."[43] He was "a businessman" with a "strong property consciousness"; he was dedicated to "the sanctity of private property."[44] Beveridge's treatment of Marshall, Parrington argued, "offer[ed] very inadequate information" about "the economics of the great contest between Federalism and Republicanism,"[45] which was, in Parrington's view, a contest between privileged "gentlemen of principle and property" and forces who sought, under the banners of democracy and egalitarianism, to break down established privilege.[46]

The "Federalism" and "nationalism" that earlier Marshall Court scholars had associated with Marshall thus acquired a different connotation for Parrington: the terms were manifestations of a "property-consciousness."[47] The Federalists were "men of property," those of acquired or inherited wealth who wanted to use their status as economic and political leverage. "Nationalism," as practiced by the Marshall Court, favored propertied elites by elevating the judiciary, ostensible protector of the national interest, to the position of a buffer against egalitarian and democratic tendencies, which tended to manifest themselves in the actions of state legislatures.[48] Thus while the Marshall Court's Federalist and nationalist doctrines were "old" (preserving the hegemony of an established elite), they were also "new," because they allowed "business men," "financial interests," "banks," and "numerous corporations" to "exploit the resources of the state."[49]

An image of the Marshall Court as having a "property consciousness" surfaced explicitly for the first time in Parrington's work, but the principal impact of the "property consciousness" label was to retain orthodox characterizations of Marshall and his Court while giving them a new meaning. Beveridge's primary goal in his biography of Marshall, Parrington claimed, was "to magnify the nationalism of [his] hero and minify the property consciousness."[50] Parrington's goal was to reorder Beveridge's focus. The interesting question about Beveridge for Parrington was not whether Beveridge's portrait of Marshall as a Federalist, nationalist, and judicial overlord offended against the shared sense of the Marshall Court. Rather, the inquiry was why Beveridge had sought to "minify," in the deceptively neutral phrase "nationalism," the property-consciousness of Marshall and his colleagues. In raising that question Parrington simultaneously revealed his "progressive" angle of vision and the earlier filiopietistic perspective of Beveridge. "Property consciousness" had become a somewhat sinister label for Parrington, Beard, and other "progressives": it connoted the machinations of propertied elites and the class consciousness of "men of property." Beveridge had simply assumed that protection for property was a basic goal of not just the Marshall Court, but America: "property consciousness" and "nationalism" were in a sense one and the same.

Scholarship in the 1930s and 1940s continued to portray Marshall and his Court in Parringtonian terms. The portrayals, in fact, become so vivid and unqualified as to amount to caricatures. Max Lerner, for example, began a 1939 article on Marshall and "the campaign of history," by asserting that "a consciousness of property and of the owning classes as the basis of social order came quite easily" to Marshall as a child, and concluded the article by stating that Marshall's "primary drive" as Chief Justice was "to protect private property from governmental encroachment."[51] Although Marshall's role as "the strategic link between capitalism and constitutionalism" was Lerner's major theme, he paid homage to other standardized views of Marshall as well.[52] Marshall was "the leading actor" of "the Federalist claque"; he had learned that "the common man, who would not respond to Federalist aristocratic theory, would respond to the same property interests when they were clothed in the rhetoric of national interest."[53] According to Lerner, Marshall was also "a magnificent dictator" as Chief Justice, "dwarfing and uniting his colleagues," "cast[ing] over his associates on the bench a spell whose persuasiveness seemed to his contemporaries almost diabolical."[54] Further, Marshall was, of course, a "nationalist."[55] But nationalism, Lerner felt, was not "the primum mobile of Marshall's being"; it was rather a rhetorical strategy "to aid and not restrain business enterprise."[56]

In 1944 Charles Grove Haines, in a book designed to show how the Supreme Court had "participated in and influenced the political and partisan activities of the time,"[57] treated Marshall in similarly vivid and caricatured terms. Marshall took on "the responsibility to preserve some of the salient principles of Federalism," Haines asserted; he created and implemented Federalist and "nationalist theories of constitutional interpretation."[58] As his tenure progressed, Haines claimed, Marshall "became more and more a partisan," a development that explained why "historians with a Federalist or nationalist bias" had "lauded [Marshall's] political efforts."[59] In Haines' view, the Court under Marshall "strengthen[ed] the bonds of the union against the growing tendencies toward particularism and the assertion of State rights," supported "the movement to develop and protect manufacturing and industrial interests," and sought "to protect property from the dangers of legislative tinkering."[60] It was the creature of its Chief Justice:

"[o]ne of the most striking phases of Marshall's long judicial career was his domineering attitude and his dictatorial control of the Court."[61]

As late as the close of the Second World War "progressive" angles of vision were dominating scholarship on the Marshall Court. A paragraph from Harold Laski's *The State in Theory and Practice,* written in 1935 and quoted with approval by Haines, embodied the dominant historiographical attitude. "Anyone who examine[d] the first fifty years of the [Marshall Court's] history," Laski wrote, would see that "the purpose of the Judges was to protect the vested interests of property from invasion by state legislatures which were being driven by the economic difficulties of their constituents to inflation, the reduction of debts, and the cancellation of property rights. . . . This epoch of judicial nationalism," he concluded, "was obviously an expression of Federalist efforts to secure the conditions under which commerce could flourish."[62]

The characterizations Laski made of the Marshall Court seemed so "obvious" to him and to other scholars of the 1930s and 1940s that one might have thought that there was nothing more to say. But in the mid-1950s a number of new studies on Marshall and the Court appeared, all of them self-consciously "revisionist." Taken together, those studies sought to qualify each of the established labels of Marshall Court historiography. Moreover, they were studies written in a conspicuously different mode: rather than advancing large generalizations or grand syntheses, they were deliberately narrow in focus and specialized in content. Their appearance signified, among other things, the "professionalization" of scholarship in legal history that had taken place since the appearance of Warren's and Beveridge's works; their angle of vision was that of the "consensus historian," a term I shall subsequently characterize.

In 1955, to commemorate the bicentennial of Marshall's birth, a number of prominent scholars delivered lectures on various themes pertaining to the Marshall Court at the College of William and Mary, Marshall's alma mater. The lectures, which were published as essays under the title *Chief Justice John Marshall: A Reappraisal,*[63] provide an excellent illustration of changes in angles of vision. Not only did the essays modify the established twentieth-century image of Marshall and the Marshall court, they were strikingly different from earlier works in their cautious posture, their qualified language, and their limited scope.

Carl Swisher's introductory essay set the tone of the volume by suggesting that standard "political labels" were not helpful in classifying Marshall and his contemporaries.[64] Marshall was not easily characterized as a "Federalist," Arthur Holcombe noted; "true Federalists" such as Patrick Henry believed that Marshall and other supporters of the Constitution were "dangerous subversives."[65] Marshall's thought was actually closer to that of Jefferson, Holcombe believed, than to the radical or reactionary "extremes" of political opinion in his day.[66] Marshall was "not a rigid party man," Joseph Dorfman argued, "Northern Federalist leaders found him too independent for orthodoxy."[67] Although Marshall's "definite constitutional theory" was "Federalist," Donald Morgan maintained, he deviated from it regularly to "maintain a solid judicial front" on his Court.[68]

Furthermore, the essays did not retain a conception of the Marshall court as being dominated by its Chief Justice. Swisher declared that the belief that Marshall "[stood] alone" on his Court, and that "the other members of the Court were nonentities and without influence," was simply "not . . . true."[69] In an essay devoted to the subject, Morgan took pains to show that "the constitutional interpretation that characterized the years 1801–1835 was the work not of Marshall, but of the Marshall Court": "[m]any judges contributed to the final result."[70] Morgan based his conclusions and explained the earlier view of Marshall's dominance on the Marshall Court's internal procedures, which stressed the suppression of concurring and dissenting opinions, thereby creating the impression that all seven justices agreed with the opinion of the Court. When those procedures broke down in the late years of Marshall's tenure, Morgan argued, divisions between individual justices, including ones between Marshall and his colleagues, were increasingly made public.[71]

But while the talismanic labels for the Marshall Court were modified by the essays, they were not abandoned. Marshall's "property consciousness" remained a theme of the essays: Swisher,[72] Holcombe,[73] and Dorfman[74] alluded to Marshall's interest in "greater security for the special interests of businessmen and property owners."[75] Moreover, Marshall continued to be identified as a "nationalist": Swisher, Irving Brant, and Morgan found that "the greatest degree of unanimity [on the Marshall Court] appeared in controversies concerning questions of . . . defending national power."[76] Further, the significance of Marshall's Federalism was retained, although the commentators reexamined the meaning of "Federalist." Although the Marshall Court was no longer portrayed as a tribunal in which "an opinion is . . . delivered as if unanimous, and with the silent acquiescence of lazy or timid associates, by a crafty chief judge, who sophisticates the law to his mind,"[77] even Morgan conceded that the Chief Justice was the preeminently influential force on his Court.

"Consensus history" was a favorite theme of writers during the late 1960s and 1970s.[78] Although I shall not attempt to review or recast that literature, one point seems to have been underemphasized by students of consensus history, the extent to which the "consensus" was of a peculiarly paradoxical sort. The essays "reappraising" Marshall and his Court were written by historians of diverse political persuasions, some of whom had previously written works whose angle of vision more resembled that of the "progressives," and also by others who had no such track record.[79] But political differences were not explicitly reflected in competing methodological approaches to the Marshall Court. On the contrary, the lectures adopted an approach that Richard Hofstadter subsequently described as "a pluralist vision," emphasizing the rediscovery of complexity in American history" and "a new awareness of the multiplicity of forces."[80] The philosophical message of the lectures may have been "life is more complicated than it has been made to appear," but the methodological message was not "everyman can therefore write his own version of history." It was, rather, "professional history is therefore best written through narrow, neutral, monographic analysis."

The term "consensus" in consensus history thus contained a paradox. Practitioners of consensus history in the 1950s, for the most part, did not convert their methodological convictions into explicit philosophical statements.[81] They rarely identified American culture as being dominated by recurrent themes or conflicts, as did the progressive historians. But the clear message of their works was that a consensual professional methodology could best capture the diversity, the complexity, and the richness of the American past. That methodology had the effect of reducing "complexity" to analytical formulas. A common frame of reference— the limited empirical inquiry designed to produce a cautious, qualified generalization about a historical topic—was assumed by the same scholars who warned about the dangers of common themes in historiography.

In 1968 Robert Faulkner's *The Jurisprudence of John Marshall*[82] appeared, a work that took considerable risks, given both the dominance of consensus history in the 1950s and early 1960s and the entrenched labels for the Marshall Court. Faulkner paid sparse attention to the shared sense of the Marshall Court. Although he argued, for example, that Marshall very likely did dominate his Court (scholarship of the 1950s notwithstanding) and that Marshall surely was a nationalist of some sort (though not the full-blown nationalist portrayed by Beveridge), Faulkner was simply not very interested in the orthodox themes historians had associated with the Marshall Court. He focused instead on Marshall's social philosophy, his jurisprudential assumptions, his language, and his interaction with other "republican" theorists. The result was a portrait of Marshall as one of the statesmen-intellectuals of the Revolutionary generation; a person who took seriously, as did Madison, Jefferson, and John Adams, questions of moral philosophy, political economy, and jurisprudence.

Faulkner thus spent as much time on Marshall's letters and his *Life of George Washington*[83] as he did on Marshall's decisions. And although he treated contemporary statement-theorists with considerable detail, especially Madison and Jefferson, he spent almost no time discussing the other justices of the Marshall Court. Faulkner's approach was to define Marshall's relationship to "republicanism," and to subsume the themes of nationalism, federalism, property-consciousness, and even personal dominance in that relationship. Republicanism was not only the key to Faulkner's interpretive structure, it was offered as a potential new "label" for the Marshall Court.

I shall subsequently consider the implication of using republicanism as a label for the Marshall Court. First, however, I should note that the relative indifference Faulkner exhibited toward the orthodox labels for the Marshall Court was also present in my own essay on Marshall in *The American Judicial Tradition,* published in 1976.[84] The twenty-seven pages I devoted to Marshall and his Court contain a few references to Marshall's theory of property rights, but scarcely a reference to Federalism, nationalism, or Marshall's alleged dominance over his fellow justices. Only one paragraph hinted at my position on the conventional characteristics ascribed to Marshall.

If he [had been] a nominal Federalist before becoming Chief Justice, he ceased being one while on the Court; on the other hand, he remained a thoroughgoing advocate of the federal union form of government. In the latter posture, however, [Marshall] was in the mainstream of his generation: as Jefferson said, the framers of the new nation were all federalists and all republicans. Marshall staked out a

discernible position and quarreled with others among the Founding Fathers primarily over the role of the judiciary in a federal union.[85]

The bulk of my essay then went on to discuss Marshall's theory of judicial review
and the ways in which he justified it in the rhetoric of his decisions.

Looking back at that paragraph, I notice a place or two where my language
concealed more than it revealed. The framers may have all been federalists and
republicans in one sense, but they are surely not all both Federalists and Republicans. Furthermore, although all the supporters of the Constitution were, by definition, committed to the conception of a "federal union," there were serious quarrels about what that conception meant in practice, and the Marshall Court was in
the thick of those quarrels. Accordingly, when I contrast the emphasis in previous
scholarship on the Marshall Court with that in the works of both Faulkner and
myself, I am simultaneously struck by the different angles of vision and motivated
to renew communication with generations; to reexamine the shared sense of the
Marshall Court.

One way to begin that reexamination is to consider the possibilities of the term
"republican" as a new talismanic label for the Court. "Republicanism" is a
theme that has, since the late 1960s, captivated the imagination of historians working in the late eighteenth and nineteenth centuries. There is now an abundance of
literature on republicanism in America,[86] both at the level of macro-theory and
the level of application; both with respect to individuals and to institutions. Moreover, this literature spans a wide expanse of time and is concerned with politics,
economics, and social trends as well as with ideas. The literature has given a new
meaning to themes, such as natural rights, natural law, and commerce, that scholars of the 1920s and 1930s associated with the Marshall Court.

If one considers the Marshall Court as a "republican" Court, concerns that
appear to have been central to republican theorists become themes worth pursuing
as clues to the Marshall Court's values.[87] One such concern was the meaning of
change in a civilized society. Like many other late eighteenth-century intellectuals, and unlike their twentieth-century counterparts, American republican theorists
thought of human societies as passing through finite and inexorable stages, from
the most "primitive" state (nomadic) through intermediate states (agricultural and
pastoral) to more "sophisticated" but corrupt states (manufacturing and commercial). They thought that although the pace of such changes in the state of society
could be altered, the changes themselves were inevitable. More significant, they
thought that change from a simple to a more sophisticated social state fostered
decay and corruption. "Progress" was a double-edged sword for them. The presence of more material goods, more "luxury," or more affluence did not necessarily signify a more enlightened or more virtuous society; indeed it often signified
the decline of civilization from a less corrupt pastoral state. Change was thus not
only not the equivalent of progress for republican theorists, it was a force to be
harnessed or resisted.

Alongside this conception of change over time should be placed the republican
theorists' attitude toward change across space. Here one comes upon a source of
late eighteenth- and early nineteenth-century attitudes toward the frontier or wil-

derness. Because the "stage" theory of civilization viewed the pastoral and agricultural states as both unsophisticated and less susceptible to corruption, the
image of vast, undeveloped land inspired republican visionaries as a setting of
pastoral and agricultural activities. The development of America across space—
westward along the frontier—became a counterpoint to fears associated with the
development of America through time. Republican theorists imagined the following scenario: if the American frontier was virtually boundless, as both the Louisi-
ana Purchase and early nineteenth-century technology suggested, perhaps a portion
of America could remain indefinitely in an agricultural or pastoral state. Moreover, perhaps the dispersal of Americans across the continent might retard the
inevitable "sophistication" of agriculture into manufacturing and commerce.
Commerce, manufacturing, and agriculture might even blend together. A nation
of yeomen farmers could have easy access to markets and foreign "luxury" items
while remaining self-sufficient and independent in their pastoral townships.

To think of the Marshall Court as a "republican" Court, then, raises the possibility that some of its conventionally ascribed features—a concern with commerce,
an interest in the protection of property, and a preoccupation with the structure
and powers of the new American nation—might take on a new meaning. It may
be that the Marshall Court was a Court bound by eighteenth-century assumptions,
although it operated in the nineteenth century. It may be that it was a Court quite
different in sensibility from any of its successors. But to take the idea that the
Marshall Court was "republican" to the point of ignoring the shared sense of the
Court seems quixotic. The labels historians have attached to the Court, although
oversimplified, are not, we have seen, meaningless. New angles of vision may
modify the meaning of these labels or point out the sense in which they appear to
be anachronistic. But the labels help define the historical context that forms part
of any interpretive structure. The attractiveness of republicanism as an interpretive
construct for the Marshall Court is dependent upon whether, as an explanatory
model, republicanism can recast the shared sense of the Court in a fresh and useful
way. Can we better understand the adjectives "property-conscious," "nationalistic," "Federalistic," and "Chief Justice-dominated" by adding another adjective—"republican"—and by asking the kinds of questions that that adjective, as
an interpretive construct, engenders?

This is not the place to explore that question in any detail. It seems worth
mentioning, however, that some of the traditional labels for the Marshall court
suggest that the label "republican" may be counterintuitive. More than one generation of historians have used labels, especially "property-conscious" and "nationalistic," that have conveyed a particular impression of the Marshall Court. That
impression is one of a Court dedicated to economic expansion, to the promotion
of manufacturing and commercial interests, to enhanced fiscal solvency of the
young American nation, and to the protection of the "propertied" classes. But
classical republican theory was deeply suspicious of commerce and manufacturing, believing them to be activities that led to luxury and corruption. It was disturbed by efforts on the part of the state to promote entrepreneurial interests, or
on the part of private citizens to enlist the state as their patron or their agent. Its
definition of what sorts of property holdings were to be encouraged in the ideal

republic was a narrow one. Thus if one is to maintain that the Marshall Court was a "republican" Court, one either has to suggest that the above impression is fundamentally mistaken, or consider the possibility that the "republicanism" of Marshall and his contemporaries had deviated significantly from classical republican theory.

It may be that the greatest value the literature on republicanism will have to studies of the Marshall Court is as a guide to the Court's language. If one uses the conventional labels as points of entry to the Marshall Court's world, questions of language and context immediately emerge. If the Court is "property-conscious," of whose property is it protective? If the Court if a "Federalist" Court, what does "Federalism" mean in the context of the early nineteenth century? If the Court is "nationalistic," what is its ideal conception of the "nation" whose interests it is promoting, and what is its conception of competing interests, such as those of the states? If John Marshall dominated his Court, what were John Marshall's attitudes toward those issues? Such questions have been raised and answered before, but new insights into the theoretical world of late eighteenth- and early nineteenth-century Americans suggest that they need to be raised and answered again.

Although those questions have been given a new dimension by the interpretations of scholars focusing on republicanism, they cannot be fruitfully addressed except through a return to the "raw materials" of the Marshall Court's record. Thus, the theory of revisionism articulated in this essay can be seen, metaphorically, as a spiral. One starts with the proposition that the record of history is often hard to treat as an entity independent of interpretations of that record. Yet successive interpretations of the same topic, while noticeably different in their angles of vision, yield common features, most obviously recognizable in oversimplified labels that form the shared sense of the topic. The labels are not the same as the raw materials of the record; they are interpretive glosses on those materials. But any "new" interpretive structure, implicitly offered as the basis for a "revised" understanding of the topic, must come to terms with the labels, and in so doing must seemingly return to that record, at least as it has commonly been interpreted. The process is not precisely circular, for one does not end up in the same place as where one began when one asked the question, "What is the meaning of the historical record?" In returning to the raw materials one is confronting the shared interpretive sense of the topic. The art of revisionism is therefore the art of fashioning an original interpretive structure that bridges a potential gap between new angles of vision and an established sense of the raw materials of a given portion of history.

Revisionism is an art because the choice of a given methodological approach to the raw materials of history cannot insure the success or failure of an interpretive structure. Whether a given interpretation is rich or flat, seminal or conventional, coherent or tortured; whether it presses the limits of, or sets new limits for, intellectual discourses or whether it remains squarely, and prosaically, in the center of established orthodoxy; and finally, whether it inspires or bores other scholars—these are questions that cannot be solved methodologically. The "revisionist" historian, like the artist, may well be fated, in most cases, to choose the materials of his day; he may even research and write, as many artists can be said to paint, within the confines of a "school" of thought. But the impact of his scholarship will depend not only on the questions that his angle of vision suggests are appropriate to ask but how imaginatively and suggestively he answers them.

NOTES

1. 2 K. POPPER, THE OPEN SOCIETY AND ITS ENEMIES 268 (4th ed. 1962).

2. *See, e.g.*, O. HANDLIN, TRUTH IN HISTORY *passim* (1979); B. TUCHMAN, PRACTICING HISTORY 16 (1981).

3. *See* White, *Truth and Interpretation in History*, 79 MICH. L. REV. 594 *passim* (1981).

4. On the changing image of Holmes, see White, *The Rise and Fall of Justice Holmes*, 39 U. CHI. L. REV. 51 (1971); White, *The Integrity of Holmes' Jurisprudence*, 10 HOFSTRA L. REV. 633 (1982).

5. *See generally*, ESSAYS ON THE AMERICAN REVOLUTION (S. Kurtz & J. Hutson, eds. 1973); THE AMERICAN REVOLUTION: EXPLORATIONS IN THE HISTORY OF AMERICAN RADICALISM (A. Young ed. 1976); B. BAILYN, THE IDEOLOGICAL ORIGINS OF THE AMERICAN REVOLUTION (1967); J. POCOCK, THE MACHIAVELLIAN MOMENT: FLORENTINE POLITICAL THOUGHT AND THE ATLANTIC REPUBLICAN TRADITION (1975).

6. H. ADAMS, HISTORY OF THE UNITED STATES OF AMERICA DURING THE ADMINISTRATIONS OF THOMAS JEFFERSON AND JAMES MADISON 1801–1816 (1891–1896).

7. F. TURNER, THE FRONTIER IN AMERICAN HISTORY (1920).

8. C. BEARD, AN ECONOMIC INTERPRETATION OF THE CONSTITUTION (1913).

9. I am arbitrarily using the masculine pronoun in a generic sense.

10. Diggins, *Power and Authority in American History: The Case of Charles A. Beard and His Critics*, 86 AM. HIST. REV. 701 (1981).

11. *Id.* at 704–10.

12. *Id.*

13. *Id.* at 701.

14. "All I mean by truth is what I can't help thinking." Letter from Oliver Wendell Holmes to Sir Frederick Pollock, in 1 HOLMES-POLLOCK LETTERS 126 (1941); "[C]ontinuity with the past is not a duty, it is only a necessity." THE OCCASIONAL SPEECHES OF JUSTICE OLIVER WENDELL HOLMES 85 (M. DeWolfe Howe, ed. 1962).

15. *See* White, *supra* note 3.

16. TURNER, *supra* note 7; BEARD, *supra* note 8; 2 V. PARRINGTON, MAIN CURRENTS IN AMERICAN THOUGHT (1927–30).

17. *See generally*, R. HOFSTADTER, THE PROGRESSIVE HISTORIANS: TURNER, BEARD, PARRINGTON (1968).

18. TURNER, *supra* note 7, at 1–38.

19. Diggins, *supra* note 10, at 702.

20. *See* PARRINGTON, *supra* note 16.

21. Diggins, *supra* note 10, at 722 n. 68.

22. *See generally* Holmes, *Response*, in 1 JOHN MARSHALL: LIFE, CHARACTER, AND JUDICIAL SERVICES 204 (J. Dillon ed. 1903) [hereinafter cited as JOHN MARSHALL]. An earlier filiopietistic biography was A. MAGRUDER, JOHN MARSHALL (1898). For accounts of Marshall by his contemporaries, see H. BINNEY, AN EULOGY ON THE LIFE AND CHARACTER OF JOHN MARSHALL (1835); J. STORY, A DISCOURSE UPON THE LIFE, CHARACTER

AND SERVICES OF THE HONORABLE JOHN MARSHALL (1835). Magruder relied heavily on these sources and on H. FLANDERS, LIVES AND TIMES OF THE CHIEF JUSTICES 279–550 (1859).

23. *See generally* JOHN MARSHALL, *supra* note 22.

24. JOHN MARSHALL, *supra* note 22, at 207.

25. 1 SELECTIONS FROM THE CORRESPONDENCE OF THEODORE ROOSEVELT AND HENRY CABOT LODGE 518 (H. Lodge ed. 1949). *See generally* Garraty, *Holmes's Appointment to the U.S. Supreme Court*, 22 NEW ENG. Q. 291 (1949), G.E. WHITE, JUSTICE OLIVER WENDELL HOLMES: LAW AND THE INNER SELF 299–306 (1993).

26. *E.g.*, Letter from Thomas Jefferson to William Johnson (June 12, 1823), *reprinted in* 12 WRITINGS OF THOMAS JEFFERSON 254 (P. Ford ed. 1905) [hereinafter cited as Jefferson Letter].

27. JOHN MARSHALL, *supra* note 22, at 205–06.

28. *See generally supra* note 4.

29. A. BEVERIDGE, THE LIFE OF JOHN MARSHALL (1916–1919).

30. 2 PARRINGTON, *supra* note 16, at 22.

31. 4 BEVERIDGE, *supra* note 29, at 473.

32. *Id.* at 59.

33. *Id.* at 1.

34. 1 C. WARREN, THE SUPREME COURT IN UNITED STATES HISTORY (1922).

35. *Id.* at v.

36. *Id.* at vii.

37. *Id.* at 451.

38. *Id.* at 814.

39. *Id.* at 2, 813–14.

40. *See* J. BRAEMAN, ALBERT BEVERIDGE, AMERICAN NATIONALIST (1971).

41. Parrington's interpretation relied heavily on Beard's AN ECONOMIC INTERPRETATION OF THE CONSTITUTION, *supra* note 8. His position had also been anticipated, to some extent, by Edward Corwin in JOHN MARSHALL AND THE CONSTITUTION (1919).

42. 2 PARRINGTON, *supra* note 16, at 20, 22.

43. *Id.* at 20.

44. *Id.* at 21, 23.

45. *Id.* at 22.

46. *Id.* at 23.

47. *Id.* at 21.

48. *Id.* at 23–24.

49. *Id.* at 21.

50. *Id.* at 22.

51. Lerner, *John Marshall and the Campaign of History*, 39 COLUM. L. REV. 396, 420 (1939).

52. *Id.* at 403.

53. *Id.* at 401, 406.

54. *Id.* at 396, 402.

55. *Id.* at 400.

56. *Id.* at 401, 429.

57. 1 C. HAINES, THE ROLE OF THE SUPREME COURT IN AMERICAN GOVERNMENT AND POLITICS 3 (1944).

58. *Id.* at 331.

59. *Id.* at 622.

60. *Id.* at 628–29.

61. *Id.* at 630.

62. H. LASKI, THE STATE IN THEORY AND PRACTICE 156–57 (1935).

63. CHIEF JUSTICE JOHN MARSHALL: A REAPPRAISAL (M. Jones ed. 1956) [hereinafter cited as A REAPPRAISAL].

64. Swisher, *Introduction*, in A REAPPRAISAL, *supra* note 63, at 3–5

65. Holcombe, *John Marshall as Politician and Political Theorist*, in A REAPPRAISAL, *supra* note 63, at 25.

66. *Id.* at 37.

67. Dorfman, *John Marshall, Political Economist*, in A REAPPRAISAL, *supra* note 63, at 144.

68. Morgan, *Marshall, the Marshall Court, and the Constitution*, in A REAPPRAISAL, *supra* note 63, at 170.

69. Swisher, *Introduction*, in A REAPPRAISAL, *supra* note 63, at 10.

70. Morgan, *Marshall, the Marshall Court, and the Constitution*, in A REAPPRAISAL, *supra* note 63, at 184.

71. *Id.* at 180–83.

72. Swisher, *Introduction*, in A REAPPRAISAL, *supra* note 63, at 9.

73. Holcombe, *John Marshall as Politician and Political Theorist*, in A REAPPRAISAL, *supra* note 63, at 28.

74. Dorfman, *John Marshall: Political Economist*, in A REAPPRAISAL, *supra* note 63, at 127.

75. Holcombe, *John Marshall as Politician and Political Theorist*, in A REAPPRAISAL, *supra* note 63, at 28.

76. Morgan, *Marshall, the Marshall Court and the Constitution*, in A REAPPRAISAL, *supra* note 63, at 175.

77. Jefferson Letter, *supra* note 26.

78. Two collections of essays on the subject are B. STERNSHER, CONSENSUS, CONFLICT, AND AMERICAN HISTORIANS (1975) and A. DAVIS AND H. WOODMAN, CONFLICT AND CONSENSUS IN MODERN AMERICAN HISTORY (1979).

79. Swisher and Dorfman had written major works in the 1930s that reflected the influence of "progressive" historiography. *See* C. SWISHER, STEPHEN J. FIELD (1930); J. DORFMAN, THE ECONOMIC MIND IN GENERAL CIVILIZATION (1946–1949); *see also* D. MORGAN, JUSTICE WILLIAM JOHNSON: THE FIRST DISSENTER (1954).

80. HOFSTADTER, *supra* note 17, at 442.

81. Two major and influential exceptions were L. HARTZ, THE LIBERAL TRADITION IN AMERICA: AN INTERPRETATION OF AMERICAN POLITICAL THOUGHT SINCE THE REVOLUTION (1955), and D. BOORSTIN, THE AMERICANS: THE COLONIAL EXPERIENCE (1958), and THE AMERICANS: THE NATIONAL EXPERIENCE (1965).

82. R. FAULKNER, THE JURISPRUDENCE OF JOHN MARSHALL (1968).

83. J. MARSHALL, THE LIFE OF GEORGE WASHINGTON (1805–1807).

84. G. WHITE, THE AMERICAN JUDICIAL TRADITION (1976).

85. *Id.* at 18.

86. For works I have found particularly suggestive on republicanism see B. BAILYN, THE IDEOLOGICAL ORIGINS OF THE AMERICAN REVOLUTION (1967); A. HIRSCHMAN, THE PASSIONS AND THE INTERESTS (1977); D. MCCOY, THE ELUSIVE REPUBLIC (1980); POCOCK, *supra* note 5; G. STOURZH, ALEXANDER HAMILTON AND THE IDEA OF AMERICAN GOVERNMENT (1970); G. WOOD, THE CREATION OF THE AMERICAN REPUBLIC 1776–1787 (1969); *see also* Stalhope, *Toward a Republican Synthesis: The Emergence of an Understanding of Republicanism in American Historiography*, 29 WM. & MARY L. Q. 49 (1972) (reviewing some additional literature, itself a source of insights). Older studies whose find-

ings are given new meaning by the literature on republicanism include C. HAINES, THE REVIVAL OF NATURAL LAW CONCEPTS (1930); B. WRIGHT, AMERICAN INTERPRETATION OF NATURAL LAW (1931), and Corwin, *The "Higher Law" Background of American Constitutional Law*, 42 HARV. L. REV. 149, 365 (1929).

87. The term "Republican theorists" is of course overbroad; there were a great many varieties of "republican" thought. But McCoy makes a good case for the prevalence of the general attitudes described in the next two paragraphs among thinkers as diverse as Hamilton, Madison, and Jefferson. *See* McCOY, *supra* note 86; *see also* STOURZH, *supra* note 86.

PART II

Doing History:
Practice

The Integrity of
Holmes' Jurisprudence*

Writing about Oliver Wendell Holmes can be likened to playing Hamlet in the theatre: it is a kind of apprenticeship that legal scholars undertake as a way of measuring their fitness to endure the academic travails ahead. Holmes himself engaged in a similar rite of passage when he wrote an essay on Plato as a Harvard undergraduate. Plato's thought, Holmes claimed, "needed a complete remodeling"; Holmes' generation "start[ed] far beyond the place where Plato rested."[1] Ralph Waldo Emerson, to whom Holmes showed a draft of his essay, suggested that "[w]hen you strike at a king, you must kill him."[2] The urge to strike at Holmes has been recurrent, and the man, as a jurist, is far from dead.

Ten years ago I suggested that Holmes' reputation was on the decline, and complained about his "articulated refusal to take pride in being human."[3] In an intellectual culture dominated by liberal humanism, I surmised, Holmes would not be likely to fare well: he was not much of a liberal and certainly not a humanist. Once again Holmes seems to have triumphed over his critics. His thought has had a capacity to contain insights sufficiently diverse and contradictory to appeal to someone regardless of prevailing intellectual fashions. And the gap between Holmes and prevailing opinion has narrowed rather than widened in the 1970s. The "disturbing dissonance" I found between Holmes' "very conspicuous social and professional success" and his "gloomy musings that . . . man has no more cosmic significance than a baboon or a grain of sand"[4] presupposed an obligation in those whom life has favored to believe in the optimistic possibilities of living. Optimism is harder to come by these days; what I called a "cranky negativism"[5] in Holmes now seems more like sensible resignation. At any rate, interest in Holmes has dramatically revived,[6] and I should not like to be thought of as having given up on him too soon.

My concern in this essay is with a feature of Holmes that, for all that has been written on him, scholars are just beginning to address. The feature involves an

*10 Hofstra L. Rev. 633 (1982). A previous version of this essay was delivered as the 1982 Hofstra University Lecture. Readers might want to compare the conclusions about Holmes and Holmes Scholarship drawn in this essay and the one that follows with my observations in *Justice Oliver Wendell Holmes: Law and the Inner Self* (1993).

apparent discontinuity between Holmes' theory of judging in the private law and public law spheres. Holmes' famous book *The Common Law*[7] reads like a credo for activist judging in pursuit of broad general principles of law; judges are to help arrange legal subjects in what Holmes called a philosophically continuous series.[8] His constitutional opinions on the Supreme Court, by contrast, extol the virtues of judicial deference. How is Holmes simultaneously the reformer of private law and the passive public law judge? How could the same judge who wanted to take all grade crossing cases away from juries[9] feel comfortable allowing legislatures to make all sorts of discriminatory classifications, so long as they were arguably rational?[10] Are these tendencies another example of the internal contradictions in Holmes' thought, which have been so regularly pointed out? Or is there a basic, if latent, integrity to Holmes' jurisprudence?

The reason this inquiry may be put as a fresh proposition so late in the history of scholarship on Holmes is that scholars have thus far given only limited attention to his experience as a judge on the Supreme Judicial Court of Massachusetts. Although Holmes was sixty-one when appointed to the Supreme Court of the United States, he remained a Justice for over twenty-nine years and made his public reputation as a Justice. Early scholarship on Holmes paid almost no attention to his years as a Massachusetts judge, and although a major biography, that of Mark DeWolfe Howe,[11] was begun in the 1950s, Howe died before he addressed the Massachusetts cases. Howe's last volume on Holmes appeared in 1963;[12] there was a gap of nearly fifteen years before any detailed treatment of Holmes' Massachusetts years appeared.[13]

The explanation for this neglect of Holmes' state court opinions is obvious. Scholarship in American legal history that emphasized private law subjects languished in the 1950s and 1960s; there was little interest in the opinions of any state court judges. Further, there was so much else in Holmes' career of interest—his early scholarship, his Supreme Court opinions, his engaging correspondence—that scholars could justify neglecting what seemed to be a collection of boring, insignificant Massachusetts cases.

Holmes himself, as we will see, found his state cases relatively trivial and dull exercises. His opinions are not particularly path-breaking, rarely detailed, and not even the rich source of aphorisms and epigrams that his Supreme Court opinions are.[14] But the experience of being a state court judge, when taken in connection with the other two major roles of Holmes' career—scholar and Supreme Court Justice—was a vital link in the forging of Holmes' jurisprudence. The experience of a Massachusetts judgeship transformed Holmes' thought from its expansive, conceptualistic, reformist early form to its cryptic, skeptical later variety. It was on the Massachusetts bench that Holmes came to adopt his familiar posture of resignation, a posture he had never expected to adopt as a judge.

This essay traces the evolution of Holmes' jurisprudence in the three major phases of his career. The first section discusses Holmes' early scholarship, which culminated in *The Common Law* in 1881, and the theory of judging that Holmes held at the time of *The Common Law*'s publication. Section II examines the process by which Holmes' ideas about judging private law cases became modified with his experiences as a Massachusetts judge, and contrasts the scholarship he produced between 1882 and 1902 with his earlier efforts. Section III discusses the relationship of Holmes' revised theory of judging, which had been developed in a private law setting, to his approach to public law cases as a Supreme Court justice. The fourth section assesses some of the implications of Holmes' jurisprudence for contemporary judging.

I The Early Scholarship: Order and Activism

Holmes' early life, as a practitioner in a Boston firm, a lecturer and professor at Harvard, and an author and editor for the *American Law Review,* has been one of the most fully examined phases of his career.[15] We know that by the 1870s Holmes had become attracted to the idea of "analys[ing] what seem to me the fundamental notions and principles of our substantive law [and] putting them in an order."[16] Beginning in 1870 he published a series of unsigned articles and book reviews, primarily in *the American Law Review,* in which he argued that the purpose of legal scholarship should be "classification," by which he meant the organization of a subject "from the most general conception to the most specific proposition or exception in the order of logical subordination."[17]

We know, as well, that Holmes found the subject of Torts a particularly fruitful one to examine in this fashion. After an original judgment that Torts was "not a proper subject for a law book,"[18] Holmes, by 1873, had concluded that "there is no fault to be found with the contents of [Torts] text-books."[19] Torts appealed to Holmes because it seemed to be a subject ripe for classification. While earlier Torts treatises had attempted to associate concepts, like trespass, evidence, and defamation, that bore no "cohesion or legal relationship" to one another, Holmes became convinced that some fundamental notions and principles could be derived.[20] He claimed that "an enumeration of the [tort] actions which have been successful, and of those which have failed, define[d] the extent of the primary duties imposed by the law."[21] This was in keeping with his belief that "form[s] of action" could be made "to correspond to every substantial duty," and thereby "embod[y] in a practical shape a classification of the law."[22] Holmes discovered that the tort writs could be divided into three groups, one requiring culpability as a prerequisite for liability, another indifferent to culpability, and a third determining culpability from "motives of policy . . . kept purposely indefinite."[23]

The last category of wrongs introduced for Holmes the standard of modern negligence, which he seized upon as a clarifying principle for tort law. Eight years after his preliminary survey of tort writs he was prepared to argue, in *The Common Law,* that the negligence principle had increasingly dominated tort law.[24] That shift from analytic classification to philosophical synthesis was characteristic of his scholarship in the late 1870s. In five articles in the *American Law Review*[25] between 1876 and 1880 Holmes revealed a new style of scholarship. His subjects and his explorations were primarily historical; his purpose, however, was not merely to clarify the historical origins of doctrine, but to claim that doctrine could not be understood apart from its historical origins. A historical exploration of a legal subject, for Holmes, revealed its essentials: its standards of liability, its core elements, its character. History, he later said, was "the first step . . . towards a deliberate reconsideration of the worth of those rules."[26] "History sets us free and enables us to make up our minds dispassionately whether the survival which we are enforcing answers any new purpose when it has ceased to answer the old."[27]

The pattern of scholarship first introduced in Holmes' articles on tort law thus continued through other subjects to culminate in *The Common Law*. As Mark Howe has shown,[28] *The Common Law* was a reformist work in two senses of the word. In his efforts to show that all the common law fields—criminal law, property, torts, and contracts—had arguably been governed by shifting external standards of liability throughout their history, Holmes was attempting to reform jurisprudence by emphasizing the derivation of general principles rather than the pleading of specific writs. Uncertainty would be reduced in the law if common law subjects were arranged according to general principles and lawyers recognized that those principles were simply manifestations of current community preferences. The study of law was thus to proceed from the individual case through history to the derivation of general principles. This would require, among other things, a basic change in the way law was taught and practiced.

Holmes was also advocating another kind of reform in the *The Common Law*. Since certainty and predictability were desirable goals for the legal profession, those institutions in the legal system that fostered certainty should be rewarded at the expense of those that appeared to hinder its pursuit. In his 1873 essay on torts Holmes expressed what he took to be the view of "many whose opinion is entitled to respect" that "negligence [was] always and in the nature of things a question for the jury."[29] This echoed a position he had taken two years earlier, when he said that "we suppose it is wholly for the jury to say whether the party has used such care as a reasonable and prudent man would have used under the circumstances of that particular case."[30] But by 1880 Holmes had changed his mind about the efficacy of allowing legal standards to be formulated by juries. In *The Common Law* he complained about "leav[ing] all our rights and duties throughout a great part of the law to the necessarily more or less accidental feelings of a jury," arguing that "the sphere in which [a judge] is able to rule without taking [jury] opinion at all should be continually growing."[31] This was in keeping with his belief that "the tendency of the law must always be to narrow the field of uncertainty."[32]

Holmes' early scholarship, in its final phases, thus envisaged a "creative epoch"[33] in late nineteenth-century American private law in which a philosophically oriented class of scholars would join with a class of judges who had acquired "a fund of experience"[34] to develop broad, predictable rules. The pursuit of order in American jurisprudence would be fostered by judicial activism. Given Holmes' confidence in the techniques of analysis he had used in *The Common Law* and in the principles he had derived as a result of their use, it was hard for him to imagine that others could not do likewise. But those others would have to be persons capable of understanding the law and its history, and dedicated to the goals of certainty, predictability, and coherence. Judges were such persons.

One of the curiosities of Holmes' early life is why, after finding his scholarly labors finally coming to fruition as he approached forty, he did not regard a life of future scholarship with more enthusiasm. After severely pressing himself to secure some scholarly achievement by his fortieth birthday—the result of which was some petty competitiveness with other scholars, a neglect of his home life, and a "fearful grip upon his work" that made him "a melancholy sight" to one observer[35]—Holmes, who had written *The Common Law* while in active law practice, was then given an opportunity to continue a life of scholarship. By November 1881, he had been offered a position on the Harvard Law School faculty, subject to the contingency of funds being raised to endow a new professorship, and had indicated his readiness to accept. In his letter of acceptance, however, Holmes reserved the right "not . . . to feel bound in honor not to consider" a judgeship should one subsequently be offered him.[36]

Less than a year later, after finally accepting Harvard's offer of a professorship in jurisprudence, Holmes resigned to go on the Supreme Judicial Court of Massachusetts. The circumstances of his resignation—he consulted no one on the Harvard faculty and accepted the judgeship three hours after it was offered—produced a good deal of bitterness at Harvard. James Bradley Thayer, who had helped raise funds for the professorship that brought Holmes to Harvard, poured out his resentment in a diary. "[W]ith all his attractive qualities and his solid merits," Thayer concluded, Holmes was "wanting sadly in the noblest region of human character,—selfish, vain, thoughtless of others."[37] Much later, when Felix Frankfurter was considering joining the Harvard faculty, Holmes wrote him that "academic life is but half life—it is withdrawal from the fight in order to utter smart things that cost you nothing except the thinking them from a cloister." He also said, in the same letter, "My wife thinks I unconsciously began to grow sober with an inarticulate sense of limitation in the few months of my stay in Cambridge."[38]

Apparently Holmes was unsure where a scholarly life would take him. He wrote James Bryce shortly after his decision to take the judgeship that he "had already realized at Cambridge that the field for generalization inside the body of the law was small and that the day would soon come when one felt that the only remaining problems were of detail"[39] The choice, he later wrote to Harold Laski, seemed to be "between applying one's theories to practice and details or going into another field."[40] Judging appeared to provide "an all round experience," and a "share in the practical struggle of life."[41] It "hardens the fibre," Holmes later said, and "is more likely to make more of a man of one who turns it to success."[42] Had he stayed at Harvard he would have felt that he "had chosen the less manly course."[43]

The striking feature of Holmes' conception of the academic and judicial worlds at this point in his career is not his sense that academic life was more cloistered or less "manly" than a judgeship. It is rather his feeling that "the field for generalization inside the body of the law was small" and that "as a philosopher" Holmes needed to "extend his range."[44] Holmes apparently believed that his labors on *The Common Law* had resulted in a comprehensive theory of jurisprudence, that he was not likely to modify that theory, and that the remainder of academic life, if he stayed in the law, would be filling in the details.[45] This was not as limited a conception of scholarship as it might first appear. Holmes was reluctant to abandon an insight once he had formulated it; nearly forty years after publishing *The Common Law* he defended its findings against critics.[46] Moreover, the seminal work of many scholars is done early in their careers, and there are temptations to rest on one's reputation and "fill in the details." Holmes may have understood that there was not much more he could do, at least in the private law subjects that held his greatest interest, after he had plumbed their depths in *The Common Law*.

But if Holmes was interested in "generalization" and the pursuit of "tempting [philosophical] themes,"[47] why did he choose to become a judge? He never made the reasons for his choice explicit, but he appears to have thought that if he were going to "apply one's theories to practice and details," performing that function in "the practical struggle for life," rather than in a "cloister," would be more satisfying. Academic detail was just nit-picking; judicial detail was "the gradual weaving of one's contribution into the practical system of the law."[48] Judging was to provide a means by which the theories of *The Common Law* were to have an impact on "business in the world."[49]

One cannot review Holmes' choice to forego academic life for a judgeship without sensing that he was proceeding under the assumption that judging would give him an opportunity to put his theories into practice. He had spent too much time deriving his views on contracts, the criminal law, property, and torts to regard them merely as "smart things"; his jurisprudence was the jurisprudence of reform. Here was an opportunity to put his reforms into action, to rewrite the corpus of Massachusetts jurisprudence. Here was an opportunity to be an activist judge creating an orderly, predictable system of laws.

II The Supreme Judicial Court: Deflated Expectations

In 1900, after nearly twenty years as a judge, Holmes asked himself "what is there to show for this half lifetime that has passed?"[50] He had considered "[a] thousand cases, many of them upon trifling or transitory matters." He "would have liked to study to the bottom and to say his say on every question which the law has ever presented." He would have liked to "invent new problems which should be the test of doctrine, and then to generalize it all and write it in continuous, logical, philosophic exposition, setting forth the whole corpus with its roots in history and its justifications of expedience." Instead he had decided a great many dull cases. That was "life," he felt; "we cannot live our dreams."[51]

The experience of judging had not conformed to Holmes' expectations. He had contemplated being able to study cases "to the bottom," to "say his say" fully on matters of common law doctrine, to use existing cases as a means of anticipating "new problems," and perhaps even to "generalize it all." For the most part he had not been able to do these things. There was not enough time to study cases in depth. Saying one's say fully ran the risk of offending one's colleagues: opinions were joint projects. Lawyers, litigants, and even judges were not interested in a case as an index of future doctrinal development; practical issues were at stake, results had to be reached and decisions made. And the common law, as it evolved in the Massachusetts Supreme Judicial Court, was hardly a "continuous, logical, philosophic" system. It was better described as a series of largely desultory cases that were decided without much attention to the "whole corpus."[52]

Decisionmaking on the Massachusetts court was best captured by the old metaphor that Holmes had first written in his 1873 essay, "The Theory of Torts,"[53] where he had speculated on the development of the law:

> Two widely different cases suggest a general distinction, which is a clear one when stated broadly. But as new cases cluster around the opposite poles, and begin to approach each other, the distinction becomes more difficult to trace; the determinations are made one way or the other on a very slight predominance of feeling, rather than articulate reason; and at last a mathematical line is arrived by the contact of contrary decisions, which is so far arbitrary that it might equally well have been drawn a little further to the one side or to the other.[54]

Rather than studying cases to their bottom, appellate courts made determinations on a "predominance of feeling." The "mathematical lines" drawn by courts were "arbitrary." Clear distinctions evolved into intuitive preferences.

A random survey[55] of Holmes' torts opinions on the Massachusetts court provides an entry to his work as a state judge. Torts had been the private law field in which Holmes had arguably made his greatest scholarly contributions. It is possible to claim that in essays such as "The Theory of Torts" and "Trespass and Negligence,"[56] and in *The Common Law,* Holmes had supplied a principle for late nineteenth-century tort law—the modern negligence principle—that allowed torts to develop its identity as a discrete branch of law. Holmes' achievement had been to see that it was possible to speak of the myriad tort writs as manifestations of a general civil duty owed by everyone not to carelessly injure others. The concept of this duty of very great generality and the limitation of the duty through the fault principle—reasonable conduct under the circumstances—were major catalysts to the growth of modern tort law. Almost all the leading torts theorists of the late nineteenth century—Thomas Cooley,[57] Melville Bigelow,[58] John Wigmore,[59] Jeremiah Smith[60]—owed their conception of the subject as dealing with universally imposed civil duties to Holmes.[61]

What were the tort cases that Holmes, with this rich scholarly background, considered on the Massachusetts court? Holmes wrote over 400 torts opinions, the most he wrote on any legal subject and nearly one-third of his entire output. Of these only three were dissents.[62] One would have thought with this amount of cases, the very high percentage of majority opinions, and Holmes' understanding of the intellectual foundations of tort law, he would have had ample opportunity to put his scholarly theories into practice. Instead his torts opinions were exceptionally routine. Two opinions in the 1883 term merely disposed of evidentiary exceptions taken by the defendant at trial.[63] A third was a conventional assumption-of-risk case that was decided on its facts.[64]

Only in *Cowley v. Pulsifer,*[65] a case testing the limits of the record libel privilege, did Holmes attempt an elaborate discussion. The case involved publication in a newspaper of the contents of a petition to remove an attorney from the bar. Before the petition had been presented to the court or entered on the docket, it appeared in the paper. Holmes stated that "no binding authority has been called to our attention which precisely determines this case, and we must be governed in our conclusion mainly by a consideration of the reasons upon which admitted principles have been established."[66] He then grounded the decision on a distinction between proceedings in open court, which could be recorded without subjecting the recorder to a libel suit, and "preliminary written statement[s] of a claim or charge."[67] The record libel privilege did not extent to the latter.

Trivial torts cases again outnumbered significant ones in the 1884 term. Of the seven cases in which Holmes wrote opinions, two simply disposed of exceptions,[68] one held that the technical requirements for a libel had been made out,[69] one allowed an action for diverting water to be maintained by a citizen of another state,[70] one refused to find contributory negligence as a matter of law where an officer in an act of arresting a person stepped into a partly covered well in the darkness,[71] and one labeled the actions of a deputy sheriff misrepresentations of facts.[72] Only in *Dietrich v. Northampton*[73] did Holmes find a case on which he could ruminate. There a pregnant woman slipped on a defective highway constructed by the town of Northampton and suffered a miscarriage. She recovered for her physical injuries, and the deceased child's administrator sought to recover for the child's death. The case raised a number of issues, including whether infants could maintain actions for injuries suffered before birth, whether an injured fetus was a "person" entitled to legal redress, and whether the common law of negligence had a different standard of liability from that imposed on towns for failure to maintain highways in proper repair. For Holmes the case turned on the proposition that "no case, so far as we know, has ever decided that, if the infant survived, it could maintain an action for injuries received by it while in its mother's womb."[74] That dictum was to survive in tort law for seventy-five years.[75]

The 1890 Term contained more cases that approximated the typical late nineteenth-century tort action: the industrial accident leading to a suit in negligence. None of the negligence cases, however, involved more than a simple application of reasonable conduct standards to their facts. An employee assumed the risk when he passed close to a band saw, slipped, and put his hand on it.[76] A conductor of a streetcar was not contributorially negligent when knocked off the car by a protruding post from an excavation barrier.[77] A husband and wife injured at a grade crossing where the gates were up and no whistle or bell was sounded by the approaching train were entitled to have the question of their contributory negligence decided by a jury.[78] A commuter who, ignoring closed gates, walked behind one train and was hit by another on a neighboring track was grossly negligent as a matter of law.[79] A town had a responsibility to repair a mudhole in a road that caused the driver of a wagon to injure himself when he drove off the road to avoid it.[80] An unauthorized person using a water closet in a railroad station was owed no duty of care by the railroad, and no liability ensued when he was killed by a train that ran off its track.[81] The maintenance of a heavy steam hammer by a car wheel company was not a nuisance.[82]

Only one case in the Term, *Burt v. Advertiser Newspaper Co.*,[83] presented Holmes with an opportunity to clarify legal doctrine. Burt was a libel action against the *Boston Daily Advertiser* for a series of articles on fraud in the New York customs house. Two brothers, James and Silas Burt, were mentioned in the articles; James Burt, a broker, was accused of "outrageous sugar frauds"[84] and Silas Burt, a naval officer, of having a "long-time connection with some of the most disreputable elements in the New York custom-house."[85] In response to a letter of protest the *Advertiser*, while conceding that Silas Burt had not been accused of any wrongdoing, said that James Burt's practices "hold the New York custom-house up as a national disgrace."[86] The question raised by the Burt case was the scope of the *Advertiser*'s privilege of "fair criticism upon matters of public interest."[87] That privilege, Holmes held, did not extend to the publication of false facts. It was the criticism—the opinions of the critics—that was privileged. Holmes distinguished between "private inquiries . . . about a private person,"[88] such as "answers to inquiries about the character of a servant"[89] and comment on public matters. The *Advertiser*'s reasonable belief that its allegations about James Burt were true did not constitute a defense, Holmes noted: "A person publishes libelous matter at his peril."[90] The Burt case furnishes a good example of nineteenth-century common law attitudes toward freedom of the press in defamation cases. Not even a showing that a reasonable editor would have believed the false facts about James Burt to be true would have helped the *Advertiser*. Strict liability was the standard in defamation cases.

The 1891 Term produced no significant torts cases. The city of New Bedford was exonerated from liability for nuisance when a homeowner who connected his drain with a sewer, which concededly had a narrow outlet, had his basement filled during a heavy rainstorm with water and sewage.[91] A person who fell down unlighted cellar stairs in the course of delivering wood was held to assume the risk of an open cellar being near the house.[92] A case where a woman fell down a lighted flight of stairs was not sufficient for res ipsa loquitur, and could be taken from the jury since its elements were "permanent, few, and simple."[93] A workman who set on fire a shafting box soaked with oil, thereby damaging the owner's premises, was negligent as a matter of law.[94] And a traveler who picked up a loose telephone wire in a road, and was injured from electric current, was considered to be owed a duty by the city of Cambridge, which had negligently allowed the wire to fall into the road.[95] In none of the above cases did Holmes' opinions extend beyond a few paragraphs.

By the 1901 Term Holmes had become Chief Justice, and his workload had increased. He wrote Sir Frederick Pollock in 1899 that he "had more to do than ever," and that he had been taking on himself "perhaps rather a lion's share."[96] But the torts cases were no more significant than they had been in the 1880s or 1890s. Holmes found no contributory negligence in a parent whose child had been run over by a wagon in a quiet road,[97] but did find it where another child was run over by an electric car in a "teeming" city street.[98] He upheld a jury's verdict that a street railway car had negligently run into a baker's wagon that had been lawfully driving on the streetcar tracks,[99] construed a dram shop act to impose liability on the owner of a bar who illegally sold liquor to a person who while intoxicated stumbled into the path of a train,[100] and refused to impute to a passenger the alleged contributory negligence of a driver of a coal wagon.[101] He found a spout that spilled water on a sidewalk, causing ice to form, to be a nuisance, and its owner strictly liable for the injuries of a pedestrian who slipped on the ice.[102] He held that proof that a woman had committed adultery was not a defense against calling her a dirty old whore.[103] He allowed recovery from emotional distress when accompanied by a slight physical injury.[104] He found a gateman who inexplicably stood between the tracks of a railroad and was killed by a freight train in the process of coupling and uncoupling cars to be contributorially negligent.[105] And he denied recovery to a postal clerk who had sued the railroad owning the train on which he was unloading mail for injuries suffered when a car from another railroad negligently hit that train.[106]

In only one torts case that Term was there a glimpse of the kind of role Holmes might have expected himself to play as a judge. In *Patnoude v. New York, New Haven, and Hartford Railway*[107] a street railway company and the New York, New Haven and Hartford Railroad had agreed to unload a streetcar at a point on the railroad's tracks near the streetcar company's barn. The unloading process required the temporary dismantling of a fence that shielded the tracks from an adjoining highway. While the fence was dismantled and the streetcar, covered with a white canvas, was resting on a flat car of the railroad, a rider drove by on the adjacent highway and his horse, startled by the sight of the streetcar, reared and threw him. The question was whether the railroad was liable in nuisance or in negligence.

"As in many cases," Holmes said in his opinion finding for the railroad, "two principles or social desiderata present themselves, each of which it would be desirable to carry out but for the other, but which at this point come into conflict." It was "desirable that as far as possible people should be able to drive in the streets without their horses being frightened, [and it was also] desirable that the owners of land should be free to make profitable and otherwise innocent use of it." A "line has to be drawn to separate the domains of the irreconcilable desires, [but] such a line [could] not be drawn in general terms."[108] In the *Patnoude* case, however, the condition of the railroad's car and fence was transitory, and its potential for frightening horses did not necessarily mean that it was unlawful.[109] Torts cases involved drawing lines, balancing irreconcilable desires, and giving common-sense interpretations to facts. General propositions were not much help in deciding them.

With *Patnoude* one can see how far Holmes' conception of judging had evolved from the one he held when first appointed to the Massachusetts court.[110] While he had enjoyed getting to the bottom of things and formulating generalizations as a scholar, such activities were not easily related to appellate judging. The facts of individual cases were so diverse, and the competing principles so generally worthy, that arbitrary line-drawing was the inevitable result. Such line-drawing could not be generalized. Setting forth "the whole corpus" of law, or "writ[ing] it in continuous, logical, philosophic exposition"[111] were tasks beyond the reach of judges, who had to decide difficult, limited, and largely trivial cases.

Holmes had learned two lessons from his experience on the Supreme Judicial Court of Massachusetts. The first lesson was that cases inevitably presented conflicts between desirable social principles, and judges simply had to choose. That choice was an act of policymaking, not an inevitable unfolding of common law principles. The second lesson was that since such choices were arbitrary, and since the process of line-drawing could not be generalized, judging was a far more modest and less creative activity than Holmes expected. These lessons fostered two judicial habits in Holmes: the habit of deferring especially arbitrary policy choices to some other body, such as a legislature or a jury, that arguably reflected community sentiment; and the habit of not agonizing over the reasoning that justified an arbitrary choice. By the time Holmes left the Massachusetts court in 1902 his opinions were already notable for their brevity, their assertiveness, and their cryptic language. It was as if Holmes recognized that his decisionmaking process was largely arbitrary and decided to get on with it.

The Massachusetts years were also notable for a significant change in the attitudes expressed in Holmes' scholarship. *The Common Law,* I have argued,[112] had been a reformist tract, seeking to show by example that a thorough canvass of private law subjects could yield some clarifying and organizing principles. One message of *The Common Law* was that such principles were there to be extracted and applied to real-life situations by judges. The meaning of a private law subject, Holmes seemed to be saying, could be found in this body of intelligible principles.

By 1897, when he delivered his address, "The Path of the Law,"[113] Holmes was offering a very different definition of the meaning of law. Notwithstanding the claims of "some text writers" that law was "a system of reason" or "a deduction from principles of ethics or admitted axioms," law could be most accurately described as "prophecies of what the courts will do in fact."[114] While the "language of judicial decision" was "mainly the language of logic," behind the "logical form" lay "a judgment as to the relative worth and importance of competing legislative grounds." Judicial decisions were "opinion[s] as to policy" that merely "embod[ied] the preference of a given body in a given time and place."[115] The "duty" of judges was to weigh "considerations of social advantage."[116]

"The Path of the Law" had stressed lesson one of Holmes' experience as a judge: while judges may attempt to cloak their decisions in logic, the decisions were instinctive policy preferences. "Law in Science and Science in Law,"[117] delivered two years later, stressed lesson two. Holmes had some faith in science as a vehicle for measuring the social desires that he saw competing in a case.[118] He conceded that an "absolutely final and quantitative determination" could only occasionally be reached "because the worth of the competing social ends which respectively solicit a judgment for the plaintiff or the defendant cannot be reduced to number and accurately fixed."[119] Since policy grounds lay behind the use of legal rules, a "quantitative comparison" of the competing social desiderata seemed desirable. Such a comparison led Holmes back to a variant on his original passage from "The Theory of Torts."[120]

In our approach towards exactness we constantly tend to work out definite lines or equators to mark distinctions which we first notice as a difference of poles. . . . When [we] ha[ve] discovered that a difference is a difference of degree, that distinguished extremes have between them a penumbra in which one gradually shades into the other, . . . [we realize that we have] to draw the line, and an advocate of more experience will show the arbitrariness of the line proposed by putting cases very near to it on one side or the other. But the theory of the law is that such lines exist. . . . We like to disguise the arbitrariness, we like to save ourselves the trouble of nice and doubtful discriminations.[121]

Thus Holmes concluded that judging ended up being the arbitrary resolution of "a conflict between two social desires, each of which seeks to extend its dominion over the case, and which cannot both have their way." In making that resolution judges were "exercis[ing] the sovereign prerogative of choice."[122] They were "weigh[ing] the reasons for the particular right claimed and those for the competing right." Their solutions could not be in general terms, because "generalities [were] worse than useless."[123] Their solutions were bound to rest on "general grounds of policy blindly felt."[124]

Such were the lessons of twenty years on the Massachusetts bench. And there were two curious, and potentially contradictory, corollaries to those lessons. Since legal decisions were at bottom choices between competing social policies, it was essential that such choices reflect the wishes and feelings of the community, so that the law might keep pace with current thought.[125] Judge-made law had a tendency to prefer the logical form to the candid policy statement, and consequently sometimes became ridden with anachronistic rules and outmoded propositions. Especially in doubtful cases, then, Holmes thought that the practice of deferring policy choices to the jury was a good one: juries were apt to "introduce into their verdict a certain amount. . . . of popular prejudice."[126] In a case like *Patnoude*, where a right to ride without fear of injury conflicted with a right to use property in a profitable manner, one could label as a question of fact whether the use that invaded the right was negligent, and let a jury decide which social desideratum it preferred. A sense of the arbitrariness of judicial decisionmaking, then, led to a desire to defer, in close cases, to a more community-minded tribunal.

At the same time, however, that sense of arbitrariness led to a desire to exercise the sovereign prerogative of choice. Holmes had no particular confidence that juries "could see further into things or form a saner judgment than a sensible and well trained judge."[127] He thought that a well-trained judge could "follow the existing body of dogma into its highest generalizations," then "discover from history how it has come to be what it is," and finally "consider the ends which the several rules seek to accomplish"[128] and make a choice. Indeed, he thought that a judge need not do all those things; he might have liked to have done them, but he had not done them often in his opinions. What he had done was to see the internal conflict presented by a case, measure the competing social desires in his mind, and make an arbitrary choice. Having done that, he had made use of logic and his own command of language, and had produced an opinion. Judging in that manner was not difficult, so long as one recognized what one was doing.

In these two peculiarly divergent corollaries lay the seeds of Holmes' constitutional jurisprudence. Holmes' opinions on the Supreme Court were of two very different types. The first type, which brought him public acclaim,[129] emphasized the unsoundness of judges substituting their judgment on social issues for that of legislatures. Legislatures, like juries, were repositories of contemporary prejudices; there was something to be said for letting them decide difficult policy questions. In this deferential stance Holmes appeared as a judge aware of his own limitations, an appearance that was deceptive. The second type of opinion that Holmes produced on the Court resembled many of his private law opinions in Massachusetts: it was a brief, cursory, and cryptic determination of a difficult and complex issue. In the first type of opinion Holmes seemed chastened by the recognition of his arbitrary power; in the second he seemed to revel in it.

III The Supreme Court: A "Job" Mentality

After being appointed to the Supreme Court in 1902 Holmes wrote Pollock of his delight with his new position. "I am . . . more absorbed, interested and impressed than ever I had dreamed I might be," he said. "The variety and novelty to me of the questions, the remote spaces from which they come, the amount of work they require, all help the effect."[130] But before long Holmes began to see recurrent themes. Most questions before the Court were questions of degree; beneath "the lion's hide" of a case was "the same old donkey of a question of law."[131] Holmes could write two opinions a week, finishing the first one assigned to him at a Saturday conference by Tuesday and the second by Saturday. In listening to counsel argue before the Court he could summarize an argument before the lawyer had finished making it. His law clerks, whom he hired from 1905 on at the suggestion of John Chipman Gray, Ezra Thayer, or Felix Frankfurter, had very little legal research to do: Holmes wrote his own opinions, asking only for an occasional citation. The clerks paid his bills, answered routine correspondence, read to him in his last years, and above all were sounding boards on contemporary issues. When another justice needed research help, Holmes lent them out.[132]

Despite the "burning themes" that appeared in constitutional cases and despite the great public attention that his opinions, especially his dissents, received, Holmes primarily thought of his work on the Supreme Court as a "job." In 1928 Holmes wrote Lewis Einstein that "when I am on my job I don't care a damn what you want or what [a President] wants."[133] Yosal Rogat once likened Holmes' attitude toward his work on the Supreme Court to that of a pony express rider who "had to undertake a dangerous and exhausting series of rides in order to insure the survival of the city." While Holmes may have ridden hard, he "was not motivated by the city's survival. . . . Rather, he executed the assignment simply because he had undertaken it and. . . . to bring back a map of the terrain."[134] Repeatedly in his Supreme Court opinions Holmes conveyed this sense of detachment. He once said in a dissent that "[t]here is nothing that I more deprecate than the use of the Fourteenth Amendment . . . to prevent the making of social experiments . . . in the insulated chambers afforded by the several States, even though the experiments may seem futile or even noxious to me.''[135]

Detachment seems the most accurate term to characterize Holmes' stance on the Supreme Court. He was not merely skeptical; his emotions were for the most part not engaged. To put it more precisely, his emotions were stimulated by the professional features of his work but not by its substance. Few judges could pack more emotion into an opinion, but the emotion was not often generated from compassion for the litigants or concern for the seriousness of the issue at stake. It was the emotion of a literary talent, a person who liked the sound of memorable phrases. Holmes' aphorisms were original and incisive; they were also repeated often.

One can see Holmes' stance of detachment as a culmination of his intellectual history. By all accounts he was not only serious about philosophy and jurisprudence as a young man; he was in dead earnest. He clung to his manuscript on Kent, taking it with him to meals; he taught himself German so as to be able to read the contribution of German jurists in the original; he worked nights on the lectures that became *The Common Law;* he allegedly married Fanny Dixwell, whom he had known most of his life, only when someone else mentioned that she was pining away out of love for him.[136] From the 1870s, when he first began to think and write about jurisprudence, to the time he went on the Supreme Judicial Court of Massachusetts, he was a passionate and zealous legal reformer, eager ''to say his say on every question which the law has ever presented.'' And then, as we have seen, the futility of his grand design revealed itself. Cases were not vehicles for propounding a grand theory, but merely clusterings around poles; judging was not writing law ''in continuous, logical, philosophic exposition'' but an exercise in the arbitrary drawing of lines. One could not live one's dreams: ''We are lucky enough if we can give a sample of our best.''[137]

Holmes' sense of his professional role thus radically contracted over time, and his reduced expectations combined with traits of personality to produce detachment. Acquaintances of Holmes had from his early years noted his apparent indifference to others. His father thought he ''look[ed] at life as at a solemn show where he is only a spectator'';[138] William James called him ''a powerful battery, formed like a planing machine to gouge a deep self-beneficial groove through life'';[139] James Bradley Thayer, embittered over Holmes' leaving Harvard for the Massachusetts court, had said that he was selfish, vain and thoughtless.[140] Holmes did not read a newspaper, paid little attention to contemporary affairs, had most of his intimate friendships with persons from whom he was physically separated, and once said that he was glad that he had no children.[141] The themes that engaged him, such as intellectual effort and war, were related to central personal experiences. Beyond that he seemed content to ''do my job in the station in which we were born.''[142]

Holmes' job at the Supreme Court consisted of, in many instances, reviewing the constitutionality of actions of a legislature. In such cases Holmes forged his famous attitude of deference, which was seen as humility and ''self-restraint'' by admirers and had the added advantage of sustaining ''progressive'' legislation about which a number of early twentieth-century intellectuals were enthusiastic.[143]

Deference to legislative policymaking was consistent with the views Holmes had developed on the Massachusetts court. In twenty years on that court he had held unconstitutional only one Massachusetts statute.[144] His general attitude was expressed in an advisory opinion on the constitutionality of the legislature's authorizing towns to buy coal and wood and sell them to their inhabitants as fuel.[145] "[W]hen money is taken to enable a public body to offer to the public . . . an article of general necessity," Holmes wrote, "the purpose is no less public when that article is wood or coal than when it is water or gas or electricity or education, to say nothing of cases like the support of paupers, or the taking of land for railroads."[146]

Deference, of course, was consistent with Holmes' belief that judging was an arbitrary exercise in policy choices, and, that being so, some policy choices were better made by more "representative" bodies of government. He may have been motivated to express his views more openly, however, by the clumsy policymaking of his contemporaries on the Supreme Court. In the first years of the twentieth century the constitutionality of a number of pieces of "welfare" legislation was tested by the Court. The legislation sought to regulate the working hours of certain occupations or persons, to insure minimum wage standards, to eliminate child labor, and other such "reforms." Holmes was not personally sympathetic to most of the legislation, but he was even less sympathetic to the treatment of it by majorities on his Court. Those majorities had invalidated the legislation by the use of the "liberty of contract" doctrine, which Holmes later called a "dogma."[147] Liberty of contract was objectionable to Holmes in that it attempted to decide "concrete cases" on the basis of a "general proposition" that was suspect as a matter of textual interpretation and debatable as a matter of economic theory.[148] The Court had sustained many legislative acts that interfered with freedom of contract, and the Constitution was "not intended to embody a particular economic theory."[149] To transform the Fourteenth Amendment into an ideological creed was to "pervert" it.[150]

It is instructive to dwell on what Holmes thought was wrong with the majority's decisions in such liberty of contract cases as *Lochner v. New York,*[151] *Adair v. United States,*[152] and *Adkins v. Children's Hospital.*[153] He did not object to the substance of the doctrine itself; he would have "to study it further and long" before endorsing it or rejecting it.[154] Nor did he necessarily object, at least as a general proposition, to the Court's substitution of its judgment for that of a legislature. What he objected to was the clumsy use of a "dogma" to decide questions that ought to have been decided by a consideration of the ends that rules seek to accomplish, the reasons those ends are desired, what is given up to gain them, and whether they are worth the price.[155] Such a consideration was presumptively suited to a legislative judgment, and if the Court were to distrust that judgment it ought to do so in a manner that did not so transparently expose the "convictions or prejudices" of its members.[156]

In deferring, Holmes thus neither espoused the worth of legislation nor expressed concern that judges ought to leave policy decisions to someone else. He merely felt that if judges were going to make arbitrary choices, they ought not to base those choices on vulnerable dogmas. Thus the principal problem with deci-

United Zinc & Chemical Company did not know that children had been in the habit of visiting the site and had not maintained the site adjacent to the road. "[I]t is at least doubtful," he wrote, "whether the water could be seen from any place where the children lawfully were." There had been no inducements, Holmes felt; there was no evidence that the water had "led [the boys] to enter the land." There was no pattern of children trespassing on the land that might have informed the United Zinc & Chemical Company of potential dangers. Even the presence of roads close to the site were not invitations: "[A] road is not an invitation to leave it elsewhere than at its end." [179]

Britt seems to have been a case ideally suited to leave to a jury, and as such raises the question why Holmes did not adopt that course of action. Child trespasser cases inevitably turn on their facts: how much of an "inducement" the dangerous substance was, how much awareness the landowner had of trespassers, how easy the dangerous substance was to reach, etc. Given the fact that landowners had long been held to owe no duty to trespassers, the child trespasser doctrine seemed designed for those circumstances where a landowner knew that he was maintaining a dangerous substance on his land and knew or should have known that it would be attractive to children. If the railroad turntable was a paradigmatic attractive nuisance, since it was adjacent to a roadway and since it was the kind of substance that would appeal to children as a place to play, a pond near an abandoned building was not far from that paradigm. The only complicating factors in the *Britt* case were that the company apparently had no experience with trespassers on the site and that the site was not adjacent to the road. But those were surely not conclusive on the question of liability, given the very dangerous condition of the pond. The case seemed designed to be decided by the "common sense" of a jury.

It appears that some of the same tendencies that motivated Holmes to lay down the "stop, look and listen" standard in *Goodman* were at work in *Britt*. In his early career Holmes had been dismayed at the unpredictability and uncertainty of jury-made rules: If the child trespasser doctrine was to be invoked or not invoked depending on the sympathies of a jury, it was not a doctrine whose existence helped landowners (or potential trespassers) plan their affairs. Holmes seems to have wanted to use the *Britt* case as a means of confining the doctrine to those cases where a landowner had notice of children trespassing near a dangerous substance on his property. So formulated, the doctrine's impact would be greatly reduced, since it could never be invoked against a landowner in a "first accident" case. Once two boys had died as a result of coming into contact with a zinc company's dangerous abandoned plant it is unlikely that the company would permit the plant to remain in that condition; at a minimum it would post conspicuous warnings. Only if the company did nothing and a second accident involving children occurred would the child trespasser doctrine come into play. That was a predictable state of affairs; it was also unlikely to happen.

Goodman and *Britt* may suggest that Holmes' "activist" decisions on the Supreme Court were confined to those instances where he had engaged himself as a scholar. But many of Holmes' most famous opinions came in areas, such as the First Amendment, that he had not addressed in his early career, and in some of these opinions he dropped his usual pose of deference to legislatures. The line of first amendment cases, stretching from *Abrams v. United States*[180] through *Gitlow v. New York*,[181] *Whitney v. California*,[182] and *United States v. Schwimmer*[183] to *Near v. Minnesota*,[184] was one set of examples: Holmes attempted to fix the outer limits of legislative regulation of speech. *Nixon v. Herndon*,[185] a case invalidating a Texas primary system that excluded blacks from participation, was another. Holmes said for the Court: "States may do a good deal of classifying that it is difficult to believe rational, but there are limits."[186] *Olmstead v. United States*[187] was yet another: there Holmes read the Fourth and Fifth Amendments to prohibit the use of illegally seized evidence in a criminal prosecution. The case invoked "two objects of desire, both of which we cannot have," Holmes said; "we must . . . make up our minds which to choose."[188] He was unwilling in that instance to let a legislature make the choice.

Nor was Holmes willing to defer to a legislative judgment in *Mahon*.[189] There the Pennsylvania legislature had passed a statute that forbade the mining of anthracite coal on land in such a way as to endanger structures erected on the surface of the land in question. A landowner sought to apply the statute to prevent the Pennsylvania Coal Company from mining on land he had bought from the company. The company had expressly reserved subsurface rights to the land and had also retained the right to remove coal from beneath the surface. Since the contract between the coal company and the landowner had been made prior to the passage of the statute, the question was whether the statute was an unconstitutional deprivation of existing property and contract rights.

Holmes, for a majority of the Court, held that it was. "The general rule," he announced, "is, that while property may be regulated to a certain extent, if regulation goes too far it will be recognized as a taking." Here the Pennsylvania legislature had provided no compensation for the mining companies, and thus had infringed their rights. "We are in danger of forgetting," Holmes noted, "that a strong public desire to improve the public condition is not enough to warrant achieving the desire by a shorter cut than the constitutional way of paying for the change." Even if the statute had been passed "upon the conviction that an exigency existed," the "question at bottom [was] upon whom the loss of the changes desired should fall."[190]

Compensation cases such as *Mahon* involved "question[s] of degree," Holmes said, and "therefore [could] not be disposed of by general propositions." That being said, he did not defer to legislative balancing. The Pennsylvania statute went "beyond any of the [compensation] cases decided by this Court." A strong public desire for property did not itself justify a taking without compensation; otherwise the legislature could invoke its police power "more and more until at last private property disappears."[191]

Mahon was not different for Holmes from the speech cases or from *Nixon v. Herndon*: there were limits to what states could do under their discretionary authority. Commentators have reacted differently to *Mahon* because Holmes protected property rights rather than personhood rights, but Holmes made no such jurisprudential distinctions. When he invoked the Constitution to invalidate a legislative restriction on rights, that was because the legislature had gone "too far."

What was "too far" was a "question of degree," but sometimes the answer was obvious. When it was, Holmes saw no reason—"exigencies" notwithstanding—to defer to legislative judgments.[192]

Neither conventional political labels nor common terms from jurisprudence help clarify Holmes' stance on the Supreme Court. Several commentators have shown that his opinions are imperfectly described as "liberal" or "conservative."[193] This article suggests that they are no more satisfactorily described as "activist" or deferential. When Holmes' tenure on the Supreme Court is subjected to detailed analysis, two striking and hitherto largely unremarked features appear. First, Holmes was nowhere near as activist in private law cases as his early scholarship suggested he might have been, but he was more activist, if anything, than he had been on the Supreme Judicial Court of Massachusetts. The *Goodman* and *Britt* opinions were in some sense throwbacks to his earlier theory, formulated as a scholar, of how negligence cases ought to be decided. Holmes retained on the Supreme Court the idea that most cases presented policy choices between competing "social desiderata," and while this led him toward deference to legislatures in many cases, it did not prevent him from making choices in others. He believed the choices to be arbitrary, but he made them anyway. Calling Holmes an advocate of self-restraint on the Court does not fully capture him.

Second, while Holmes saw that at the bottom of nearly every Supreme Court case was a choice between competing public policies, he was not deterred by that realization from making a prompt decision. If he chose to defer to a legislature, he spent very little time justifying the legislature's actions: the simplest bow to minimal rationality generally sufficed. Sometimes, in cases like *Patsone v. Pennsylvania*,[194] Holmes did not even seem to be lingering over the question of legislative rationality. In that case he blithely accepted the legislature's premise that aliens were more dangerous to wildlife than citizens. Nor was Holmes any less peremptory when he chose to upset a legislative judgment. That the Texas legislature had gone too far in *Nixon v. Herndon* was "too clear for extended argument."[195] That the Pennsylvania statute in *Mahon* went "beyond any of the cases decided by this Court" needed only to be stated.[196]

The overwhelming impression of Holmes' performance on the Supreme Court, then, is the same impression one gets of his performance in Massachusetts. Here was a judge whose principal interest seems to have been in having cases decided, written up, and disposed of. The vivid sentence with which Holmes ended his opinion in *Britt,* "a road is not an invitation to leave it elsewhere than at its end,"[197] captures the mood in which Holmes appears to have written most of his opinions. The sentence is striking, but it is not much help, either as a general statement or as an explanation of the case. Travelers leave roads at a variety of places—indeed almost no one who travels on a road leaves it at its end. A road, in fact, is not an "invitation" to leave it at all; if anything, it is an invitation to take it somewhere, as being an easier place on which to travel than a field or a stream. But the sentence is designed to dismiss the argument that the presence of the road in *Britt* may have been an enticement to travel near the poisoned site. The sentence does "dismiss" that argument, but only through a largely erroneous statement that captures our attention. It is as if having turned a phrase Holmes decided that he had said enough, and could get on to something else. Holmes makes cases seem like toys scattered in a child's room: The idea is to pick them up and put them in place, not to linger over the differences among them nor to give some more special meaning than others. When the job is over, the room is clean; the toys are "put away."

IV Remembering Holmes: What Does He Leave Us?

However much Holmes is written about or ignored, his reputation seems secure. I have suggested that his reputation may contain some erroneous components, such as the idea that he was consistently an apostle of judicial self-restraint, but that is not to suggest that it will not endure. Three of Holmes' contributions seem so significant as to resist even the most aggressive form of historical debunking. First, he identified judging as an exercise in intuitive policy choices at a time when few other judges or jurists were prepared to concede that judging was anything other than finding and applying preexistent legal principles. For Holmes to see that cases were repositories of clashing policies was a keen enough insight; for him to come upon that insight in the midst of a jurisprudential climate that denied any policymaking component to judging was remarkable.

Second, Holmes helped develop a significant corollary to his insight that judges were policymakers. The corollary was his theory of deference, and while he did not originate the theory nor practice it exclusively, several of his opinions were powerful arguments for its use. This was particularly true in the public law area, and most particularly true in Supreme Court cases, where Holmes' version of good sense was juxtaposed against tortured judicial efforts to preserve "dogma" at all costs. The accident of Holmes' being on the Supreme Court at a time when legislatures had become more active, and the Court had not developed a theory of responding to that activism, made him one of the original spokesmen on the Court for a theory of constitutional adjudication that was to have great influence in the twentieth century. While Holmes was never as zealous a proponent of self-restraint as some of his disciples, his opinion in *Lochner* gave deference intellectual respectability.

Third, as the last sentence from *Britt* illustrates, Holmes had a distinctively arresting style. No Supreme Court Justice matched Holmes in this regard; only Robert Jackson occasionally came close. The holdings of Holmes' opinions may be forgotten, but the epigrams remain. "A word is . . . the skin of a living thought";[198] "[g]reat cases like hard cases make bad law";[199] "[t]he Fourteenth Amendment does not enact Mr. Herbert Spencer's Social Statics";[200] "the best test of truth is the power of the thought to get itself accepted in the competition of the market";[201] "[t]hree generations of imbeciles is enough."[202] Not one of these sentences was necessary to the decision in the case in which it appeared; all contain overstatements or ambiguities. Each, however, helps to universalize the act of opinion writing, to make it a process of communicating at the deepest levels of human experience. When a judge can write in that fashion subsequent generations will be gripped by his style. No notes of dissatisfaction with his opinions as guidelines for future conduct will fully detract from his appeal. Holmes wrote lines that spanned time.

But can one remember Holmes as more than the author of arresting epigrams? Does his jurisprudence leave us a foundation for thinking about judging? Here it seems that on some issues Holmes seems so overwhelmingly right that one wonders how a contrary position was ever seriously maintained, and on other issues Holmes seems so disinclined to explore questions once he has raised them that one is tempted to conclude that an important function of his jurisprudence is to cut off thinking at preliminary stages.

Holmes may have thought, when he was at the fever pitch of his scholarly efforts in the 1870s, that, while absolute certainty might be unattainable, fields of private law could be made more certain, in the sense of being more regularized and predictable. The impulse toward certainty is a strong one in legal scholarship: recently we have seen the "laws" of welfare economics offered as yet another source of regularizing the common law. But we should have learned the lesson Holmes had learned after sixteen years as a judge: "[c]ertainty generally is illusion, and repose is not the destiny of man."[203] Too many variables exist for certainty in the law to be realizable: the discrete personalities and idiosyncracies of judges and other lawmakers; the changing intellectual climates in which research is conducted, which affect the normative dimensions of research and thereby insure that scholarly contributions will never be timeless; the fortuitous allocation of talent and incentives among counsel for one side or another; the strange ways in which the facts of a case compel a rule, which then evaporates when the facts fade into memory. Holmes may have been sensible, as a young scholar, to search for certainty; had he not thought it attainable he might not have tried to study private law subjects to their bottom. But he was even more sensible to abandon certainty as a judge. His metaphor of "growth" in the law, a series of decisions clustering around two poles and finally being separable only by an arbitrary line, rings truer than all the pronouncements that law can be made "scientific." I would not call Holmes' metaphorical description a process of growth, merely one of change, but I think as a description it is uncontroverted.

Does it follow, then, that since certainty in jurisprudence is elusive, humility and deference are the only appropriate lawmaking postures? Here I think Holmes' own indifference and the misguided labors of his disciples have contributed to lend prominence to a theory of judging that possesses serious limitations. During Holmes' tenure judicial deference resulted in legislation that helped alleviate some of the inequalities of rampant industrialism; in the 1950s and 1960s a similar version of deference would have perpetuated malapportioned legislatures, racially segregated facilities, the absence of legal representation for impoverished persons, and restrictions on the use and dispensation of birth control devices. The simple truth that law cases in America serve as a forum for testing conflicting ideas about public policy does not suggest that all such decisions should be made by "representative" or "community-minded" bodies, such as legislatures or juries. Sometimes the choices of the public are benighted or hasty or prejudiced; sometimes the majority oppresses those who differ with it. Holmes taught us that judges, if unchecked, will make justice synonymous with their own prejudices. The Warren Court taught us that legislatures will do the same.

Deference or activism is thus a function of time and place and of the seriousness of the issues at stake. Sometimes a court does well to defer: the issues are volatile, the public divided, the principles hard to grasp. At other times a court seemingly has an obligation not to defer: a more representative body has forgotten elementary principles of justice and needs to be admonished by an institution whose popularity is not so dependent on majoritarian whim. It stretches Holmes beyond recognition to make him a Warren Court Justice, but he had his own areas, ranging from speech to subsurface mining, where he found majoritarian solutions defective. Still, while one would like to blame Holmes' disciples for the agonized state in which self-restraint theory found itself after World War II, Holmes set it on that path.[204] He found legislative rationality in too many mere pretexts, he tolerated repression in the name of democracy too often. Before long judges who considered themselves intellectuals and "liberals" in the tradition of Holmes were allowing legislatures to compel school children to salute the flag and to require that college professors go on record as opposing Communism.[205] Holmes' theory of deference had led them there; his having scrapped the theory when it suited him did not excuse his putting it on the market for others to misuse.

Linked to Holmes' beliefs that certainty was an illusion and that deference was often a sensible judicial posture was his conviction that judicial decisions were at bottom arbitrary exercises. As we have seen, the discovery of arbitrariness led Holmes in two directions, toward deference and also toward a "job mentality" that emphasized deciding cases so that they could be decided. Arbitrariness raises two separate issues: are we resigned to its presence, and, if so, what can we do about it? As to the first, to sense that human decisionmaking is arbitrary seems to me the beginning of wisdom about the way persons conduct their affairs. All of us have our memories of a nakedly arbitrary decision, ranging from a situation when two devotees of one side of an issue forgot the date of a meeting and the other side won by a single vote, to a situation where a committee was deeply divided on the resolution of an academic matter and finally decided in accordance with the views of the sole member who prepared written comments. Beyond those examples, all of us sense that many decisions are made that would have been made differently had different personnel been involved, had the timing of events been different, or had the issue been presented in different form. Holmes was right to see arbitrariness built into every discretionary decision; he was also right not to be afraid of it.

But does arbitrariness provide a justification for the kind of limited explanations for decisions that Holmes so regularly produced? Here it seems to me that one can advance two interpretations of the purpose of a judicial decision, and the explanations that one produces for one's results will be affected by the interpretation one chooses. One can see the decisions of cases as single existential phenomena: They occur, they dispose of a controversy, they cease to have an existence. Or one can see such decisions as communications beyond the immediate controversy, directed, potentially, at future litigants, future judges, commentators, the general public. If one holds to the first view there is not much point in advancing extensive justifications for one's results. New cases will necessarily be different; a whole host of variables will serve to distinguish them from the past, and prior explanations will not prove much use. I think that in many instances Holmes adopted this view, or at least was sufficiently skeptical of the utility of extensive explanations and sufficiently motivated to get on with the job that he acted as if he adopted it. On other occasions, of course, Holmes regarded a decision as a means of communicating more extensively; he did not dissent just to see how many memorable phrases he could turn.

The idea that judicial opinions communicate to audiences beyond the immediate parties in the dispute is one that once led me to characterize constitutional adjudications as a dialectical process.[206] The dialectical theory holds that judicial decisions, at least when they interpret the Constitution, are in a kind of provisional state of acceptance; they possess the authority of the court that delivers them but their eventual acceptance—their legitimacy—has not been achieved. The process of legitimation involves a testing, over time, of the justifications advanced for the given interpretation. Of course the interpretation yields a definite result, and the controversial nature of the result will play a part in how swiftly or how searchingly the interpretation is tested. But the process occurs to some extent in all decisions.

When a decision is being "tested," the pressure points of its explanatory apparatus may make a difference in how fully it becomes legitimated. To take a contemporary example, an opinion that seems not yet to have reached the status of being legitimated is *Roe v. Wade*,[207] which is eight years old at this writing. *Roe v. Wade*'s indeterminate status is partially a function of the controversial nature of the issue it purports to resolve: abortion is not an issue easily "settled" in one fashion or another. The decision's indeterminate status seems also linked, however, to its explanatory strategy, which chose to emphasize the state of medical knowledge about when a life is "in being" as a crucial determinant for when an abortion is permissible. Such an emphasis, of course, renders the decision vulnerable to changes in the state of medical knowledge. If the time a life is said to come into being were to recede, in the view of a dominant number of qualified medical practitioners, until a point so close to conception that any abortion would be a termination of "life," *Roe v. Wade*'s guidelines for abortion, which allow a mother unrestricted autonomy to terminate a pregnancy in the first trimester, might be threatened. In that instance *Roe v. Wade* could be taken as a communication into the future that was eventually found lacking in persuasive power due to the outmoded assumptions on which it rested.

Such seems to be the fate of many constitutional opinions. But one might argue that this form of communication, regardless of its vulnerability, is preferable to the cryptic, assertive form adopted by Holmes in many of his opinions. An explanation like that advanced in *Roe v. Wade* seems to be saying: "Here are my choices, between life and the autonomy of personhood; my decision to choose one over the other is necessarily arbitrary, but is influenced by some assumptions about the medical nature of 'life'; if those assumptions are subsequently called into question, another arbitrary choice may result." Holmes' explanations rarely sought to communicate in so extended a fashion. Indeed when Holmes retreats to the kind of language he used to explain his results in such cases as *Patsone*—a reasonable man might well think aliens are dangerous to wildlife[208]—one gets the impression that his tongue is in his cheek; that he is using the convention of deference to cut off communication rather than to open it up.

Here, finally, I come back to Holmes' job mentality. There are many cases, he seems to be saying, where the choices are between generally desirable policies that happen to conflict; we must prefer one or the other; we will surely not invariably prefer that one on every occasion; we have a case to decide; let's get on with it. But that method tells us precious little about why one policy should prevail over another even in this case. It seems to tell us, in fact, only that the judge made a choice; another judge might have decided differently. That message leads us to *The Path of the Law* and the "prophecies of what the courts will do in fact,"[209] to the idea that law is synonymous with the arbitrary fiats of officials, and to related cynical revelations. If we end up endorsing such cynicism, Holmes can take some of the credit.

But I think Holmes intended to convey something more in his cryptic explanations. I think he was attempting to show that in a truly "hard" case, if you force an extended explanation, that explanation will crumble to pieces on reflection. And as one explanation after another crumbles, one is left with the fact of judicial power, the force of judicial intuition, and the way the law has of correcting itself over time. After a while, Holmes seems to say, it is not the explanations that count—they all crumble, eventually—but the decisions. One's job as a judge becomes to decide—that is what people count on one to do; that is what judges have the power to do where ordinary people do not—and not to agonize about why. Cryptic explanations, then, are intended to cut off thinking about issues that are sufficiently complicated and difficult to benumb one's mind. At some point one has to stop thinking and choose. It may be that Holmes' view of judging makes sense—and if it does, the concept of a dialectic of constitutional adjudication seems so much academic gossamer—but even if it cuts off thought and explanation too soon, it may not be the easy way out. The easy way out may be to pretend that sooner or later some disinterested, reasoned justification will emerge mysteriously out of one's ruminations as one tries to decide a case. Holmes looked to the bottom of cases and saw only his own reflection. Should we probe so far, we might conclude that reasoning in epigrams was preferable to more extended ratiocinations. Length is not the equivalent of depth.

NOTES

1. Holmes, *Plato,* 2 U.Q. 205, 206 (1860).
2. Letter from Oliver Wendell Holmes to Elizabeth Shepley Sergeant (Dec. 7, 1926), *quoted* in 1 M. HOWE JUSTICE OLIVER WENDELL HOLMES 54 (1957).
3. White, *The Rise and Fall of Justice Holmes,* 39 U. CHI. L. REV. 51, 77 (1971).
4. *Id.* at 76.
5. *Id.* at 77.
6. In the past two academic years, Harvard Law School, Northwestern University

School of Law, the University of Illinois School of Law, and the American Society for Legal History have devoted lectures or symposia to Holmes' work, and Professors Patrick Atiyah, Robert Cover, Grant Gilmore, Robert Gordon, Morton Horwitz, Saul Touster, and Jan Vedder, as well as Judge Benjamin Kaplan, have delivered papers on various features of Holmes' career.

7. O.W. HOLMES, THE COMMON LAW (1881).

8. O.W. HOLMES, *The Solider's Faith,* in OCCASIONAL SPEECHES 73, 78–79 (M. HOWE ed. 1962).

9. *See infra* text accompanying notes 171–78.

10. *See infra* text accompanying notes 161–66.

11. M. HOWE, JUSTICE OLIVER WENDELL HOLMES (vol. 1, 1957; vol. 2, 1963).

12. 2 *id.*

13. *See* Tushnet, *The Logic of Experience: Oliver Wendell Holmes on the Supreme Judicial Court,* 63 VA. L. REV. 975 (1977).

14. There are a few exceptions. *See, e.g.,* Crocker v. Cotting, 170 Mass. 68, 71, 48 N.E. 1023, 1024 (1898) ("The jurisdiction is not affected by a defendant's recalcitrance"); Laplante v. Warren Cotton Mills, 165 Mass. 487, 489, 43 N.E. 294, 295 (1896) ("A boy who is dull at fifteen probably was dull at fourteen"); Lincoln v. Commonwealth, 164 Mass. 368, 378, 41 N.E. 489, 491 (1895) ("All values are anticipations of the future").

15. *See, e.g.,* 1 M. HOWE, *supra* note 11, at 245–86 (Boston law practice); 2 *id.* at 26–95, 253–83 (Harvard years); *id.* at 1–95 (*American Law Review* experience).

16. Letter from Oliver Wendell Holmes to James Bryce (Aug. 17, 1879), *quoted in* 2 M. HOWE, *supra* note 11, at 25.

17. *The Arrangement of the Law—Privity,* 7 AM. L. REV. 46, 47 n.2 (1872).

18. Book Notices, 5 AM. L. REV. 341 (1870).

19. *The Theory of Torts,* 7 AM. L. REV. 652, 659–60 (1873).

20. Book Notices, *supra* note 18, at 341.

21. *The Theory of Torts, supra* note 19, at 659–60.

22. Book Notices, 5 AM. L. REV. 359 (1871).

23. *The Theory of Torts, supra* note 19, at 659.

24. O.W. HOLMES, supra note 7, at 89.

25. *See* 2 M. HOWE, *supra* note 11, at 136.

26. O.W. HOLMES, *The Path of the Law,* in COLLECTED LEGAL PAPERS 167, 186–87 (1920).

27. O.W. HOLMES, *Law in Science and Science in Law,* in COLLECTED LEGAL PAPERS 210, 225 (1920).

28. 2 M. HOWE, *supra* note 11, at 196–97.

29. *The Theory of Torts, supra* note 19, at 658.

30. Book Notices, 5 AM. L. REV. 536 (1870).

31. O.W. HOLMES, *supra* note 7, at 124–26.

32. *Id.* at 127.

33. *Id.* at 89.

34. *Id.* at 124.

35. Letter from Mrs. Henry James to Henry James, Jr., *quoted in* 1 R. PERRY, THE THOUGHT AND CHARACTER OF WILLIAM JAMES 519 (1935).

36. Letter from Oliver Wendell Holmes to Charles W. Eliot (Nov. 1, 1881), *quoted in* 2 M. HOWE, *supra* note 11, at 261.

37. Thayer, Memorandum (Dec. 22, 1882), *quoted in* 2 M. HOWE, *supra* note 11, at 268.

38. Letter from Oliver Wendell Holmes to Felix Frankfurter (July 15, 1913), *quoted in* 2 M. Howe, *supra* note 11, 282.

39. Letter from Oliver Wendell Holmes to James Bryce (Dec. 31, 1882), *quoted in* 2 M. Howe, *supra* note 11, at 280.

40. Letter from Oliver Wendell Holmes to Harold Laski (Nov. 17, 1920), *quoted in* 2 M. Howe, *supra* note 11, at 281.

41. Letter from Oliver Wendell Holmes to James Bryce (Dec. 31, 1882), *quoted in* 2 M. Howe, *supra* note 11, at 280–81.

42. Letter from Oliver Wendell Holmes to Felix Frankfurter (July 15, 1913), *quoted in* 2 M. Howe, *supra* note 11, at 282.

43. Letter from Oliver Wendell Holmes to James Bryce (Dec. 31, 1882), *quoted in* 2 M. Howe, *supra* note 11, at 281.

44. *Id.* at 280.

45. *Id.*

46. Letter from Oliver Wendell Holmes to Harold Laski, (Feb. 1, 1919), *quoted in* 2 M. Howe, *supra* note 11, at 137.

47. Letter from Oliver Wendell Holmes to Harold Laski (Nov. 17, 1920), *quoted in* 2 M. Howe, *supra* note 11, at 281.

48. Letter from Oliver Wendell Holmes to Lady Clare Castletown (Mar. 5, 1897), *quoted in* 2 M. Howe, *supra* note 11, at 282.

49. Letter from Oliver Wendell Holmes to Felix Frankfurter (July 15, 1913), *quoted in* 2 M. Howe, *supra* note 11, at 282.

50. O. W. Holmes, *Speech at Bar Dinner,* in Occasional Speeches 122, 123 (M. Howe ed. 1962).

51. *Id.*

52. *Id.*

53. *The Theory of Torts, supra* note 19.

54. *Id.* at 654.

55. Even the term "random survey" may impart too much rigor. I have examined Holmes' torts opinions in three time periods from 1881 to 1902. Adjustments were made if the number of opinions in a given year seemed too low to be revealing. I was interested in the significance or insignificance of the case, as suggested by Holmes' opinion and subsequent treatment of the opinion, and in comparisons between Holmes' jurisprudential perspective in one time frame and another.

56. Holmes, *Trespass* and *Negligence,* 14 Am. L. Rev. 1 (1880).

57. *See* T. Cooley, A Treatise On The Law Of Torts 628–58 (1880).

58. *See* M. Bigelow, The Law of Torts 106–16 (8th ed. 1907).

59. *See* 1 J. Wigmore Select Cases On The Law of Torts 7–8 (1912).

60. *See* Smith, *Tort and Absolute Liability—Suggested Changes in Classification,* in Selected Essays On The Law Of Torts 176, 189–90 (1924).

61. *See* G. White, Tort Law In America 6–62 (1980).

62. May v. Wood, 172 Mass. 11, 14, 51 N.E. 191, 192 (1898) (Holmes, J., dissenting); Nash v. Minnesota Title Ins. & Trust Co., 163 Mass. 574, 586, 40 N.E. 1039, 1042 (1895) (Holmes, J., dissenting); Hanson v. Globe Newspaper Co., 159 Mass. 293, 299, 34 N.E. 462, 464 (1893) (Holmes, J., dissenting).

63. McMahon v. O'Connor, 137 Mass. 216 (1884); McAvoy v. Wright, 137 Mass. 207 (1884).

64. Williams v. Churchill, 137 Mass. 243 (1884).

65. 137 Mass. 392 (1884).

66. *Id.* at 393.

67. *Id.* at 394.

68. New Salem v. Eagle Mill Co., 138 Mass. 8 (1884); Purple v. Greenfield, 138 Mass. 1 (1884).

69. Hurley v. Fall River Daily Herald Pub. Co., 138 Mass. 334 (1885).

70. Mannville v. Worcester, 138 Mass. 89 (1884).

71. Learoyd v. Godfrey, 138 Mass. 315 (1885).

72. Burns v. Lane, 138 Mass. 350 (1885).

73. 138 Mass. 14 (1885).

74. *Id.* at 15.

75. The first case to extend a right of action for prenatal injuries was Verkennes v. Cornifa, 229 Minn. 365, 38 N.W.2d 838 (1949). Dietrich v. Northampton, 138 Mass. 14 (1884), was not limited until Keyes v. Construction Serv., Inc., 340 Mass. 633, 165 N.E.2d 912 (1960).

76. May v. Whittier Mach. Co., 154 Mass. 29, 27 N.E. 768 (1891).

77. Powers v. Boston, 154 Mass. 60, 27 N.E. 995 (1891).

78. Merrigan v. Boston & A. R.R., 154 Mass. 189, 28 N.E. 149 (1891).

79. Debbons v. Old Colony R.R., 154 Mass. 402, 28 N.E. 274 (1891).

80. Pomeroy v. Westfield, 154 Mass. 462, 28 N.E. 899 (1891).

81. Dillon v. Connecticut River R.R., 154 Mass. 478, 28 N.E. 899 (1891).

82. Wesson v. Washburn Car Wheel Co., 154 Mass. 514, 28 N.E. 679 (1891).

83. 154 Mass. 238, 28 N.E. 1 (1891).

84. *Id.* at 241, 28 N.E. at 3.

85. *Id.* at 239, 28 N.E. at 2.

86. *Id.* at 241, 28 N.E. at 3.

87. *Id.* at 242, 28 N.E. at 4.

88. *Id.* at 243, 28 N.E. at 4.

89. *Id.* at 242, 28 N.E. at 4.

90. *Id.* at 245, 28 N.E. at 5 (citations omitted).

91. Buckley v. New Bedford, 155 Mass. 64, 29 N.E. 201 (1891).

92. Walker v. Winstanley, 155 Mass. 301, 29 N.E. 518 (1892).

93. Pinney v. Hall, 156 Mass. 225, 226, 30 N.E. 1016 (1892).

94. Perry v. Smith, 156 Mass. 340, 31 N.E. 9 (1892).

95. Bourget v. Cambridge, 156 Mass. 391, 31 N.E. 390 (1892).

96. Letter from Oliver Wendell Holmes to Frederick Pollock (Dec. 1, 1899), in 1 HOLMES-POLLOCK LETTERS 98 (M. HOWE ed. 1941).

97. Walsh v. Loorem, 180 Mass. 18, 61 N.E. 222 (1901).

98. Cotter v. Lynn & B.R.R., 180 Mass. 145, 61 N.E. 818 (1901).

99. Vincent v. Norton & Taunton St. Ry., 180 Mass. 104, 61 N.E. 822 (1901).

100. McNary v. Blackburn, 180 Mass. 141, 61 N.E. 885 (1901).

101. Murray v. Boston Ice Co., 180 Mass. 165, 61 N.E. 1001 (1901).

102. Davis v. Rich, 180 Mass. 235, 62 N.E. 375 (1902).

103. Rutherford v. Paddock, 180 Mass. 289, 62 N.E. 381 (1902).

104. Homans v. Boston Elev. Ry., 180 Mass. 456, 62 N.E. 737 (1902).

105. Tirrell v. New York, N.H. & H.R.R., 180 Mass. 490, 62 N.E. 745 (1902).

106. Stoddard v. New york, N.H. & H.R.R., 181 Mass. 422, 63 N.E. 927 (1902).

107. 180 Mass. 119, 61 N.E. 813 (1901).

108. *Id.* at 120–21, 61 N.E. at 814.

109. *Id.*

110. *See supra* text accompanying notes, 50–61.

111. O. W. HOLMES, *supra* note 50, at 123.

112. *See supra* text accompanying notes 28–32.

113. O. W. HOLMES, *supra* note 26, at 167.

114. *Id* at 172–73.

115. *Id.* at 181.

116. *Id.* at 84.

117. O. W. HOLMES, *supra* note 27, at 210.

118. *Id.* at 226.

119. *Id.* at 231.

120. For the original passage from *The Theory of Torts,* see *supra* text accompanying note 54.

121. O. W. HOLMES, *supra* note 27, at 232–33.

122. *Id.* at 239.

123. *Id.* at 242.

124. *Id.* at 232.

125. *Id.* at 238.

126. *Id.* at 237–38.

127. *Id.* at 237.

128. O. W. HOLMES, *supra* note 26, at 198.

129. *See, e.g., Dewey, Justice Holmes and the Liberal Mind,* 53 NEW REPUBLIC 210, 211 (1928); Frankfurter, *The Constitutional Opinions of Judice Holmes,* 29 HARV. L. REV. 683, 691–94 (1916); Pound, *Judge Holmes' Contributions to the Science of Law,* 34 HARV. L. REV. 449, 450 (1921).

130. Letter from Oliver Wendell Holmes to Frederick Pollock (Dec. 28, 1902), in 1 HOLMES-POLLOCK LETTERS, *supra* note 96, at 109.

131. Letter from Oliver Wendell Holmes to Frederick Pollock (Dec. 11, 1909), in 1 HOLMES-POLLOCK LETTERS, *supra* note 96, at 156.

132. For the reminiscences of one of Holmes' law clerks on these matters, see Derby, *Recollections of Mr. Justice Holmes,* 12 N.Y.U.L. REV. 345, 349–50 (1935).

133. Letter from Oliver Wendell Holmes to Lewis Einstein (Apr. 1, 1928), in HOLMES-EINSTEIN LETTERS 279 1964

134 ROGAT *The Judge as Spectator,* 31 U. CHI. L. REV. 213, 244 (1964).

135. Truax v. Corrigan, 257 U.S. 312, 344 (1921) (Holmes, J., dissenting).

136. *See* C. BOWEN, YANKEE FROM OLYMPUS 259–61, 270–74 (1945). Bowen's account of Holmes's life is partially fictionalized and undocumented, so one cannot be sure the conversation ever took place.

137. O. W. HOLMES, *supra* note 50, at 123–24.

138. O. W. HOLMES, SR., 3 THE COMPLETE WRITINGS OF OLIVER WENDELL HOLMES 142 (1900).

139. Letter from William James to Henry James (July 5, 1876), *quoted in* 1 R. PERRY, *supra* note 35, at 371.

140. Thayer, *supra* note 37.

141. *See* 1 M. HOWE, *supra* note 11, at 8.

142. *Holmes-Cohen Correspondence,* 9 J. HIST. IDEAS 10 (1948).

143. *See* White, *supra* note 3, at 56–61.

144. Lorden v. Coffey, 178 Mass. 489, 60 N.E. 124 (1901).

145. Opinion of the Justices, 155 Mass. 598, 607, 30 N.E. 1142, 1146 (1892) (opinion of Holmes, J.).

146. *Id.*

147. Adkins v. Children's Hosp., 261 U.S. 525, 568 (1923) (Holmes, J., dissenting)

(overruled in West Coast Hotel Co. v. Parrish, 300 U.S. 379 (1937); *see* G. WHITE, THE AMERICAN JUDICIAL TRADITION 164–67 (1976).

148. Lochner v. New York, 198 U.S. 45, 76 (1905) (Holmes, J., dissenting).

149. *Id.* at 75 (Holmes, J., dissenting).

150. *Id.* at 76 (Holmes, J., dissenting).

151. 198 U.S. 45 (1905).

152. 208 U.S. 161 (1908).

153. 261 U.S. 525 (1923) (overruled in *West Coast Hotel Co. v. Parrish*, 300 U.S. 379 (1937)).

154. 198 U.S. at 75 (Holmes, J., dissenting).

155. *See, e.g., Adkins,* 261 U.S. at 568 (Holmes, J., dissenting).

156. *Lochner,* 198 U.S. at 75 (Holmes, J., dissenting).

157. *Id.* (Holmes, J., dissenting).

158. *Id.* (Holmes, J., dissenting).

159. *Id.* at 76 (Holmes, J., dissenting).

160. Patsone v. Pennsylvania, 232 U.S. 138 (1914).

161. Buck v. Bell, 274 U.S. 200 (1927).

162. Bartels v. Iowa, 262 U.S. 404, 412 (1923) (Holmes and Sutherland, JJ., dissenting).

163. Schenck v. United States, 249 U.S. 47, 52 (1919).

164. *Summary of Events, The Gas-Stokers' Strike,* 7 AM. L. REV. 582, 583 (1873).

165. *Id.*

166. *See, e.g.,* F. FRANKFURTER, MR. JUSTICE HOLMES AND THE SUPREME COURT 36–45 (1938).

167. 275 U.S. 66 (1927).

168. 258 U.S. 268 (1922).

169. 260 U.S. 393 (1922).

170. O. W. HOLMES, *supra* note 7, at 128–29.

171. *Id.* at 129.

172. *Id.*

173. *Id.*

174. *Id.*

175. *Id.* at 70.

176. *Id.*

177. Pokora v. Wabash Ry., 292 U.S. 98, 106 (1934).

178. *See supra* text accompanying notes 108–109.

179. 258 U.S. at 276.

180. 250 U.S. 616, 628–31 (Holmes, J., dissenting) (stating that defendant had right to publish leaflets supporting Russian revolution and attacking United States policy).

181. 268 U.S. 652, 672–73 (1925) (Holmes and Brandeis, J J., dissenting) (stating that Socialist Party member should not have been convicted of criminal anarchy merely because he advocated a proletarian dictatorship).

182. 274 U.S. 357, 379 (1927) (Brandeis and Holmes, J J., concurring) (overruled in Brandenburg, v. Ohio, 395 U.S. 444 (1969) (per curiam)) (stating that mere advocacy of the desirability of proletarian revolution is protected speech but intent to commit serious present crimes is not protected).

183. 279 U.S. 644, 653–55 (1929) (Holmes, J., dissenting) (stating that a Quaker should not be denied United States citizenship because of her pacifist views).

184. 283 U.S. 697 (1931) (Minnesota statute authorizing ''previous restraints'' of peri-

odicals that publish defamatory or malicious articles held unconstitutional infringement of freedom of press).

185. 273 U.S. 536 (1927).

186. *Id.* at 541.

187. 277 U.S. 438, 469 (1928) (Holmes, J., dissenting) (overruled in Katz v. United States, 389 U.S. 347 (1967)).

188. *Id.* at 470 (Holmes, J., dissenting).

189. 260 U.S. 393 (1922).

190. *Id* at 412–16.

191. *Id.* at 415–16.

192. See, *e.g., id.*

193. For a recent collection of such efforts, see D. Burton, What Manner of Liberal? 155–56 (1979).

194. 232 U.S. 138 (1914).

195. 273 U.S. at 541.

196. 260 U.S. at 416.

197. 258 U.S. at 276.

198. Towne v. Eisner, 245 U.S. 418, 425 (1918).

199. Northern Securities Co. v. United States, 193 U.S. 197, 400 (1904) (Holmes, J., dissenting).

200. Lochner v. New York, 198 U.S. 45, 75 (1905) (Holmes, J., dissenting).

201. Abrams v. United States, 250 U.S. 616, 630 (1919) (Holmes, J., dissenting).

202. Buck v. Bell, 274 U.S. 200, 207 (1927).

203. O. W. Holmes, *supra* note 26, at 181.

204. *See* White, *supra* note 3, at 64–71.

205. For an example of one justice's agonized attempts to adopt Holmes' theory of deference to mid-twenth-century cases, see H. Hirsch, The Enigma of Felix Frankfurter (1981).

206. White, *The Evolution of Reasoned Elaboration: Jurisprudential Criticism and Social Change,* 59 Va. L. Rev. 279, 296–98 (1973).

207. 410 U.S. 113 (1973).

208. *See supra* note 161 and accompanying text.

209. *See supra* note 114.

Looking at Holmes in the Mirror*

The ubiquity and endurance of Justice Holmes as a figure of historical interest has begun to rival the prominence of Holmes during his lifetime. It seems that each time the direction of American scholarship takes a new turn, a group of scholars emerges with some "fresh" thoughts on Holmes; it seems that no matter how much Holmes has been dissected or analyzed, he provides commentators with something new to write about. The appearance of a series of scholarly assessments of Holmes in the 1980s provides another example of this phenomenon. In an essay published in 1982[1] I noted that four lectures and symposia had been devoted to Holmes since 1980; in addition, two books devoted entirely to Holmes,[2] another in which Holmes figures prominently,[3] and a series of law review articles[4] on Holmes have appeared in the decade. Once again the scholarly process of generational revisionism has included Holmes. In seeing themselves and their work anew commentators have also seen the image of Holmes in altered form.

This essay considers four of the recent commentaries on Holmes, lectures by Benjamin Kaplan, Patrick Atiyah, and Jan Vetter, and an extended essay by Frederic Rogers Kellogg.[5] In each of the commentaries the treatments of Holmes are different in their substantive emphasis and their points of view. But I think it is possible to identify some features the commentaries have in common, and to suggest that these features are in a sense representative of the state of scholarly commentary on Holmes in the 1980s.

Holmes has, of course, been all things to all commentators. He is one of the few jurists in American history whose career was long enough, and whose impact pervasive enough, to have functioned as a kind of repository of changing juristic attitudes. Holmes' role as a repository has in part been a function of the seminality of his thought and the memorable quality of his style, but it has also been a function of deeply ambivalent character of his jurisprudence and the cryptic nature of his expressions. One can seize upon a Holmes aphorism—of which there is an abundant supply—as a crystallization of a point of view, but there is often another aphorism that points in a very different direction. These features of Holmes have made him a rich subject, and may provide an explanation for why numerous scholars continue to be motivated to say something about Holmes even though so much has already been said.

*4 Law and Hist. Rev. 439 (1986).

Nonetheless, commentary on Holmes has had different emphases at different times. I think it is possible to characterize the emphasis of this decade as having been encapsulated in four characterizations of Holmes: as private law theorist, as ancestor of Legal Realism, as "impoverished" judge, and as fallen hero. I will discuss each characterization separately. I want to first say a word about the characterizations themselves.

The characterization are, of course, oversimplifications, representing tendencies in commentary rather than the sole emphasis of any one commentator. Holmes as private law theorist refers to the tendency in recent scholarship to be less concerned with his theory of constitutional adjudication, which elicited considerable commentary from the 1930s through the 1960s,[6] and more concerned with his early scholarship, which focused on private law topics, ultimately culminating in the series of essays that became *The Common Law*.[7] Holmes as ancestor of Realism emphasizes the commentators' interest in exploring connections between Holmes' jurisprudence and the Realist movement of the 1930s, whose nature and implications have been a subject of great interest for current scholars. Holmes as improverished judge illustrates an emphasis, first suggested by Yosal Rogat's essays on Holmes in 1963 and 1964,[8] on Holmes's apparent indifference to human rights during his tenure on the Court, which, Rogat argued, made Holmes' jurisprudence "fundamentally impoverished."[9] Holmes as fallen hero takes as a starting point Holmes's diminished reputation in the 1960s, when constitutional theorists scorned his passive stance toward judicial review and liberals bewailed his indifference to minorities,[10] and suggests that Holmes' stature can be revived if one approaches the world from the philosophical stance of resignation.

The obvious connection between the characterizations of Holmes and the ideological tendencies of our own times is worth noting. We have witnessed the growth of a body of scholarship in the "private law" dimensions of legal history; it is not too much to say that legal history came of age as a discipline in American scholarship when its practitioners distinguished themselves from constitutional historians and defined their principal focus to be on the social, economic, and intellectual dimensions of private law.[11] We have also seen that the two principal innovative forces in current scholarship, the law and economics movement and the critical legal studies movement, both claim descent from Realism. We have been privy to a decisive shift in scholarly opinion with respect to the proper role of the judge in constitutional adjudication, one in which the earlier idea of judicial "self-restraint," with which Holmes was conspicuously identified, has lost stature, and debates now rage on the nature and limits of judicial "activism," a stance that is taken as a given by most commentators. Finally, the loss of reputation Holmes suffered in the 1960s was largely based on the fact that his values seemed remote from those of modern liberalism, but it is now liberalism that is under severe attack, and both Holmes' intellectual radicalism and his skeptical philosophic stance seem more in vogue. With this brief backdrop, I now turn to the commentaries on Holmes under review.

I

For several years historians have been interested in resurrecting the essays on private law that Holmes wrote between 1870 and 1880, when he recast several of them as the lectures that were published as *The Common Law.* The renewed interest in Holmes' early essays has been, principally, for what they say about the growth of his ideas or his personal life during a period that his biographers have suggested was pivotal in his career.[12] While it is surely interesting to know that Holmes thought Torts "not a proper subject for a law book" in 1870,[13] but worth general theoretical treatment two years later,[14] or that Holmes carried the manuscript of his edition of Kent's *Commentaries* to the dinner table and was characterized by contemporaries as having a "pallid face" and a "fearful grip upon his work,"[15] the major emphasis of recent scholarship has been to attempt to locate Holmes in the intellectual revolution that took place in late nineteenth-century America.

There seems to be little doubt that at the time Holmes began editing the *American Law Review,* and contributing essays to its pages, he and his close contemporaries regarded themselves as engaged in a thoroughgoing critique of established intellectual orthodoxy. There has been much less agreement about that critique itself: its origins, its character, its implications. Morton White linked Holmes to a group of "anti-formalists" whose central intellectual purpose was to replace universalistic doctrines and concepts with relativistic ones designed to have greater relevance and practicality in a world perceived to be in a constant state of change.[16] The origins of anti-formalism, White argued, came in the perceived dissonance late nineteenth-century intellectuals felt between received orthodoxy and an altered cultural environment.

The contribution made by White was to redirect scholarly attention toward Holmes' early career as an intellectual radical. White's treatment appeared in 1947, a time when Holmes was seen principally as a Supreme Court justice and constitutional theorist, and his earlier career as a scholar neglected. But White's characterization subsequently proved unsatisfactory for scholars who wished to pursue the concepts of anti-formalism and formalism in more detail. While the meaning of "anti-formalism" became clear enough as White progressed through Holmes to other associated theorists, the meaning of "formalism" remained obscure. White never defined the term, and his description of the common elements in the "revolt" against formalism raised some difficulties. Chief among them, as applied to Holmes, was the assertion that the critics of formalism rebelled against its use of static concepts. Formalism, in White's analysis, appeared as an orthodoxy that was both "frozen" in time, thus being unresponsive to changing social conditions, and overly general and abstract, thus being unresponsive to the particularities of experience.

While Holmes' comment, in his dissent in *Lochner v. New York,* that "general propositions to do decide concrete cases."[17] would seem to identify him as suspicious of abstract generalizations, the thrust of his early scholarship had been toward the extraction and promulgation of "scientific" general principles. One of Holmes' self-appointed tasks as a scholar was to make the legal subjects he studied more "scientific" or "philosophical" (words he used interchangeably) by developing classifications, systems, and other schema for organizing a field. If the formalists were conceptualistic in their orientation, so was Holmes.

Despite these difficulties with White's interpretation, scholars in the 1950s continued to emphasize the same feature of Holmes as White: his philosophical skepticism and his apparent distaste for dogma, especially in constitutional adjudication. Thus Mark Howe and Henry Hart debated whether Holmes' approach to judging rendered him a "positivist" who rigidly separated law from morals and deferred to majority rule.[18] The critical question in their essays, as in White's treatment, was whether a jurisprudential point of view that distrusted absolutes and accepted the inexorability of change could affirm any values as universal or permanent. In a sense this question lay at the bottom of Yosal Rogat's searching critiques of Holmes in the 1960s.[19] Rogat found Holmes deficient as a civil libertarian and ultimately as a humanist because his skepticism was bred in a profound detachment. "To a remarkable degree," Rogat argued, "Holmes simply did not care."[20] Holmes was able to defer to the majority, Rogat intimated, because he was basically indifferent to minority rights; he was skeptical of absolutes because there were no values whose primacy he insisted upon.

Despite the penetrating quality of Rogat's attack on Holmes, his analysis left much unexplained, particularly the intensity of Holmes' early immersion in scholarship. If Holmes was simply a fatalist or a skeptic or a positivist, why were he and his colleagues in the Metaphysical Club so passionately engaged in the pursuit of cosmic truths? Why were they so critical of the religious "twaddle" of their parents' generation? Why was Holmes consumed by his efforts to bring out an edition of Kent's *Commentaries?* And why, for that matter, had he fought in the Civil War?

Mark Howe's two volumes in Holmes' early career[21] sought to answer some of these questions. For a variety of reasons, not the least of which was his own skill as a biographer, Howe produced a rich account of Holmes' struggle to separate himself, as a person and as an intellect, from the lustre of his famous father. But Howe's treatment of Holmes, while admirably dense in some respects, was incomplete in others; that incompleteness was caused largely by the nature of Howe's project, a multivolumed effort cut short by Howe's death. In particular, Howe did not explore in detail the intellectual context of Holmes' early scholarship, especially its cross-cultural features, nor did he seek to explain how the jurisprudential perspective Holmes developed from his immersion in private law topics in the 1870s squared with the perspective he exhibited as a twentieth-century constitutional theorist.

For it was clear that Holmes the commentator on private law was quite different from Holmes the apostle of judicial self-restraint in constitutional adjudication. In Torts he argued for the primacy of negligence, not merely as an issue to be delegated to the jury but as a standard to be laid down by the courts, and in his notorious "stop look and listen" decision, *Baltimore and Ohio R.R. v. Goodman,*[22] attempted to establish an absolute rule for all motorists approaching railroad crossing. In Contracts he sought to promote doctrines, such as the "bargain" theory of consideration and the idea that all contracting parties had the option to breach and pay damages, which would have had the effect of regularizing and objectifying standards of liability.[23] And in Property he attempted to reduce the problem of possession to a single inquiry, whether the alleged possessor had sought to exclude others from access to the object in question. If an intent to exclude existed, Holmes argued, it was fruitless to speculate about whether the person seeking to exclude others had a "right" to do so.[24] The purpose of each of these inquiries was to establish broad, "objective" rules and standards that would replace subjectivist inquiries into morality, human idiosyncrasy, or "intent." Holmes the private law theorist was an apostle of certainty, predictability, rule-orientation, and judicial power.

Because of Howe's death, and because of the relative lack of interest among twentieth-century scholars in the history of private law subjects, an important link between Holmes the late nineteenth-century scholar and Holmes the twentieth-century Supreme Court justice, his twenty years of service on the Supreme Judicial Court of Massachusetts, was largely ignored. Beginning in the late 1970s, however, commentators began to look again at Holmes' Massachusetts decisions.[25] Grant Gilmore, who had been chosen to succeed Howe as Holmes' authorized biographer, published two volumes of lectures that had been stimulated in part by his exploration of Holmes as a state judge. It is fair to say, in fact, that the perception of Holmes Gilmore derived from his exposure of Holmes' private law decisions prevented his ever completing the biography, since the exercise stripped Gilmore of any sympathy with his subject. "Put out of your mind," Gilmore wrote in 1977,

> the picture of the tolerant aristocrat, the great liberal, the eloquent defender of our liberties, the yankee from Olympus. All that was a myth, concocted principally by Harold Laski and Felix Frankfurter, about the time of World War I. The real Holmes was savage, harsh, and cruel, a bitter and lifelong pessimist who saw in the course of human life nothing but a continuing struggle in which the right and powerful impose their will on the poor and weak. . . . In this bleak and terrifying universe, the function of law, as Holmes saw it, is simply to channel private aggressions in an orderly fashion.[26]

While that image of Holmes may have dogged Gilmore as he sought to pursue his subject through the fifty-odd years of life Howe had left unreported, it did not prevent Gilmore from noticing that the thrust of Holmes' early scholarship, and of his private law decisions on the Massachusetts court, was toward erecting broad rules whose purpose was to maximize certainty and predictability and to minimize liability. In Contrasts and Property damages for breach or for the unauthorized assertion of possessory rights were to be kept to a minimum; in Torts losses from accidents were to lie where they fell. In Gilmore's treatment Holmes, as a private law theorist, was the archetypical conceptualist, a blood brother of Christopher Columbus Langdell. His doctrines, Gilmore argued, perfectly harmonized with the general tendency of late nineteenth-century Americans to applaud a "theoretical structure which would leave the masters of the new wealth free to do their own thing in their own way."[27]

Gilmore, of course, had his own conceptualistic structure, into which he fitted Holmes, Langdell, and anyone else who suited his thematic purposes.[28] But Gilmore was able to see what early generations of scholars had not been inclined to look for: the paradox of Holmes the deferential "realist" justice who had been Holmes the activist conceptualist scholar and state judge.

Gilmore's interest in Holmes as a private law theorist also signified the emergence of a new era in Holmes historiography. Since 1977 only a single scholarly treatment of Holmes has had as its principal focus his theory of constitutional adjudication or his career as a Supreme Court justice, and that treatment may be said to be the exception that proves the rule, since it is quite consciously intended as a retrospective to unfinished work Yosal Rogat had begun on Holmes in the 1960s.[29] All the principal works under review in this essay spend far more time on Holmes' stance toward private law issues than on his attitude toward constitutional questions. Part of this emphasis can be traced to the fact that 1981 was the centennial of the publication of *The Common Law,* a work that did not deal with constitutional issues. But the decision of Harvard Law School to devote the Holmes Lectures of 1981 to a reexamination of *The Common Law* signified a judgment that Holmes' contributions to private law were worth scholarly attention. The rediscovery of Holmes the private law theorist was part of a larger rediscovery of the history of private law.

Frederic Rogers Kellogg maintains that Holmes' early essays in private law contain the germ of his jurisprudential philosophy. Kellogg's argument is basically the following. As early as his nineteenth year, Holmes had been interested in "an intellectual movement whose mission was seen as . . . that of advancing the cause of empirical science and freeing all human knowledge from traditional and unverifiable assumptions of religion and metaphysics."[30] After his return from the Civil War, Holmes took up the critique of mid nineteenth-century intellectual orthodoxy in earnest, devoting his attention to "legal science," which he then identified with "universal system[s] of logical classification" of legal subjects.[31] The idea that law should be separated from religion or metaphysics and classified "scientifically" had come to Holmes from Auguste Comte, Jeremy Bentham, and especially John Austin. But while Holmes' earliest essays represented efforts to formulate logical classifications of legal subjects (such as classifications based on "duties" of various kinds owed by persons to one another), he soon abandoned an emphasis on "logic" for one on evolutionary history. Holmes' substitution of history for logic as his point of methodological emphasis came, Kellogg believes, because he found "that the framework of logic across the body of current law contained fundamental inconsistencies,"[32] and that those inconsistencies could be best explained historically. Being an enthusiast for the principle of evolution, as were others of his generation, Holmes subjected legal doctrines to a historical analysis, demonstrating that much of their "nonlogical" character could be explained by the context of their origins.[33]

"Evolutionism" was hence one strand of Holmes' jurisprudence. The other strand was pragmatism. By the late 1870s Holmes' contacts with other members of the Metaphysical Club in Cambridge, notably Charles S. Peirce, had led him to the belief that "the actual operative effects" of a legal concept defined what that concept was.[34] If, in practice, possession was synonymous with an intent to exclude others, then the concept of possession was that intent: "what the law does is what the law conceptually is."[35] Holmes' claim in "The Path of the Law" that law was basically the predictions of what courts would do was, for Kellogg, "a trademark of the pragmatic reduction of concepts to effects."[36] Kellogg believes that Holmes eventually came to a recognition that history demonstrated the inability of law to conform with logic, and empirical observation demonstrated that legal doctrines were synonymous with their effects. Hence the only accurate definition of "law" was what courts, given the "sovereign prerogative of choice," could be expected to decide at a given point in time.[37]

If one accepts Kellogg's formulation, Holmes' jurisprudence becomes clearly linked to two major intellectual movements of the late nineteenth century, evolutionism and pragmatism; becomes "authentically American" since evolutionism (Social Darwinism) flourished in America and pragmatism has often been described as the only philosophical position invented by Americans; and can be distinguished from both legal realism (which Kellogg describes as an "extreme" form of pragmatism) and conceptualism (the "logic" Holmes saw history as undermining).

I think there are some difficulties with Kellogg's argument. First, despite Holmes' famous comment about law being determined by the felt necessities of the times rather than by logic, it is hard to see his early writings, including *The Common Law,* as embracing cultural determinism. The analyses of common law subjects offered in the early writings are directed toward a common end, the formulation of general rules. The rules (fault in torts, bargained-for consideration in contracts, an intent to exclude others from possession in property) are empirically observable, "objective," and intended to be universal in their application. Holmes' use of history in the early writings is not, contrary to Kellogg's claims, intended to illustrate the arbitrariness and contingency of doctrine. It is rather to demonstrate the primacy of the rules Holmes is propounding. Thus the fault principle has always been the governing standard of liability in Torts, notwithstanding some cases suggesting the presence of an "act at peril" standard; the balance-wheel theory of consideration is confirmed by history; the historical existence of possessory rights in bailees confirms the "intent to exclude" principle as the basis of possession. As Gilmore noted, *The Common Law* lectures are noteworthy for their "repeated insistence that the principles of liability appropriate to the late nineteenth-century United States had been laid down in the English yearbooks of the fourteenth and fifteenth centuries."[38]

In his early writings, then, Holmes is an "evolutionary" historian in the same sense as were Langdell, Ames, and the other late nineteenth-century conceptualists: he used history to confirm the primacy of principles that he was asserting to be philosophically sound.[39] His history was by no means hermeneutic. Doctrinal inconsistencies or anomalies were dismissed as anachronisms; current ideology was read into the past; historical "progressions" were created as self-fulfilling prophecies. History, in short, was in the service of contemporary theory. Thus while it seems fair to call Holmes an "evolutionist"—for him history confirmed the universality of external standards of liability just as for the Social Darwinists history confirmed that life was a struggle in which the fittest survived—it does not follow that Holmes "sought to confine legal concepts . . . to the limits of . . . historical operation."[40] His concepts overwhelmed history.

A second difficulty with Kellogg's analysis comes in his characterization of Holmes as a "pragmatist." It is, of course, possible to extrapolate from Holmes' writings some ideas consistent with pragmatism, beginning with his aphorism that the life of the law has been experience.[41] But it is possible to find a Holmes aphorism in support of nearly any intellectual position. Those who would classify Holmes as a pragmatist must first reckon with his explicit disassociation of his ideas from those of William James, who popularized pragmatism and whose philosophy Holmes called "amusing humbug."[42] Disassociation of himself from intellectual colleagues, however, was a familiar Holmesian device: he regularly denied being influenced by anyone else, even when he obviously had been, although he was remarkably sensitive to the possibility that others might be influenced by him and not give him credit.[43] A more serious barrier to seeing Holmes as a pragmatist comes from the lack of evidence that gave serious attention to the effects of legal rules or doctrines he supported. As part of his deferential stance toward legislation under constitutional attack, for example, Holmes endorsed the so-called "rational basis" standard of judicial review, where a judge asked whether the legislation in question had been grounded on "reason" rather than mere legislative prejudice. In a case where the Pennsylvania legislature solemnly announced that aliens should be given more limited access to firearms than citizens in order to protect wildlife, Holmes said that while he would not scrutinize the legislative's motives, "popular speech" suggested that the association of alien status with a greater propensity to endanger wildlife made sense.[44] And in *Baltimore & Ohio R.R. v. Goodman* Holmes announced a grade crossing rule whose effects rendered it absurd: on many occasions getting out of one's car to ascertain whether a train was coming was more dangerous than taking no action at all.

In short, I think that Kellogg has made a contribution in demonstrating that Holmes' early scholarship shifted in its emphasis from purely analytical to historical, and that the shift demonstrated a recognition by Holmes of the limits of logic as a classification device. But the shift did not mean that Holmes abandoned the goal of classification, and his adoption of a historically oriented methodology did not mean that he saw legal doctrines as necessarily limited by their temporal and cultural context. At the time of the appearance of *The Common Law* Holmes was still a conceptualist in his jurisprudence, albeit one who had found evolutionary history useful in the promulgation of his conceptual schema.

I do not believe that any of the other treatments of Holmes under review would dispute the conceptualistic quality of Holmes' work as a private law theorist. Benjamin Kaplan sees *The Common Law* as a book dominated by the belief that "all law, in its historical development, aspired by and large to a condition in which the inner states of mind of individuals were irrelevant and the standard by which they were to be judged was objective."[45] Patrick Atiyah identifies Holmes as one of a group of late nineteenth-century theorists who were interested in restructuring private law subjects in accordance with "general principles."[46] Jan Vetter is most explicit: he argues that "the theory of natural selection" was "the largest single influence on The Common Law and that Holmes is best seen . . . as a kind of Social Darwinist.''[47] All these commentators agree that the thrust of Holmes' early scholarship was to replace interpretations of legal doctrine based on morals, metaphysics, or "logic" with interpretations based on his (evolutionary) version of late nineteenth-century legal science.

II

There is a sense in the essays by Atiyah, Vetter, and Kellogg that Holmes' most important work was done as a private law theorist. Atiyah and Kellogg do not discuss Holmes' attitudes toward constitutional adjudication at all, and Vetter chooses to characterize the body of Holmes' work in terms most easily applicable to his private law writings. But while Holmes may be most interesting to current scholars as a private law theoretician, there was much more to Holmes' career than his early writings, and there is much more to his legacy than *The Common Law*. Of particular interest to contemporary academicians is Holmes' relationship to the legal Realists, who are themselves under close scrutiny as the nature and meaning of Realism is being reassessed.

Kaplan recaptures the spirit with which his generation of law students, who entered law school at a time (1930) when Realism represented the cutting edge of intellectual discourse, approached Holmes. The great contribution of Holmes for his contemporaries, Kaplan notes, was "The Path of the Law." As Kaplan describes his first encounter with Holmes:

> My class entered Columbia Law School . . . in 1930. The place was in ferment as a vanguard of a movement that came to be called "legal realism"—1930 was in fact the year of publication of those provocative realist tracts, Karl N. Llewellyn's *The Bramble Bush* and Jerome Frank's *Law and the Modern Mind*. Realism claimed inspiration and derivation from Holmes, and the professors gave emphasis to the point of making Holmes's striking essay "The Path of the Law" required reading for us as we started out.[48]

Here we see Holmes as the ancestor of Realism, a position he occupied well into the 1940s, and, as a result of changing ideological currents, arguably occupies once more in the 1980s. The links between Holmes and Realism were, for members of the Realist moment, clear enough. He defined law as it "really" was—the prophecies of what the courts will do in fact, not the elaboration of abstract rules. He insisted on a sharp separation between law and morals: what the Realists called the divorce of "Is" and "Ought." As an explanation for the content of legal doctrines, he disdained "logic" and offered the observation of current social attitudes and conditions—the "felt necessities of the times." And he appeared to endorse social science research, the special favorite of the Realists, as the methodology most conducive to enlightened lawmaking. "The man of the future," he suggested, would be "the man of statistics and the master of economics."[49]

Before exploring the history of Holmes' image as ancestor of Realism, it is worth asking how the positions that linked him to the Realists squared with positions he had previously taken in his early scholarship. With the exception of his suggested replacement of ''logic'' with cultural observation, all of the positions came from his ''Path of the Law'' essay or from ''Law in Science and Science in Law,''[50] written two years later. In some respects the positions tracked Holmes' earlier views, but one important modification had taken place. Holmes had no truck for ''morals,'' which is associated with metaphysical and religious dogma, as early as his days at Harvard College, and while his earliest private law essays showed some interest in analytical logical classifications, that emphasis, as Kellogg notes, was soon abandoned. His critique of logic and his endorsement of ''experience,'' while put cryptically in *The Common Law,* could have been said to anticipate his call for study of experience through social science research in ''The Path of the Law'' and ''Law in Science.'' In holding those positions in the 1890s, then, Holmes had not departed very far from his views in the 1870s.

But in equating law with prophecies of what courts will do in fact Holmes seems to have abandoned his earlier rule orientation. Predicting what courts would do appeared to shift focus from rules to a battery of other issues, such as the personalities of judges, the existential nature of fact situations, or the behavior of decisionmakers holding authority. The definition also intimated that ''law'' was merely an aggregate of individual court decisions; rules were not guides to its content. Had Holmes really come to believe, as the Realists took him to believe, that legal rules were meaningless? If so, much of his early effort to develop universal, objective principles of liability was in vain; if so, his attempts to reserve rulemaking authority for the courts in such areas as grade crossing accidents appeared to be quixotic.

I have argued,[51] and continue to believe, that Holmes had largely lost his faith in rules by the time he wrote ''The Path of the Law.'' Mark Howe, in an ingenious gloss on that essay, suggested that Holmes' ''bad man theory'' of law, and his positivistic definition of law as prophecies of judicial behavior, were just heuristic devices to get his audience's attention, and that his comment last in the essay that ''I take it no man will accuse me of the language of cynicism'' provides a clue to his heuristic purpose.[52] But Howe's attention, when he wrote that analysis of ''The Path of the Law,'' had not yet been directed to Holmes' years on the Supreme Judicial Court of Massachusetts, years in which his experience as a judge, I think, undermined his faith in rule orientation. One cannot read Holmes' Massachusetts opinions, which are for the most part cryptic, assertive, and delphic, without concluding that if Holmes believed that courts and scholars had an obligation to reduce legal subjects to a ''philosophically continuous series'' he was going about it in a remarkably perverse way.

The Massachusetts court was a collegial body, with a busy docket and personnel of uneven quality, functioning as the last appeal for most of the cases it decided. In this atmosphere, I believe, Holmes soon learned that he could not study cases ''to the bottom'';[53] that, above all, he was called upon to make a judgment, to decide, and that that was basically what judging was about—deciding cases and getting them off the docket. Not only was there not time to formulate rules of great universality and philosophical continuity, those rules might not be attractive to every judge in the context of every new case. Judging was much more arbitrary, fortuitous, and contingent than Holmes the scholar may have imagined. I believe "The Path of the Law" was written in a mood conductive with those insights. I do not find it a cynical essay, but a resigned essay. The "bad man" may be a vivid image, but the basic question about lawmaking is not "what are the rules," but "what will the courts do?"

The Realists' impression of Holmes, then, was incomplete but accurate. It left out his conceptualism in the interest of claiming Holmes, by the 1930s a legendary figure, as a patron. But the Realists did not misread Holmes as an apostle of resignation. When Holmes "deferred" to state legislation, he saw it as the deference of one who recognizes where power lies and what uses power can be put to. Deference was neither an endorsement of liberal social policies nor a legitimation of racism, genocide, or Darwinism. It was simply a recognition that "the sovereign prerogative of choice" was in this instance being exercised by a legislature rather than a court. The Realists were not as much interested in theories of judicial review as they were in common law rules.[54] To the extent they spent time on Holmes as a constitutional theorist, they tended to exhibit sympathy to his posture because it either produced liberal results or attacked conceptualistic opinions such as the majority argument in *Lochner v. New York*. But they did not parse many of Holmes' opinions. Instead they conveniently ignored his early private law scholarship and most of his Massachusetts opinions and warmed to "The Path of the Law."

When Holmes got into posthumous trouble in the 1940s, it was for the same reasons as did the Realists. Resignation on issues such as the legitimacy of power, and advocacy of a separation of law and morals, could easily be associated with totalitarianism, and the association was made. Most Realists took back the implicit suggestion of moral relativism in their earlier statements that "is" and "ought" could be fruitfully separated, and Holmes' defenders suggested that a man who fought to abolish slavery or at least to preserve the Union would hardly have been passive about Hitler. But the critics of Holmes were right in one sense: the very issue that linked Holmes to the Realists was a deep distrust of the permanency of legal rules and the moral claims of settled doctrine. Holmes did not think that rules were legal truths, let alone moral ones, and the Realists agreed with him. The difficulty with that position, in the 1940s, was that it seemed to ignore the role of law as a structural embodiment of the values of American culture, values such as hostility to racial genocide, brutality, oppression, and the parceling out of freedoms by a police state. Holmes had said, in places, that law had nothing to do with morals and that he was the supple tool of power; but he had also said that he hoped he would die for freedom. His urging that law be cleansed of metaphysical twaddle did not mean that he denied that law in America would necessarily be the repository of "democratic" values. Those values were among the felt necessities of the time.

Thus as an ancestor Holmes was both a benefit and a burden to the Realists. He was useful as a legitimating figure: the "completely adult jurist"[55] to a group of youthful iconoclasts who could claim that they were doing no more than elaborating upon the wisdom of one of the great men of the law. In his resignation, however, he was also a source of what appeared as moral relativism and even amorality. Those latter postures were fine in the late 1920s, when a certain self-conscious nihilism was fashionable, but they went down far less well in the late 1930s and 1940s, when moral values served to differentiate the Allies from the Axis.

Holmes and the Realists suffered through the 1940s and were nearly buried in the process literature of the 1950s (Holmes was hardly the model for "reasoned elaboration" in a judge, and the insights of the Realists were domesticated in such metaphors as judicial "balancing"). But a turn of events has once more brought Realism to the fore, and sparked another assessment of the relationship between Holmes and the Realists. This is the effort by the two leading current movements deviating from process theory, law and economics, and critical legal studies, to claim descent from Realism. The nature of the claims reveals the ambivalent posture of the Realists: one claim originates in the "scientific" side of Realism, with its emphasis on empirical research into "real" social and economic behavior; the other claim originates in the philosophical message of Realism that rules are indeterminate and contingent.

Holmes himself has played a part in the revival of interest in Realism. Through the Realist, he can be seen as a kind of ancestor of law and economics. Holmes identified the task of fashioning legal policy as one of cultural observation, not the mere invocation of rules, and even hinted that the policymaker of the future will be an economist; the Realists particularized his task as that of empirical social science research; the law and economics movement has carried out that research and is now in a position to reformulate rules. That the rules, in the current version of law and economics, are mainly those of the "marketplace" is not even a massive departure from Holmes: he had, after all, referred to successful ideas as those that have the power to become accepted in the marketplace of thought.[56]

How about Holmes as a "crit"? One may laugh at the image of Holmes reading Duncan Kennedy's *Legal Education and the Reproduction of Hierarchy,* but the image of Holmes reading Richard Posner on wealth-maximization may be just as ludicrous. As he often said, Holmes believed in "can't helps": ideas and values that, for inexplicable reasons, were so much a part of one's being as to be beyond dispute. He also, eventually, held to a deterministic theory of cultural change: his "felt necessities" can be seen as his version of the "deep structures" critical scholarship has identified. His excursus into history in *The Common Law,* as Kellogg points out, was partially designed to reveal the irrational origins of legal rules. There are affinities, in short, between Holmes and both the instrumentalist and irrationalist wings of the critical legal studies movement.

Of course making Holmes into either a patron of law and economics or critical legal studies has some serious difficulties. There is no evidence that Holmes cared about empirical research, let alone believed in the concept of utility maximization. When Brandeis took Holmes' comments about statistics and economics seriously, and recommended that Holmes spend part of his summer looking at the reports of state industrial commissions, Holmes originally concluded that the experience would improve his mind. But when cartons came to his summer home filled with commission reports, Holmes unpacked them, looked at them, and went back to his favorite literature, which included racy French novels and detective stories. Moreover, in his later years Holmes was opposed, as his *Lochner* dissent suggests, to the idea that law could be organized around a single comprehensive theory. He may have originally had the hope of reducing private law subjects to a philosophically continuous series, but that hope had not survived his experience as a judge.

By "The Path of the Law," in fact, Holmes was something of a positivist, an orientation that would sharply distinguish him from advocates of critical legal studies. Holmes embraced the idea of revolution (he often recalled a comment that the masses were most likely to revolt over the price of beer),[57] but he also embraced repression, the status quo, liberalism, hegemony, and other bugaboos of critical legal studies. He was fundamentally indifferent to the content of majoritarian values, although not indifferent to the power of majorities. In this sense he was an arch-positivist, one whose philosophy was designed to reinforce the values of those in power simply because they were in power. Thus the strongest disaffinity between Holmes and the critical legal studies movement is not that he thought of leftist politics as "drool";[58] but that he was prepared to legitimate any set of political beliefs on the theory that the dominance of ideas is a question of force rather than of content.

As the revival of interest in Realism sheds new light on that movement, the differences between Holmes and the Realists may come into stronger focus. The Realists now seem to have been two things Holmes decidedly was not: political reformers and enthusiasts for social science. While the surface thrust of Realism appeared to be jurisprudential rather than political, the Realists' recognition that certain legal doctrines were sterile or rigid had been precipitated by their finding those doctrines unresponsive to the conditions of contemporary life. In calling for the implementation of "real" rather than "paper" rules Realists were also calling for rules that were "relevant" and "up to date." Their sympathies were with administrative agencies, social welfare legislation, and the New Deal; their bête noir was a legal system organized around the outmoded and untested assumptions of the nineteenth century.

The Realists' distinction between "paper" and "real" rules suggested that empirical research and political reform went hand in hand. By studying the behavior of lawmakers and their constituents jurists would not only learn what the law "really" was, they would be identifying rules that were more responsive to social conditions and hence more "modern." In what has come to be pictured as the caricature of Realist empirical research, Underhill Moore and his affiliates observed the behavior of persons seeking parking spaces in New Haven. The image of a law professor solemnly counting the number of times an aspiring parker circled a block may be a source of amusement, but Moore's research had, for the Realists, the desirable dual purpose of ascertaining how people actually behaved under a system of rules and of eventually refashioning rules to be more congruent with that behavior.[59]

Holmes, of course, was neither a social scientist nor a political reformer. His role as an ancestor of Realism therefore needs qualification. I would describe the relationship between Holmes and the Realists as follows. In the midst of a late nineteenth- and early twentieth-century jurisprudence that was resolutely conceptu-

alist in its methodology and Darwinist in its premises, the later Holmes was virtually alone in his conviction that the end of conceptualism—clear, predictable,
universal rules—was unattainable because of the inevitability of social change and
the arbitrariness of rulemaking. Holmes held this conviction despite being a Darwinist himself. The Realists, two generations removed from Holmes, had repudi-
ated Darwinism and were determined to expose conceptualism on grounds similar
to those that had forced Holmes to abandon it. They thus felt a kinship to Holmes,
claimed him as an ancestor, and attempted to make him into a twentieth-century
liberal and a kind of behavioral scientist, neither of which he had ever been.
Nonetheless, the most penetrating of all the insights of Realism—that however
rigorous one's methodology, legal rules were inescapably contingent rather than
universal—had been glimpsed by Holmes, and the remarkable fact about Holmes'
having glimpsed that insight was that he had done so in a world whose juristic
energy was radiating in the opposite direction.

III

Holmes was, of course, not primarily a scholar, an analyst, or a philosopher. He
was for fifty of his sixty-odd professional years a judge. What kind of a judge
was he, and how well has he been regarded? The answer to the first question
seems more finite than the second, but the two are related. Holmes developed a
judicial style on the Supreme Court of Massachusetts that he was maintain on the
United States Supreme Court: the context and issues changed, but his style remained constant. Kaplan has a brief description of it in his Holmes lecture. "He
can be short on the facts," Kaplan suggested, "uninterested in putting the fair
cases for either side, cryptic or highly allusive in his reasoning, apt to finesse hard
points by a mere form of words." [60] I want to comment briefly on each of the
features described by Kaplan, and to add a few of my own.

Facts were uninteresting to Holmes in two respects: because as a common law
judge his initial search was for rules into which factual situations could be fitted,
and because he was usually not engaged by the human elements of a case. His
lack of interest in facts led him to follow precedent more than one might have
expected: Kaplan notes that in nearly 1800 signed opinions during his years as a
Massachusetts judge Holmes only dissented twelve times. Notwithstanding his
aphorism in Lochner that general propositions do not decide concrete cases,
Holmes was not interested in the interplay of generality and particularity that has
engaged many common law judges. If he was inclined toward a result, he framed
a general rule to accompany it; if the rule served poorly in a later case, he framed
another one. Here, as in many instances, Holmes's working style belies his observations as a commentator. The above comment about general propositions suggests he might have been fact-specific in his approach, and the Realists, enamored
of fact specificity, may have taken him as such, but facts were dreary details
for Holmes.

Despite Holmes's indifference to facts, he was not above presenting them so as to reinforce the result he would reach. Consider his statement of the facts in *Schenck v. United States*.[61]

> The document [that formed the basis of the indictment in Schenck] upon its first printed side recited the first section of the Thirteenth Amendment, and said that the idea embodied in it was violated by the Conscription Act, and that a conscript is little better than a convict. In impassioned language it intimated that conscription was despotism in its worst form and a monstrous wrong against humanity in the interest of Wall Street's chosen few. It said "do not submit to intimidation," but in form at least confined itself to peaceful measures such as a petition for the repeal of the act. The other and later printed side of the sheet was entitled "Assert Your Rights." It stated reasons for alleging that anyone violated the Constitution when he refused to recognize "your right to assert your opposition to the draft". . . . It denied the power to send our citizens away to foreign shores to shoot up the people of other lands, and added that words could not express the condemnation such cold-blooded ruthlessness deserves, etc., etc. . . . Of course the document would not have been sent unless it had been intended to have some effect, and we do not see what effect it could be expected to have upon persons subject to the draft except to influence them to obstruct the carrying of it out.
>
> We admit that in many places and in ordinary times the defendants in saying all that was said in the circular would have been within their constitutional rights. But the character of every act depends upon the circumstances in which it is done. . . . When nation is at war many things that might be said in time of peace are such a hindrance to its effort that their utterance will not be endured so long as men fight, and that no Court could regard them as protected by any constitutional right.[62]

The defendants in *Schenck*, according to Holmes, had asserted that the Conscription Act was unconstitutional; that it should be repealed; that persons had a right to oppose the draft; and that the draft itself was an unauthorized use of Congressional power. That was all. Holmes then added that the circular making these assertions "could not have been sent unless it had been intended to have some effect" and the only effect he could see was to influence persons to obstruct the carrying out of the draft. He then went on to suggest that the possession of constitutional rights was a matter of "circumstance," and that, in war, the test of whether one had a constitutional right to speak was, basically, whether what one said "will be endured."

The dispositive "facts" of *Schenck* were thus that the defendants had voiced constitutional and sociological objections to the draft; that a war was going on; and that such talk would "not be endured" in wartime. No effort was made to inquire as to whether the circular had any effect on the conscription process; whether it had been accompanied by any obstructive acts; or whether any moderately large number of persons took it seriously or even knew about it. No effort was made to justify the assertion that constitutional rights were a function of circumstance, or that the test for whether a speech could be barred was whether it could be endured. Under Holmes' *Schenck* test a statement made in America in

1942 to the effect that Nazi Germany was an efficient secular regime could have been made the basis for a criminal prosecution.

Holmes' approach in *Schenck* enhances in interest when compared with his statement of the facts in *Abrams v. United States,*[63] where, of course, he came out differently. *Abrams*, like *Schenck*, was a prosecution for obstructing the war effort through the distribution of inflammatory circulars. As Holmes described the circulars,

> The first of these leaflets says that the President's cowardly silence about the intervention in Russia reveals the hypocrisy of the plutocratic gang in Washington. . . . It says that there is only one enemy of the workers of the world and that is capitalism; that it is a crime for workers of America etc., to fight the workers' republic of Russia. . . . The other leaflet . . . tells the Russian emigrants that they now must spit in the face of the false military propaganda by which their sympathy and help to the prosecution of the war have been called forth. . . . The leaflet winds up by saying, "Workers, our reply to this barbaric intervention has to be a general strike!"[64]

Holmes then characterized the circulars as "poor and puny anonymities" whose "only object" was "to help Russia and stop American intervention there against the popular government." Their purpose, he concluded, was "not to impede the United States in the war that it was carrying on." He required a "specific intent" to curtail or cripple the United States in the prosecution of the war to make out a conviction. He then went on to suggest that "the expression of opinions" should not be curtailed "unless they so imminently threaten immediate interference with the lawful and pressing purposes of the law that an immediate check is required to save the country."[65]

The *Schenck-Abrams* sequence is a good example of Holmes' investing facts with a tone helpful to his result. In *Schenck* he makes a great deal of affinity between writing a circular attacking the draft and an intent to obstruct the draft; in *Abrams* he found no evidence that a circular attacking "the prosecution of the war" had any intent to impede the war effort. He advanced no reasons why the intent he found lacking in *Abrams* was present in *Schenck*. He admitted that the context of wartime was decisive in *Schenck*, but *Abrams* was also a wartime case. Finally, his standard for curtailment of free expression (that an immediate check be required to save the country) would seem to invalidate the conviction in *Schenck*. No one suggested that the leaflet in *Schenck* had produced any effect whatsoever.

The *Schenck-Abrams* sequence also brings us to a third characteristic of Holmes's style noted by Kaplan, namely the tendency to "finesse hard points" through appeal to vivid language. In *Schenck* Holmes formulated the standard for restricting free expression as the "clear and present danger" test: whether "the words are used in such circumstances and are of such a nature as to create a clear and present danger that they will bring about the substantive evils that Congress has a right to prevent."[66] Then in *Abrams* he reformulated the test as requiring "imminent" and "immediate interference" with a law, so that "an immediate check'' was required ''to save the country.'' Under that standard, as noted, it is hard to imagine that the defendants in *Schenck* could have been convicted; and under ''clear and present danger'' the defendants in *Abrams* might well have been.

The *Abrams* reformulation was also presented after some eloquent, emotional, and abstract language. The sentence before the reformulation read as follows:

> But when men have realized that time has upset many fighting faiths, they may come to believe even more than they believe the foundations of their own conduct that the ultimate good desired is better reached by free trade in ideas—that the best test of truth is the power of the thought to get itself accepted in the competition of the market, and that truth is the only ground upon which their wishes safely can be carried out. That in any rate is the theory of our Constitution. It is an experiment, as all life is an experiment. Every year if not every day we have to wager our salvation upon some prophecy based upon imperfect knowledge. While the experiment is part of our system I think we should be eternally vigilant against attempts to check the expression of opinions that we loathe and believe to be fraught with death, unless. . . .[67]

Next came the reformulation. Here Holmes appears to be hiding in some excellently turned phrases. It is, of course, not at all clear that the best test of truth is the power to get one's ideas accepted in the marketplace, witness advertising, political campaigning, and the like. There is no evidence that the framers of the Constitution adopted a ''market'' approach to free speech, whatever their First Amendment theories. ''Wagering salvation'' on ''imperfect knowledge'' is simply an elegant way of saying that at some level all beliefs amount to guesswork and beliefs are all that we have. Eternal vigilance on behalf of opinions that one loathes sound fine, but Holmes had hardly adopted that posture in *Schenck*. In short, the eloquence of the *Abrams* dissent was primarily a distraction, a device to engage the reader emotionally about the value of free speech at a point in the opinion where Holmes was in deep waters.

Schenck and *Abrams* are in this sense examples of what Kaplan calls Holmes' cryptic or highly allusive reasoning. The quoted passages are not ''reasoning'' in the conventional sense at all; they are efforts to create emotional imbalances. In *Schenck* the emotional imbalance is tilted against the defendants by suggestions that there is a very close line between vigorously opposing the draft and encouraging others to resist it. In *Abrams* the imbalance is tilted the other way. By his noble talk about free speech Holmes prepares the reader for his reformulation of the standard for suppressing speech; and after the reformulation, with its emphasis on immediacy, it appears ludicrous to convict supporters of the Russian Revolution for criticizing the American government for not sharing their support. The emotional tipping is achieved by allusions—to the marketplace, the founding fathers, ''poor and puny'' leaflets, the images of thousands laying down their arms because they see that as conscripts they are convicts.

Do these characteristics of Holmes' style make him an unsatisfactory judge? The simple answer to that question is that it depends on what one wants in a judge, but there is a more complex answer. It is clear that in times when juristic commentators admire irreverence, blinding insight, and a critical attitude toward official dogma, allusive opinion writing may curry favor. Holmes was dubbed the "Great Dissenter" in the 1920s and 1930s not because he dissented often—his colleague John Clarke, to whom no one has attacked a memorable epithet, wrote far more dissents than Holmes in the years of their joint service—but because his dissents, at the time, were on fashionable liberal issues such as free speech and liberty of contract. Admirers liked his eloquence, his ability to cut through solemn doctrinal pronouncements, and above all his point of view. In the 1950s, however, when jurists became more interested in fostering the "maturing of collective thought"[68] and in parsing the elaborated reasons for decisions, Holmes' allusiveness began to pall. He had a disturbing way of using an eloquent phrase as a substitute for analysis, and his majority opinions were often quite poor in giving guidance to lower courts or commentators. In a universe in which enlightened judicial opinions were supposed to be ones resting on articulated principles of neutrality and generality that "quite transcend[ed] the immediate result,"[69] Holmes was not much of a model.

From the sense that Holmes was "cryptic" or "allusive" it was a small step to Yosal Rogat's conclusion that Holmes, as a judge, gave a "fundamentally improverished account of legal phenomena." The shift was basically the result of a coupling of the 1950s perception that Holmes' opinions were insufficiently elaborated with a 1960s perception that he was hostile or indifferent to civil liberties. When one appreciates the results a judge reaches, as liberals in the 1930s did of Holmes in free speech cases, hiding difficulties behind eloquence can make a judge "great." But when one deplores the results, as those influenced by the civil rights movement did when they looked back at Holmes' opinions on aliens, blacks, children, and disabled persons, allusive and cryptic reasoning becomes a symptom of an "improverished" sensibility. Tossing off the due process claims of a person facing sterilization with the aphorism "three generations of imbeciles is enough"[70] appears gratuitously cruel if one believes in the sanctity of those claims. Calling the Equal Protection Clause "the usual last resort of constitutional arguments"[71] offends those who would make the clause a shield against social injustice. "Impoverished" to Rogat meant not only indifferent to human needs, it meant indifference to the obligation to ground one's results in more than an epigram. Over and over again Rogat found Holmes deficient in giving guidance:

> Nowhere in any of the cases that we have considered did Holmes help in framing a remedy to serve a constitutional right. . . . Nor did he ever perceive new interests that were relevant to the determination of rights and liberties.
>
> Instead he habitually upheld government action by pointing to the most general powers that government had already exercised, giving little indication of how the Court might determine the limits of those powers, and sometimes leaving it unclear whether any such limits existed.[72]

Of the commentators under review, only Vetter alludes to Rogat's image of Holmes as an impoverished judge, and finds Rogat's critique "ahistorical." Vetter is puzzled why "liberals like Frankfurter and Laski made a hero of Holmes," and believes that Rogat's criticism can be reduced to the proposition that "Holmes was not a fit member of the Warren Court of 1964."[73] I think Vetter is partially right and partially wrong. Rogat, and others who have adopted his view of Holmes as an enemy of civil liberties, have surely judged Holmes by the standards of their own time. One might equally take Holmes to task for being a male chauvinist, for never learning to drive a car, or for wearing high buttoned shoes and wing collars. He was born in 1841; his experience and sensibility were light years away from Selma and Little Rock. He did not see that the criminal justice system was systematically biased against blacks or that segregated schools were inherently unequal; neither did his colleagues. If anything, Holmes was somewhat more catholic in his contacts and friendships than his privileged WASP contemporaries.

But Vetter too easily dismisses the improverishment critique. Holmes' opinions, as noted, played fast with facts, substituted vivid writing for analysis, often replaced intellectual inquiry with assertions, and ignored the human dimensions of cases. When John Noonan, in his *Persons and Masks of the Law,*[74] chose famous examples of judges who contributed to the process by which the law depersonalizes those who come into contact with it, Holmes was one of his choices. Rogat is correct, I believe, in claiming that "to a remarkable degree, Holmes simply did not care." He did not care about the persons engaged in the litigation before him; he did not care particularly about giving fair treatment to both sides of a case; he did not care about precision or consistency in his legal tests and standards; he often did not care how the case was decided so long as it was. He was in some respects the antithesis of a "lawyer's judge" or a "judge's judge," and he was certainly not a litigant's judge. He wrote his opinions to indulge his very considerable talents for expression, to communicate an occasionally strongly held belief, to puncture levels of sophistry and dogmatism, and to get cases disposed of. I am unwilling to go so far as to call this mode of judging improverished. But it is the mode of a judge who is not deeply engaged with all the levels of judging, most notably its technical and human levels.

IV

With Rogat's critique came the decisive "fall" of a heroic reputation that had reached its apex in the 1930s and had been gradually going downhill ever since. In exploring whether Holmes' reputation has revived itself in the 1980s it is worth recalling the original sources of his image as a hero. Holmes was "heroic," to the generation of the 1930s, because he was a "liberal," as manifested in his role as the "Great Dissenter," because he had transcended the values of his class and was thus a humanitarian, and because he was a gifted prose stylist and a sophisticated, "adult" jurist. Each of these components of Holmes' heroism had been qualified or rejected by scholarship in the next three decades. The first critique focused on Holmes' liberalism, as manifested in his attitudes toward power and legitimacy. Holmes was too willing to defer to those in power, critics suggested; too quick to conclude that might made right. He was thus soft on totalitarianism: a Fascist sympathizer rather than a liberal. In his "adult" skepticism he had forgotten the elementary truth that law and morality are inseparable and that at some point even "sophisticated" thinkers have to take a stand.

Holmes as the transcendent Brahmin was an attractive image to a generation in which class values were still deeply embedded and in which the kind of benevolent paternalism practiced by such figures as the Roosevelts was applauded. Holmes, after all, had supported labor unions, advocated First Amendment protection for Bolsheviks and pacifists, and included Jews and Orientals in his correspondence friendships. The critics of the 1960s, however, did not consider those tendencies "democratic" or "liberal." They were evidence of a different and less admirable quality in Holmes: detachment. Holmes encouraged labor's opportunities to combat capital because he was indifferent to labor-management struggles; he supported free speech without regard to who was speaking because he thought the expressions of radicals were "silly" and would not have any impact; he was willing to write to anyone whose ideas he found interesting, so long as he did not have to entertain the correspondent at home. Holmes was, in short, the embodiment of rather than the transcender of class values: the cold, disinterested WASP.

With Holmes' deficiencies as a liberal and a humanitarian in mind, critics of the 1960s reexamined his style and his jurisprudence. They found that in both instances Holmes was "impoverished": his style substituted aphorisms for analysis and his juristic stance was the stance of the indifferent spectator. Holmes was more interested, commentators suggested, in turning a memorable phrase than in seeing that justice was done or that litigants were fully and fairly heard. He was more interested in deferring to majoritarian views than in examining the soundness of those views. In short, his attitude as a judge was designed to cut off intellectual, and especially emotional, inquiry rather than to further it. Some critics found his indifference particularly shocking in light of his own great gifts, good luck, and love of praise. Holmes the celebrated nonagenarian contemplating humans as so many grains of sand was an image to which I once attributed a "disturbing dissonance."[75]

Are the views of Holmes encompassed in this criticism still dominant? One recent study has suggested that, at least with respect to civil liberties issues, a "new orthodoxy" has emerged since the 1940s that has emphasized Holmes's indifference.[76] A similar attitude appears to inform Gilmore's portrait: Holmes is a "bitter and lifelong pessimist," looking on life as a struggle in which only the fittest survive.

Two trends in the 1980s literature, however, appear to be moving in a different direction, and can be taken as a signal that Holmes' reputation is once again on the upswing. First is what one might call the domestication of Holmes' skepticism. This point of view is vividly expressed in Kaplan's description of his successive "encounters" with Holmes. After his initial excitement at being exposed to "The Path of the Law" as a law student, Kaplan reread Holmes in 1937, inspired by Jerome Frank. Holmes, on second reading, appeared to Kaplan "as a bleak, harsh figure," who "saw out of his window a Darwinian world." He was "a tough old party, quite aware that he was deficient in empathy." He believed that "a person justifiably preferred himself to other people" and that "might made right, or nearly so." He "appeared to accept simplistic justifications for capitalism and economic individualism.'' And he ''thought . . . morality . . . at bottom a matter of personal taste.''[77]

But in his 1981 lectures Kaplan turned again to Holmes, and sought a ''more balanced appreciation.'' He then spoke as Holmes might have against his generation of critics:

> When I said that morality was a matter of taste, I was referring with perhaps undue emphasis to the difficulty, if not the impossibility, of arriving at an ethical system that would be accepted by everyone everywhere as ''true.'' But when, in *The Common Law,* I held that even criminal liability might be cast on a person who was blameless in an inner sense, I was not being amoral; rather I was asserting that the stiff treatment of individuals might in given cases be justified as incidental to a large public good—surely a respectable utilitarian judgment. . . .
> The figure of the ''bad man'' was ill chosen if it was taken to recommend that lawyers advise clients to do their worst within the letter of the law: such advice would be not only morally offensive but improvident, because a judge tries to do as a good man would. . . . The notion ''might makes right'' and its variants were cryptic and ironic. I did not delight in force, but recognized it for what it truly is—the ultimate ratio, although a poor one.[78]

One is tempted to dwell on the most obvious of the Kaplanesque glosses here: can one imagine Holmes saying ''with perhaps undue emphasis'' or justifying one of his pronouncements as ''a respectable utilitarian judgment''? But the theme of domestication is not unique to Kaplan.[79] I would suggest that it has emerged, as so much of Holmesian commentary does, from factors external to the text. Prominent among those factors is what might be called the rediscovery of indeterminancy in legal and moral judgments.

What endeared Holmes to the commentators of the 1930s—and disappointed his critics from the 1940s through the 1960s—was his insistence that were no determinate principles on which legal decisions could habitually be grounded. This was a far thing from saying that all legal principles were meaningless or that naked power was all that counted in life, and Holmes was seriously misread; but it was also a far thing from the conceptualistic schemes that Holmes had once tried to implement and had largely abandoned as a judge. Holmes' nineteenth-century intellectual radicalism was refreshing to those who had become convinced in the 1930s that conceptualism was sterile and rigid; but his refusal to affirm the universality of beliefs was chilling to later critics. How one could fail to be determinate about issues such as genocide or racial prejudice was a puzzle to Holmes' post-World War II critics.

Holmes' perception of the indeterminancy of belief seems to have struck new chords in the 1980s. One explanation for the revival may be that there has been an implicit narrowing of the issues that seem overwhelmingly capable of being resolved by a single ''right answer.'' Apartheid, for the present writer, is one such issue. But against such ''easy'' moral issues are the countless ones, such as abortion, euthanasia, or pornography, where ''solutions'' appear indeterminate and historically and culturally contingent. To claim that Holmes was clearly ''wrong'' in taking one stance or another, and to thereby suggest that one knows what is clearly "right," seems less easy than it once may have been. The revolution in attitudes engendered by the civil rights movement in the 1960s appeared to engender a sudden wisdom about human relations that made one capable of making moral judgments on numerous issues of the past and present. That wisdom may still operate at some fundamental level. But its premises of moral absolutism and universal determinate criteria for judging "right" from "wrong" are at least debatable. Where Holmes may once have appeared "impoverished," he now seems something like "wise" in his recognition that the leap from strong belief to universal moral proposition is a treacherous one.

The revival of indeterminacy explains, for me, the popularity of both of the current movements in legal scholarship, law and economics and critical legal studies. The former movement is an effort to resist indeterminacy by introducing a new set of conceptualistic criteria into legal analysis, the criteria purportedly being "scientific" and "objective" in character and therefore determinate. The latter movement begins with the perception of indeterminacy and presses it beyond traditional doctrine to methodology and metatheory, with the purpose of exposing what is taken to be the contingent and political character of even the most determinedly objective scholarship. In this sense, Holmes is a law and economics type and a crit after all.

It is the perception of indeterminacy that lies at the bottom of renewed interest in Holmes as a private law theorist. Consider the encomiums to Holmes in the works under review. Kaplan suggests that Holmes' "vision of law . . . informs all that we do as lawyers"; that "we move to the measure of his thought."[80] Atiyah states that Holmes' "ideas and influence may have been so deeply felt that they have passed into the common currency of legal thought."[81] Vetter speaks of a "Promethean gift of self awareness" in Holmes that "warms and burns us still."[82] Kellogg claims that "Holmes has had a profound impact on those who have since attempted to frame a body of legal theory, and his thought continues to affect decisions long after his death."[83] Why should Holmes be a figure of continuing "influence" if the premises on which his juristic attitude was built—Darwinist and Malthusean premises, coupled with a reaction to early nineteenth-century moral philosophy—are so decisively out of fashion? Why should anyone care about Holmes the private law scholar if his grand theories of tort liability, possession, and consideration have all come to naught?

It may be that generation after generation of scholars comes to care about Holmes simply because of his striking accomplishments, his elegant style, and his cryptic and ubiquitous discourse. But I think this generation will continue to care about Holmes because his career, especially in its early and middle stage, represents an effort to identify, to combat, and finally to accommodate the indeterminancy principle. There is Holmes and Harvard undergraduate and Civil War soldier, believing that he had made sense of the universe in a novel way from his father's generation and then experiencing the much less "sensible" tableau of wartime. Holmes the enthusiast for "science" and "philosophy," seeking codes and arrangements of private law subjects, using history to demonstrate the apparent universality of certain general organizing principles. Holmes the judge and essayist, finding the universality elusive and discovering in its place the "sovereign prerogative of choice" and the inexorability of majority rule. Holmes insisting on getting on with the job notwithstanding indeterminacy. Holmes saying that he would die for some beliefs but that no generalized belief was worth a damn. Whether this stance makes Holmes skeptical, resigned, indifferent, or bitter depends on how much one hopes that the world will be a conceptually tidy and morally resonant place. Above all, the stance makes Holmes a figure of continuing interest.

NOTES

1. G. Edward White, "The Integrity of Holmes's Jurisprudence," 10 *Hofstra Law Review* 633 (1982).

2. Howard Pohlman, *Justice Oliver Wendell Holmes and Utilitarian Jurisprudence* (Cambridge, Mass., 1984); David H. Burton, *Oliver Wendell Holmes, Jr.* (New York, 1980).

3. G. Edward White, *Tort Law in America: An Intellectual History* (New York, 1980).

4. Saul Touster, "Holmes a Hundred Years Ago," 10 *Hofstra Law Review* 673 (1982); Robert Gordon, "Holmes's *Common Law* as Legal and Social Science," 10 *Hofstra Law Review* 719 (1982); David H. Burton, "Justice Holmes and the Jesuits," 27 *American Journal of Jurisprudence* 32 (1982); E. Donald Elliott, "Holmes and Evolution," 13 *Journal of Legal Studies* 113 (1984); Patrick J. Kelley, "A Critical Analysis of Holmes's Theory of Torts," 61 *Washington University Law Quarterly* 681 (1983); Joan I. Schwartz, "Oliver Wendell Holmes's "The Path of the Law": Conflicting Views of the Legal World," 29 *American Journal of Legal History* 235 (1985).

5. Benjamin Kaplan, "Encounters with O.W. Holmes, Jr.''; Patrick Atiyah, "The Legacy of Holmes Through English Eyes''; Jan Vetter, "The Evolution of Holmes: Holmes and Evolution," in *Holmes and the Common Law: A Century Later* (Occasional Pamphlet #10, Cambridge, Mass., Harvard Law School, 1983). The Kaplan, Atiyah, and Vetter lectures are hereinafter cited as *Holmes and the Common Law*, which is paged consecutively. Frederic R. Kellogg, *The Formative Essays of Justice Holmes* (Westport, 1984).

6. For a compilation of sources, see G. Edward White, "The Rise and Fall of Justice Holmes," 39 *University of Chicago Law Review* 51 (1971).

7. See Frederic R. Kellogg, supra note 5 at x–xii.

8. Yosal Rogat, "Mr. Justice Holmes: A Dissenting Opinion," 15 *Stanford Law Review* 3, 254 (1983); Yosal Rogat, "The Judge as Spectator," 31 *University of Chicago Law Review* 213 (1964).

9. Yosal Rogat, 31 *University of Chicago Review* at 225.

10. See infra text at notes 68–71.

11. See G. Edward White, Book Review, 59 *Virginia Law Review* 1130 (1973).

12. See Mark De Wolfe Howe, *Mr. Justice Holmes: The Shaping Years* (Cambridge, 1957); David H. Burton, supra note 2 at 13–50.

13. [Oliver W. Holmes], Book Notice, 5 *American Law Review* 340, 341 (1871).

14. Oliver W. Holmes, "The Theory of Torts," 7 *American Law Review* 652 (1873).

15. Mrs. Henry James to Henry James, Jr. (1873), quoted in Ralph Barton Perry, *The Thought and Character of William James* 2 vols. (Boston, 1935) i, 519.

16. Morton White, *Social Thought in America: The Revolt Against Formalism* (Boston, 1947) 67–74.

17. Lochner v. New York, 198 U.S. 45, 76 (1905).

18. Mark De Wolfe Howe, "The Positivism of Mr. Justice Holmes," 64 *Harvard Law*

Review 529 (1951); Henry Hart, "Holmes's Positivism: An Addendum," 64 *Harvard Law Review* 929 (1951); Mark De Wolfe Hose, "Holmes's Positivism—A Brief Rejoinder," 64 *Harvard Law Review* 937 (1931).

19. Yosal Rogat, supra note 8.

20. Yosal Rogat, 31 *University of Chicago Law Review* at 255.

21. Mark De Wolfe Howe, supra note 12; Mark De Wolfe Howe, *Mr. Justice Holmes: The Proving Years* (Cambridge, Mass., 1953).

22. 275 U.S. 66 (1927).

23. Grant Gilmore, *The Death of Contract* (Columbus, 1974) 14–21, 37–43; John P. Dawson, *Gifts and Promises* (New Haven, 1980) 199–205. See also the discussion by Patrick Atiyah in *Holmes and the Common Law,* supra note 5 at 63–66.

24. Mark De Wolfe Howe, supra note 21 at 201–22. See also the discussion in Frederic Kellogg, supra note 5 at 48–57.

25. See Grant Gilmore, supra note 23; Grant Gilmore, *The Ages of American Law* (New Haven, 1977); Mark Tushnet, "The Logic of Experience: Oliver Wendell Holmes on the Supreme Judicial Court," 63 *Virginia Law Review* 975 (1977).

26. Grant Gilmore, supra note 25 at 49. In a footnote Gilmore suggested that while "some admirers of Holmes" had taken his comments as "an attack on Holmes," Gilmore had come to believe that "Holmes, to the extent I can follow the dark outlines of his thought, [appeared] both a greater man and a more profound thinker than the mythical Holmes ever was." *Id.* at 127.

27. Grant Gilmore, supra note 25 at 66.

28. See Peter R. Teachout, "Gilmore's New book: Turning and Turning in the Widening Gyre," 2 *Vermont Law Review* 229 (1977).

29. James M. O'Fallon, "Mr. Justice Holmes: A Dissenting Opinion—The Speech Cases," 26 *Stanford Law Review* 1349 (1984).

30. Frederic R. Kellogg, supra note 5 at 4.

31. Ibid. at 6.

32. Ibid. at 7–10.

33. Ibid. at 37–42, 56.

34. Ibid.

35. Ibid.

36. Ibid. at 69.

37. Ibid. at 74.

38. Grant Gilmore, supra note 25 at 54.

39. For a searching discussion of Langdell's methodological assumptions, see Thomas Grey, "Langdell's Orthodoxy," 45 *University Pittsburgh Law Review* 1, 30–32 (1983).

40. Frederic R. Kellogg, supra note 5 at 57.

41. E.g., Note "Holmes, Peirce, and Legal Pragmatism," 84 *Yale Law Journal* 1123 (1975).

42. Holmes to Sir Frederick Pollock, June 17, 1908, in Mark DeWolfe Howe, ed., *Holmes-Pollock Letters* 2 vols. (Cambridge, 1946) i: 139.

43. "Holmes never acknowledged any debt to [Charles] Peirce or for that matter to any one else." Gilmore, supra note 25 at 51. For an example of Holmes's sensitivity about having his work recognized, see John P. Reid, "Brandy in his Water: Correspondence Between Doe, Holmes, and Wigmore," 57 *Northwestern Law Review* 522 (1962).

44. Patsone v. Pennsylvania, 232 U.S. 138, 144 (1914).

45. Benjamin Kaplan in *Holmes and the Common Law,* supra note 5 at 2.

46. Patrick Atiyah in ibid. at 40.

47. Jan Vetter in ibid. at 96, 97.

48. Benjamin Kaplan in ibid. at 8–9.

49. Oliver W. Holmes, "The Path of the Law," 20 *Harvard Law Review* 457, 469 (1897).

50. Oliver W. Holmes, "Law in Science and Science in Law," 23 *Harvard Law Review* 421 (1899).

51. G. Edward White, supra note 1.

52. Mark DeWolfe Howe, "The Positivism of Mr. Justice Holmes," supra note 18.

53. "I look into my book in which I keep a docket of the decisions of the full court which fall to write, and find about a thousand cases. . . . A thousand cases, when one would have liked to study to the bottom and to say his say on every question which the law ever has presented." Oliver W. Holmes, speech to the Bar Association of Boston, March 7, 1900, in Oliver W. Holmes, *Collected Legal Papers* (New York, 1920) 245.

54. Very little Realist scholarship was directed at constitutional law. Consider the private law emphasis in Karl Llewellyn, *The Common Law Tradition: Deciding Appeals* (Boston, 1960), the culmination of Llewellyn's scholarly efforts.

55. Jerome Frank, *Law and the Modern Mind* (New York, 1930) 253.

56. "[T]he best test of truth is the power of the thought to get itself accepted in the competition of the market." Holmes in Abrams v. United States, 250 U.S. 616, 630 (1919) (dissent).

57. "I always have said that the rights of a given crowd are what they will fight for. I once heard the older Agassiz say of some place in Germany that there would be a revolution if you raise the price of a glass of beer." Holmes to Harold Laski, July 23, 1925 in Mark DeWolfe Howe, ed., *Holmes-Laski Letters* 2 vols. (Cambridge, Mass., 1953) ii: 762.

58. "I never read a socialist yet from Karl Marx down, and I have read a number, that I didn't think talked drool." Holmes to Harold Laski in ibid. at i: 96.

59. On Moore see John H. Schlegel, "American Legal Realism and Empirical Social Science: The Singular Case of Underhill Moore," 29 *Buffalo Law Review* 195 (1980).

60. Benjamin Kaplan in *Holmes and the Common Law,* supra note 5 at 17.

61. 249 U.S. 47 (1919).

62. Ibid. at 50–52.

63. Supra note 56.

64. 250 U.S. at 625–26.

65. Ibid. at 630.

66. 249 U.S. at 52.

67. 250 U.S. at 630.

68. Henry Hart, "The Time Chart of the Justices," 73 *Harvard Law Review* 84, 100 (1959).

69. Herbert Wechsler, "Toward Neutral Principles of Constitutional Law," 73 *Harvard Law Review* 1, 15 (1959).

70. Holmes in Buck v. Bell, 274 U.S. 200, 207 (1927).

71. Ibid. at 208.

72. Yosal Rogat, 15 *Stanford Law Review* at 305–06.

73. Jan Vetter in *Holmes and the Common Law,* supra note 5 at 86.

74. John Noonan, *Persons and Masks of the Law* (New York, 1976).

75. G. Edward White, supra note 6 at 73.

76. David M. Rabban, "The First Amendment in its Forgotten Years," 90 *Yale Law Journal* 514–80 (1981).

77. Benjamin Kaplan in *Holmes and the Common Law,* supra note 5 at 12–14.

78. Ibid. at 15–16.

79. "[Holmes'] hesitancy to adopt final standards was a logical outcome of his skepti-

cism. It reflected even more the essential humility which his investigations of cosmic truth had demanded of him." David H. Burton, supra note 2 at 142.

80. Benjamin Kaplan at 25.
81. Patrick Atiyah in ibid. at 27.
82. Jan Vetter in ibid. at 101.
83. Frederic R. Kellogg, supra note 5 at ix.

Revisiting the New Deal Legal Generation*

I Introduction: Definitions and Qualifications

The title of this essay may seem to some to constitute a welcome break from the qualified prose of ordinary academic language, but to others it may serve to revive the specter of naked scholarly overstatement. A series of assumptions seems embedded in the title: that one can talk meaningfully about "generations" in American history; that the phrase "legal" conveys something intelligible about the composition of a class of a persons; that the identification of a group of lawyers with a political movement, roughly characterized by a slogan of Franklin Roosevelt's, gives that group a discernible cast. Methodological problems, in short, seem to abound in the title. This essay is not about methodology, and thus I will address those assumptions only briefly, but they deserve some preliminary attention.

The essay assumes that generations are relevant and meaningful ideological units in the study of American history. Morton Keller once suggested that perhaps the most striking feature of American political life has been the juxtaposition of a remarkably stable and enduring institutional structure of government with constant and dramatic social change.[1] The collective memory[2] of political change in America, in this view, has not been a memory of one governmental apparatus displaced by another, but rather a memory of a virtually extant governmental apparatus superimposed on what seems, for each successive group of persons coming to maturity, to be a radically new set of cultural experiences. For the maturing group, the political culture of its elders appears both recognizable and alien. According to this line of argument, "Vietnam" or "Watergate" are best seen not as events that temporarily transformed American political institutions, but as events that temporarily transformed political consciousness. The events can be seen as bringing to an end the legitimacy and thus the power of a generation of elite political leaders, and at the same time stimulating the emergence of leadership. Vietnam and Watergate were thus "generational" in their impact.

The essay assumes further that "legal" can be given a precise meaning in the

*17 Cap. U. L. Rev. 37 (1989). A previous version of this essay was delivered as the 1987 Sullivan Lecture at Capital University.

context of the generation of persons who acceded in the 1930s to elite positions of political leadership. Legal designates not so much a profession in its entirety— indeed the word is intended to refer to a particular subsegment of that profession— as a professional ideology, an orientation toward the management of public affairs by persons with legal training. Persons with this orientation assumed that law could provide a unique response to the perceived social problems of the 1930s, and that elite lawyers had a special competence in problem solving. This sense that law was "special" not only reinforced a high sense of self-esteem held by those who had been conspicuously successful in the legal profession, it gave elite lawyers a confidence that their influx into the public sector of American society, together with the growing legalization of American public life in the 1930s, would have a beneficial effect on American political culture.

Finally, the essay assumes that with the presidency of Franklin Roosevelt came a political transformation in America, a transformation suggested by the phrase "New Deal." Among the elements of that transformation were the emergence of previously scattered political voting blocs, such as racial minorities and members of academic communities, as relatively cohesive units; the delegitimation of "free" market capitalism as an economic ideology whose "natural" predominance had hitherto been taken to be beyond dispute; the identification of the Republican party with the discredited version of market capitalism; and the tacit acceptance by the electorate of strategies and programs designed to increase dramatically the presence of the federal government as a regulatory force in the American economy. However centrist and evolutionary the thrust of the New Deal may have been in terms of the specific content of its policies, it was revolutionary in its rhetorical rejection of the unregulated economic structure that had supposedly collapsed with the crash of 1929.[3]

"New Deal lawyers," as used in this essay, were thus persons who shared the assumptions of the Roosevelt policymakers that various sorts of experiments in market regulation were economically feasible and ideologically progressive, and that such experiments could be implemented through the legal system. In sum, the New Deal legal generation was composed of persons sympathetic to the new politics of the 1930s, trained in the law and imbued in the ideology of legalization, and of an age such that they perceived the purported collapse of market capitalism in the late 1920s as a deeply formative experience in shaping their political consciousness. Not all persons graduating from law school and entering law practice in the late 1920s and 1930s can be said to be members of this "generation"; not even all conspicuously successful graduates of elite law schools, who had the widest number of career options in a rapidly shrinking market, can be said to qualify. The New Deal generation, for my purposes, was composed of lawyers and law graduates whose educational status and achievements presented them with a wide number of options, but whose political consciousness impelled them to seek positions in the public sector. In entering public service in large numbers, in occupying positions of responsibility early in their careers, and in becoming intimately involved with experiments in regulating market functions and redistributing economic benefits on a relatively large scale, such persons were unique in the history of their profession in America.

II The New Deal Legal Generation: Career Patterns

When the careers of some individuals in this generation of lawyers are subjected to closer scrutiny, some striking patterns emerge. The purpose of this essay is to explore the presence and the meaning of those patterns. My effort is to seek a cultural explanation for the patterns: an explanation that deemphasizes individual idiosyncrasy in its focus on the professional and political context in which members of the New Deal legal generation came to maturity and prominence.

The first distinctive characteristic of members of the generation of lawyers that entered public service in the 1930s was their relative social marginality. Until the close of the 1920s graduates of elite law schools—a limited circle of institutions that could fairly be confined to Harvard, Yale, and Columbia—were overwhelmingly sons of upper and upper-middle class Protestants.[4] Felix Frankfurter, who graduated from Harvard in 1905, was one of the few Jews attending any elite law school at the time. Law school was for Frankfurter an entry into WASP society and culture: it was a means of distancing himself from his ethnic heritage.[5] Harvard, in the early twentieth century, did not serve a similar function for many of its graduates. They were, before they came to law school, and remained after they left, scions of wealthy and socially prominent New England families.[6]

In contrast, the Harvard graduates who entered public service in the early 1930s were far more diverse in their social origins. Not only had Harvard widened its geographic pool of students, it had begun to admit, selectively and not without opposition, qualified sons of ethnic minorities. For persons such as Thomas Corcoran, the scion of a working-class Catholic family in Rhode Island, Harvard Law School was a gateway to a professional world that had not been available to his parents. When Corcoran completed his education at Harvard, with a distinguished record, he was rewarded not only with a clerkship with Justice Oliver Wendell Holmes but with an offer from a Wall Street law firm. For him and several of his contemporaries academic distinction at an elite law school had been a means of surmounting the barriers of class and ethnicity.

In 1983 Katie Louchheim, whose first husband Walter had been one of the first employees of the Securities and Exchange Commission when it came into being in 1934, published a book entitled *The Making of the New Deal: The Insiders Speak,* in which she interviewed several "employees" of the early Roosevelt administration (1932–1940) who reminisced about their experiences. Of the twenty-seven lawyers Louchheim interviewed, fifteen were from Jewish or Catholic backgrounds; eight came from a background that could be described as affluent.[7] For persons from lower middle-class backgrounds, professional eduction provided a means of escaping relative poverty and attendant social marginality in the stratified society of the 1920s.[8] For members of ethnic minorities, it also offered a means of escaping the stigma of prejudice. When the public market for legal services expanded dramatically in the 1930s, those who profited most from that expansion were Jewish graduates of elite law schools, whose ethnicity had limited their career opportunities in private practice. The federal government was not subject to similarly perceived constraints.

The social upward mobility of many of the New Deal generation of lawyers was symptomatic of a fundamental transformation in the status alignments of American elite culture that was underway by the late 1920s. That transformation, reduced to its essentials, constituted the substitution of education and professionalization for previous indices of high status, such as family heritage and lineage. As educational institutions widened their geographic base of students and began to function as barriers to entry into professions such as medicine, law, and higher education, educational achievement at high status institutions became the equivalent of social prestige. By the 1930s, lineage rankings of students at such universities as Harvard, common in the eighteenth century, had given way to meritocratic rankings, with high grades becoming a surrogate for high social standing. Meritocratic education assumed a correlation between high grades, vocational success, and eventual social prestige: academically talented members of ethnic minorities profited from a meritocratic standard.[9]

One of the indications that meritocratic standards had become established in elite legal education by the 1930s was the altered nature of placement networks. Such networks had been a characteristic of late nineteenth- and early twentieth-century upper-class urban culture, but they were social in nature: identification with socially prestigious clubs at elite universities was critical in the placement process.[10] In the 1930s class rank emerged as the principal criterion for placement decisions in elite law schools. Academically distinguished graduates of elite law schools were placed in jobs in public service by networks composed of previous graduates of that school who had joined the public sector, professors at the school who demonstrated an interest in the placement of graduates in public service, and others in a position to evaluate the qualifications of a particular graduate for a particular job.

The most active and best known of the placement networks was that which functioned to place Harvard Law School graduates with New Deal agencies. Felix Frankfurter and Thomas Corcoran were the central figures in the Harvard network, with Frankfurter identifying and evaluating promising graduates and Corcoran funnelling them into particular positions. Numerous New Deal lawyers were products of the Harvard network, many of them members of ethnic minorities and nearly all of them persons with distinguished academic records. Once in place, the recruitees often participated in the recruitment of new graduates.[11] While the Harvard network was the most extensive and ubiquitous of those that emerged in the 1930s, Yale and Columbia Law Schools had similar networks.[12]

The New Deal lawyer, then, was often a person for whom educational and professional achievement had served as a vehicle for social mobility. Even more often, the New Deal lawyer was a person who had distinguished himself[13] academically in college and especially in law school; and very often a person who owed his first job in the public sector to the sponsorship of one or more members of a network that placed graduates of his law school in public service.

The parallels in the careers of members of the New Deal legal generation were not confined to their preparation for public service. The members of the generation who entered law practice in the public sector in the 1930s also tended to hold jobs of disproportionately greater power and responsibility than those held by their counterparts practicing in the private sector. To a large extent this phenomenon was a product of the fortuities of politics. The Roosevelt administration, because of the close identification of the Republican party with the failed system of market capitalism that supposedly produced the Great Depression, entered office with a substantial mandate for change and responded by significantly expanding the presence of the federal government as a regulatory and distributive force.[14] Each of the law agencies that came into being in the early years of Roosevelt's presidency required lawyers to help create the New Deal's regulatory apparatus, to staff the newly created federal regulatory agencies, to articulate and to implement the policy of expanding the power of the federal government to improve economic conditions, and to provide help for the numerous persons disadvantaged by the Depression.[15]

The jobs created by the expansionist regulatory policies of the Roosevelt administration involved drafting of legislation intended to have very wide impact; drafting rules and regulations for federal agencies envisaged as active regulatory forces; formulating policies to provide relief to disadvantaged persons, such as tenancy sharecroppers in the South, who had been reduced to a state of penury by the Depression; and advising the Executive and Congress as to how best to go about implementing their electoral mandate for change. These were heady positions of power, in most instances occupied by persons only recently graduated from law school.[16] One graduate of Harvard who first went to Washington in 1932, recruited by Corcoran, described his experience as representing "life, excitement, movement, growth, creation, high endeavor."[17]

The significant responsibilities undertaken by lawyers who first entered public service in the 1930s were to have an effect on their later careers. While many who first came to Washington during Roosevelt's first term remained there throughout the duration of his presidency, staffing the legal institutions of the New Deal and then those that emerged as a result of the outbreak of the Second World War, almost all left public service when the war ended in 1945. Of the twenty-seven lawyers sampled by Louchheim, all but one had left government service for private practice or academics by 1946. In many instances the lawyers remained in Washington, forming law firms and orienting their practice toward the relationship of private sector clients to government agencies. One could characterize this generation of lawyers as having brought immediate stature to their role as private practitioners; they were advising clients about governmental institutions with whose formation they had been intimately involved and with whose structure and deliberative practices they were intimately acquainted.[18]

Two other characteristics of the New Deal legal generation are thus suggested by their career patterns after public service. The first was that many New Deal lawyers, as they passed from positions of firsthand responsibility for the creation of a federal regulatory agency to positions of expertise in the internal workings of that agency, never had a period in their professional lives where they were not perceived as "experts," with the power and prestige commensurate with that epithet. The second was that the New Deal lawyers had functioned in two distinctive markets for legal services that had originated with their generation: an expansive market for legal services in the public sector and a market for the services of lawyers who operated in the private sector but were knowledgeable about the regulatory public sector. The professional development of the New Deal lawyers was thus ultimately tied to the formation of an expanded public sector of legal services in the 1930s and the blurring of lines between that sector and the private sector after the Second World War.

III Casualties of the New Deal Legal Generation: Some Brief Case Studies

Of all the career patterns of the New Deal legal generation, however, none is more striking than the tendency of some of its most visible members to be identified with legal or ethical difficulties that adversely affected their careers. Several case studies are suggestive, but before those careers are sketched, a preliminary comment is in order.

The identification of prominent lawyers with potential legal or ethical misconduct has, of course, been a recurrent theme in American legal history, dating back at least to Chief Justice John Marshall's surreptitious participation in *Martin v. Hunter's Lessee*,[19] a case in which he officially recused himself but nonetheless drafted a petition for a writ of error for one of the litigants.[20] No claim is being made in this essay that the members of the New Deal legal generation were uniquely unethical. Nor is a claim being made that most New Deal lawyers, over the course of their careers, found themselves in difficulties relating to their ethical conduct. In short, many lawyers in America have been involved in ethical or legal misconduct who were not members of the New Deal legal generation, and many members of the New Deal legal generation were not involved in ethical or legal misconduct.

Nonetheless, the case studies that follow are striking, I shall be arguing, in four respects. First, all the subjects involved participated in public service, where their clients were ostensibly not private individuals but the public at large, and in all cases but one their alleged ethical misconduct amounted to a breach of public trust rather than too zealous a pursuit of the private interests of a client. Second, all the alleged ethical misconduct participated in by the subject occurred after they had left a career with the New Deal to work in a capacity that was not directly related to their early positions in the public sector. Third, in all but one case the alleged ethical or legal misconduct of the subjects was, even allowing for changes in conceptions of lawyers' roles, of a rather blatant kind. The conduct, on its face, raised questions about why a reasonable person in the distinctly advantaged position of the subject would conceivably have engaged in it. Fourth, despite the apparently obvious irregularity of the conduct with which they were identified, most of the subjects of the case studies publicly claimed that their conduct was not in fact irregular, or that they had been inappropriately singled out for censure by their political enemies.

The first of the suggestive careers is that of Alger Hiss,[21] a descendant of an impoverished Baltimore family that had once enjoyed social prominence, a graduate of Harvard Law School (where he served on the Law Review), a clerk for Justice Holmes, and a protégé of Frankfurter. Hiss joined the staff of the Agricultural Adjustment Administration in 1933, and was involved in the controversial efforts on the part of AAA staffers to establish protection for tenant sharecroppers against the exploitation of their landlords. Hiss went from the AAA to the Solicitor General's office of the Justice Department and later to the State Department, where he played an important part in the inauguration of the United Nations. At the end of the Second World War, he left government service to become President of the Carnegie Endowment for International Peace. Hiss was regarded at that time as one of the leading diplomats and international policymakers of his generation.

In 1950, Hiss was indicted and convicted of perjury as a result of his testimony before the House Un-American Activities Committee the preceding year. The Committee had confronted Hiss with evidence, largely based on testimony by journalist Whittaker Chambers, that Hiss had been a member of the Communist Party and an agent for the Soviet Union while employed by agencies of the United States government. Hiss denied the charges, was convicted of perjury (he was never tried for espionage), and served four years in prison. He was disbarred until 1974, when he was readmitted to the Massachusetts bar, and has spent much of the remainder of his life as an obscure salesman for a stationery company, all the while maintaining his innocence. In 1978 a historian reviewing Hiss' case, who had begun his inquiry inclined to believe that Hiss was innocent of the espionage charges, concluded after reexamining the evidence that Hiss had been guilty,[22] but very recently evidence from a former Soviet intelligence agent has suggested that Hiss had no connection with the Soviet Union.

The next career is that of Abe Fortas,[23] the son of a Jewish cabinetmaker from Memphis who attended Yale Law School on a scholarship, distinguished himself as editor-in-chief of the Law Journal, and became a protégé of William O. Douglas, then on the Yale faculty, who recruited Fortas for the AAA and later the Securities and Exchange Commission. Fortas subsequently joined the Department of Interior, where he was Under Secretary during the Second World War.

In 1946, Fortas formed his own law firm in Washington, Arnold, Fortas, and Porter, where he remained until President Johnson appointed him to the Supreme Court in 1965. In 1967, Johnson appointed him Chief Justice, but the Senate declined to confirm his nomination, citing his unduly close ties with the Johnson White House while a member of the Court. That same year, information came to light that while a member of the Court, Fortas had entered into a secret agreement with the Wolfson Foundation, an organization whose benefactor, Louis Wolfson, had been indicted on criminal charges and faced the prospect of litigation in the federal courts. The agreement paid Fortas and his wife, Washington tax attorney Carol Agger, $20,000 a year each until death; the duties of Fortas and Agger under the agreement were not specified. As a result of the information about his connection with the Wolfson Foundation, impeachment proceedings were contemplated against Fortas, and he eventually resigned from the Court, opening a private law practice in the District of Columbia. He maintained until his death in 1982 that he had been hounded from office for political reasons.

A third case is that of James Landis,[24] the son of a Methodist missionary, who preceded Hiss at Harvard and was also an editor of the Law Review and a Frankfurter protégé. Landis spent a year clerking for Justice Louis Brandeis, then returned to Harvard to take an S.J.D. degree, studying with Frankfurter and exploring the new field of legislation. After that year, Landis was appointed to the Harvard faculty, where he remained until 1933, when he was appointed to the Securities and Exchange Commission. Landis became Chairman of the S.E.C. in 1935, and returned to Harvard as Dean in 1937, at that time only thirty-eight years old. A year later, he published *The Administrative Process,* a justification of the New Deal regulatory agencies as "[t]he mode [for] provid[ing] . . . the efficient functioning at the economic processes of the states."[25]

In 1942, while technically remaining on the Harvard faculty, Landis assumed positions with a series of government agencies, including the Office of Civilian Defense and the Civil Aeronautics Board. Four years later, beset by marital problems, he resigned from Harvard, and in 1948 was dismissed as Chairman of the Civil Aeronautics Board. He then became Joseph P. Kennedy's personal lawyer, performing a number of legal services for Kennedy and the Kennedy family. Beginning in the late 1950s Landis unaccountably failed to file his income taxes, a fact that came to light when President John F. Kennedy sought to appoint him to a federal post in 1961. Eventually Landis was prosecuted and convicted of wilful tax evasion in 1962 and spent over a year in federal prison. On his release in 1963, he sought to reenter the practice of law, but in 1964 he was found drowned in the swimming pool of his home in Westchester County, New York, apparently the victim of a heart attack.

A fourth case involving a New Deal lawyer who was subsequently involved in legal or ethical difficulties is that of Edward Prichard, a native of Kentucky who attended Princeton and then Harvard Law School, graduating with distinction in 1938 and serving as law clerk to Frankfurter in 1939.[26] After his term with Frankfurter, Prichard joined the Attorney General's Office in the Justice Department, and during the war years worked for the Office of Economic Stabilization. In 1945, he left Washington to enter private practice in Kentucky, where he became involved in Democratic Party politics. In 1949, he was indicted for voter fraud, a result of stuffing ballot boxes in a 1948 Senatorial election. He was convicted and sentenced to two years in federal prison, and was pardoned five months after beginning his sentence by President Truman. Eventually Prichard resumed his law practice and his involvement in politics, and in the 1950s and 1960s functioned as an advisor to Governors Bert Combs and Edward Brethitt.

In addition to the above examples of careers destroyed or disabled because of apparent ethical or legal violations, there are two suggestive cases of New Deal lawyers who did not actually face censure but who came close to doing so. After Fortas' resignation from the Court, pressure mounted to secure the impeachment of Justice William O. Douglas, who had himself been a member of the New Deal legal generation.[27] Douglas, who had grown up in poverty and obscurity in Yakima, Washington, had worked his way through Columbia Law School in the late 1920s, graduating second in his class and narrowly missing out on a clerkship with Justice Harlan Stone. After a brief interval in law practice Douglas joined the Columbia faculty in 1928, and a year later went to Yale, where he was sufficiently successful to be named Sterling Professor of Law in 1931. Three years later, Douglas left academic life to become affiliated with the Securities and Exchange

Commission, eventually becoming a Commissioner in 1936 and replacing Landis as Chairman in 1937.

In 1939, Douglas was nominated to the Supreme Court, where he remained for thirty-six years, emerging early in his tenure as an outspoken liberal activist and a supporter of dissident causes. Douglas also maintained a controversial lifestyle for a Justice, marrying four times, participating in protest movements, and writing numerous books, one of which, *Points of Rebellion,* expressed sympathy for the radical ideas of New Left supporters in the 1960s. In the early 1960s, Douglas entered into a relationship with the Albert Parvin Foundation that was similar to the relationship Fortas had established with the Wolfson Foundation. The agreement stipulated that Douglas would be paid a yearly salary for unspecified services. Albert Parvin, unlike Louis Wolfson, was not a litigant in the federal courts, but was an associate of gambling interests who had repeated problems with the Internal Revenue Service; Douglas had on one occasion offered him tax advice.[28] In 1970, a resolution to impeach Douglas was brought in the House of Representatives and referred to the House Judiciary Committee, which eventually cleared Douglas of all charges. Douglas had previously resigned from the Parvin Foundation.[29]

The second case is that of Thomas Corcoran, who had gone from Pawtucket, Rhode Island, and Brown University to Harvard Law School in 1922, graduating first in his class three years later.[30] After Harvard, Corcoran clerked for Justice Holmes, and then went into private practice in New York until 1931, when he joined the Hoover administration in the Reconstruction Finance Corporation. The Roosevelt administration perpetuated the RFC, and Corcoran remained at that agency until 1933, when he became involved in drafting the Securities and Exchange Act, which created the Securities and Exchange Commission a year later. For the next several years, Corcoran was a member of the White House staff, responsible for a variety of political and legal tasks, and was also one of the chief recruitment officials for legal talent for the New Deal. He was heavily involved in both the Court-packing plan of 1937 and Roosevelt's third term effort in 1940, and aspired, after that effort had succeeded, to become Solicitor General. His candidacy was blocked as a result of opposition among Roosevelt intimates, including Justice Felix Frankfurter, to Corcoran's style of blending legal policymaking with politics.

In 1941, Corcoran left public service to enter private law practice in Washington. His private practice was uniquely informal and unstructured, consisting of liaison efforts with government agencies and Congress on behalf of corporate clients. Among the clients he represented regularly during the next decades were the "China Lobby," composed of various political and entrepreneurial interests in Nationalist China and then in Formosa, and various utilities, who sought favorable treatment from Congress or regulatory agencies.

In 1969, Corcoran allegedly approached Justices Hugo Black and William Brennan in private conversations, seeking their support on behalf of one of his clients, the El Paso Natural Gas Company, that the Supreme Court had ordered divested the previous term.[31] El Paso Natural Gas was seeking a rehearing on the divestiture order; Corcoran reportedly urged Black and Brennan to "do something'' for the company. The conversations were not made public until 1979, when they were revealed in the book *The Brethren*, whose authors based their information on confidential sources within the Supreme Court.[32] After the conversations were made public, one of Corcoran's longtime opponents, Admiral Hyman Rickover, demanded an investigation into Corcoran's conduct, and the matter was referred to the Board of Professional Responsibility of the District of Columbia Bar, who conducted an inquiry and recommended, partly on the ground of Corcoran's advanced age and infirm health, that no disciplinary action be taken.[33]

Corcoran's case may at first glance appear to differ sharply from most of the others sketched. The legal and ethical difficulties of the other subjects were directly related to their having held public office; Corcoran's difficulties stemmed from an allegedly overzealous representation of a client while in private practice. Moreover, all the other subjects, save Douglas, were not only charged with legal or ethical violations, they suffered severe professional reverses because of these violations.[34]

On reflection, however, Corcoran's case more resembles the others than might first appear. The salient feature of Corcoran's career as a private practitioner was that he traded on the political and personal connections he had made as a public official. He was, in his words, ''an entrepreneur''[35]; others claimed he was a lobbyist;[36] he might also be described as an influence-trader. In short, he was hired by private clients because of his long experience in public service. Before his alleged ex parte conversations with Black and Brennan, he had been accused, although never formally charged, of other efforts to secure favorable treatment for private clients from old acquaintances in positions of public responsibility. While lawyers are supposed to advance the causes of their clients, and the expertise of Washington lawyers is supposed to make them more effective in their representation of clients who deal with agencies of the government, there is a line between ''experienced'' advocacy and ex parte contacts with old friends who happen to be the judges deciding a client's case. Bar Association grievance committees assume the existence of that line.

Thus there seems little difference between the judge in the public sector who breaches a public trust by accepting favors from or dispensing advice to potential litigants (as one might characterize Fortas or, with more difficulty, Douglas) and a lawyer in the private sector who, outside of court, encourages a judge to do him and his client a favor. The lawyer is also breaching a public trust: he or she is an officer of the Court and taking undue advantage of that role. Corcoran was not censured or disbarred, to be sure, just as Douglas was not impeached. But the parallels between the cases sketched do not cease simply because the consequences of the subjects' conduct were not always the same.

IV The Symbolic Meaning of the Careers: Some Preliminary Thoughts

I have argued that the careers sketched above are suggestive in that each represents an example of a conspicuously successful lawyer who held positions of considerable responsibility in public agencies at an early age, but who found his later professional life tarnished or threatened by the spectre of legal or ethical impropriety. It remains to suggest an explanation for these parallel career patterns that rests on more than the idiosyncracies of personality or on reflexive characterological labels. Any such explanation will necessarily require much more space and time than is afforded here. What follows are some preliminary and tentative observations.

One theme surfacing in most of the careers sketched is a sense that members of the New Deal legal generation may have believed that they were somehow specially favored persons, given great opportunities for power and influence early in their lives because of their own intrinsic merit. Hiss, when first questioned by the House Un-American Activities Committee, appeared without a lawyer, assumed a posture of defiance, and summarily denied any participation in Communist activities. His credibility was subsequently undermined when he was forced to admit that he had, in fact, known his accuser, Whittaker Chambers. Fortas, to his death, refused to acknowledge publicly that he had committed any ethical improprieties while on the Court. Landis claimed that he had simply forgotten to file over five years' worth of tax returns.[37] Prichard, reminiscing about his voter fraud conviction in 1979, said that his New Deal experience had been "heady wine," that "I got to feeling . . . that I was bigger than I was, that the rules didn't always apply to me."[38] Douglas, alone among Fortas's close friends, counseled Fortas to stay on the Court and to fight impeachment; he believed that both he and Fortas were simply the scapegoats of politics.[39] On Corcoran's death in 1981, a friend said that he had "worked . . . in the same ways for his clients as he once did for the President"; that he had "never been able to make a distinction between them, or to realize that what might be justified within the Government cannot be from outside it."[40]

The sense of being "special," of being beyond the rules, was one that, in retrospect, one can associate with the unique situation in which certain members of the New Deal legal generation found themselves. Individuals like the subjects sketched were the "best and the brightest" of their era; they had succeeded at the top law schools and been rewarded with the sponsorship of influential academics and prestigious clerkships. They were entering a political culture seemingly filled with opportunities: to change the political course of the nation, to replace outmoded policies with fresh experiments, to improve the lives of countless downtrodden persons. They were themselves the architects of the programs of that new culture. They were participants in a society whose public sector was dramatically expanding and in which the lines between "public" and "private" activity were becoming blurred. They were, in short, a "chosen" group: chosen by their age, their education, their talent, and their participation in a transformative experience. With so much at stake, who was to say that they were beholden to antiquated rules and practices? They were making the rules and policies for the future.

With hindsight, one gets the sense that, for accomplished persons of the New Deal legal generation, power came so rapidly, policies changed so fast, and the old guidelines of the moribund market capitalist order collapsed so suddenly, that law, politics, ambition, and self-esteem all became blurred together, and the only restraints on one of the chosen group were seen to be the limits of his intelligence and his acumen. From the insight that the nation was ripe to be directed along different paths, and that a new class of persons was eligible to be the directors, it was perhaps a small step to the perception that this class of persons was not subject to the same rules as less specially favored mortals. Legal skills, honed in a meritocratic educational subculture, interacted with political ideology and the promise of new leadership in a "heady" fashion; law students, research assistants, and junior technicians suddenly became policymakers for the future. A familiar twentieth-century pattern of elite leadership began: the nobility or popularity of political ends was made an implicit justification for bypassing existing canons of accountability.

The last comments suggest that the cultural experience of elite members of the New Deal legal generation may well have been unprecedented. The mix of sociological modernization and political ideology that created a plethora of new opportunities for persons such as the subjects sketched was undeniably distinctive. Previous generations, such as the generation that survived the Civil War, had witnessed decisive transformation in American political culture; other generations, such as that which returned after World War I, had confronted the dramatic modernization of Western world societies that produced new definitions of status and power. The New Deal legal generation, however, faced the experience of both phenomena occurring simultaneously and in an apparently self-reinforcing fashion. As meritocratic criteria replaced lineage criteria as indices of professional prominence, the same ideological forces that had facilitated that change began to encompass traditional American politics as well. The emergence of professional service in the public sector for elite lawyers was related not only to new definitions of elites in America but to new conceptions of the functions lawyers could perform. The New Deal legal generation was arguably the first in American history to have the benefit of both of these developments.[41]

The comments also suggest that the experience of elite members of the New Deal legal generation was not unique in its effects. Subsequent generations of lawyers have also rested their justifications for conduct that has been perceived as breaching a public trust on ends-means arguments. The Watergate and Iran-Contra episodes come immediately to mind, but there are numerous other examples. The continued association of elite lawyers in the public sector, not themselves members of the New Deal generation, with alleged ethical or legal misconduct might suggest that the association is endemic to the profession or to all persons holding positions of prominence in public service. One can conjure up "scandals" throughout American history, from the XYZ affair to the Teapot Dome incidents, in which public officials used allegedly noble ends to justify irregular or illegal conduct.

The singular feature of the parallel careers of casualties of the New Deal legal generation is thus not their justificatory rhetoric, nor the fact that they were lawyers who were associated with legal or ethical misconduct. It is that they were "chosen" members of a new class of professionals: a class whose clients were the public at large and whose rule was to serve not as advocates for particular interest groups but as enlightened policymakers in a society to be organized around the ideological assumptions of modern liberalism. They were to be the architects of an increased federal regulatory apparatus, of federal social welfare legislation, of internationalism and humanitarianism in foreign affairs, and of more "realistic" and policy-oriented judging. Federal regulatory statutes and agencies of the New Deal, the Social Security system, the United Nations, and the plan to "pack" an "old" and recalcitrant Supreme Court with more "enlightened" judges were their legacies.

In this vein, the careers that have been sketched above can be seen as symbolic. Hiss, whose career in public service began in the domestic arena with the AAA, eventually moved into the area of foreign policy, and it was there that he arguably made his greatest impact. He was functioning, in his years with the State Department and most notably during his tenure as organizer of the San Francisco conference that resulted in the U.N., as the prototypical elite lawyer as liberal internationalist. The attack on Hiss by Chambers and the House Un-American Activities Committee can be seen, in retrospect, as an effort on the part of those who felt excluded from the foreign policy apparatus on grounds of status or ideology to strike out at a vulnerable representative of the policymaking elite. Hiss became a symbol of "Communists in government"; the State Department a symbol of a governmental institution whose elitist character had made it "soft" on Communism. McCarthyism can be seen as an example of this sort of social protest, and as a movement fueled by people who saw themselves displaced from or excluded from policymaking by Hiss and his kind.[42]

Fortas' and Douglas' careers can be seen as symbolic of another legacy of the New Deal legal generation—the judge as activist policymaker. As the insight that judges made law, on which the New Deal lawyers had been nurtured,[43] became conventional jurisprudential wisdom, the judicial community reacted in a variety of ways, one of which was by continuing an active interest in political issues but expressing that interest in a covert fashion. Thus, Justice Brandeis, who functioned in a culture in which judicial involvement with political issues was severely downplayed, nonetheless held soirees, lobbied for political programs, and hired the services of Felix Frankfurter to promote lobbying efforts for causes he supported.[44] Frankfurter, whose announced jurisprudential philosophy followed that of Brandeis in emphasizing the importance of judicial "self-restraint" where political issues were concerned, continued Brandeis' pattern of covert lobbying, using the network of former clerks and other intimates that he had helped create during the New Deal period.[45] Later Justices were more openly activist. Notable were Douglas, who made no secret of his views on a variety of political issues and encouraged his fellow justices to take on controversial questions,[46] and Fortas, who continued to advise the Johnson administration on matters of foreign and domestic policy while sitting on the Court.[47] The attacks on Fortas that surfaced after he was named Earl Warren's replacement as Chief Justice in 1969, and resulted in his nomination being successfully filibustered in the Senate, were in this sense attacks on the image of judges as policymakers, an image compatible with the jurisprudential assumptions of the New Deal generation but which made judges themselves vulnerable to political opponents.

The symbolic role of Landis for future generations came in his close identification with the idea of governmental regulation of the economy.[48] That idea had been alien to the generation that preceded the New Deal lawyers, had been one of the major contributions of the Roosevelt administrations, and had encountered complexities in the years of economic growth that marked the decades after World War II. In particular, the theory of economic regulation posited by the New Deal generation had placed great reliance on the administrative and regulatory agency as the unit of government best suited to achieve the goals of a regulated capitalist society. Agencies, in the minds of the New Dealers, combined the flexibility and pragmatism they believed was desirable in government with the disinterestedness associated with a proper regulatory stance. Landis, we have seen, was perhaps the lawyer of his generation most visibly identified with the growth of agencies to prominence. Agency government, however, came under attack in the 1950s and 1960s, as agencies were accused of becoming captured by the interests of the industries they were regulating and losing sight of their original mandate to serve the public interest.[49] The public disgrace of Landis, ironically at the hands of the most pervasive federal administrative agency of modern America, the Internal Revenue Service, was a reminder of the distance that had passed since Landis' generation first went to Washington.

Finally, in the careers of Prichard and Corcoran, one can see a fourth symbolic function of the New Deal lawyer. This function was that of the public servant who adapts techniques of political strategy and management to the private sector. As Prichard put it in an interview late in his life, he was of "two natures," one of which was the altruistic public servant, seeking to do good; the other was the political strategist, for whom the ends justified the means.[50] Prichard's stuffing of ballot boxes or Corcoran's lobbying of Supreme Court justices were, at one level, merely applications of a familiar technique of management in a different context; they were, in another sense, examples of a sensibility that found the lines between public and private obligations difficult to draw. By not appreciating the difference between working for the President and working for a local politician or a corporate lobbyist Prichard and Corcoran raised again the possibility that the cultural experience of the New Deal legal generation fostered a sense among some of its members that the traditional boundary lines of American professional and political life did not apply to their world. Examples of such boundary lines were that between the private and public sectors of the economy, or that between judging and policymaking, or that between regulators and regulatees, or that between accountable and unaccountable elite public servants.

Rather than simply stereotype persons such as Hiss, Fortas, Landis, and the rest as "crooks" or "political victims," we need to undertake a more detailed exploration of the professional and political culture in which they came to prominence. The New Deal remains a profound force in its effect upon contemporary America; at the same time it is now as much a part of our past as it is an element in our current consciousness. Elite lawyers continue to serve in prominent positions of public policymaking, and yet the relatively narrow elite educational subculture that produced the "casualties" discussed above has itself been transformed. Issues involving the ethics of lawyers and the accountability of public servants remain prominent features of contemporary life, but we rarely investigate those issues from the comparative perspective of history. It is time to take a fresh look at the New Deal legal generation in order to take a more discerning look at ourselves.

NOTES

1. Morton Keller, "Reflections on Politics and Generations in American," 107 Daedallus 123, 125 (1978).

2. I am using the term memory to signify the collective understanding by one generation of the meaning of its immediate past. The term emphasizes the shared images that result from a collective reconstruction of the past and deemphasizes individual variations in the reconstruction process, which of course are invariably present. See Frederick Somkin, *Unquiet Eagle: Memory and Desire in the Idea of American Freedom, 1815–60* (1987).

3. See generally Paul Conkin, *The New Deal* (2d ed., 1975); William Leuchtenberg, *F.D.R. and the New Deal* (1963); Arthur Schlesinger, Jr., *The Coming of the New Deal* (1958).

4. See Robert Stevens, *Law School* 99–103 (1983); Jerold Auerbach, *Unequal Justice* 102–29 (1976).

5. See Michael Parrish, *Felix Frankfurter and His Times: The Reform Years* (1982); H. N. Hirsch, *The Enigma of Felix Frankfurter* (1981). For more details on this theme, see G. Edward White, "Felix Frankfurter, The Old Boy Network, and the New Deal," 39 Ark. L. Rev. 631 (1986).

6. See the unconscious confirmation of this feature of the early twentieth-century Harvard student body in Harvard Law School Association, *Centennial History of the Harvard Law* 128–39 (1918).

7. Katie Louchheim, *The Making of The New Deal: The Insiders Speak* (1983). The lawyers interviewed by Louchheim were Thomas Corcoran, Alger Hiss, Donald Hiss, James H. Rowe, Jr., Herbert Wechsler, Joseph Rauh, Jr., Edward F. Prichard, Jr., David Riesman, Robert L. Stern, Charles A. Horsky, David A. Morse, Paul A. Freund, Frank Watson, Kenneth Crawford, Milton Katz, Gerhard A. Gesell, Milton V. Freeman, Francis Thornton Greene, Charles A. Kaufman, Thomas H. Eliot, Gerard D. Reilly, Thomas I. Emerson, Paul M. Herzog, Abe Fortas, Henry Hamill Fowler, Telford Taylor, and Arthur Goldschmidt. Of these the Hissess, Riesman, Gesell, Greene, Emerson, Fowler, and Taylor came from affluent backgrounds, although the Hiss family was undergoing financial difficulties by the time Alger and Donald attended law school. See sources cited *infra*, note 20.

8. See Frank Freidel, "Foreword," in Louchheim, *The Making of The New Deal: The Insiders Speak, supra* note 7, at xii.

9. See generally Michael Young, *The Rise of Meritocracy* (1959); Daniel Bell, "Meritocracy and Equality," 29 the Public Interest 29 (1972); David Riesman, "Educational Reform at Harvard College: Meritocracy and Its Adversaries," in Seymour M. Lipset and David Riesman, *Education and Politics at Harvard* (1975).

10. *See* E. Digby Baltzell, *Philadelphia Gentlemen: The Making of a National Upper Class* (1958); G. Edward White, *The Eastern Establishment and the Western Experience* 1–35 (1968).

11. For details, see White, "Felix Frankfurter, The Old Boy Network, and the New Deal," *supra* note 5.

12. *Id.* at 658–59.

13. The archetypal lawyer described in this paragraph was also usually a man. A few

women attended Yale and Columbia Law Schools in the 1930s, see Karen B. Morello, *The Invisible Bar: The Woman Lawyer in America* 93–100 (1986), and a high percentage of those women entered public service upon graduation, *see id.* at 96–99, but the overwhelming number of New Deal lawyers were male.

14. *See generally* Leuchtenberg, *supra* note 3.

15. Auerbach, *supra* note 4, at 190–230; Peter Irons, *The New Deal Lawyers,* 3–14 (1980).

16. Auerbach, *supra* note 4 at 1880–85; Irons, *supra* note 15, at 6–10.

17. Milton Katz in Louchheim, *supra* note 7, at 129.

18. *See* Irons, *supra* note 15, at 297–300.

19. 1 Wheat. 304 (1816).

20. The ethical impropriety of Marshall's conduct is not taken for granted here: his conduct may not have breached the then existing canons of judicial ethics. *See* the discussion in G. Edward White, *The Marshall Court and Cultural Change, 1815–35* 165–73 (1988). The point of the example is that Marshall's conduct was potentially improper.

21. For the outlines of Alger Hiss' career see Tony Hiss, *Laughing Last* (1977); Allen Weinstein, *Perjury* 70–141 (1978).

22. *See* Weinstein, *supra* note 21, at xvii–xxi.

23. On Fortas *see* Bruce Murphy, *Fortas* (1988); Laura Kalman, *Abe Fortas* (1990); Robert Shogan, A *Question of Judgment* (1972): Abe Fortas, Oral History, Lyndon B. Johnson Library, Austin, Texas; Charles Edmundson, "The Great Persuader," Memphis *Commercial Appeal,* December 11, 1966.

24. An excellent source of information on Landis is Donald Ritchie, *James M. Landis: Dean of the Regulators* (1980). *See* also Thomas McCraw, *Prophets of Regulation* 153–209 (1984).

25. James Landis, *The Administrative Process* 13–14 (1938).

26. Relatively little has been written on Prichard. An illuminating treatment is Arthur Schlesinger, " 'Prich': A New Deal Memoir," *New York Review of Books,* March 28, 1983.

27. The best biography of Douglas is James Simon, *Independent Journey* (1980). Douglas produced two volumes of autobiography, William O. Douglas, *Go East, Young Man* (1975) and *The Court Years* (1980). See also G. Edward White, "The Anti-Judge: William O. Douglas and the Ambiguities of Individuality," 74 Va. L. Rev. 17 (1984), reprinted in *The American Judicial Tradition* (1988 ed.).

28. Simon, *supra,* note 26, at 399.

29. I am not concerned at this point with exploring the question why Fortas was unsuccessful in defeating a challenge to his presence on the Supreme Court and Douglas was. The cases can be distinguished in several respects, and the distinctions may be significant. Suffice it to say here that both extrajudicial relationships raised the appearance of judicial impropriety.

30. Very little historical scholarship has been written on Corcoran. The most comprehensive treatment is Monica L. Niznik, "Thomas G. Corcoran: The Public Service of Franklin Roosevelt's 'Tommy the Cork'," Ph.D. diss., Department of History, University of Notre Dame, 1981. Niznik had access to the private papers of Corcoran, which are now in the Library of Congress. Corcoran's career is also treated briefly in Frank Freidel, *FDR: Launching the New Deal* (1973); Charles E. Jacob, *Leadership in the New Deal* (1967); Leuchtenberg, *supra* note 3, and Schlesinger, *supra* note 3. *See also* Joseph Lash, *Dealers and Dreamers* (1988).

31. *Utah Public Service Commission v. El Paso Natural Gas Co.,* 395 U.S. 464 (1969).

32. Bob Woodward and Scott Armstrong, *The Brethren*, pp. 89–95 (1979).

33. *See* "Thomas G. Corcoran, Aide to Roosevelt, Dies," *New York Times*, December 7, 1982.

34. Shogan, *supra* note 23, at 264, does not believe Fortas would have been successfully impeached, but believes an impeachment trial would have disabled Fortas' career on the Court.

35. Quoted in *New York Times, supra* note 33.

36. *Id.*

37. Ritchie, *supra,* note 24, at 197–99.

38. Quoted in Schlesinger, *supra,* note 26, at 23.

39. Simon, *supra* note 27, at 396, quoting an interview Simon had with Abe Fortas, July 23, 1976. *See also* Douglas, *The Court Years, supra* note 27, at 358.

40. Quoted in "Thomas G. Corcoran, Aide to Roosevelt, Dies," *supra* note 33.

41. One can, of course, identify other generations that experienced new roles for lawyers and new definitions of status and power in American society. An example would be the post-Civil War generation itself. See Robert Gordon, "Legal Thought and Legal Practice in the Age of American Enterprise, 1870–1920," in Gerald Geison, ed. *Professions and Professional Ideologies in America* (1983). Intragenerational comparisons are treacherous because changes in the cultural context of professional activity render efforts to make linear comparisons between generations problematic. ("The New Deal was the ancestor of the New Frontier" would be an example of a linear comparison fraught with difficulties.)

Despite these difficulties, I would argue that no generation prior to the New Deal had experienced the effects of modernization on political culture and professional status criteria at virtually the same moment in time. When "new" aspirants to elite professional status graduated from law schools in the late 1920s and early 1930s, they encountered a "new" political culture with "new" professional options. No previous generation of American lawyers had had this experience.

42. McCarthyism was, of course, a movement subsuming a number of ideological and sociological perspectives. See generally the essays collected in Earl Latham, ed. *The Meaning of McCarthyism* (1973).

43. The coincidence of the rise of Realism as a jurisprudential orthodoxy in the 1930s and the emergence of the New Deal has often been noticed. See, e.g., G. Edward White, *Patterns of American Legal Thought* 129–139 (1978); Edward Purcell, *The Crisis of American Democratic Theory* (1973). For a contemporary statement explicitly linking Realism and New Deal policymaking, see Jerome Frank, "Realism in Jurisprudence," 7 Am. L. School Rev. 1063 (1934).

44. *See* Bruce Murphy, *The Brandeis-Frankfurter Connection* 40–44 (1982).

45. *See, id.,* at 304–40; White, "Felix Frankfurter, The Old Boy Network, and The New Deal," *supra* note 5; Elman, "The Solicitor General's Office, Justice Frankfurter, and Civil Rights Litigation," 100 Harv. L. Rev. 817 (1987).

46. *See* Douglas, *The Court Years, supra* note 27.

47. *See* Shogan, *supra* note 34, at 135–42.

48. *See generally* McCraw, *supra* note 24.

49. *See* Louis Jaffe, "The Illusion of the Ideal Administration," 86 Harv. L. Rev. 1183 (1973).

50. Quoted in Schlesinger, *supra,* note 26, at 23.

Felix Frankfurter, the Old Boy Network, and the New Deal: The Placement of Elite Lawyers in Public Service in the 1930s*

We may be inclined to forget—partly because of the now considerable distance between the 1930s and our own times, and partly because of the professional culture we encounter today—that it is possible to advance two generalizations about lawyers in public service in twentieth-century America. The first generalization is that there was a time when practically no lawyers went into public service; the second is that there was a time when public service work was perceived as one of the most prestigious and important employment opportunities offered recent graduates of American law schools.

Of these generalizations, the most surprising feature of the second may be how odd it sounds in today's world. Many of the individuals who considered public service their most exciting professional option, and who came to regard time in public service as an essential prerequisite of an elite lawyer's[1] professional training, have reached retirement age in law schools and law firms. On many law faculties a pattern of clerkships, government service, and subsequent entry into academic life has been replaced by a pattern of clerkships and subsequent entry into academics, with government service, often in the form of a judgeship, coming after an academic reputation is established. Recent graduates of law schools have tended overwhelmingly to work in the private sector: a career option law graduates in the 1930s and 1940s routinely chose because it apparently provided the greatest amount of flexibility and the most numerous opportunities for advancement has now been tacitly installed as a low rung on current graduates' ladder of priorities.

These recent developments may suggest that the experience of the New Deal generation of lawyers[2] who entered public service was more unique, and less recurrent, than once thought. When those lawyers first entered the public sector,

---

*39 Ark. L. Rev. 400 (1986). A previous version was delivered as the 1985 Hotz Distinguished Lecture, University of Arkansas at Fayetteville.

they were conscious of their role as pathmakers: their collective decisions had, they believed, created a whole new dimension to the career of being a lawyer. What they have been less conscious of, as they have moved through or out of public service in the course of their professional lives, is the fact that their experience will not necessarily be duplicated in the future. One of my arguments in this essay is that their experience was a product of a cultural context peculiar to America in the early twentieth century, a context that may not replicate itself.

The structure of the above argument can be briefly summarized. The cultural context that fostered the placement of lawyers in public service in the 1930s contained four significant components. The first component was the growth of the public sector of the American economy as a market for legal services. The second was the triumph in early twentieth-century elite American culture of the ideal of ethnic assimilation, symbolized in the concept of America as a "melting pot." The third was the primacy among academics, younger professionals, and self-defined members of the intelligentsia, in the 1930s, of a "reformist" political ideology. The fourth was the emergence in those years of a version of the principle of meritocracy as the leading criterion for the career placement of law students and younger lawyers.

The above factors combined to facilitate the emergence of a network[3] for the placement of elite law school graduates in public service. The graduates had in common one or more of the following characteristics: a disinclination to enter or a difficulty in entering private practice; an ethnic background that adversely affected their employment opportunities; a commitment to the politics and ideology of the New Deal; and the sponsorship of influential lawyers in academics or public service.[4] The network functioned to ensure that graduates possessing such characteristics would have their entry into public service facilitated; it also functioned to perpetuate the idea that the entry of such persons into public service would enhance the quality of legal services in the public sector and, ultimately, enhance the visibility and prestige of public service itself. This idea was to evolve, as placement networks expanded and solidified after the Second World War, into a belief in the primacy of "the best and the brightest" as public policymakers. The questioning of that belief in the 1960s has had significant consequences for the stature of public service as a career option for recent law school graduates.

The central figure in the growth of the 1930s placement network was Felix Frankfurter, who from the First World War until his appointment to the Supreme Court in 1939 was intimately involved with every stage of the process by which graduates of Harvard and other elite law schools secured public service jobs.[5] But while Frankfurter's influence has regularly been noted by participants in the placement process and others, little attention has been paid to the cultural dimensions of Frankfurter's presence. Those dimensions form the basis of my second argument in this essay. I argue that Frankfurter's influence was not simply a function of his energy, industry, and commitment to public service, as has often been suggested.[6] Frankfurter's career was itself an embodiment of the factors that coalesced in early twentieth-century American society to bring the network into being and to give it a distinctive character. The network, and Frankfurter's role in it, are thus treated in this essay as cultural symbols: peculiarly evocative features of a phase of the history of the elite stratum of the American legal profession in the twentieth century. For reasons of chronology, the two arguments just summarized are presented in inverse order.

I Frankfurter and the Origins of the Network

In 1936 George Peek, the first chairman of the Agricultural Adjustment Administration, wrote what has come to be a famous caricature of the entry of recent law school graduates into public service at the time of the New Deal. "A plague of young lawyers settled on Washington," Peek observed. "They all claimed to be friends of somebody or other and mostly of Felix Frankfurter. . . . They floated away into offices, took desks, asked for papers and found no end of things to be busy about. I never found out why they came, what they did or why they left." [7] Peek's identification of Frankfurter as the patron of New Deal lawyers was only slightly exaggerated. One commentator has suggested that Frankfurter was "the proprietor of an organization for filling government positions of every kind, from a Cabinet page to a clerkship," [8] and Frankfurter himself wrote an article in 1936, "The Young Men Go to Washington," in which he claimed that "the best men of the graduating classes of the leading law schools" had been "freed from [the] complicated ramifications of private life" and had entered public service "diverted by minimum of vanities and jealousies." [9] The magazine in which that article appeared, *Fortune,* called Frankfurter "the most famous legal employment service in America." [10]

Frankfurter was, of course, not himself a member of the New Deal generation. He was fifty when Roosevelt was elected president, and he served the New Deal entirely as a patron and unofficial advisor, turning down Roosevelt's offer to be Solicitor General of the United States in 1933 and remaining on the Harvard law faculty, which he had joined in 1914, until 1939, when he was appointed to the Supreme Court. [11] Thus Frankfurter was a full generation older than most of the "best men" he sponsored. This fact is crucial to an understanding of his role: he saw the placement of young lawyers in public service in the 1930s as a replication, and a vindication, of his own early career. The early years of Frankfurter's professional life can be seen as having been affected by the same cultural features that were to affect the 1930s placement network. In an almost uncanny fashion Frankfurter saw his career beginning again in those of his protégés; and where differences of time, place, and personality existed, the network process he helped create functioned to deemphasize them.

Frankfurter was one of the few members of his class at Harvard Law School, which graduated in 1906, to enter public service directly after law school. There was a brief period of three months after his graduation during which Frankfurter joined a New York City law firm, but he soon abandoned private practice for a job in the United States District Attorney's office for the Southern District of New York, and never returned. After spending five years at the District Attorney's office, Frankfurter joined the legal staff of the War Department in Washington, where he remained until being appointed to the Harvard law faculty. In 1917 he took leave from Washington to be counsel to the War Labor Policies Board, returning to Cambridge in 1919. Of the first thirteen years of his career, Frankfurter was in public service for ten. By the age of 37 he had spent only three years in academics and three months in practice.[12]

The degree of Frankfurter's immersion in public service was unprecedented among one visible and powerful set of persons: lawyers of his generation who were graduates of elite law schools and returned to teach on elite law school faculties. Similarly unprecedented in Frankfurter's case was the close connection between his entry into public service and the theme of anti-Semitism. Frankfurter was neither the first Jewish Harvard graduate nor the first to enter public service: Louis Brandeis, among others, had preceded him in both categories.[13] But Frankfurter was the first Jewish graduate of Harvard to teach on the Harvard faculty. He was also the first Jewish law professor at an elite school to encounter the significant influx of Jewish applicants to elite schools after World War I and the wave of anti-Semitism at Harvard and other elite institutions that emerged, not coincidentally, during the same time period.

Anti-Semitism, in early twentieth-century elite American culture, was a double-edged phenomenon. The negative stereotyping of persons with Jewish backgrounds[14] that was part of the ideology of anti-Semitism was engaged in by Jews as well as others. Anti-Semitism can be seen as the underside of a powerful set of attitudes that fostered the ideal of ethno-cultural assimilation and was symbolized by the concept of America as an ethnic "melting pot." The "positive" dimension of assimilationism manifested itself in an assumption that the tolerance of Americans for "foreign" ethnic cultures had resulted in the integration of successive waves of immigrants into mainstream American life; the "negative" dimension manifested itself in an assumption that the cultural price aspiring immigrants paid was an implicit renunciation of their "foreignness" and acceptance of "American" mores, specifically the mores associated with middle- and upper-class gentile society.[15] In the case of Jews the two dimensions of assimilation were clearly articulated. Jews were stereotyped as "bright" and "energetic" and thus capable of cultural assimilation, especially through the process of higher education; Jews were also stereotyped as "pushy," "money-grubbing," and "unethical," "foreign" in their behavior patterns and value orientation.[16]

The status of Jews in early twentieth-century America was further complicated by immigration patterns. The first significant wave of Jewish immigrants came to America in the years between the 1840s and the 1870s, with Germany being the country of origin for most emigres. In contrast, the second wave, which began in the 1870s and lasted through the First World War, was primarily made up of immigrants from Russia and the Balkan states.[17] A demarcation between "German" and "Russian" Jewish immigrants has regularly been advanced in characterizations of the Jewish community in northeastern America: the demarcation reflects, among other things, contrasting attitudes toward ethno-cultural assimilation.[18] "German" Jewish immigrants have been characterized as more entrenched within mainstream American culture and thus more inclined to downplay their religiosity and ethnicity than "Russian" immigrants. A New York "German" newspaper's editorial has been offered as illustrating the difference in attitudes.

"The thoroughly acclimated American Jew," the *Hebrew Standard* declared, "has no religious, social or intellectual sympathies with [the new "Russian" immigrants]. He is closer to the Christian sentiment around him than to the Judaism of these miserable darkened Hebrews." [19]

The "German-Russian" division, while an oversimplification, helps locate Frankfurter within the early twentieth-century elite northeastern Jewish community. His parents were of German extraction, having come to New York from Vienna in 1894, when he was twelve. His father, the descendant of six generations of rabbis, was a retail furrier and an agnostic. Frankfurter was by all accounts a brilliant student, but not a wealthy one: public school and City College of New York were all his family could afford. Seven years after arriving in American he graduated from City College of New York, ranking third in his class. While at CCNY he encountered students with "Russian" backgrounds, and identified them as more speculative, less practical, and far more engaged in left collectivist politics than their "German" counterparts. [20]

Frankfurter's pre-legal career, then, had poised him between the "German" and "Russian" sectors of the New York Jewish community. He was neither a wealthy "German," such as his contemporary Walter Lippmann, [21] nor a "Russian," such as one of his roommates at Harvard, Morris Raphael Cohen, later to become a renowned philosopher and intellectual cult figure. [22] In a 1953 oral interview Frankfurter stated that his decision to go to law school was a recoiling from the "Russians" and an affirmation of his practical "German" roots, [23] but in fact his father's temperament was more "speculative" than practical, and few "Germans" had pursued politics and public affairs, which Frankfurter identified with the study of law. [24] In sum, Frankfurter was fully conscious of his Jewish heritage and neither disinclined to ignore it nor to fully discard it. He went to law school, he said, to learn the skills to right the injustices around him and to make his mother proud: by "injustices" he meant, among other things, ethnic prejudice. [25]

On coming to Harvard Law School in 1902, then, Frankfurter was already deeply immersed in the issue of ethnic identity and, through it, the issue of political consciousness. Both issues were to resurface later in his career. As the "German"-"Russian" division suggested, a particularly evocative issue for Jews in the early twentieth century was political ideology. But the political demarcations existing in the Jewish community during that time period tended to be overlooked in elite gentile opinion after World War I, which took on a xenophobic cast. "Foreign" ideologies of all kinds were stigmatized, especially those associated with the collectivist left; ethnicity and ideology were indiscriminately linked. The result was a loose identification of Jews with socialists, Bolsheviks, and other "alien" groups whose existence was perceived as threatening American capitalism and American democracy. [26] Frankfurter's involvement with political issues after World War I will subsequently be discussed.

Frankfurter's career at Harvard exposed him, for the first time, to the issues of "meritocracy" and professional marketability. In Cambridge his roommates, Samuel Rosensohn and Morris Cohen, were New York Jews, [27] but his circle of friends and acquaintances rapidly expanded to include middle- and upper-class gentiles. He "went to this and that, went to the library, read, roamed all around,

and . . . satisfied a gluttonous appetite for lectures, exhibitions, concerts'' during
his first semester, but after not performing well in a series of mid-year practice
exams, ''buckled down and ended up . . . being first in the class [for] the three
years'' of his law school career.''[28] By being first in the class he was elected to
the Law Review and was asked to serve as a summer research assistant for Professor John Chipman Gray. Through Gray, Frankfurter became closely acquainted
with two of his early mentors, James Barr Ames, who had succeeded Christopher
Columbus Langdell as Dean in 1895, and, later, Oliver Wendell Holmes, who
had been appointed to the Supreme Court of the United States a year before and to
whom Gray subsequently wrote a letter of introduction on Frankfurter's behalf.[29]

Harvard, during Frankfurter's years as a law student, was still comparatively
small, with between 700 and 764 students and 9 full-time professors;[30] it was also
overwhelmingly gentile in its ethnic composition. Harvard University, in the years
between 1902 and 1904, was almost unique among institutions of higher education
for its official tolerance of diverse religious and political beliefs. Under the presidency of Charles W. Eliot, Harvard had appointed socialists and Jews to the faculty, admitted blacks and Jews to the student body, abolished compulsory chapel,
and had become conspicuously involved with the defense of academic freedom.[31]
During Frankfurter's student years Harvard undergraduates became significantly
involved in settlement work in immigrant ghettos. In 1903 William James of the
Philosophy Department characterized Harvard as having a ''persistently activistic
constitution'' that stressed ''tolerance of exceptionality and eccentricity.''[32] But
Harvard Law School was not entirely reflective of the university as a whole. One
historian has characterized it, perhaps too severely, as a place where ''waist-
coated doyens of the legal profession . . . attempted to make gentlemen and
lawyers out of the scions of the Anglo-Saxon establishment and a handful of
immigrants,'' an ''institution [that] prized logical thinking, private property, and
brutal competition, all within a framework of social privilege and unabashed
snobbery.''[33]

Whether Harvard Law School, in Frankfurter's student years, was a bastion of
snobbishness and a competitive sweatshop, or an institution that had absorbed
some of the catholicity and ideological permissiveness of Eliot's university ultimately depends on one's point of view. But one fact is clear: in Frankfurter's
memory the Harvard of his student years had a vivid and uniform image. It was a
school whose faculty members were ''the best products of civilization,'' examples
of ''dedication of lives of great powers to the pursuit of truth, and nothing else,''
of ''complete indifference to all the shoddiness, pettiness and silliness that occupies the concern of most people who are deemed to be important or big.''[34] It had
an ''atmosphere, first, of professionalism and, [second, of] . . . the democratic
spirit. What mattered was excellence in your profession to which your father or
your face was equally irrelevant.''[35] It was a place where ''[a]ll this big talk about
'leadership' and character, and all the other things that are nonascertainable, but
usually are high-falutin' expressions for personal likes and dislikes, or class, or
color, or religious partialities or antipathies—they were all out.''[36] It was, in
short, a ''meritocracy'' in which ethnicity played no part.

The above comments about Harvard were made by Frankfurter in 1953, but as early as 1921 he had forged the image. In a letter to Roscoe Pound that year, written in the context of efforts on the part of the president of Harvard University and some members of the law faculty to restrict the number of Jewish students, Frankfurter said: "The great thing about the School when I was a student was that Skull & Bones, Hasty Pudding, wealth, family fortune, skin, creed—nothing particularly mattered, except scholarship and character objectively ascertained." [37] Frankfurter, in short, had a strong desire to see the Harvard of his student days as blind to matters of ethnicity or class or all such "nonascertainable" features of the student body, and directed only to "scholarship and character objectively ascertained." His dual use of the term "character" in the 1953 and 1921 comments is particularly suggestive. In 1921 character is something that can be "ascertained . . . objectively"; in 1953 character is listed as one of the "things that are nonascertainable." The change suggests that Frankfurter may have initially felt that positive judgments on his "scholarship" were also relevant judgments about his character: by being first in his class he was "worth something." If so, the association had disappeared by 1953: character was simply a fancy expression for judgments about personality, ethnicity, or class. [38] In both statements, however, Harvard emerged as a meritocratic institution.

The term meritocracy requires clarification, for it is capable of subsuming two quite distinguishable ideas. One is the idea of perpetuating elites whose membership has been based on "intangibles," such as class or ethnicity, through the assimilation of new members whose eligibility is based on allegedly "tangible" rather than "intangible" criteria, such as grades on "objective" examinations and academic rankings based on those grades. The other is the idea of replacing elites whose membership was based on intangibles with elites whose membership is based on tangibles. The term "merit" is ambiguous enough to embrace both subjective ("intangible") and objective ("tangible") factors. The two ideas have been represented in sociological literature by the terms "aristocratic meritocracy" and "democratic meritocracy." [39]

The latter version of meritocracy may be perceived as more consistent with democratic principles, but it has only rarely been taken seriously by elite opinion in American society. The "aristocratic" version of meritocracy was clearly in place during Frankfurter's student years at Harvard: Frankfurter's own career was evidence of that. But Frankfurter did not, in his later characterizations of his student life, distinguish between the aristocratic and democratic versions of the term. On the contrary, he confused the versions, and claimed that "the democratic spirit" pervaded Harvard Law School. [40] What he had encountered as one of the "bright men" in his class, however, was not democracy but sponsorship.

Sponsorship was the concept through which the aristocratic version of meritocracy was put into operation at Harvard Law School and at other elite educational universities in the early twentieth century. Sponsorship involved the creation of a symbiotic relationship between an older man, the "patron" or "mentor," and a younger man, the "protégé" or "disciple." [41] The pairs of terms convey different aspects of the relationship, with the patron/protégé pairing reflecting the occupational dimensions of the relationship and the mentor/disciple pairing reflecting its ideological dimensions. Ames, Gray, and James Bradley Thayer "sponsored"

Frankfurter's student career at Harvard, but in quite different ways. Ames was a patron in his official capacity as Dean and a mentor in his accessibility and generosity to students.[42] Gray was a patron in his singling Frankfurter out for a research assistantship and a mentor in promulgating a "pragmatic interpretation of the origin of legal rules" that Frankfurter would adopt in his own later scholarship.[43] Thayer, whom Frankfurter never met, was strictly a "mentor": his 1893 essay, "The Origin and Scope of the American Doctrine of Constitutional Law,"[44] was later identified by Frankfurter as the single greatest influence on his approach to "public law" questions.[45]

The sponsorship of persons such as Ames and Gray and others, such as Brandeis, Holmes, and Harvard Law faculty members Samuel Williston, Edward H. Warren, and Joseph Beale, was eventually to secure Frankfurter a professorship at Harvard. But in 1905, when Frankfurter sought employment in New York after graduation, his assimilation into the elite sectors of the legal profession appeared problematic, notwithstanding his sponsors. In the experience of seeking permanent employment Frankfurter was to encounter, for the first time, the "negative" dimensions of ethnic assimilation. He "went from office to office" in New York in the spring of 1905, and "was made to feel as though I was some worm going around begging for a job."[46] He presented letters of introduction from Ames, and one lawyer responded that he had forged Ames' signature.[47] He was made to feel "that the fact that I did very well at the Harvard Law School really didn't amount to much."[48]

Then came, as Frankfurter later recalled, an incident that changed his whole attitude. Dwight Morrow, a young practitioner from an upper-class background who had also graduated from Harvard, reportedly told Frankfurter to "just remember that a good office needs a good man just as much as a good man needs a good office."[49] Morrow's colloquial articulation of the principle of aristocratic meritocracy "was a revelation from heaven" for Frankfurter. In remembering the incident in 1953 he said that Morrow's remarks

> put the thing in proper perspective, that I wasn't a mendicant, that I had something they wanted as much as they something I wanted. There was one office, Hornblower, Byrne, Miller and Potter, that was one of the best offices at the time. Lots of Harvard people were in there. I'd heard that they had never taken a Jew and wouldn't take a Jew. I decided that that was the office I wanted to get into. . . .[50]

One could be hard put to find a more fertile series of associations in a reminiscence than the series in the above paragraph. In Frankfurter's structuring of the incident, Morrow states the meritocracy principle. Frankfurter reflects on it and realizes that, after all, he is not begging the gentile legal establishment for a job, that "they" need him as much as he needs them. He comes to understand that he has "something" they want, namely demonstrated success at Harvard Law School; that he has that "something" despite being Jewish; and that he can thus "get into" the world of New York gentile law practice. His reference to Hornblower, Byrne, Miller and Potter comes immediately after his realization that he, as well as they, has "something" the other wants. The reference specifies that he has converted this realization to a determination to be offered employment by the Hornblower firm because "they had never taken a Jew and wouldn't take a Jew." The story is told in 1953, when the ending is already known. The Hornblower firm offered him a job.

But there is an unanswered question left in the air by the paragraph. Did the Hornblower firm offer Frankfurter employment in spite of his being Jewish or because they expected his "Jewishness" to vanish? If they "wouldn't take a Jew," had they taken one in Frankfurter? The question is not merely rhetorical, for a page later in his reminiscences Frankfurter reveals that one of the partners at the Hornblower firm asked him to change his name, and that he refused to.[51] Moreover, two pages later Frankfurter notes that after spending three months with the Hornblower firm he left to take a job at Henry Stimson's U.S. Attorney's office. The position with Stimson required a salary cut,[52] but, as Frankfurter puts it, he "could practice law without a client."[53] By that comment Frankfurter doubtless meant practicing law in an independent, nonaccountable fashion,[54] but he also meant "client" in a narrower and more specific sense: practicing law without having to be a Jew seeking clients in a gentile world.

By 1906, Frankfurter had encountered all the themes that were to shape his conception of the placement network for lawyers that he helped construct in the 1930s. The only theme not figuring prominently in Frankfurter's life as a Harvard law student and beginning lawyer was reformist politics, although there has been speculation that he considered himself a political reformer while a law student.[55] But with his association with Stimson's office, Frankfurter entered what was to become a widening circle of early twentieth-century reformist politicians and intellectuals. The story of Frankfurter's career between 1906 and 1913 is a story of constant preoccupation with Progressive, or as Frankfurter sometimes styled it, "liberal" politics.[56] He assisted Stimson in the prosecution of sugar and railroad corporations for corruption and bribery; he helped Stimson in the latter's unsuccessful campaign for Governor of New York in 1910; after moving to Washington in 1911, on Stimson's urging, to be legal adviser to the Bureau of Insular Affairs of the War Department, he covertly advised Theodore Roosevelt in Roosevelt's 1912 presidential campaign, notwithstanding being a member of the Taft administration.

A symbol of Frankfurter's political concerns in his early Washington years was his residence on 19th Street, the "House of Truth," which he shared with Robert Grosvenor Valentine, Taft's Commissioner of Indian Affairs; Wilfred Denison, whom Frankfurter had first met in Stimson's U.S. Attorney's Office; and others.[57] The "House of Truth," so designated because it was a center for dissident Progressives within the Taft administration, became a kind of political and intellectual salon, numbering among its visitors Holmes, Brandeis, the Progressive theorists Herbert Croly and Walter Lippmann, and assorted sculptors, journalists, diplomats, and lawyers. Frankfurter once described the House of Truth as having "started out in the most innocent fashion, but it became a fashionable thing. . . .

The magnet of the house was exciting talk. . . . How or why I can't recapture, but almost everybody who was interesting in Washington sooner or later passed through the house."[58]

One can see, in retrospect, that the House of Truth was more than "a fashionable thing" for Frankfurter. It was the center of a series of concentric circles of people who were "interesting," a word Frankfurter variously associated with intelligence, social prominence, a commitment to political reform, or all of the above. The visitors and residents at the house were of different generations, ranging from Holmes, born in 1841, to Lippmann, fifty-eight years Holmes' junior and seven years younger than Frankfurter. They occupied different positions in the Washington legal and political community, ranging from Supreme Court justices through power brokers, such as Brandeis then was, to apprentices such as Frankfurter. They were nonetheless drawn together by "exciting talk," a euphemism for reformist political and cultural dialogue. In short, the "atmosphere" of the House of Truth incorporated, in an amorphous and unselfconscious fashion, the themes of sponsorship, meritocracy, and "liberal" politics; and the sociological mix of the house was a mix of upper-and upper-middle class gentiles and "German" Jews. The House of Truth can thus be seen as a precursor to the network Frankfurter would later help assemble: a "center of liveliness"[59] that anticipated the center of legal and political power the network represented.

II Toward the Formation of the Network: The Playing Out of Earlier Themes

With Frankfurter's departure from Washington to join the Harvard Law School faculty in 1914 a phase of his career appeared to have ended, and in a sense it had: Frankfurter the political reformer and public service lawyer had become Frankfurter the academician, a role he would not formally relinquish until 1939, when he was appointed to fill Benjamin Cardozo's seat on the Supreme Court. But in several other respects the move to Cambridge was a continuation of Frankfurter's public service career. First, no sooner had Frankfurter returned to Harvard than World War I broke out, and by 1917 he had returned to Washington as special assistant to Newton Baker, the Secretary of the War Department.[60] Frankfurter remained in Washington until the fall of 1919, holding a series of jobs, which ranged from drafting labor codes for the clothing industry in wartime to accompanying Henry Morgenthau, Sr., a former ambassador to Turkey, on a quixotic mission to split Turkey from the Central Powers alliance. By 1918 he had been named chairman of the newly created War Labor Policies Board, a position in which he first encountered Franklin D. Roosevelt.[61] A year later, with the war concluded, thousands of veterans returned to the labor market, and the Wilson administration bogged down in its ill-fated League of Nations venture, Frankfurter had had enough. The Wilson administration, he said, was "paralyzed," and had "practically announced bankruptcy and . . . invited the Republicans as receivers."[62] But before returning to Harvard he made it clear to a friend that he was going back, in part, because "I should have only six hours of teaching with the expectation of being very active in public affairs in my field of interest."[63]

Second, as the above letter suggests, Frankfurter did not think of his academic role as that of a scholar, but as that of a trainer of prospective public servants and a participant in public affairs. He had said before accepting Harvard's original offer that he was "not a scholar, qua scholar," but that he was "struck with the big public aspect of what should be done by our law schools."[64] His going into law teaching was, he felt, not "a final choice between public and academic work": the work of a law professor "*is* public work—our universities increasingly should be in politics—with the emphasis on sustained thinking along . . . questions of public affairs."[65] In another letter at the same time, this one to Holmes, he said that

> I would not go [to Harvard] for a conventional professorship. Academics are neither my aptitude nor the line of my choice. . . . The thing is rather different and what challenges me is to bring public life, the elements of reality, in touch with the university, and, conversely, to help harness the law school to the needs of the fight outside.[66]

Third, Frankfurter's career at Harvard from 1914 through the 1930s was marked by persistent involvement with external public issues. In that period he was an advisor to the "liberal" magazine *The New Republic*, which began in 1914; helped organize a campaign to defend Brandeis against critics who attacked his nomination to the Supreme Court in 1916; argued *Bunting v. Oregon*,[67] in which the constitutionality of state minimum wage and maximum hour legislation was tested; became informally and then formally involved in the American Zionist movement;[68] and publicly announced his support for the Progressive candidate Robert La Follette in the presidential election of 1924.[69] To those activities should be added his most significant political ventures in the period: his overt engagement with the Sacco-Vanzetti trial[70] and his covert partnership as a lobbyist for public policy proposals[71] with Brandeis. The first erroneously branded him, in elite legal opinion, as a "radical"; the second expanded and solidified his role as a reformist political strategist. The 1928 presidential election demonstrated the depth and breadth of Frankfurter's political involvement. While Frankfurter campaigned vigorously for Al Smith, when Herbert Hoover defeated Smith he turned to Frankfurter for advice on a nomination for Undersecretary of State, and Frankfurter, working behind the scenes, was able to secure the post for Joseph Cotton.[72]

In the decades from the opening of the Great War to the election of Franklin Roosevelt, then, Frankfurter, although based at Harvard, could be said to have remained in public service. But his role had shifted from that of officeholder to that of advisor, and the shift was a crucial one. Frankfurter had come to believe, by 1919, that his greatest strengths were in "handling" people and in bringing people together;[73] and also that he needed "freedom" to work with a minimum of occupational or financial constraints. Private practice, with clients, represented one set of constraints for him; formal government service another. Academic life was the most "free" in his sense of the term; it was also the life, he felt, in which he could most easily advise and "manage" others. The primary purpose of his advice and management was liberal politics and policymaking.

There was, however, a secondary and perhaps a less conscious purpose shaping Frankfurter's professional activity between 1919 and 1932. This was the playing out of the themes of his earlier career in a fashion that both vindicated that career and bequeathed it, as it were, to a younger generation. Law teaching was, for Frankfurter, a version of public service, but it was also a form of sponsorship. At Harvard in this period he encountered men younger than himself, just as at his earlier time at Harvard older men had encountered him. Older men had sponsored him; he would be a sponsor in this turn. Put most sharply, older elite gentile law professors had sponsored a "bright" young Jew in an overwhelmingly gentile professional and social world; now that "bright" young person, assimilated into the world, could sponsor others. But what did sponsorship, with its premise of ethnocultural assimilation, mean to the adult Frankfurter? Did sponsorship signify an implicit abandonment of his ethnic heritage, a tacit version of the name change suggested to him earlier? Or did it signify a more complex, and potentially self-contradictory, repetition of earlier themes: a sponsorship whose purpose was not simply to foster the career of protégés or disciples but to solidify the special qualities of the patron/mentor? The meaning Frankfurter gave to sponsorship was the latter one: an "old boy" network was the result.

Before turning to the details of the placement network, three additional facets of Frankfurter's career in its transitional years need to be briefly mentioned. The first, already described, was the emergence in his correspondence of the idea of elite legal education as a meritocracy. The second was his continued concern with the issue of anti-Semitism, especially in higher education, which embroiled him in bitter disputes with Harvard University President A. Lawrence Lowell and, eventually, Harvard Law School Dean Roscoe Pound.[74] The third was his use of the network concept itself. As early as 1917, when he was appointed chairman of the War Labor Policies Board, Frankfurter already had become active in securing positions within the Wilson administration for recent Harvard graduates. That year, he wrote his then ally, Pound, that two such graduates had "made good with a bang with the Shipping Board"; and that "[a]ll the other boys" were "doing nicely."[75] The most thorough study of Frankfurter's early career claims that during World War I Frankfurter's Harvard protégés "formed a network of intelligence and intrigue that stretched from the Justice Department to the Emergency Fleet Corporation."[76] That claim is overstated, at least in the sense that "network" is used in this article: the graduates were not numerous and their jobs temporary. But the pattern had begun.

III The Placement Network of the 1930s

While the themes of Frankfurter's early career had been played out during the 1920s in a manner that deepened and solidified his conception of sponsorship, comparatively few graduates of Harvard Law School had entered public service between 1921 and 1929. The principal reason for this placement pattern was the

American economy and the set of cultural attitudes that nurtured it. The private sector of the economy was booming in those years; the public sector, especially at the federal level, was stagnant. The idea of an increased federal regulatory apparatus was still viable among Frankfurter and other "liberals," [77] but that idea was not embraced by the national Republican Party. Jobs for lawyers in the corporate sector expanded dramatically, a fact that gave Frankfurter concern, but that concern was apparently not shared by many of his students. [78] The prospects for exciting public service employment in the 1920s were perceived so skeptically by Frankfurter, in fact, that he devoted his energy to attempting, with occasional success, to steer his protégés from Supreme Court clerkships or graduate programs directly to tenure-track positions on the Harvard law faculty. [79]

But the stock market crash of 1929, the ensuing economic depression, and the national political and ideological realignment those events helped precipitate were to combine with other factors to reinstitute public service as a career option, one of unprecedented scope. Between 1929 and early 1933, when Roosevelt, having defeated Hoover for the Presidency, took office and instituted the first New Deal legislation, all the themes of Frankfurter's earlier career seemed to coalesce for him and his sponsorees. The private sector market expanded with the creation of federal agencies that needed legal staffing. In a tight private economy ethnicity remained a significant job barrier; in the federal government overt ethnic discrimination was less entrenched and less easily justifiable. Reformist "liberal" politics became mainstream politics with the formation of the Democratic "coalition" and the delegitimation of traditionalist cultural symbols such as "captains of industry" or "Napoleons of finance." [80] And, perhaps most significantly, the primacy of elite gentile class values, whose persistence through the twenties could be seen in the debates about Jewish applicants to Harvard, was severely shaken by the symbolic ramifications of the Depression. Roosevelt, a gentile aristocrat, surrounded himself with advisors of multifarious social and ethnic backgrounds, "welcomed the hatred" [81] of Wall Street, and was branded "a traitor to his class." The implicit attack on elite gentile class consciousness brought with it a corollary, the resurgence of the concept of meritocracy, especially in its "aristocratic" version.

All these factors made possible the formation, by Frankfurter and his associates, of an "old boy" placement network. The term "old boy" is used advisedly: the model Frankfurter had in mind was that long employed by the British universities and civil service, a model that simultaneously perpetuated gentile class values and fostered professionalism through informal connections developed in the hierarchical British education system. Frankfurter was a lifelong anglophile, whose "childlike passion for England [and] English institutions" [82] was only partially satiated by his spending the 1933–34 academic year in Oxford as the George Eastman Professor at All Souls' College. For him the British "old boy" model was a resonant one. But the network he helped create was, necessarily, Americanized. In particular, its participants were not aloof from partisan politics, as British civil servants ostensibly were, but openly and resolutely partisan. Frankfurter's network functioned to place only certain types of elite lawyers in public service, those who were perceived as having a reformist inclination.

As noted, Frankfurter had from his earlier years as a lawyer been engaged in the recruitment of "eligible" young men into public service:[83] "eligibility" came to have a special definition for him. The characteristic Frankfurter recruit, or sponsoree, was a graduate of Harvard Law School, politically liberal, usually highly ranked in his class, and either an obvious product of upper-class gentile culture or an obvious product of a radically different cultural environment who was "comfortable" in the upper-class gentile world. The two symbolic linchpins of Frankfurter's network were Holmes and Brandeis, both of whom selected their law clerks, during the 1920s and 1930s,[84] from Harvard graduates recommended by Frankfurter. Holmes the Brahmin gentile and Brandeis the "German" Jew who had penetrated, and then defied, the New England gentile establishment, were sent a variety of clerks, including upper-class Protestants Mark De Wolfe Howe and Alger Hiss, along with Thomas Corcoran, a Rhode Island Catholic, who served Holmes; and James Landis, the son of a Methodist missionary, and David Riesman, from an upper-class "German" Jewish Philadelphia family, who were dispatched to Brandeis. The clerks may at first appear to be a diverse, even disparate group, but on closer scrutiny they can be seen as embodying the polarities of Frankfurter's "melting pot" vision: the upper-class gentile intellectual and the upwardly mobile "outsider" who both aspires after and reinvigorates elite gentile culture.

Holmes' and Brandeis' clerks occupied special roles within the network: beyond that "charmed" circle Frankfurter appeared to be less conscious of symbolic ethnicity, although rarely less conscious of "merit" or politics. Among the Frankfurter sponsorees who entered public service in the 1930s were Paul Freund, Henry Hart, Dean Acheson, Telford Taylor, Joseph Rauh, Edward Prichard, David Morse, Charles Kaufman, Philip Graham, Erwin Griswold, Charles Wyzanski, and Lee Pressman. The first three (a "German" Jew from St. Louis, a miner's son from Montana, and the son of an Episcopal bishop from Connecticut) were Brandeis clerks: the rest, a more diverse group sociologically, were all members of the Harvard Law Review and all "liberals" by 1930s standards.[85]

The pervasiveness of Frankfurter's influence in funnelling young lawyers to Washington in the 1930s can be seen in a series of reminiscences by "insiders" about the New Deal. Of twenty-three lawyers interviewed about their entry into public service, thirteen stated that Frankfurter was directly responsible, and another three identified Corcoran, who after joining the Roosevelt administration in 1933[86] consulted Frankfurter on most Harvard applicants. Among the comments made by the lawyers were the following: "I'm a total product of . . . Frankfurter, because if it weren't for him I would be a fat corporate lawyer in Cincinnati, Ohio. He changed the course of my life."[87] "Most people don't appreciate the gigantic influence Felix had in the early New Deal days."[88] "My relatively early departure [from government service] caused Professor Frankfurter, who had appointed me, to call me a black sheep."[89] "Frankfurter sent me to Tom Corcoran, which was the classic way to get a job in the New Deal."[90] "All during the period of Roosevelt's campaign, and for some time before, those of us who'd been under the influence of Felix Frankfurter thought of Roosevelt as a great man."[91] "Felix Frankfurter was into the life of almost every Law Review student who passed through Harvard for three years. . . . Felix was good to me in every professional material way. I have to thank Felix for everything."[92]

By 1934 a number of persons were highly placed in New Deal agencies whom Frankfurter had taught at Harvard or otherwise knew well—Jerome Frank in the Agricultural Adjustment Administration; Nathan Margold at the Interior Department; James Landis in the Securities and Exchange Commission; Charles Wyzanski in the Department of Labor; Harold Stephens in the Justice Department; and Corcoran in the Reconstruction Finance Corporation and later the Public Works Administration. Each of those individuals, when positions became available in his department, consulted Frankfurter and invariably received a recommendation; some, such as Landis and Corcoran, involved themselves in the staffing of other agencies. Occasionally Frankfurter intervened directly with Roosevelt on a personnel matter. In July 1933 he asked Roosevelt to "retain in the Solicitor General's office two young men of really unusual ability," Erwin Griswold and Paul Miller. Griswold and Miller were "being strongly tempted by outside offers."[93] Nine days later Homer Cummings, the Attorney General, responded to Roosevelt that "Messrs. Griswold and Miller . . . are both good men," and "[the Solicitor General] would like to keep both of them, at least for a considerable time."[94]

While the network occasionally resulted in the placement of lawyers who were several years removed from law school, it primarily functioned to create opportunities for graduating students. This fact should not be surprising, since the kind of legal jobs that were created in the public sectors in the 1930s tended to be of temporary duration and to offer comparatively low salaries. Those features of the employment effectively precluded recruitment of senior lawyers, who could not afford to take salary cuts for jobs whose tenure was uncertain. The recruitment pool for such jobs was thus limited to recent law school graduates or the occasional lawyer, such as Jerome Frank, whose political sympathies motivated him to enlist in the New Deal. Since the average job prospect lacked experience in a given area of practice, the major source of information about him was his performance in law school. Prospective employers thus required, above all, evaluations of applicants by persons who were in a position to assess their academic performance and whose judgment was perceived as being reliable. Frankfurter, of course, filled that role: he had widespread contacts among New Deal agencies and he made it his business to become acquainted with Harvard students who had distinguished themselves academically. But while Frankfurter's involvement was unusual, his role could be filled by other academics: the network was nothing more than a sharing of information by law professors at elite law schools and agencies inclined to hire their students.

Consequently, versions of Frankfurter's network soon spread to Yale and Columbia law schools, as faculty members of those institutions joined the New Deal and recruited their former students. Wesley Sturges of the Yale faculty, who had gone to the Department of Agriculture in 1933, recruited Abe Fortas for the Agricultural Adjustment Administration that year. Fortas later went to work for William O. Douglas, another former Yale law professor, at the Securities and Exchange Commission.[95] Subsequently Gerhard Gesell, another Yale student, joined the SEC. Later Douglas named Gesell special counsel to the Temporary National Economic Committee largely because, as Gesell put it, "I was a known entity."[96] Similar relationships between Walter Gellhorn and Herbert Wechsler (two former clerks for Harlan Fiske Stone) and staff members of New Deal agencies, facilitated the placement of Columbia graduates.

Virtually none of the recruitees expected their jobs to be permanent. As one put it, "[w]e all felt we were going to have to leave just as soon as things got back to normal. We were going into the world to earn some real money."[97] Most, in fact, did not stay long, leaving government service to enter Washington law firms or to return to academic life. Fortas, Landis, Corcoran, Freund, Hart, Acheson, Taylor, Rauh, Prichard, Morse, Kaufman, Graham, Griswold, and Pressman left for teaching or private practice, and Douglas, Frank, Gesell, and Wyzanski became judges. Of the Frankfurter protégés listed, only Alger Hiss remained principally in government service, and Hiss' career was curtailed after his conviction for perjury in 1950.

The above characterization is, however, somewhat misleading. Many whose early careers were spent in government service returned to the public sector later in their careers. Fortas became a justice of the Supreme Court; Landis Chairman of the Civil Aeronautics Board; Freund an assistant in the Solicitor General's office; Taylor general counsel for the Federal Communications Commission; Wechsler an assistant attorney general in the Justice Department; and Acheson Secretary of State. The pattern Frankfurter had established in his own career—that of a lawyer in academics or in private practice taking periodic leave to work in a government agency—was followed by the New Deal lawyers.[98] While recruitees may have contemplated, in the 1930s, that their stay in the public sector would be temporary, the experience instilled in many of them an inclination to reenter government service as a response to a national emergency or just as an opportunity to recharge their batteries. As one recruitee said of his experiences in government service in the 1930s: "to me and my age group [the experience] represented life, excitement, movement, growth, creation, high endeavor."[99]

IV The Cultural and Intellectual Legacy of the Network

This essay has thus far emphasized the unique combination of cultural factors that produced the "old boy" placement network in its Frankfurterian and other versions. That uniqueness has, of course, another dimension: no other generation of law students since the New Deal has encountered a similar combination of circumstances. There has been no economic depression comparable to that of the late 1920s and early 1930s, and thus the supply of jobs in the private sector has remained relatively high. Anti-Semitism among law firms and their clients has gradually lessened between the 1930s and the present, so that ethnicity has been increasingly less a bar to employment. The salary gap between private practice and public service still exists, but has narrowed so that salaries in government service are no longer at a level that only very recent graduates can afford.

But there has been an important intellectual legacy of the network, a legacy that appears to have transcended its cultural setting. An implicit assumption of the placement network, embedded in the idea of meritocracy, was that the infusion of "bright young men" into legal positions in the government would have a positive effect because the recruitees were "bright." Frankfurter was the most visible advocate of this point of view. Over and over again in the course of his career as a recruitment agent, evaluator of talent, and sponsor, Frankfurter stressed the idea that the principal criterion for marketability ought to be demonstrated merit, not "intangible" factors such as wealth or status. "Election to the Harvard Law Review," he wrote in his reminiscences, "followed academic rank, an automatic affair. . . . If one fellow got 76, and another 76.5, there's no use saying the 'the 76 man is better.'"[100] We have seen that Frankfurter believed that his own success at Harvard had been due to the fact that the law school was a meritocracy, but that belief took for granted that he was "bright" and that his intelligence would not only overshadow "nonascertainable" qualities such as physical size, wealth, or ethnicity, it would lead to professional competence.

The idea that merit could be objectively determined, and the corresponding idea that "merit" should replace "nonascertainable" factors as the basis for the placement of lawyers, thus led to a corollary. Since one could objectively determine that one prospective lawyer was "better" than another, the choice of a given individual for a particular job would make a difference in how competently that job was performed. These assumptions can be said to represent the intellectual premises of the placement networks. When New Deal agencies sought to staff themselves with lawyers, they wanted the "best" applicants. The "best" were those who ranked high in their classes in the "best" law schools. By identifying and recommending the "best" students, Frankfurter and others were helping to insure that the quality of work at a given agency would be high, because the theory of meritocratic placement assumed a clear correlation between high grades and competence as a lawyer or policymaker. Getting the "best" students thus insured that an agency would do "good" legal work and thereby facilitate the programs of the New Deal and increase the power and prestige of the public sector.

The belief that individuals "made a difference" in politics and government was reinforced by Legal Realism, the jurisprudential movement that came into prominence in American law schools in the late 1920s and 1930s. The dominant jurisprudence of the period preceding Realism, which the Realists reacted against, had assumed that a properly "scientific" approach to the law could yield governing "principles" that were universal in their application. Once such principles had been extracted from authoritative sources and identified, a mechanistic application was all that was necessary. Thus while legal science required ingenuity and perhaps talent in its earlier, "extractive" stages, once the scientists had done their work the rest was largely rote. As a jurisprudence, legal science placed a great value on the content of legal doctrine and relatively little value on the individual characteristics of those who applied it.

Realists rebelled against this emphasis. The "law," they argued, was nothing more than the aggregate of individualized applications and interpretations; doctrinal rules were meaningless abstractions. The practices and customs of indus-

tries, the interpretive techniques of courts and agencies, the personalities of decisionmakers had more to do with "the law" as it "really" was than disembodied
doctrine.[101] Frankfurter was not closely identified with the Realist movement.[102]
But on the issue of whether law was a collection of disembodied rules or the
aggregate of individualized decisions, he was far closer to the Realists than to
those who embraced the jurisprudence of legal science. His own career, his vision
of a meritocracy, his emphasis, as a commentator on the Supreme Court, on personalities and political orientations, all suggested that he believed that men, far
more than doctrine, "made a difference" in the law.

In their conclusion that "objective" criteria, such as law school examinations,
could determine whether one person was "better" than another, in their assumption that "better" law students would be more competent lawyers, and in their
conviction that the presence of more competent lawyers would have a favorable
effect on the performance of the government agency who hired them, Frankfurter
and his fellow participants in the placement network seemed to have ignored or
discounted a phenomenon that may be of critical importance in assessing the efficacy of meritocratic placement networks. The phenomenon is the tendency of the
individuals and institutions who participate in such networks to reflect the "cultural filters" of a particular generation sharing tacit ideological premises. One can
see the phenomenon at work in Frankfurter's contrast between class or color or
religion and numerical grades on examinations. He claimed that leadership and
character were "nonascertainable," but that there was "no use saying" that a
person scoring lower on an examination was "better" than a person scoring
higher. Frankfurter asked, rhetorically, "How do you know the [lower scorer] is
better"; one might ask how he "knew" the higher scorer was. Frankfurter would
have had an answer: "because he had received a higher grade on an objective
examination whose only purpose was to determine merit." But that answer presupposes that the skills tested on "objective" examinations are not themselves
culturally determined; that distinctions between "76.5" exams and "76" exams
are not arbitrary, and that "merit" is associated with high exam scores rather than
"intangibles." To put the point another way, Frankfurter's tacit ideological premises prevented him from considering the possibility that a group of "bright" lawyers, recruited from elite schools, would make "better" decisions only if "better"
was defined culturally. They would make the decisions that their collective ideology deemed to be "better," using techniques that their professional culture rewarded.

As the placement networks of the 1930s expanded throughout the Second
World War and the 1950s, and as the public legal sector also expanded, graduates
of elite law schools increasingly came to occupy significant policymaking positions in the federal government. With the advent of the war in Vietnam the networks confronted what might be called their first cultural crisis. The staffing of
high-level advisory positions in the years of the Vietnamese war was determined
by a process roughly comparable to the placement of lawyers in public service in
the 1930s. Through a "meritocratic" network, reflecting the political culture of
the 1950s and early 1960s, the "best and brightest" of a generation of persons
who had come to maturity after the Second World War were placed in national

security advisory positions.[103] One assumption of the networks that placed those persons in such positions was that of the 1930s networks: "better" people would make "better" decisions about national security and foreign policy. And in one sense the decisions made about Vietnam were "good" decisions: they were carefully thought through, fully debated, and represented a canvass of a number of able and experienced individuals. The problem with the decisions was that all of the participants conceived the world of foreign policy and national security in the same fashion—as a "bipolar" world divided between the "free world" and the "communist bloc"—and formulated policy in Vietnam in accordance with that conception. The conflict in Vietnam did not fit easily into the "bipolar" model, and as a result a number of high-level policy decisions were made for which there was a decisive consensus at the time but which in retrospect appear to have been "bad": bad in the sense of dominated by assumptions that were simply not tenable.

While the recognition of "cultural blinders" has become a commonplace feature of academic discourse since the 1960s, the phenomenon of shared ideological premises serves to characterize the placement process of the 1930s in a different way from that which it appeared to the participants. Each of the premises on which the 1930s placement networks were based—the idea of meritocracy, the assumption that merit could be objectively determined, the correlation between performance in law school and competence as a lawyer, and the belief that individuals with higher grades were "better" and would therefore "make a difference" in the performance of the institutions they joined—appears to be vulnerable to the claim of latent cultural bias. The "meritocratic" system, as applied to elite legal education, in fact rewards one kind of skill, performance on a particular kind of analytical exercise; and that skill is tested by those who themselves have demonstrated an aptitude for such exercises. The skill is then transposed into an "objective" criterion for "merit," as if "anyone" could recognize that those who demonstrate the skill are "better" lawyers than their peers. Other skills arguably as important in the effective practice of law, such as empathy, judgment, dedication, or reliability, are deemed incapable of "objective" measurement. As structured, the meritocratic system insures its self-perpetuation, since the qualities deemed important for placement and advancement in the legal profession are the "objective" qualities that make one "better" in the first place. Thus, those who emerge in positions of power within the system will have demonstrated the qualities, and by insisting on the "importance" of such qualities those persons justify their own success.

From a contemporary perspective, then, the placement process of the 1930s seems to have been structured to ensure that the entry of certain lawyers into public service would "make a difference," but in a different sense from that which the participants imagined. The process ensured that the entrants would be products of a meritocratic system that assumed a high correlation between good performance on law school exams and good lawyering, and thus ensured that such an assumption would continue to be made by the individuals participating in the system. With this feature of the placement process in mind, one can understand why so many lawyers who began their careers in government service in the 1930s returned to work in the public sector later in their lives. Those individuals believed that their returning to public service would "make a difference" because of their "merit." In many cases, we have noted, individuals originally recruited in the 1930s returned to government service in the Second World War, believing that the national emergency required them to lend their expertise to the war effort. While their reentry was based on motives of patriotism and self-sacrifice, it was also premised on the belief that their attachment to governmental institutions would make those institutions "better."

Thus the placement network of the 1930s, when viewed from a contemporary perspective, leaves us with a troubling intellectual legacy, one capable of two quite different interpretations. One interpretation of the "old boy network," an interpretation premised on cultural relativism, might argue against future participation by lawyers in public service. If the only way that lawyers who "succeed" in an allegedly meritocratic system "make a difference" to the institutions they serve is to transfer to those institutions the tacit biases of that system, there is no real hope that the "best and the brightest" will make the quality of legal services in the public sector "better." All that will occur is that the cultural blinders already embedded in the meritocracy will be perpetuated. Thus one cannot expect that one's presence in the public service will "make a difference" except in the sense that an already established ideology will continue to be established. Given the very limited sense in which one can make a difference, one might as well direct one's energies to the accumulation of one's own wealth, something that many current graduates seem inclined to do.

On the other hand, one might interpret the placement experience of the 1930s somewhat differently. Many of the lawyers recruited by Frankfurter and others in that decade testified to the degree of responsibility suddenly thrust upon them and to their conviction that they were engaged in work of an importance and gravity incommensurate with their experience. As one recruitee said:

> The thing I remember most about those times is . . . the sense that we were doing something worthwhile, that it was important, that it was important to do it the very best way you could. . . . This was the spirit of the New Deal. We felt we were going to change the United States and make it a better place. And we did, damn it, we did.[104]

While the recruitees' sense of their importance and their accomplishments may have been premised on debatable assumptions, there is no question that they took satisfaction in participating in a transformation of American life. They entered public service at a time when the nation was in economic turmoil and the regulatory apparatus of the federal government was embryonic; they left, in many cases, having seen the economy rebound and the administrative apparatus of the New Deal made a permanent fixture of American government. While historians may believe that the correlation between economic recovery and the growth of federal administrative regulation was fortuitous, the participants did not believe that. They believed that when they entered public service numerous Americans were starving, without jobs, and without hope, and when they left many of those persons were better off. They could leave public service with the conviction that they had "made a difference"; that their presence had made the United States a "better place."

This attitude can fruitfully be contrasted with the passivity and cynicism cultural relativism engenders. Whether or not one's reasoning is circular or self-deceptive, there is something to be said for believing that taking action to improve the conditions of human life may actually result in those conditions being improved, not simply being shifted to another point on the graph of marginal utility. While one may be tempted to view the organizers of the American "old boy" networks as parochial and self-preoccupied, and the participants in those networks as either smug and elitist or trapped in their own biases, there is a sense in which the enthusiasm and esprit de corps of the 1930s graduates contrasts favorably with the silent careerism and materialism of their current counterparts. For all its difficulties, the "old boy" networks of the New Deal produced a generation of persons who could look back on their experience in public service with genuine enthusiasm and pleasure; who could feel that they had done something to help others and to help America become a more enlightened society. Will current graduates, fifty years from now, be able to look back at their careers with comparable sanguinity?

NOTES

1. The term "elite lawyers," for the purposes of this essay, refers to a graduate of one of the law schools perceived to be at the top of the status hierarchy of legal education, and thus to afford to its graduates a wide range of professional opportunities. Between 1900 and 1940 the number of such schools was comparatively small: Harvard, Columbia, and Yale. *See* R. STEVENS, LAW SCHOOL 73–91, 131–54 (1983). After 1940 the term encompasses graduates of several additional schools.

2. "New Deal generation" refers to lawyers who graduated from law school between the mid 1920s and the Second World War. These individuals encountered the political and cultural transformations of the 1930s, represented in the shorthand term "New Deal," somewhere in their early professional lives. For a more precise definition of the term, *see* "Revisiting the New Deal Generation," *supra*, at 132–33.

3. "Network" may well have a precise meaning in social science literature, *see, e.g.*, D. DANELSKI, A SUPREME COURT JUSTICE IS APPOINTED (1964). Here the term is used, preliminarily, to signify the existence of an informal cluster of persons united by a common desire to identify "eligible" graduates of elite law schools as candidates for jobs in the public sector, and to secure positions for such graduates. Subsequent refinements on this definition are developed in the article as a whole.

4. The graduates had one other characteristic in common: they were all white males. Masculine pronouns are used in this article to reflect the gender dimensions of that characteristic.

5. Frankfurter's involvement with the "networking" process did not stop on his being appointed to the Court, but his activity after 1939 is beyond the scope of this essay. *See infra*, note 98.

6. *See, e.g.*, FROM THE DIARIES OF FELIX FRANKFURTER 35–36, 52–54 (J. Lash ed. 1974); L. BAKER, FELIX FRANKFURTER 153–55 (1969).

7. Peek, *In and Out: The Experiences of the First AAA Administrator*, 208 THE SATURDAY EVENING POST 7 (May 16, 1936).

8. E. JANEWAY, STRUGGLE FOR SURVIVAL 140–41 (1951).

9. Frankfurter, *The Young Men Go to Washington*, 13 FORTUNE 61 (January 1936), *reprinted* in LAW AND POLITICS: OCCASIONAL PAPERS OF FELIX FRANKFURTER 1913–1938 238 (A. MacLeish & E. Prichard eds. 1939).

10. *Felix Frankfurter*, 13 FORTUNE 83, 90 (January 1936).

11. Throughout this essay I have significantly relied on M. PARRISH, FELIX FRANKFURTER AND HIS TIMES: THE REFORM YEARS (1982) and H. HIRSCH, THE ENIGMA OF FELIX FRANKFURTER (1981) for biographical information about Frankfurter. While I differ from Professors Parrish and Hirsch on some matters of interpretation, as will be evident, my debt to them is considerable, as is the debt of anyone seeking to assess Frankfurter's early career. Two other important secondary sources for Frankfurter's early life are Sanford Levinson's note, *The Democratic Faith of Felix Frankfurter*, 25 STAN. L. REV. 430 (1973), and Lash, *supra* note 6. Relevant and accessible primary sources include ROOSEVELT AND FRANKFURTER, THEIR CORRESPONDENCE 1928–1945 (M. Freedman ed. 1967); OF LAW AND MAN (P. Elman ed. 1956); FELIX FRANKFURTER REMINISCES (H. Phillips ed. 1962); and OF LAW AND LIFE AND OTHER THINGS THAT MATTER (P. Kurland ed. 1965). My observations on Frankfurter's early career in G. WHITE, THE AMERICAN JUDICIAL TRADITION 325–27 (2d ed. 1988) identify some themes pursued in greater detail in this essay.

12. *See* PARRISH, *supra* note 11, at 27–149; HIRSCH, *supra* note 11, at 22–64.

13. On Brandeis' career *see* M. UROFSKY, A MIND OF ONE PIECE (1971); A. GAL, BRANDEIS OF BOSTON (1980); P. STRUM, LOUIS D. BRANDEIS (1984); L. PAPER, BRANDEIS: AN INTIMATE BIOGRAPHY (1985).

14. The term "Jewish background" is used advisedly: this essay does not explore the question of whether a person's Jewish "heritage" is primarily religious, cultural, or ethnic in character. In the period under discussion in the article "Jews" tended to be perceived by most elite gentiles as an ethnic or even a racial group, and I have sometimes employed the terms "ethnicity" to reflect that perception. But the use of that term should not be taken to signify any view on the "essence" of "Jewishness," a question I regard as unanswerable and perhaps irrelevant.

15. A classic study of ethnic assimilationism is J. HIGHAM, STRANGERS IN THE LAND (1955). *See also* J. AUERBACH, UNEQUAL JUSTICE 125–27, 184–88 (1976), for a discussion of anti-Semitism among elite gentile lawyers in the early twentieth century.

16. *See* AUERBACH, *supra* note 15, and sources therein cited.

17. *See* HIGHAM *supra* note 15, at 26–28; M. RISCHIN, THE PROMISED CITY: NEW YORK'S JEWS, 1970–1914 19–20 (1962).

18. The demarcation is made in RISCHIN, *supra* note 17, at 95–111; D. HOLLINGER, MORRIS R. COHEN AND THE SCIENTIFIC IDEAL 17–19 (1975); and PARRISH, *supra* note 11, at 11–16. New York's Jewish community also included Sephardic Jews, originally from Spain, of which Justice Benjamin Cardozo was one: cultural assimilation was a less dominant theme in Sephardic families. *See* Kaufman, *Benjamin Nathan Cardozo*, in MR. JUSTICE 251–52 (A. Durham & P. Kurland eds. 1964); WHITE, AMERICAN JUDICIAL TRADITION *supra* note 11, at 254–56.

19. Hebrew Standard, *quoted in* PARRISH, *supra* note 11, at 15.

20. *See* PARRISH, *supra* note 11, at 14–19.

21. On Lippmann's relationship to the early twentieth-century New York Jewish community, and on his reaction to anti-Semitism, *see* R. STEEL, WALTER LIPPMANN AND THE AMERICAN CENTURY 6–11, 186–96 (1980).

22. On Cohen, *see* HOLLINGER, *supra* note 18.

23. Frankfurter, Oral History Transcript (May & November 1953, Felix Frankfurter Papers, Manuscripts Division, Library of Congress), *quoted in* PARRISH, *supra* note 11, at 16.

24. PARRISH, *supra* note 11, at 16.

25. Frankfurter, *supra* note 23; PARRISH *supra* note 11, at 16.

26. HIGHAM, *supra* note 15, at 254–63; AUERBACH, *supra* note 15, at 122–29.

27. PARRISH, *supra* note 11, at 16; HIRSCH, *supra* note 11, at 19.

28. Frankfurter in Phillips, *supra* note 11, at 18–19.

29. On the connection between Gray and Holmes, *see* HIRSCH, *supra* note 11, at 21. On the transition at Harvard from Langdell's deanship to that of Ames, *see* Stevens, *supra* note 1, at 59–61; A. SUTHERLAND, THE LAW AT HARVARD 204–14 (1967). The Sutherland volume, a semi-"official" history of Harvard, should be supplemented, for the period when Frankfurter was a student, by C. WARREN, HISTORY OF THE HARVARD LAW SCHOOL (1908) and the remarkable CENTENNIAL HISTORY OF THE HARVARD LAW SCHOOL (1918), a collectively (and anonymously) authored volume that remains the best "internal" history of an American law school yet written.

30. SUTHERLAND *supra* note 29, at 215, 223.

31. H. HAWKINS, BETWEEN HARVARD AND AMERICA 133–35, 180–90 (1972); S. LIPSET AND D. RIESMAN, EDUCATION AND POLITICS AT HARVARD 99–102 (1975).

32. W. James, *The True Harvard,* 12 HARVARD GRADUATES' MAGAZINE 5, 6 (1903), *quoted in* LIPSET, *supra* note 31, at 118.

33. PARRISH, *supra* note 11, at 17.

34. Frankfurter in Phillips, *supra* note 11, at 24.

35. *Id.* at 26–27.

36. *Id.*

37. Frankfurter to Roscoe Pound (August 28, 1921, Roscoe Pound Papers, Harvard Law School), *quoted in* PARRISH, *supra* note 11, at 156.

38. In a 1930 letter to Learned Hand Frankfurter said that while he knew "the dangers of giving the past a golden hue," he felt "smugly safeguarded against that danger." Frankfurter to Hand (January 16, 1930, Learned Hand Papers, Harvard Law School), *quoted in* PARRISH, *supra* note 11, at 153.

39. *See generally* David Riesman's insightful essay, *Educational Reform at Harvard College: Meritocracy and Its Adversaries,* in LIPSET, *supra* note 31. A distinction between "aristocratic" and "democratic" meritocracy is made by Riesman at 287–89.

40. Phillips, *supra* note 34, at 26.

41. D. LEVINSON, THE SEASONS OF A MAN'S LIFE 97–101 (1978) discusses the psychological ramifications of sponsorship.

42. In remembering his student years, Frankfurter said of Ames that "[y]ou would sort of walk off on clouds as a result of a talk with [him]." Frankfurter in Phillips, *supra* note 11, at 20.

43. PARRISH, *supra* note 11, at 20.

44. 7 HARV. L. REV. 129 (1893).

45. *See* Freedman, *supra* note 11, at 10–11.

46. Frankfurter in Phillips, *supra*, note 11, at 35–36.

47. *Id.* at 36.

48. *Id.*

49. *Id.*

50. *Id.* at 37.

51. *Id.* at 38.

52. From $1000 to $750 a year. *See* PARRISH, *supra* note 11, at 39.

53. Frankfurter in Phillips, *supra* note 11, at 39.

54. As suggested by HIRSCH, *supra* note 11, at 24.

55. PARRISH, *supra* note 11, at 20–22.

56. "Liberal" was the term Frankfurter tended to use to characterize his political stance in his early years in Washington and at Cambridge, although he equated it with "progressive." An example is a memorandum Frankfurter wrote for Herbert Croly when the latter was founding *The New Republic*. In it Frankfurter identified *The New Republic*'s purpose as "to give a . . . vigorous, consistent, comprehensive, and enlightened expression to the Progressive principle," and "to embody a single-minded, whole-hearted and well-balanced liberalism." Frankfurter, Memorandum to Herbert Croly (undated, 1913 or 1914, Frankfurter Papers, Library of Congress), *quoted in* PARRISH, *supra* note 11, at 66–67.

57. On The House of Truth, *see id.* at 51–52; O'Connell & Dart, *The House of Truth: Home of the Young Frankfurter and Lippmann,* 35 CATHOLIC U. L. REV. 70 (1985). Denison had gone on to be Secretary of the Interior for the Philippines in the War Department under Taft. *See* PARRISH, *supra* note 11, at 45–46.

58. Frankfurter in Phillips, *supra* note 11, at 106–07.

59. *Id.* at 106.

60. *Id.* at 114.

61. PARRISH, *supra* note 11, at 108. Eleanor Roosevelt wrote her mother, after meeting Frankfurter on one occasion, that he was "[a]n interesting little man but very jew." Eleanor Roosevelt to Sara Delano Roosevelt (May 12, 1918, Eleanor Roosevelt Papers, Hyde Park, N.Y.), *quoted in* PARRISH, *supra* note 11, at 108.

62. Frankfurter to Learned Hand (January 21, 1919, Learned Hand Papers, Harvard Law School), *quoted in* PARRISH, *supra* note 11, at 117.

63. Frankfurter to Herbert Croly (undated, 1918 or 1919, Frankfurter Papers, Library of Congress), *quoted in* HIRSCH, *supra* note 11, at 67.

64. Frankfurter to Henry L. Stimson (June 26, 1913, Frankfurter Papers, Library of Congress), *quoted in* HIRSCH, *supra* note 11, at 38.

65. Frankfurter to Stimson (July 7, 1913, Frankfurter Papers, Library of Congress), *quoted in* HIRSCH, *supra* note 11, at 39. (Italics in original.)

66. Frankfurter to Oliver Wendell Holmes (September 6, 1913, Oliver Wendell Holmes Papers, Harvard Law School), *quoted in* HIRSCH, *supra* note 11, at 41.

67. 243 U.S. 426 (1917). Frankfurter represented the National Consumers' League, as had Brandeis in the earlier case of Muller v. Oregon, 208 U.S. 412 (1908).

68. On Frankfurter and Zionism, *see* PARRISH, *supra* note 11, at 129–49.

69. Frankfurter, *Why I Shall Vote for La Follette,* NEW REPUBLIC, October 22, 1924, *reprinted in* MacLeish and Pritchard, *supra* note 9, at 314.

70. *See* HIRSCH, *supra* note 11, at 90–94; PARRISH, *supra* note 11, at 176–96.

71. *See* B. MURPHY, THE BRANDEIS-FRANKFURTER CONNECTION (1982); HIRSCH, *supra* note 11, at 85; PARRISH, *supra* note 11, at 162.

72. Frankfurter in Phillips, *supra* note 11, at 218.

73. HIRSCH, *supra* note 11, at 61–64.

74. For the details *see* PARRISH, *supra* note 11, at 155–59; HIRSCH, *supra* note 11, at 67–69.

75. Frankfurter to Roscoe Pound (May 3, 1917), Roscoe Pound Papers, Harvard Law School), *quoted in* PARRISH, *supra* note 11, at 108.

76. PARRISH, *supra* note 11, at 108.

77. *See* Frankfurter in Phillips, *supra* note 11, at 190–91.

78. *Id.*

79. One success was James M. Landis, who had done an S.J.D. thesis under Frankfurter in the 1924–25 academic year and who was appointed an assistant professor in the fall of 1926. *See* HIRSCH, *supra* note 11, at 96–97. One failure was Nathan Margold, who was appointed to an assistant professorship in 1928, only to have President Lowell intervene to block his appointment, and to have Dean Roscoe Pound eventually back Lowell. *See* PARRISH, *supra* note 11, at 157–58.

80. *See generally* D. WECTER, THE AGE OF THE GREAT DEPRESSION (1948); W. LEUCHTENBERG, FRANKLIN D. ROOSEVELT AND THE NEW DEAL (1963).

81. *Quoted in* LEUCHTENBERG, *supra* note 80, at 184.

82. Isaiah Berlin, who met Frankfurter in Oxford in 1933, made this observation about him. *Quoted in* FELIX FRANKFURTER: A TRIBUTE 30 (W. Mendelson ed. 1964).

83. *Fortune* magazine claimed in 1936 that it had known about Frankfurter's activity for some time:

[I]f his relation to the annual recruiting for . . . New York [law] offices was close, his relation to the rarer recruiting for the public services was even closer. . . . Harvard Law School infiltration in Washington, begun under Taft, reached a high point during the [First World] War, when the demand for good young lawyers was enormous . . . and rose to a record peak with the legal demand created by the New Deal. And Harvard Law School, from the Washington point of view, meant *out of* Harvard Law School *by* Felix Frankfurter.

FORTUNE, *supra* note 10, at 90. (Italics in original.)

84. *See* HIRSCH, *supra* note 11, at 85–86; PARRISH, *supra* note 11, at 160–62.

85. Parrish has argued that Frankfurter's protégés "did not form a monolithic, ideologically coherent block of sentiment within the New Deal. . . . One might distinguish them by the cut of their clothes . . . but not by their devotion to one political creed." The argument is clearly correct in cautioning against too uniform a definition of 1930s "liberalism," but at the same time none of Frankfurter's protégés was an opponent of the New Deal or, for that matter, an opponent of early twentieth-century reformist political theory.

86. Corcoran had first served in the Hoover administration at the Reconstruction Finance Corporation. In 1933, he joined the Treasury Department under Roosevelt, was pressured out by Henry Morgenthau, and returned to the RFC. *See* PARRISH, *supra* note 11, at 225.

87. Joseph Rauh, *quoted in* K. LOUCHHEIM, THE MAKING OF THE NEW DEAL: THE INSIDERS SPEAK 56 (1983).

88. Rauh in *id.* at 63.

89. Robert Stern in *id.* at 149.

90. Thomas Emerson in *id.* at 206.

91. Alger Hiss in *id.* at 237.

92. Telford Taylor in *id. at 241.*

93. Frankfurter to Franklin D. Roosevelt (July 10, 1933) in Freedman, *supra* note 11, at 139.

94. *See* Homer Cummings to Felix Frankfurter (July 19, 1933) in *id.* at 144.

95. *See* Abe Fortas in LOUCHHEIM, *supra* note 87, at 220. Douglas himself was not only a prototype of the 1930s law professor turned public servant; he was, at the time he recruited Fortas, an admirer of Frankfurter's efforts to build bridges between the academic community and the New Deal. On hearing that Frankfurter had been appointed to the Supreme Judicial Court of Massachusetts in 1932 (an appointment Frankfurter declined), Douglas wrote Frankfurter that he "realize[d] the great loss that would entail for . . . the veritable host of young men whom you inspire and stimulate in your incomparable fash-

ion,'' but that ''the call to public service is strong and insistent.'' William O. Douglas to Felix Frankfurter (June 24, 1932, William O. Douglas Papers). Eighteen months later Douglas, now at the SEC, wrote Frankfurter, in residence at Oxford, that:

> I would have been happier if I could have been in constant touch with you during the last few months. I could have been sure that there were no blind spots in my reasoning and no naivete in my assumptions. And however the battle lines are drawn in the future you may be assured that I am ever at your call to serve the cause of the public interest.

William O. Douglas to Felix Frankfurter (December 8, 1933, William O. Douglas Papers). The collection of the William O. Douglas Papers in which the above letters appear is currently in the possession of Professor Melvin I. Urofsky of the Department of History at Virginia Commonwealth University. My thanks to Professor Urofsky for permission to use excerpts from the letters.

96. Gerhard Gesell in LOUCHHEIM, *supra* note 87, at 137.

97. Frank Watson in *id.* at 107.

98. When several New Deal lawyers returned to Washington during the Second World War, there was Justice Frankfurter, now on the Supreme Court of the United States. In the 1940s a version of The House of Truth sprang up. Prichard, Graham, and Adrian Fisher, all Frankfurter protégés, rented ''Hockley,'' a large house in Arlington, Va., along with several other ''bright young bachelors,'' MURPHY, *supra* note 71, at 225. ''Hockley'' parties became a 1940s version of The House of Truth's soirees, with many prominent Washington figures, including Frankfurter, attending. *See* O'Connell, *supra* note 57, at 93–95; MURPHY, *supra* note 71, at 225–26.

99. Milton Katz in LOUCHHEIM, *supra* note 87, at 129.

100. Frankfurter in Phillips, *supra* note 11, at 26–27.

101. The generalizations in the last two paragraphs are documented in G. WHITE, TORT LAW IN AMERICA: AN INTELLECTUAL HISTORY 20–113 (1985 ed.).

102. *See* Llewellyn, *Some Realism About Realism,* 44 HARV. L. REV. 1222, 1226 (1931).

103. *Cf.* D. HALBERSTAM, THE BEST AND THE BRIGHTEST (1969).

104. David Morse in LOUCHHEIM, *supra* note 87, at 88.

Recapturing New Deal Lawyers*

The title of this essay speaks of "recapturing" rather than "revisiting" or "reassessing" the professional and cultural experience of lawyers in public service in the 1930s. The choice of metaphor in the term "recapture" is intended to be taken seriously. It suggests the investment many current commentators on the New Deal generation of lawyers have in the subjects of their commentary. It also highlights the deep ambivalence in current New Deal historiography, an ambivalence that this essay seeks to explain. Current commentary on the New Deal is both nostalgic, emphasizing a purported contrast between the altruistic idealism of the New Deal and the cynical materialism of the 1980s, and futuristic, seeking to extract from the experience of the New Dealers political and epistemological messages that will continue to resonate in the years ahead. This essay suggests that the current meaning of the New Deal, and the experiences of a generation of lawyers who entered public service as the New Deal came into being, can best be discerned by probing this impulse to recapture.

The current meaning of the New Deal has not only been rendered in an ambivalent fashion, however; it has also been masked and diluted by the persistence of two strains in New Deal scholarship. These strains may be designated the "survivor" strain and the "legacist" strain. While significantly different in their approaches, these strains share a tendency to prevent appreciation of the importance of the New Deal as an episode in cultural history. In brief, the survivor strain of commentary is characterized by a celebratory mode of analysis in which the New Deal is rendered as a uniquely exhilarating experience for its participants, and, at the same time, by the absence of speculation as to what cultural or ideological factors produced that sense of exhilaration. The survivor strain is nostalgic and retrospective in its tone, emphasizing the distinctive atmosphere of the New Deal and, implicitly, the contrast between that atmosphere and the atmosphere of the present day. The legacist strain of commentary, by contrast, emphasizes continuity between the New Deal and successive "reform" movements in twentieth-century America, with reform being equated with "liberalism," and liberalism being projected backward in time from a post-World War II egalitarian perspective.

Neither strain of commentary is interested in probing the sources of the New

*102 Harv. L. Rev. 489 (1988).

Deal's uniqueness as a cultural episode. In place of such probing, the survivor strain offers vivid personal recollections of participants in an experience the novelty and importance of which is taken for granted, but never explained. The legacist strain does not see the New Deal as unique, but rather as one of many episodes in a linear progression of American liberalism stretching from the 1930s through the "Great Society" reforms of the 1960s and perhaps beyond. Any sense of uniqueness about the New Deal is obliterated in the legacist strain by folding the New Deal years into a tradition of twentieth-century reform.

The result is that recapturing the world of significant actors in the New Deal, many of whom were lawyers, has too commonly been an exercise in survivors' nostalgia or in the facile creation of a linear history of twentieth-century American liberalism. A central dimension of the cultural experience of New Deal lawyers has been obscured in the process. The experience of New Dealers was significantly affected by the availability to them, on entering public service, of a new epistemological orthodoxy—modernism [1]—to explain and to justify their new professional roles, and by the apparently overwhelming vindication of modernist epistemological assumptions by the political and economic "success" of New Deal policies. Ultimately the confirmation of modernism as an orthodoxy in the generation in which New Deal lawyers came to positions of professional prominence can furnish an explanation not only for the special quality commentators attributed to the experiences of those lawyers, but also for the ambivalence present in current commentary on the New Deal.

Recapturing the world of New Deal lawyers, in short, can be seen as an exercise in confronting changes in epistemology over time. This essay begins with an evaluation of the two current strains of commentary that seek to recapture the lives of New Deal lawyers, but fail to illuminate the cultural context of those lives. It then progresses to a further exploration of that context, and to an extrapolation of the novel epistemological underpinnings of elite ideology in the 1930s. It concludes with a reflection upon the extent to which we may now be witnessing the passing of the modernist epistemology of the New Deal from a status of intellectual orthodoxy to one of potential obsolescence.

Joseph Lash's *Dealers and Dreamers: A New Look at the New Deal* (1988), and Bruce Alan Murphy's *Fortas: The Rise and Ruin of a Supreme Court Justice* (1988), books that are reviewed in this essay, both represent unwitting examples of the two predominant strains in current New Deal commentary. Lash's history of the New Deal, while openly celebratory in its tone, was intended to be more than an idiosyncratic memoir; unfortunately, Lash's death while the book was being completed, and the subsequent decision to publish his unfinished manuscript, resulted in *Dealers and Dreamers* being an ironic example of "survivor" literature. Murphy's central purpose in *Fortas* was to provide details of the behind-the-scenes events that led to the defeat of Abe Fortas's nomination as Chief Justice in 1968 and Fortas's subsequent resignation from the Court; Fortas's connection with the New Deal occupies only a small portion of Murphy's narrative. Nonetheless, the explanation Murphy advances for both the "rise" and the "ruin" of Fortas's career is one that emphasizes Fortas's role as a "child of the New Deal" and the connections between the New Deal generation of lawyers and successive generations. As representative of the two dominant strains of New Deal commentary, Lash's and Murphy's works invite reflections on the role of those strains in perpetuating current images of the New Deal.

I Current Commentary on New Deal Lawyers: Predominant Strains

The Survivor Strain: Lash's Dealers and Dreamers

In his preface to *Dealers and Dreamers,* Lash announces that he wrote the book from the perspective of a "member of the Left [i]n the thirties" who believed with Benjamin Cohen, one of his principal subjects, that "'our New Deal years were the best years of our lives'" (Lash p. 8.).[2] Lash's purpose in *Dealers and Dreamers* is to describe the spirit and enthusiasm of the generation of Americans who, having graduated from colleges and professional schools in the twenties and early thirties, went to Washington to "roll up their sleeves and make America great."[3] Lash seeks not only to convey the uplifting experience that he and his contemporaries encountered in the 1930s, but also that life since the New Deal pales significantly in comparison.[4]

Lash's perspective on the New Deal in *Dealers and Dreamers* is that of one who participated in the culture he describes, and who recollects the New Deal in a celebratory mode, with no particular pretense of detachment, little effort at completeness, and a strong implicit sense of nostalgia for a more uplifting era. His account is that of a "survivor." The appearance in the 1980s of survivor accounts of the New Deal marks a new stage in New Deal historiography.[5]

A recent book, *The Making of the New Deal: The Insiders Speak,*[6] provides another example of the survivor strain. Edited by Katie Louchheim, Vice-Chairman of the Democratic National Committee during the Roosevelt administration, *The Making of the New Deal* came into being when Louchheim realized that there might be "no link between [contemporary] generation[s] and those eventful years" in which "the triumphant recovery known as the New Deal" came into being.[7] Louchheim recorded the comments of forty-nine New Dealers, ranging from Alger Hiss to Lady Bird Johnson, and collected memories of the atmosphere in which the New Deal came into being, as described by many of those survivors.

A representative comment was that of Milton Katz, who had been in the New Deal with the Securities and Exchange Commission and the Justice Department.[8] Katz first came to Washington in 1932 to work for the legal division of the Reconstruction Finance Corporation, which had been established by the Hoover administration to respond to the growing number of bank failures during the early 1930s.[9] He described his initial impression:

> Then came the great crisis, the closing of all the banks and the arrival of Mr. Roosevelt as President. I can only describe the change as physical, virtually physical. The air suddenly changed, the wind blew through the corridors, a lot of old air blew out the windows. You suddenly felt, "By God, the air is fresh, it's moving, life is resuming . . ." I had lived in a world in which, for practical purposes, there appeared to be no government, in which there was an almost

demoralized people who had the feeling that there was no one to whom they could turn. . . .

To me and my age group, FDR represented life, excitement, movement, growth, creation, high endeavor. This was supplemented by an intense esprit-de-corps. [10]

In this passage can be found many of the themes of the survivor mode. There is the sense of a unique, transformative cultural experience ("The air suddenly changed . . . a lot of old air blew out the windows."). There is the heady recollection of having lived in a time in which America rejuvenated itself (a "demoralized people who had the feeling that there was no one to whom they could turn" were being given new hope). Above all, there is the feeling of being a specially favored generation, one with an "intense esprit-de-corps," one that had experienced "life, excitement, movement, growth, creation," and, because they had helped a demoralized people, one with "high endeavor."

It is that generation to which Lash seeks to pay homage in *Dealers and Dreamers*. His original plan was to recreate the world of the New Deal through a joint biography of two of its central figures, Benjamin Cohen and Thomas Corcoran. The plan to focus on Cohen and Corcoran made sense: although Corcoran and Cohen were the focus of an outpouring of popular literature in the 1930s and 1940s,[11] they have received little scholarly attention in recent years.[12] Lash knew both Cohen and Corcoran well, had privileged access to Corcoran's papers, which have been deposited in the Library of Congress but whose use is restricted, and had similar access to Cohen's papers. Lash's great success in writing histories about his other acquaintances in the thirties—most notably Eleanor Roosevelt[13] and Felix Frankfurter[14]—augured an account that would present a far more rounded and interesting picture of Cohen, Corcoran, and their relationship to the New Deal than had previously appeared.[15]

But no such portrait appears in *Dealers and Dreamers*. After some promising early explorations into the lives of his two principal subjects,[16] Lash seems to give up any effort at achieving the kind of integrated portrait of individuals and their culture he had accomplished in his earlier works. About two-thirds of the way through the book, he appears to lose interest in Cohen and Corcoran altogether, discussing instead the coming of World War II and the role of labor, blacks, and Communists in the New Deal. By the closing chapters, Corcoran's departure from public service and Cohen's temporary affiliation with the wartime Office of Economic Stabilization are simply mentioned in passing, as if the reader should regard them as unimportant.

The lack of thematic consistency in *Dealers and Dreamers* is less troublesome, however, than the lack of adequate documentation. When coupled with obvious errors and omissions, Lash's erratic documentation eventually results in the collapse of the book as a scholarly history of the New Deal.

In a chapter entitled "The Brains Trust," for example, Lash seeks to explain Felix Frankfurter's role as an advisor to Franklin Roosevelt by fusing observations about Frankfurter's personality with descriptions of the social and ideological context in which Frankfurter and other advisors functioned. Early in the chapter he introduced Columbia law professor Raymond Moley, "the chief member of [Roosevelt's] original Brains Trust" and seeks to compare and contrast Moley's advisory role with that of Frankfurter. Lash details the consternation among Moley and his allies on hearing, shortly after Roosevelt's reelection as Governor of New York, that Frankfurter had visited Roosevelt. "None of them liked it," Lash suggests. Each in later writings was to "place [his] resistance to Frankfurter's influence on the grounds of principle." It becomes apparent that Lash's purpose in the passage is to sketch the rivalry between Moley and Frankfurter as part of a more general argument that "[t]wo schools of progressive thought," one far more committed to a planned economy than the other, "competed for Roosevelt's soul" during the New Deal. But his effort to employ the relationship between Moley and Frankfurter in this fashion is marred by a distractingly inept use of his sources.

At one point, Lash asserts that

> Moley . . . was unhappy over Frankfurter's influence with Roosevelt, and Frankfurter in a letter to Brandeis in 1934 indicated that his cultivation of Moley was "another case of working with the tools we have." But whatever the reservations on each side, the two worked together, a collaboration that was pursued the more aggressively by Frankfurter. That was his nature.

A footnote appears at the end of this passage, making reference to two books by Moley; the Frankfurter letter to Brandeis is not cited. Lash then continues in this vein throughout the rest of the chapter, quoting sources that are not footnoted, listing references that on their face are not germane to his comments in the text, and, in general, thoroughly baffling a reader seeking to evaluate the plausibility of his claims. By the end of the chapter, Lash's approach has reduced his narrative to a version of oral history, seriously damaging *Dealers and Dreamers* as a contribution to current scholarly understanding of the New Deal.

The damage becomes apparent in one of the chapter's concluding passages:

> Occasionally Frankfurter wondered, and it was a sign of how strongly the Great Depression was beating away at settled intellectual convictions, whether Edmund Wilson who was then getting ready to vote for the Communist presidential candidate . . . might be getting "at the root of things—more trenchantly and fearlessly" than he did. Nevertheless [Frankfurter] did not "embrace, and indeed distrusted, a full-blown, 'rational' countersystem."
>
> . . .
>
> It is important to take cognizance of this basic Frankfurter affirmation. Not only did his proteges, deputies, foster sons, call them what you will, [Thomas] Corcoran, [Ben] Cohen, [James] Landis, [Max] Lowenthal, [David] Lilienthal, [Dean] Acheson, [Charles] Wyzanski, and so on, share his gradualism but it was the rock to which his friendship with Roosevelt was anchored.

A great deal is at stake for Lash in this passage. It contains the skeleton of his general argument in *Dealers and Dreamers* that the New Deal was a battleground between collectivist idealists, represented by such figures as Moley, and pragmatists, such as Frankfurter and his disciples Cohen and Corcoran. According to

Lash, Frankfurter was tempted to embrace far more radical political alternatives in the 1930s, but ultimately abandoned them for a philosophy of "gradualism" in domestic affairs. His disciples shared that gradualism, Lash maintains, and a gradualist political philosophy linked Frankfurter with Roosevelt while helping Frankfurter and his disciples emerge as the leading New Deal advisors and policymakers.

Lash's claim, while not a startling one, justifies his focus on Cohen and Corcoran, the main subjects of the book, to the exclusion of other arguably prominent and influential New Deal lawyers. But the passage with which Lash ends the "Brains Trust" chapter collapses as the source of a plausible argument. It is not surprising to the reader, at this point, that none of the quotations in the passage is footnoted, or that the only apparent candidate for the source of Frankfurter's observations, a 1932 letter to Walter Lippmann, is cited in connection with a different quotation at another place in the chapter. The reader may well have ceased to trust the accuracy of Lash's references altogether, and, if so, he or she may have concluded that Lash's entire argument about the nature of the New Deal—his entire effort to recapture "the 350-odd men and women, the New Dealers, who helped Roosevelt put through the social transformation of the thirties"—is simply an extended reminiscence of his own.

A possible explanation for the incomplete documentation of *Dealers and Dreamers* is that after Lash's death, a decision was made to publish his manuscript in its unfinished state. Lash died on August 22, 1987;[17] he suffered for several years from a variety of illnesses. Lash's sources for *Dealers and Dreamers* indicate that he continued to conduct interviews[18] and make use of letters[19] as late as the end of 1986. Although Lash may have been highly motivated to complete *Dealers and Dreamers,* the research for which he had begun at least as early as 1974,[20] he was still investigating sources for the book about six months before his death. The decision to publish quickly also explains the obvious errors that stand out in many places in the book.[21] Particularly suggestive in this regard is the index to *Dealers and Dreamers,* which, while otherwise thorough, contains no references at all to material in the footnotes, as if Lash's notes were insufficiently complete at the time of indexing to permit references to them.

The unfinished state of *Dealers and Dreamers* thus prevents Lash's last book from approaching the stature of his earlier ones. But the state of his manuscript remains interesting. The work, in its published version, represents an example of the "survivor" strain of New Deal commentary: an effort to recapture, partly as an exercise in nostalgia and partly as a pointed contrast to the atmosphere of the 1980s, the "exhilarating days"[22] of public service in the 1930s. It may be that Lash's motivation in beginning the book was simply to celebrate the memory of his youth at a time when he sensed that those who retained that memory were diminishing in number. But after having resolved to engage in that celebration, Lash, judging from the structure of his manuscript, seemed a little at a loss about how next to proceed. In particular, he seemed to vacillate between a conception of a joint biography of Cohen and Corcoran, tracing the social, professional, and personal significance of their extremely close relationship, and a conception of a more impressionistic kind, capturing the spirit of the New Deal.

The latter conception eventually comes to dominate *Dealers and Dreamers*, but in the incomplete and unsubstantiated fashion previously outlined. This makes the book what it might have been intended to be all along: a survivor's retrospective. Seen in this fashion, it leaves those who seek a more searching examination of the world of New Deal lawyers in a state of frustration. Taken together with *The Making of the New Deal* and other examples of the survivor strain of commentary, *Dealers and Dreamers* conveys an unmistakable sense that there was something special about the experience of the generation of lawyers who entered public service in the 1930s. Just what that is remains elusive, however, despite the eloquent rhetoric of Katz and other interviewees in the Louchheim volume, and despite Lash's own efforts. All the survivor strain seems to be able to offer is the vivid personal recollections of participants in "the social transformation of the thirties." Missing is any effort to reconstruct the meaning of that social transformation.

The Legacist Strain: Murphy's Fortas

"Legacist" commentary on the New Deal resembles "survivor" commentary in emphasizing particular features of the New Deal years that have a resonance for succeeding generations, but failing to probe the uniqueness and time-boundedness of the New Deal as a cultural episode. The legacist strain of commentary differs markedly from the survivor strain, however, in its mode of recapturing the New Deal. Survivor commentators implicitly employ a recapturing mode that emphasizes contrasts between the New Deal and the present; legacist commentators employ a mode that emphasizes continuity.

A recent version of the legacist strain is Bruce Alan Murphy's *Fortas: The Rise and Ruin of a Supreme Court Justice*. As noted, in the legacist strain of commentary the image of the New Deal is that of an episode in the history of American "reform," with the "legacy" of the New Deal emerging as a commitment to civil liberties, affirmative government, equality, and the other goals of mainstream voices in the Democratic party's intellectual constituency in the mid-twentieth century. A passage from a history of the New Deal written in 1967 encapsulates the lagacist perspective:

> The New Deal stopped growing. It did not disappear. A subsidized, regulated welfare capitalism still stands, thirty years later, as the core of American domestic policy. The United States has neither moved beyond it nor searched for valid alternatives. . . . The changes of the thirties were not only numerous but prophetic, setting the themes for subsequent political disclosure.[23]

Murphy's *Fortas* appears over twenty years after the work just quoted, but Murphy's vision, although informed by the passage of time, is legacist nonetheless. That is apparent in Murphy's explanation of why he wrote the book:

> As I examined what little literature existed on the topic [of extrajudicial activities of Supreme Court Justices] I was puzzled by the constant comparisons of the

revered Louis D. Brandeis and Felix Frankfurter, who represented for many the "paragons of judicial virtue," with the sometimes brutally criticized Abe Fortas, who represented for these same people a judge who had become tainted by his involvement in politics. These comparisons puzzled me greatly because I was also finding hints in that same literature that Brandeis and Frankfurter might well have been heavily involved in private politicking while serving on the Supreme Court. . . . So I was left with two unresolved questions: Were Brandeis and Frankfurter really all that different from Abe Fortas in their off-the-bench activities? And did Fortas get a raw deal in 1968?

In Murphy's view the extrajudicial activities of Brandeis, Frankfurter, and Fortas were linked. Brandeis had served on the Court during the first years of the New Deal. Frankfurter was named to the Court by Roosevelt in 1939, and Fortas was appointed as an Associate Justice in 1965 and nominated as Chief Justice in 1968 by Lyndon Johnson. The activities of all three Justices were premised on an attitude that extrajudicial involvement with politics was appropriate, but should be covert. Fortas's attitude was the legacy of Brandeis and Frankfurter's attitude. Murphy does not, however, explain the source of the shared attitude, nor why the similarity of their attitudes should constitute a defense of Fortas as opposed to an indictment of all three Justices. Exploration of those questions reveals the conception of New Deal culture and of its legal actors that informs Murphy's book.

Fifteen pages into the book, Fortas, at the age of twenty-three, has graduated from Yale Law School and entered the New Deal in the Legal Division of the Agricultural Adjustment Administration. Murphy seeks to convey the symbolic meaning of Fortas's first job:

> It was an exciting time to be in Washington. In the first hundred days of his new presidency in 1933, Franklin Delano Roosevelt had infused in the best young men and women a crusading spirit, as they joined the pilgrimage to Washington and fought to end the Depression. In better times these people would have been working in the nation's industries, law firms, universities, and elsewhere. Now they had answered the call from their president to help the nation. It was as if these young people believed that through hard work and ingenuity they could rewrite the rules, remake the social order, and bring about a recovery.

Here again is the sense of excitement, of a unique opportunity, of a new generation coming into prominence that is also characteristic of survivor accounts. But Murphy has added something to the portrait of New Dealers such as Fortas: the idea that they believed they could "rewrite the rules" and "remake the social order" through "ingenuity."

In the next sixty-five pages of *Fortas,* Murphy attempts to use his subject's early career as a New Dealer to illustrate this characterization. Fortas drafted documents regulating prices and production schedules in the canned peach industry, defended AAA codes in federal district court,[24] worked with William O. Douglas in an SEC study of the fraudulent use of "protective committees" by failed businesses,[25] supervised the breakup of holding companies for the SEC under the Public Utility Holding Company Act of 1935, and, at the age of thirty, was named

Director of the newly created Division of Power in the Department of the Interior, charged with regulating federal hydroelectric power. By 1942, at the age of thirty-one, Fortas had become Under Secretary of the Interior Department.[26]

Murphy ascribes Fortas's rapid rise to his perfection of the management techniques of his generation of New Dealers, techniques that harmonized with Fortas's own temperament. Fortas "developed a certain confidence that came with bending and breaking the old rules and writing new rules to govern society." He had an "ability to skirt the minefields of the governmental bureaucracy." He functioned as "the 'technician,' designing the solutions regardless of the ends being sought." The chief beneficiary of Fortas's techniques appeared to be himself: Murphy claims that Fortas's later years in the New Deal had been marked by "raw ambition," demonstrated by his willingness "to sacrifice [the careers of others] for his own."

According to Murphy, by the time Fortas founded the law firm of Arnold, Fortas, and Porter in the years after World War II, his role as a lawyer had been shaped by his New Deal service. He was a member of the latter of "two camps of alumni from the Roosevelt era in 1946: those who labored further for a New Deal for the nation, and those who wanted a 'new deal' for themselves." After leaving government, Fortas used the techniques of bureaucratic politics that he had developed in the public sector to serve his private clients. "Once more," Murphy suggests, "he was simply the technician, now bending laws that he had once helped to make."

Having linked Fortas closely with the New Deal culture in which he came to professional prominence, and having suggested that Fortas's years in private practice from 1946 until his appointment to the Supreme Court in 1965 can be seen as an extension into the private sector of the roles he had previously played in public service, Murphy then radically shifts his emphasis. He abandons any effort to see Fortas' judicial career in the context of his earlier professional life, focusing instead on a series of behind-the-scenes political maneuvering.

Murphy first details the machinations leading to Fortas's reluctant agreement to be nominated to the Court; followed by those resulting in his nomination as Chief Justice; then, in great detail, those enabling his political opponents to prevent the Senate's confirming that nomination; and, finally, those culminating in his decision to resign from the Court.[27] In a narrative of nearly 600 pages, these events occupy about two-thirds of them; Murphy's focus on these events transforms Fortas from a biography to a study of political intrigue, "just as interesting," in his view, "as Allen Drury's classic *Advise and Consent*," and "made even more so by the fact that it was real and that real people's lives had been changed and even destroyed." This shift in the focus has significant consequences, not only for the general worth of *Fortas* as a scholarly contribution but also for any effort to understand Abe Fortas' resignation from the Court.

From the outset of *Fortas,* it is clear that Murphy's strength as a scholar lies in his ability to extract meaningful information from nearly inaccessible documents. He earlier had demonstrated this strength in *The Brandeis/Frankfurter Connection,*[28] in which he sifted through material in the Library of Congress to reconstruct relationships in which Frankfurter, while on the Harvard Law School faculty, acted as Justice Brandeis' paid agent to promote public issues. Murphy demonstrated considerable ingenuity in piecing the evidence of this arrangement together, even if he was not the first scholar to be aware of it in scattered form.[29] In *Fortas,* Murphy demonstrates that he continues to be a persistent and thorough researcher.[30] He also demonstrates, unfortunately, that his skill at research is not matched by comparable skills as an analyst or stylist.[31]

It may be that Murphy truly found the political maneuvering that took place in connection with Fortas's judicial career to be the stuff of high drama. But the fact is that not much information unearthed by Murphy in his accounts of the successive episodes is new, and its appeal seems confined to those who appreciate close studies of the way professional politicians acquire, trade off, and dispense with power and patronage.[32]

More important, although most of the information revealed by Murphy conveys a good deal about how the political process of nominating and confirming Supreme Court Justices operated during Lyndon Johnson's presidency, it shows precious little about Fortas himself. In short, Murphy's narrative of the "ruin" of Fortas's judicial career emphasizes neither Fortas's temperament, nor the tendencies of his pre-Court career, nor the nature of his extrajudicial conduct. Instead it emphasizes the politics of Fortas's effort to be confirmed as Chief Justice and the immediate aftermath of that effort.

Murphy's labored emphasis on the behind-the-scenes political maneuvering in *Fortas* thus appears designed to do more than simply narrate a "real life" version of an Allen Drury novel. It also advances the thesis that Fortas's resignation from the Court can primarily be explained by the vicissitudes of national politics. It was national politics that forged Fortas's relationship with Lyndon Johnson, that made Johnson a lameduck President and his nominee to be Chief Justice a more vulnerable target in the Senate, and that spawned the key relationships—ranging from Johnson to Richard Russell to Robert Griffin to Everett Dirksen to Richard Nixon to John Mitchell—that affected Fortas's candidacy and precipitated his demise.

In his epilogue, Murphy makes this explanation of Fortas's resignation explicit by conducting what he calls the "political autopsy of Abe Fortas." After dismissing various theories for Fortas's downfall—avarice, hubris, indiscretion, and overconfidence—Murphy advances his own:

> The truth is that the forces that did Abe Fortas in were much greater than any one individual. . . . His fate was beyond his control in 1968 and 1969 because the nation was at what might be called a "triple critical period" in its history. . . .
>   There are periodic shifts in the institutional, political, and generational relationships in Washington. Institutionally, there is always a struggle between the president and Congress for power to set the political agenda . . . politically, there is a seesawing relationship between the conservatives and the liberals, with one side leading and the other following at any given time. . . . And finally, generationally, it is axiomatic that just as all the rest of us are born, grow old, and die, so do politicians. At certain points in our history, certain groups of politicians who have dominated the national scene will grow old together. . . .

When any one of these shifts occurs, there is instability . . . and when two or three of them occur at the same time, there can be chaos.

If one was to name the disease that killed Abe Fortas, then, it would have to be classified as political progeria—a kind of premature aging. . . . Because of the combination of circumstances, vulnerabilities, and bad luck, Fortas aged and died politically before his time (Murphy pp. 594–96 [footnotes omitted]).

Murphy admits in his author's note and acknowledgments to *Fortas* that he developed the above explanation for his subject's demise "perhaps too early one morning, partially in a fit of desperation." His self-assessment may well ring true.

One difficulty with Murphy's "triple critical period" hypothesis for Fortas's demise is that while the ingredients of the hypothesis—political, institutional, and generational change and conflict—are endemic to American political culture, only one Supreme Court Justice has been forced to resign.[33] One could argue that a similar "triple critical period" had occurred in the early 1930s, when the New Deal came into being. One could argue further than Justices McReynolds, Butler, Sutherland, and Van Devanter were identified with a discredited "older generation" far more than was Fortas. One could even argue that those Justices were pressured to resign from the Court, the pressure taking the form of the Court-packing plan. But then one would need to make the same argument with respect to Justice Brandeis, who was even older than the others but who was not identified with the "older generation." In sum, Murphy's hypothesis, on its face, proves far too much.

There is another, perhaps unintended, meaning one can extract from Murphy's "political autopsy" of Fortas. That meaning is suggested by another excerpt from Murphy's epilogue:

While it is true that [Fortas] was involved in advising Lyndon Johnson, the relationship was not unlike those that other justices maintained with other presidents. But Louis Brandeis, Felix Frankfurter, William O. Douglas, Fred Vinson, and Roger Taney were not caught, and Fortas was. . . .

Being a judge requires that one be removed from the political fray, out of the action. This preserves both the independence of the entire institution and the reflective detachment necessary to fulfill the adjudicative role. Fortas never came to this understanding. Rather than changing this manner of action and ethical code once on the court, he continued to follow the same standards that had previously guided his legal career. . . .

All in all, how different would his life have been if this child of the New Deal had not cockily ignored the fact that the rules he had once helped to fashion governed him as well?

The above passage at first seems inherently contradictory. How can Fortas, in failing to "change his manner of action" once named to the Court, be distinguished from Brandeis and Frankfurter, who had likewise failed to change their involvement with politics and political issues, but had simply not "gotten caught"? If he was not "removed from the political fray," neither were they. How can Murphy simultaneously seek to defend Fortas by association with other and to criticize him for "cockily ignor[ing]" rules of judicial conduct? And how did Fortas himself "fashion" such rules?

Murphy reconciles these contradictions through his characterization of Fortas as "this child of the New Deal." The "rules" Fortas "helped to fashion" are not meant to refer to any legislative or administrative standards or regulations, but to implicit rules of conduct that followed from the assumption of Fortas's generation of New Deal lawyers and judges that judging, like other forms of lawmaking, was inescapably political. The canons of impartiality and "reflective detachment" Murphy associates with the "adjudicative role" are canons made necessary by the interaction of a longstanding image of American judges as being "independent" from politics and the belief of the New Deal generation of lawyers that judges were political beings.[34]

This reading of Murphy's "autopsy" helps explain his marked emphasis on Fortas's comment, made to Murphy in a 1981 interview, that he was "dying on the court."[35] Fortas intended "dying" to convey his loss of involvement with the interface between law and politics that had characterized all of his pre-Court career. He was a New Deal lawyer and as such had believed in and practiced pragmatic political activism. In order to avoid dying, he continued that activism on the Court in the form of covert extrajudicial activities.

Murphy, however, supplies an additional meaning to "dying": he means to suggest that Fortas was "killed" along with the rest of his generation of New Deal lawyers when political conditions changed such that that generation's political and institutional primacy was challenged. Fortas "got caught," and Brandeis and Frankfurter did not, because the political culture of the late 1960s overwhelmed him and his fellow New Dealers, including Lyndon Johnson. In the penultimate sentence of *Fortas*, Murphy brings his explanation of Fortas's demise forward into the 1980s: the rejection of Robert Bork's candidacy was another example of a "modern nomination [being] rejected for ideological reasons."

Murphy's explicit identification of Fortas with Brandeis and Frankfurter and his labeling of Fortas as a "child of the New Deal" thus reveal his vision in *Fortas*. It is a legacist vision, with the legacy stretching backward to Brandeis and Frankfurter and forward to Bork. The "legacy" for Murphy is the inextricable connection between Supreme Court Justices and politics that was taken for granted by Fortas and his contemporaries. But Murphy's vision makes his defense of Fortas extremely awkward. If the only difference between Brandeis, Frankfurter, and Fortas was a matter of political timing, what does Murphy mean when he says such things as "[t]he intellect was certainly there [in Fortas], but not the temperament," or when he contrasts Fortas's "manner of action and ethical code" with those "necessary to fulfill the adjudicative role"?

What Murphy means to say, but never says, is that the New Dealers's insight that the professions of lawyer and judge are necessarily involved in the practice of politics led to a corollary: given the intrinsically political nature of judging, judges could not avoid involvement in politics, but it was nonetheless necessary for them to adopt strategies to conceal or to minimize their political behavior.[36] Among those strategies was the creation of canons such as "judicial self-restraint," to which both Brandeis and Frankfurter subscribed. Brandeis', Frankfurter's, and Fortas's covert extrajudicial activities can be seen as another such strategy, premised on a belief that the close relationship between judging and politics they assumed would be threatening if overtly revealed.

And—here Murphy transforms his legacist vision into a normative position— why should we necessarily blame such judges for their surreptitious involvement? In particular, why should we distinguish between the careers of Brandeis, Frankfurter, and Fortas simply because Fortas "got caught" and the others did not?

The above proposition raises a number of difficulties, including whether the extrajudicial activities of Brandeis, Frankfurter, and Fortas can be linked in so summary a fashion.[37] But whether Murphy has succeeded in his defense of Fortas's extrajudicial conduct or not, the question that I am primarily interested in is whether Murphy's implicit claim that Fortas's career can only be understood by seeing him as a "child of the New Deal" and a successor to the legacy of Brandeis and Frankfurter illuminates our understanding of Abe Fortas.

My answer is a mixed one. On the one hand, Murphy's obsession with the relationship between judging and politics, and his own penchant for behind-the-scenes political intrigue, have produced a book that can be seen as lacking in balance, both with respect to thematic coverage and analytical judgment. The reader learns too much about the machinations of national politicians in the debates over Fortas's confirmation as Chief Justice[38] and not enough about Fortas as person[39] or as a Supreme Court Justice.[40] This emphasis is disquieting because the principal reason why Fortas's life continues to be of great interest is that he was a Justice forced to resign because of alleged ethical violations. Yet Murphy, while greatly interested in the process leading to the resignation, does not seem particularly interested in the personal dimensions of Fortas's conduct,[41] or in his work on the Court.[42] Without adequate information about those features of Fortas's life, the reader is virtually forced to accept Murphy's hypothesis that Fortas was a conspicuously talented "child of the New Deal," who had the dual misfortune of being placed on the Supreme Court by Lyndon Johnson and then encountering a "triple critical period" in which New Deal liberalism lost its primacy as a political ideology.

Yet in identifying Fortas as a "child of the New Deal," in emphasizing the parallels between his extrajudicial behavior and that of Brandeis and Frankfurter, and especially in unconsciously using Fortas to demonstrate a conceptual paradox at the heart of New Deal jurisprudence, Murphy may have illuminated Fortas's career. The paradox, of course, is that the New Deal canon of "judicial self-restraint" followed from an assumption that judges were intrinsically political beings. Yet if the canon was responsibly adhered to, the political dimension of judging was suppressed. But what then, did judging consist of?

Brandeis' and Frankfurter's response to that paradox was to continue to pay service (in varying degrees of intensity) to the "self-restraint" canon in their opinions, while covertly engaging in political activity.[43] Fortas's response was to pay less deference to that canon,[44] and to engage intensively in covert political activities.[45] It appears that Fortas's behavior rendered the paradox unintelligible. His extrajudicial activities so blurred the distinction between overt and covert political involvement, indeed between activities that were appropriately "judicial" and appropriately "extrajudicial," as to suggest that efforts to eschew judicial political involvement (the self-restraint canon) and efforts to conceal judicial political involvement were one and the same: politically inspired efforts.

In Fortas's demise, then, may have been the demise of the delicate jurisprudential paradox that had framed the conduct of politically minded judges since the New Deal. Murphy's book thus invites us to see Fortas's unfortunate career on the Court as the career of a "New Deal judge," and to probe further into what that encapsulation means.

II Toward a Cultural History of New Deal Lawyers

The strains of commentary represented by Lash's and Murphy's efforts to recapture the lives and the world of New Deal lawyers thus end up being more revealing of the perspectives of their authors than of the subjects of their commentary. One emerges from the books with little sense of the nature of the cultural experience encountered by Cohen, Corcoran, and Fortas in the 1930s, of why the atmosphere in which they functioned as government lawyers was perceived by their contemporaries as so exhilarating and transformative, or of how their roles as "child[ren] of the New Deal" affected their subsequent professional careers. The challenge the Lash and Murphy books present is that of creating a different mode of analysis by which the experience of New Deal lawyers can be recaptured. The remainder of this essay sketches the form such an analysis might take.

The methodology of the analysis employs techniques derived from cultural anthropology and the sociology of knowledge. It focuses on the New Deal as a "slice" of history, with distinctive cultural and ideological characteristics, rather than as an event capable of being universalized in the form of a subsequent "social transformation" or encompassed in a linear progression of modern American reform. Central to the analysis is an association of the New Deal with the triumph of the ideology of modernism as an epistemological structure in which events are cast and given meaning by elites. The process by which events are thus structured produces "cultural narratives" in which external phenomena are invested with significance, and the responses of elite policymakers to those phenomena explained and justified.

The remainder of this essay describes the central features of modernist ideology and suggests how several phenomena central to the experience of New Deal lawyers could have been invested with a distinctive meaning by modernist cultural narratives. It then proceeds to consider how the triumph of modernism as an ideological orthodoxy in the years during and after the New Deal has served to shape current commentary on New Deal lawyers. Finally, it suggests that the status of modernism as an ideological orthodoxy, serving as the epistemological basis of a system for structuring cultural narratives, may currently be in a precarious position. The very precariousness of modernism as an ideological orthodoxy, this essay concludes, should stimulate efforts to recapture the world of New Deal lawyers from a perspective different from that of survivors or legacists.

Modernist Narratives of New Deal Culture

According to a recent symposium on modernist culture, American modernist epistemology "begins with the premise of an unpredictable universe where nothing is ever stable, and where accordingly human beings must be satisfied with knowledge that is partial and transient at best." [46] From that premise follow two controlling beliefs: that "[t]o create [moral] values and garner whatever knowledge is available, individuals must repeatedly subject themselves . . . to the trials of experience," and that "[a]bove all, [individuals] must not attempt to shield themselves behind illusions or gentility, as so many did during the nineteenth century." [47] In an interpretation of events, the modernist invests with significance those episodes that confirm the inevitability of social impermanency, the necessity of subjecting value judgments to experiental testing, and the illusory quality of a priori value systems or unexamined established codes of conduct, such as gentility. The assumptions of modernism thus serve both to shape the events selected to be narrated and to provide the explanation of their meaning.

An example can be found in the meaning ascribed to two events invested with great significance by Americans in the 1930s—World War I and the Great Depression. Both events were identified as cataclysmic phenomena, occurrences that shook twentieth-century American civilization at its foundations. Both were read as modernist "lessons." The War confirmed the illusion of permanency, as embodied by the breakdown of the "permanent" codes and alliances of "civilized" nations, producing a war in which poison gas figured prominently. The Depression likewise revealed the impermanency of the economic institutions of unregulated capitalism, previously regarded as inevitable and inviolate. The "lesson" of both episodes was seen as the need to abandon illusions, to confront impermanency, and to gain a keener understanding of the relationship between a priori values and experience.

If this interpretation of World War I and the Great Depression by American elites of the 1930s is kept in mind, several features of the cultural experience of New Deal lawyers take on added significance. One feature was a tacit shift in criteria for success in elite sectors of the legal profession, in which the "meaning" of ethnicity was redefined so as to permit greater entry by Irish or Jewish individuals into those sectors.

Both Lash's and Murphy's books provide evidence of a complex attitude toward the relationship between ethnicity, professionalism, ideology, and social mobility in place at the time the New Deal came into being. On several occasions Lash and Murphy allude to the fact that Corcoran, Cohen, and Fortas were members of ethnic minorities whose affiliation with elite law schools and entry into government service enhanced not only their professional but their social standing. But at the same time, Lash and Murphy suggest that ethnic stereotyping of Irish and Jewish lawyers persisted during the New Deal, and that all three of their New Deal subjects labored under the burden of ethnic prejudice. [48]

The ambiguities revealed by Lash and Murphy were generally present in elite sectors of American society in the 1930s, and they reflected a pervasive but incomplete transformation of the criteria for social and professional success in those

sectors. In 1910, the year of Fortas's birth, when Cohen was seventeen and Corcoran nine, a Catholic had never run for President and a Jew had never sat on the
Supreme Court. By 1933, when all three men were working for New Deal agencies, Al Smith had run against Herbert Hoover, and Brandeis and Cardozo were
both Supreme Court Justices. In those years, however, Jewish quotas had been
imposed at some elite educational institutions, and prejudice against Irish Catholics continued to be an important part of the climate at such universities.[49] Moreover, ethnic self-consciousness and ethnic stereotyping often were internalized by
prominent Jewish lawyers, including Frankfurter[50] and Jerome Frank.

In sum, the New Deal years were marked both by an opening up of professional opportunities for ethnic lawyers and by the persistence of discriminatory
practices. As many commentators have suggested, the 1930s marked the first decade in American society during which significant numbers of ethnic lawyers who
had habitually encountered discrimination in private firms were able to secure
employment in the public sector.[51] A conventional explanation for this phenomenon is that the New Deal created a market for legal jobs in the federal government,
and the federal government could not discriminate on ethnic grounds in hiring.
But there is no evidence that those responsible for recruiting lawyers in the New
Deal felt themselves bound not to discriminate. On the contrary, there is ample
evidence that recruiters, even those who were Jewish, were concerned about hiring
too many Jewish candidates, or about hiring persons whose behavior was regarded
as unduly conforming to negative stereotypes.[52]

It thus appears that the increased use by ethnic minorities of educational and
professional achievement as a vehicle for enhanced status in the 1930s, and the
simultaneous persistence of ethnic selfconsciousness or stereotyping during that
decade, were complementary phenomena. Both resulted from the replacement of
a status hierarchy in which lineage was a necessary criterion for prominence by a
status hierarchy in which more functional characteristics, such as educational and
professional achievement, were given more weight. The shift did not so much
displace lineage as the basis for prominence as it precipitated a reconsideration of
what lineage signified. Lineage began to signify a code of attitudes and conduct
as much as a family association. As the lineage criterion implicitly was subjected
to a functional analysis, lineage was recast in terms of "positive behavioral characteristics," rather than the "negative" characteristics of those lacking the
proper background.[53]

The resulting judgment was that non-WASPs should not be excluded automatically from consideration for positions of prominence in America. What was once
thought of as an inexorable social deficiency was reformulated in terms of behavioral characteristics, and, as a consequence, a non-WASP could achieve prominence by exhibiting WASP behavioral patterns. This subtle transformation of status criteria in the 1930s can be seen as signifying a shift from the assumption of
the permanence of certain value judgments (such as the primacy of lineage) to an
assumption that such judgment should be subjected to functional analysis. If non-
WASP lawyers were professionally qualified and properly "WASP" in their behavior, they could achieve prominent positions hitherto reserved for WASPs.[54]

The reformulation of status criteria that took place at the time of the New Deal can be seen as inspired by the assumptions of modernism. Skepticism about the necessary importance of lineage (reflected in the assumption that "gentility" was an illusory value), coupled with the belief that all values needed to be confirmed in experience, provided observers of social stratification with a different perspective. The idea that Irish or Jewish lawyers should be excluded from positions of power because of their place in an assumed "natural order" became one that needed to be tested functionally.

Indeed, it is possible to see the coming of the New Deal itself as susceptible to being explained by contemporaries in terms that confirmed the primacy of modernist assumptions. From the perspective of contemporaries, the New Deal brought to prominence a "new breed" of lawyers, most of them young, many from ethnic groups never before allowed into elite sectors of the legal profession, to construct a new explanation for the perceived failure of the American political and economic order in the late 1920s. The cultural failure against which the "New Deal" was to be juxtaposed, signified by the stock market crash and the Great War, became in this narrative a failure caused by too long a belief in premodernist values. Those values had disintegrated; the New Deal, with its modern "liberal" ideology of pragmatism, experimentalism, and professional expertise was offered as an alternative.[55]

Several additional features of the New Deal years can be seen as similarly confirming modernist premises. One feature was the emergence of Realism as a claimant of educational and jurisprudential prominence in elite law schools at roughly the same time as the New Deal's emergence as a political movement. Realism, with its emphasis on empirical and functional methodologies and its thoroughgoing skepticism about moral or epistemological absolutes, would seem to be a quintessentially modernist jurisprudence.[56] Graduates of law schools in the 1930s, however, did not necessarily join the New Deal because they had been imbued with Realist messages, nor did the existence of New Deal programs necessarily provide a stimulus for the articulation of Realist jurisprudential theories. Rather, New Deal policies and Realist messages simultaneously exemplified modernist explanations of contemporary experience, reinforcing but not creating one another.

Another feature was the increased importance, from the New Deal through the 1960s, of "meritocratic" criteria in the admissions process for elite law schools and in the placement of elite graduates in practice.[57] In the 1950s, Felix Frankfurter supplied an explanation for the emergence of "meritocratic" criteria by linking it to democratic values. In his opinion, institutions such as the Harvard Law School, where "merit" was determined by "ascertainable" criteria such as grades, were embodiments of "the democratic spirit." In such institutions "class, or color, or religious partialities or antipathies . . . were all out." Academic rank at Harvard and other "meritocratic" institutions was "an automatic affair." If "one fellow got 76, and another 76.5," Frankfurter claimed, "there's no use saying 'the 76 man is better.' "[58]

But it is possible to see the shift to meritocratic criteria not as bearing a relationship to democratic theory, but as resting on the modernist presumption that "merit" can be empirically and functionally determined. Such a shift might represent a narrowing of the grounds for eligibility to high status positions in legal education, to those who could achieve high numerical grades on law schools examinations. From Frankfurter's perspective, the emergence of meritocratic criteria was inevitably "democratic" because it resulted in persons such as himself, a Jew who might have been excluded from high status positions on the basis of lineage, having the opportunity to achieve such status. But in expanding professional opportunities for some, the shift restricted them for others. Its significance resided less in its democratizing effects than in the fact that it changed the criterion for success. Success, it was believed, could and should be functionally determined.

Two other prominent features of the 1930s appear susceptible to a similar analysis. One is the rise of federal regulatory and administrative agencies during the New Deal, and the consequent emergence both of administrative law as a doctrinal category and of agency practice as a career specialty for lawyers, especially former New Dealers. The creation of federal agencies was among the most distinctive and significant public policy initiatives of the New Deal,[59] and the agency form of government was explicitly premised on modernist assumptions. Experimental regulation of the economy was taken as preferable to the earlier belief in unregulated market capitalism. Moreover, the principal justification offered for the enhanced power of regulators and administrators was that they possessed "expertise," that is, knowledge based on experience; conversely, the functional methodology of the agencies was assumed to invest their staffers with a disinterested perspective.[60] In short, the New Deal agencies were conceived as modernist governmental institutions.

Another event confirming modernist perspectives was the "crisis" that produced the Court-packing episode of 1937. The recognition of a "crisis" has conventionally been described as a belief that an "old Court" was declaring constitutional doctrine that was "outmoded" because it failed to legitimate the legislative and administrative experiments of the New Deal.[61] But the belief that a "crisis" existed reflected more than dissatisfaction with specific Court decisions. It also encompassed an intuitive rejection of the Court's reasoning that the New Deal legislation offended the Constitution. The Court's critics intuited that the Constitution must have been erroneously interpreted in the New Deal cases because their Constitution was a modernist document that could accommodate change and respond to political and economic chaos. If the Court failed to perceive the modernist nature of the Constitution, it was because its Justices were "outmoded" in their sensibility. They were trapped in a premodernist theory of Constitutional interpretation that stemmed from a premodernist conception of the document.

A similar analysis may be made of Roosevelt's response to the Court's actions. The Roosevelt administration's plan to "reform" the Court envisaged the addition of up to five new Justices, each of whom would, of course, be appointed by the President.[62] The plan assumed not only that Roosevelt appointees would be sympathetic to the New Deal, but, more significantly, that the question of whether the Constitution permitted or prohibited New Deal legislative experimentation did not have a definitive, timeless answer. Instead, interpretation of the Constitution changed as circumstances and the composition of the Court changed. "Packing" the Court, in this narrative, was simply a recognition that some Justices, being ideologically "outmoded," had not perceived that the Constitution must adapt to changed circumstances, rather than those circumstances to the Constitution. The Court-packing plan has been repeatedly characterized as a political blunder by the Roosevelt administration, because of its failure to grasp that such a radical transformation of the Court would be unpalatable to the public.[63] But within the framework of modernist premises regarding the Constitution and its interpretation, the transformation was not radical at all.

In sum, it appears that the function of legal institutions, the composition of elite sectors of the legal profession, and ideas about law itself were being explained in new terms in the 1930s. Of course that decade was also witnessing unprecedented economic and political instability, which not only helped create new roles for young lawyers associated with the New Deal but contributed to the more general sense that the nation was encountering a revolutionary period in its history. There is little wonder that survivors recall their entry into the New Deal as "heady" and subsequent years as anticlimactic; little wonder that they perceived the cultural atmosphere as fresh, exciting, and transformative. They were entering a professional world whose meaning was being redefined to conform to the tenets of modernism, and they were asked to put those tenets into practice. Having, in most cases, little previous professional experience, and not being identified with "outmoded" epistemological attitudes, they were "new" at a time when to be "old" was to be "demoralized."[64]

The Decline of Modernism and the Ambivalence of New Deal Historiography

To conceive of New Deal lawyers as belonging to the first generation entering practice when modernist narratives of cultural experience had become orthodox is to begin to recapture their sense of uniqueness. But identifying the emergence of New Deal lawyers with the triumph of a modernist epistemology does not fully explain the ambivalence that current commentary exhibits toward the New Deal. In some respects that ambivalence appears to have more to do with current perceptions of the New Deal than with its character as a cultural and ideological episode. Here again, however, a focus on the close identification of the New Deal generation with the triumph of modernism proves fruitful.

Describing the course of modernist epistemology in the decades following the New Deal, Daniel Joseph Singal suggests that modernism's status as epistemological orthodoxy may be declining. In his view, there is a "growing inability" among contemporary Americans "to tolerate the formidable demands made by Modernist culture, especially its abiding lack of resolution and certainty." At the same time he suggests that while a "desire to find a stable point of reference . . . to rest our perceptions and values" may augur a dissatisfaction with modernism, "postmodernist initiative[s] [have] taken place within an essentially Modernist framework."[65] Two propositions advanced in that commentary are germane to the present discussion. One is the association of contemporary dissatisfaction with modernism and a search for a stable reference point from which to ground substantive values. The other is the claim that despite the decline of modernism, as yet no clear epistemological alternative to modernism has surfaced.[66]

The ambivalence toward the New Deal demonstrated by Lash and Murphy is best understood in relation to the current dissatisfaction with modernism. An example may serve to illustrate this observation. One of the singular aspects of the careers of several prominent New Deal lawyers was that they were accused of allegedly improper legal or ethical practices after they left government service. Fortas's alleged ethical misconduct as a judge is discussed in detail by Murphy, but Fortas was by no means unique among his contemporaries. Alger Hiss, James Landis, Edward Prichard, and Corcoran himself were each investigated for legal or ethical improprieties, and the first three were convicted of crimes and sent to prison.[67] As noted, Murphy suggests that Fortas's alleged improprieties were less a product of idiosyncratically deviant behavior than of two other factors: his belief, as a "child of the New Deal," that somehow the "rules had once helped to fashion" did not apply to him, and changes in the political culture of the late 1960s, which made Fortas, and others of his generation, suddenly more vulnerable to attack.

While I have argued that Murphy's interpretation is analytically flawed, it nevertheless is instructive with respect to the current crisis of modernist epistemology. If a core proposition of modernism is the absence of fixed or permanent values and the consequent necessity of adopting a relativistic and experimentalist approach to moral as well as other issues, then a situational and "pragmatic" conception of the ethical or legal obligations of lawyers might seem to follow.[68] Likewise, if one then associates current dissatisfaction with modernist epistemology with a recoil from unconstrained relativism and a search for more permanent and fixed values, an interest in exploring the possibility of formulating more absolutist standards of professional ethics might seem to follow.

Thus Fortas, as a member of a generation in which modernist narratives of experience predominated, might genuinely wonder what he had "done wrong" in maintaining as a judge a "pragmatic" approach to conflict-of-interest and separation-of-powers issues. Moreover, Murphy, as a legacist, might also wonder what Fortas had "done wrong," even in the course of documenting the number of occasions on which Fortas concealed or flatly misrepresented the breadth of his extrajudicial activities. In this view, Murphy becomes a commentator in an academic culture in which the shift from modernism to post-modernism remains partial and incomplete. He meticulously documents Fortas's transgressions, but then suggests that they might not have been transgressions at all. His premises about the relationship between judging and politics are modernist, but his explanation for Fortas's demise emphasizes a cultural change that made Fortas suddenly prematurely "old." While Murphy characterizes this change primarily in terms of political alignments, Fortas's resignation from the Court can also be seen as taking place in an atmosphere marked by enhanced scrutiny of situational definitions of judicial ethics.

One can chart a similar ambivalence in Lash's account of the New Dealers. He applauds their "sixth-sense feeling for the programs that were politically feasible not simply ideally desirable." He reminds the reader that the lesson he learned anew in writing about Cohen and Corcoran is that the political feasibility of ideas counts more than their substantive virtue—a relentlessly modernist lesson.[69] But in the last pages of *Dealers and Dreamers* he defends Corcoran against the charge that "Tom was the epitome of the public interest lawyer who [after the New Deal] was working against what he had done." In Lash's defense of Corcoran, a commitment to the primacy of "humanistic values" is offered as a justification for a use of informal discretionary power. This defense suggests a stable point of reference for values—a postmodernist thrust.

We can thus begin to see the impulse to recapture the world of New Deal lawyers as part of a more general effort to make sense of modernist narratives in a culture masked by a nascent postmodernist epistemology.[70] In both the survivor and legacist strains of commentary, one can sense the conviction that the New Deal was a powerfully generative moment in American culture interfused with bafflement or frustration as to why that moment has passed.[71]

III Conclusion: Reflections on the Impulse to Recapture

The place to start in recapturing New Deal lawyers and the culture in which they functioned is with an understanding of the recapturing impulse itself. For commentators in the 1980s, the New Deal appears simultaneously relevant and obsolete because it represents the formative episode of modernism as a twentieth-century ideological orthodoxy, as perceived through the lenses of a culture in which modernist epistemology remains extant but precarious. If the relativistic and empiricist assumptions of modernism are to survive, the New Deal represents the roots of policies premised on those assumptions; if modernism is to be perceived as an orthodoxy in decay, the transformative energy of the New Dealers can be appealed to as inspiration for another epistemological transformation; if the New Deal is to be made into an "outmoded" "old order" to serve as a baseline against which "new" perspectives and policies are to be tested, an understanding of the precise ways in which the assumptions of New Dealers "failed" is necessary to the critique.

However the New Deal is recaptured, it needs to be recaptured not as a series of nostalgic memories or as a link in the chain of American reform movements, but as a vivid manifestation of a modernist narrative of culture experiences. The fact that the New Deal can be recaptured in those terms at all suggests that we have passed from a culture in which modernism remained an unquestioned ideological orthodoxy to a culture in which the orthodoxy of modernism may itself have come to be perceived as a historical event.[72] Recapturing the New Deal, in short, is interesting and vital precisely because the central meaning of the New Deal is a meaning that directly relates to our current epistemological predicament.

NOTES

1. For a definition of modernism, *see infra*, text accompanying notes 46–72.

2. Quoting Address by Benjamin V. Cohen at New Dealers Reunion Dinner (Mar. 4, 1977).

3. THE MAKING OF THE NEW DEAL: THE INSIDERS SPEAK xviii (K. Louchheim ed. 1983) [hereafter INSIDERS] (quoting Lady Bird Johnson).

4. "I can't tell you how exciting life is down here," Thomas Corcoran once said to Benjamin Cohen during the 1930s. "I am afraid that after this all life will be anti-climax" (Lash p. 466). Years later, Cohen said to Lash: "You don't know how . . . painfully true [Corcoran's fear was]" (Lash p. 466).

5. See, e.g., P. CONKIN, FDR AND THE ORIGINS OF THE WELFARE STATE (1967); O. GRAHAM, TOWARD A PLANNED SOCIETY (1976); W. E. LEUCHTENBURG, FRANKLIN D. ROOSEVELT AND THE NEW DEAL, 1932–40 (1963); NEW DEAL THOUGHT (H. Zinn ed. 1966); A. M. SCHLESINGER JR., THE COMING OF THE NEW DEAL (1959).

6. INSIDERS, supra note 3.

7. Id. at xix.

8. See id. at 323.

9. See id. at 120.

10. Id. at 121, 129 (quoting Milton Katz).

11. See, e.g., "Twins": New Deal's Legislative Architects: Corcoran and Cohen, NEWSWEEK, July 13, 1935, at 24–25; Krock, Are the Two 'Wunderkinder' About to Re-emerge? N.Y. TIMES, Apr. 2, 1937, at 22, col. 5; Necks In: Irishman and Jew Keep Quiet Behind To-Day's Rooseveltian Brain Trust, LITERARY DIG., May 22, 1937, at 7; A Glimpse into the Nation's Backstage Government: Two Brilliant Young Men Who Run the Show for the President, AM. MAG. Aug. 1937, at 4; Flynn, Circles Around the Throne—Punches for Corcoran and Cohen, NEW REPUBLIC, Aug. 18, 1937, at 5.

12. One recent scholarly treatment is Monica Nisnik, Thomas G. Corcoran (Ph.D. dissertation, Univ. of Notre Dame, 1981).

13. See J. LASH, ELEANOR AND FRANKLIN (1971), ELEANOR: THE YEARS ALONE (1972).

14. See J. LASH, FROM THE DIARIES OF FELIX FRANKFURTER (1975) (an extensive biographical essay, "A Brahmin of the Law," followed by annotated excerpts from Frankfurter's diaries, in the Library of Congress).

15. In a recent appreciative article on Lash, Robert Caro described his earlier works as having made an "indelible contribution to American letters and American history." Caro, Starting Late, Finishing First, N.Y. TIMES, June 12, 1988, § 7 (Book Review), at 12.

16. After reviewing Cohen's early life as the son of a Polish Jew who made his living selling scrap iron in Muncie, Indiana, and who moved to Chicago so that his son could attend University High School in Hyde Park and then the University of Chicago, Lash concludes:

Despite [Cohen's] unique academic record at the university and law school, he did not have a commanding presence, and, as a classmate said, "Ben was very awkward physically."

. . .

There already was in young Ben Cohen a haunting sense of insufficiency. . . . He read, analyzed, understood better than everyone around him and his sweet nature made him a delight to those who appreciated intelligence and sensitivity, but the ideas and visions that thronged his brain required others to bring them to fruition (Lash p. 14).

Or consider this observation on Corcoran as a young man:

He was the eldest son of an eldest son of an eldest son and among the Irish that conferred a special status that carried with it a sense of responsibility not only for himself but for [other members of his family].

. . .

He was also an ascetic about women, called himself a "Christer and Puritan."
"Mummy had given me an abiding discomfort about women. Don't become a male
spider," she cautioned him, referring to that insect's ability to entangle its prey in
its silken strands. Women liked Tom . . . But he was a self-described "worka-
holic" and in 1922 when he entered Harvard Law School in Cambridge, "I was the
complete scholar. All I did was study." . . . He concentrated on his books and
avoided social life, Tom said, out of "the fear of being shunned. I do recall Professor Williston's, the Brahmin authority on contracts, comment, 'I've just read a most
remarkable paper by a man with the most unpromising name of Corcoran' " (Lash
pp. 54–57).

17. *See* Pitt, *Joseph P. Lash Is Dead,* N.Y. Times, Aug. 23, 1987, at 40.

18. Lash cites interviews with Ida Klaus in August 1986, Hope Dale Davis in September 1986, and Joseph Clark in November 1986 (Lash p. 492 nn. 19, 3, 5).

19. Lash cites a letter from Rexford Tugwell to Leon Keyserling as evidence that Tugwell retained his emphasis on a planned economy, which in Lash's view "went to the heart
of [Tugwell's] controversies with the Brandeis-Frankfurter progressives in the thirties,"
fifty years later (Lash p. 4).

20. Lash's sources include an interview he had with Benjamin Cohen on April 8, 1974
(Lash p. 493 n 16).

21. One error occurs in the very first line of Lash's text, where he lists 1932, instead
of 1930, as the year of Franklin Roosevelt's reelection as Governor of New York. Two
additional examples have been chosen merely as illustrations. On page 20 of *Dealers and
Dreamers,* Lash referred to Benjamin Cohen's having "f[allen] deeply in love with Ella
Winters" while in London in 1919. He then goes on to discuss the Cohen-Winters relationship, and quotes two comments on Winters, one by Margery Abrahams and one by Stella
Frankfurter, made to Lash in 1983 (Lash p. 21). Both comments refer to "Ella Winter,"
and Lash's reference to his conversations with Abrahams and Frankfurter also spells Ella's
last name "Winter." At page 452 in *Dealers and Dreamers,* Lash again mentions "Ella
Winter." The index entries, however, contain the last name "Winters."

A second example can be found on page 474 of *Dealers and Dreamers,* where Lash
gives two footnote references to interviews with Judge Simon Rifkind. The first lists the
date of one of the interviews as July 28, 1983. The second spells the judge's last name
Rifkin and lists another interview with him as taking place on April 21, 1933.

Few books published in the 1980s are free from typographical errors, and thus the
disconcertingly inaccurate quality of Lash's references can be attributed in part to the fact
that the manuscript was very likely prepared for publication by a person or persons who
were not especially familiar with its contents and would thus not recognize typographical
errors that would come to the attention of a specialist reader. But surely any person lingering over a page in a manuscript would question two different spellings of the same name
on the same page or within a page of each other, and two interviews cited on the same
page alleged to have taken place fifty years apart.

22. INSIDERS, *supra* note 3, at xxi (quoting Katie Louchheim).

23. P. CONKIN, *supra* note 5, at 103.

24. *See* P. Irons, New Deal Lawyers 142 (1982).

25. Fortas played a significant role in drafting the eight-volume *Report on the Study
and Investigation of the Work, Activities, Personnel and Functions of Protective and Reor-
ganization Committees,* eventually issued by the SEC in 1937 (Murphy p. 26).

26. Fortas had remained at the SEC until 1939, when he accepted the position of general counsel to the Public Works Administration. That agency was scheduled to be liqui-

dated, however, so that same year Fortas moved to the Bituminous Coal Division of the Department of the Interior, where he remained until 1941 and became acting director of the Division of Power. One year later, Fortas became Undersecretary of Interior (Murphy pp. 34–41).

27. The facts of Fortas's resignation are sufficiently well known to require only the barest recapitulation. During the Senate confirmation hearings on Fortas's nomination for the Chief Justiceship in 1968, charges were made that Fortas, while a sitting Justice, had advised the Johnson administration on matters of national policy such as the conduct and public relations defense of the war in Vietnam. Fortas appeared as a witness at the hearings and denied the charges, but his nomination was successfully filibustered by opponents in the Senate and ultimately withdrawn by the Johnson Administration in October 1968. Fortas then resumed his seat on the Court as an Associate Justice, but critics continued to press him for details about another of his extrajudicial activities that had come to light during the confirmation hearings: participating in a seminar at American University, for which he was paid a fee of $15,000 out of money raised by one of his law partners, Paul Porter. Then in May 1969, an article appeared in *Life Magazine,* written by journalist William Lambert, that disclosed a relationship between Fortas and financier Louis Wolfson, who was under investigation by the SEC, in which Fortas had been paid $20,000 from the Wolfson Family Foundation for work on "educational and civil rights projects." The *Life* article was first made public on May 4; Fortas resigned from the court on May 15. The next day the *Los Angeles Times* revealed that the $20,000 payment to Fortas by the Wolfson Family Foundation was to be repeated on an annual basis for the rest of Fortas's life.

28. B. MURPHY, THE BRANDEIS/FRANKFURTER CONNECTION (1982). Most of the sources Murphy relied upon were in the Felix Frankfurter Papers at the Library of Congress, a voluminous collection.

29. Some reviews of THE BRANDEIS/FRANKFURTER CONNECTION claimed that the information Murphy discovered had already been disclosed. *See, e.g.,* Danelski, Book Review, 96 HARV. L. REV. 312, 312 n.4 (1982).

30. One example will suffice: Murphy's discovery of documents in the Earl Warren Papers, now available at the Library of Congress, that reveal that the Justice Department, in the early days of the Nixon administration, had obtained a copy of the $20,000 annual retainer between financier Louis Wolfson and Fortas. The documents contain no new evidence, but nonetheless represent a significant discovery. The existence of an agreement between Fortas and Wolfson had already been revealed at the time of Fortas's resignation from the Court, but no copy of the Wolfson-Fortas contract had been made public, and no one at the time other than Earl Warren knew that a copy of that contract, which had been included in documents presented to Warren by Attorney General John Mitchell on May 7, 1969, and returned to Mitchell one week later, had remained in Warren's court papers. Indeed all knowledgeable sources of the investigation into the Wolfson-Fortas relationship believed that, as Fortas said to Wolfson in a secretly recorded conversation in 1977, all the relevant documents "ha[d] been sealed in the Department of Justice so that [they] will not get out." *See* Woodward, *Fortas Tie to Wolfson Is Detailed,* Wash. Post, Jan. 23, 1977, at A12, col. I.

31. Murphy's analytical deficiencies are discussed below at pp. 296–300. The stylistic deficiencies of *Fortas* can perhaps be traced to an attempt to reach a popular audience through efforts at vivid writing. The results are some strained metaphors, such as "Fortas was caught in a riptide of history, and no matter how strong his swimming skills, there was no possibility of escape" (p. 594), or "[w]hile Fortas was justified in lowering his cannons, he chose only to fire shots across Black's bow in two minor cases" (p. 514).

32. At times Murphy writes as if sensational revelations are about to take place, only to disclose information whose content, if not necessarily predictable, is far from startling. For example, Murphy takes 20 pages to discuss the impact of a latter written by Senator Richard Russell to President Johnson on Fortas's nomination as Chief Justice (pp. 329–49). The contents of the letter are not disclosed in those pages, although Murphy later claims that the letter "was a turning point in the life of Abe Fortas", but the letter only revealed that Russell's support for the Fortas nomination was closely tied to the Johnson administration's appointment of a Russell protégé, Alexander Lawrence, Jr., to a federal district judgeship. Such *quid pro quos* are not uncommon and their revelation hardly earthshaking.

33. *See generally* Keller, *Reflections on Politics and Generations in America*, DAEDALUS, Fall, 1978, at 123.

34. The belief that judges were as inclined to be affected by politics and political attitudes as any other decisionmakers was vividly exemplified by the Realist movement in American jurisprudence, which emerged in elite law schools in the 1920s and 1930s. *See infra* note 56, and accompanying text.

35. In his author's note and acknowledgement Murphy recounts the impact that the phrase had on him:

> In the middle of this conversation, almost entirely out of context, Fortas began speaking in a sad voice about the isolation felt by members of the "court. . . . [I]t" was then that he spoke about "dying on the court" . . . .
>
> The phrase that kept rolling around in my head was his "dying on the court." In a very real sense, I realized, Fortas *had* "died" on the court, and not just in the way he understood (Murphy p. 687 [emphasis in original]).

36. *See id.* at 505.

37. One could argue that there is a significant ethical difference between a judge hiring a lobbyist to promote causes in which the judge believes, as Brandeis did, and a judge accepting a retainer from a person who anticipated litigating before the federal courts, as Fortas did.

38. More than half the book covers the events between Fortas's nomination as Chief Justice in 1968 and his resignation from the Court in 1969. Given the nature of the information Murphy supplies, that emphasis is not warranted. Although many of the details Murphy uncovers from the Lyndon Johnson papers are not generally accessible, the story of Fortas's judicial demise has been previously described in Robert Shogan's *A Question of Judgment,* the findings of which Murphy does not contradict. *See* R. SHOGAN, A QUESTION OF JUDGMENT (1972).

39. Fortas's early life, education, law school career, marriage, and first six years in government service is covered in 30 pages of a 598–page book (Murphy pp. 3–32).

40. Forty pages are devoted to Fortas's career on the Court, which spanned four Terms, from 1965 through 1968. In contrast, 72 pages are devoted to Fortas's role as a White House advisor while sitting on the Court.

41. Murphy hints in early chapters that Fortas had difficulty making decisions under pressure, and that this indecision may have had some connection to a latent insecurity that stemmed from Fortas's social marginality as the son of an immigrant Jew in Louisville in the 1920s. He fails to further develop this theme, however, and he offers no explanation for why this insecurity somehow evolved into the "cockiness" he attributes to Fortas as a lawyer and Supreme Court Justice.

42. This lack of interest may be a function of Murphy's unfamiliarity with legal doctrine. In his chapter on the Warren Court during Fortas's tenure, he seems content to rest on conventional characterizations of the Justices. He claims, for example, that the Court

during Fortas's tenure was "perfectly balanced" between the "liberal wing" and "four conservatives," but cites no cases in support of that proposition, resting content with generalities such as "[the] conservative bloc had attempted to stem the tide of social reforms created by their liberal colleagues, and to limit the government's legal powers over the corporate world" (p. 213).

43. *Cf* Ashwander v. TVA, 297 U.S. 288, 345–48 (1936) (Brandeis, J., concurring) (arguing that judges should, where possible, avoid passing on the constitutionality of legislative acts); West Virginia State Bd. of Educ. v. Barnett, 319 U.S. 624 (1943) (Frankfurter, J., dissenting) (declaring that "[a]s a member of this Court I am not justified in writing my private notions of policy into the Constitution").

44. *Cf. In re* Gault, 387 U.S. 1 (1967); Time v. Hill, 385 U.S. 374 (1967) (Fortas, J. dissenting).

45. Murphy documents, through the use of Lyndon Johnson's papers, the very high number of occasions on which Fortas visited or telephoned the White House while on the Court. These findings seriously undermine the credibility of Fortas's denial of his involvement with the White House.

46. Singal, *Towards a Definition of American Modernism*, 39 AM. Q. 7, 15 (1987). See also the collection of essays edited by Singal, David J. Singal, ed., *Modernist Culture in America* (1991).

47. *Id.*

48. Two additional illustrations of this attitude can be found in incidents involving Franklin Roosevelt's effort to recruit lawyers. In 1936 Roosevelt wrote to Charles C. Burlingham, an established Wall Street lawyer and professional Democratic political advisor, soliciting his help in recruiting young lawyers. "Dig me up fifteen or twenty youthful Abraham Lincolns from Manhattan and the Bronx to choose from," Roosevelt told Burlingham. "They must be liberal from belief and not by lip service. . . . They must have no social ambition." Letter from Franklin D. Roosevelt to C.C. Burlingham (Feb. 6, 1936), *quoted in* Lash at 38. And in 1942, when Fortas's name was proposed to Roosevelt by Harold Ickes for appointment as Undersecretary of the Department of Interior, Roosevelt asked Ickes, according to Murphy, if he "[c]ould afford to appoint another 'Hebrew' to a position of high authority." Ickes assured Roosevelt that Fortas was "one of the quiet, unobtrusive types," and "one of the ablest lawyers in Washington." The exchange between Roosevelt and Ickes was recorded in Ickes' unpublished diaries on May 31, 1942, and quoted in Murphy at 41.

If one assumes that the term "Abraham Lincolns" in Roosevelt's letter to Burlingham, when taken in connection with the comment about the prospective recruits having "no social ambition," refers to non-WASP lawyers, both incidents suggest that Roosevelt assumed that ethnicity was not a bar to recruitment, but a salient characteristic that might prove troublesome if the individual possessed "social ambition" or was not "one of the quiet, unobtrusive types.

49. *See generally* M. SYNNOTT, THE HALF-OPENED DOOR (1979) (describing discriminatory admissions policies at Harvard, Yale, and Princeton in the twentieth century).

50. In 1923 Frankfurter, while on the Harvard Law School faculty, had written his close friend Emory Buckner of a Jewish candidate for a position with Buckner's firm: "I assume that you have all the Jews that the traffic can bear but you're letting a rare thing go in Birnbaum." Letter from Frankfurter to Emory Buckner (Apr. 1923), *quoted in* H. N. HIRSCH, THE ENIGMA OF FELIX FRANKFURTER 76 (1981).

51. *See* J. AUERBACH, UNEQUAL JUSTICE 6, 173, 184–88 (1976); K. LOUCHHEIM, *supra* note 3, at xii–xiii.

52. Jerome Frank, then at the Agricultural Adjustment Administration, is quoted by

Lash as responding to the proposal of these candidates, named Schachner, Muravchick, and Timberg, for positions at the AAA by saying "Goddam it . . . I've got to be careful. You've got too many Jews in here now" (p. 219).

53. Thus, the "Abraham Lincolns" in Roosevelt's letter to Burlingham, *see supra* note 48, were expected to have "no social ambition," and "Hebrews" such as Fortas, referred to in his exchange with Ickes, *see id.*, were expected to be "quiet and unobtrusive."

54. One of the apparent difficulties in efforts to unpack the epistemological premises of past generations is that of attaching precise periodization to "shifts" in the tacit premises from which discussions, such as that between Roosevelt and Burlingham or between Roosevelt and Ickes, *see supra* note 48, are conducted. While one can produce symbolic evidence, such as the "eligibility" of Catholics or Jews for high-status offices, of a modification of the lineage criterion for social advancement in the early twentieth century, examples of functional redefinitions of lineage criteria might also be summoned from earlier periods. Epistemological shifts tend to be vast, gradual, irregular, and often unnoticed by those participating in them; the deepest premises of a prevailing epistemology are often only recognizable by those operating in a subsequent generation that challenges its axioms. The concluding sections of this essay suggest that the emergence and decline of modernism as an epistemological orthodoxy can be associated with the years between the 1930s and the 1980s, although examples of individuals exhibiting a modernist sensibility can surely be found outside those years. Periodization can serve as much as a barrier to historical observation as a refinement of it.

55. Earlier reform ideologies, most notably Progressivism, had advocated an empirical approach to social issues and stressed the value of professional elites as policymakers. Nonetheless, Progressivism was not a fully modernist ideology, principally because its adherents sought to employ the techniques of early twentieth-century social science to restore the vision of a homogeneous, virtuous American culture. Representative Progressives, such as Brandeis, were firmly committed to traditional moral values. *See* P. STRUM, LOUIS D. BRANDEIS: JUSTICE FOR THE PEOPLE 132–202 (1984). On the relationship of Progressivism to the New Deal, see generally O. GRAHAM, AN ENCORE FOR REFORM: THE OLD PROGRESSIVES AND THE NEW DEAL (1967), which analyzes the theoretical foundations of the New Deal and its relationship to Progressivism.

56. On the characteristics of Realism, see G. E. WHITE, PATTERNS OF AMERICAN LEGAL THOUGHT 116–35, 137–44 (1978).

57. *See* R. STEVENS, LAW SCHOOL 191–231 (1983).

58. The quotations from Frankfurter are taken from an oral history he gave in the 1950s, published as FELIX FRANKFURTER REMINISCES 26–27 (H. Phillips ed. 1960).

59. *See* Sunstein, *Constitutionalism After the New Deal,* 101 HARV. L. REV. 421, 440 (1987).

60. *See* J. LANDIS, THE ADMINISTRATIVE PROCESS 11–12, 23–26 (1938)

61. *See, e.g.,* A. SCHLESINGER, THE POLITICS OF UPHEAVAL 451–67, 486–96 (1960).

62. *See id.*

63. *See, e.g.,* W. E. LEUCHTENBERG, *supra* note 5, at 233.

64. Katz, *From Hoover to Roosevelt,* in K. LOUCHHEIM, *supra* note 3, at 121.

65. Singal, *supra* note 46, at 21, 22, 23. The decline of modernism is sometimes identified with the emergence of a "postmodernist" epistemology, although commentators have not agreed on the precise content of postmodernism. *Compare* Jameson, *Postmodernism, or The Cultural Logic of Late Capitalism,* 146 NEW LEFT REV. 53 (July-Aug. 1984) *and* Wolin, *Modernism vs. Postmodernism,* 62 TELOS 9 (Winter 1984–85) *with* Graff, *The Myth of the Postmodernist Breakthrough,* 26 TRIQUARTERLY 383 (Winter 1973).

66. One can find a suggestive example of contemporary trends in legal scholarship that

lends support to these observations. Central to the modernist assumption that values need to be tested experientially was a belief that empirical methodologies could yield objective data (the data of "experience") which could then be used to test "subjective" rules or policies. The law and economics movement in contemporary scholarship apparently became energized along a similar assumption, that empirical data about the economic behavior of actors in the legal system could be introduced as a test of the effectiveness of legal rules. Recently, however, skepticism about the objectivity of even the "hardest" empirical data (that of the physical sciences) has surfaced, *see* T. KUHN, THE STRUCTURE OF SCIENTIFIC REVOLUTIONS (2nd ed. 1970), and the normative dimensions of law and economics scholarship have been conceded by its adherents, *see, e.g.,* R. POSNER, ECONOMIC ANALYSIS OF LAW (3rd ed. 1986). The apparent objectivity of empirical analysis represented a stable reference point for modernists in the 1930s. As that reference point has been revealed to be another "illusion," one of the energizing assumptions of modernist work would seem to have been enervated. Yet the claim that "objective" empirical research is possible has not been fully discredited, and the law and economics movement remains attractive to many contemporary scholars.

67. *See generally* D. RITCHIE, JAMES M. LANDIS: DEAN OF THE REGULATORS (1980); A WEINSTEIN, PERJURY, 70–141 (1978); B. WOODWARD AND S. ARMSTRONG, THE BRETHREN 79–85 (1979); Schlesinger, *'Prich': A New Deal Memoir,* N.Y. REV. BOOKS, Mar. 28, 1985, at 21; *Thomas A. Corcoran, Aid to Roosevelt, Dies,* N.Y. TIMES, Dec. 7, 1981, at D18.

68. Fortas once made the following defense of legal advocacy:

Lawyers are agents not principals; and they should neither criticize nor tolerate criticism based upon the character of the client whom they represent or the cause that they prosecute or defend. They cannot and should not accept responsibility for the client's practices. Rapists, murderers, child-abusers, General Motors, Dow Chemical—and even cigarette manufacturers and stream polluters—are entitled to a lawyer; and any lawyer who undertakes their representation must be immune from criticism for so doing.

Fortas, *Thurman Arnold and the Theatre of the Law,* 79 YALE L. J. 988, 1002 (1970).

69. Pragmatism, Lash says, was a lesson he learned "in the thirties [as] a member of the Left" and "learned . . . anew in the course of writing [his] book" (Lash pp. vi–vii).

70. It is important to distinguish, in discussions of "postmodernism," between a reaffirmation of the a priori primacy of substantive values, which could amount to a revival of premodernist epistemology, and a recoil from a relativistic, experiential conception of values, especially without the "resting place" of "objective" empiricism. Behind the methodological self-consciousness of contemporary scholarship there may exist a desire to develop a point of reference in which methodology and substance are fused so that the primacy of certain substantive values is again affirmed. But the very diversity of methodological persuasions, and the attraction of contemporary scholars to methodologies that emphasize the difficulties in deriving substantive values from sources external to the deriver's own framework, suggest that generalizations about postmodernist epistemology are hazardous and premature at this point.

71. To those strains of commentary one could add a third strain, just recently surfacing, in which distance between the New Deal and the 1980s is more explicitly perceived, the problematic nature of the solutions of the New Deal lawyers and judges more clearly recognized, and in which a yearning to construct a different narrative of the cultural experiences of the New Dealers can be discerned. Three examples of this strain can be seen in recent works by Peter Irons, Thomas McCraw, and Cass Sunstein. *See* P. IRONS, *supra* note 24,

at 295–96 (1982); T. McCRAW, PROPHETS OF REGULATION, 212, 217 (1984); Sunstein, *supra* note 59, at 421–23; Sunstein, *Lochner's Legacy,* 87 COLUM. L. REV. 873, 891–93 (1987); Sunstein, *The Beard Thesis and Franklin Roosevelt,* 56 GEO. WASH. L. REV. 114, 122–23 (1987).

72. One could cite, as an example of the precarious state of modernist epistemology in contemporary elite culture, the unsuccessful Supreme Court nomination of Robert Bork, which Murphy described as an instance of a nomination being defeated on "ideological" grounds, as he believes Fortas's was.

Crucial to Judge Bork's defeat was the victory of one argument at the expense of another. His supporters argued that so long as a nominee to the Court was "professionally qualified," the substance of his or her ideological views should not play a factor in the confirmation process. This argument took as a given that Presidents had a prerogative to name nominees of similar ideological persuasions, and asked that attention be directed only to whether a nominee met other ostensibly apolitical criteria.

The above argument collapsed in the face of an argument advanced by opponents, who maintained that whatever Bork's "professional" qualifications, his substantive views on legal issues were "extreme" and potentially dangerous.

The Bork debate can be said to have been conducted on modernist terms in the sense that both sides assumed that ideology made a difference in Supreme Court judging; that justices were political beings; and that the Constitution was an adaptive document. But the elevation in the debate of certain substantive values (such as privacy or equality of race and gender) to a litmus test of eligibility, so that Bork's apparent failure to endorse them was regarded as disqualifying him for the Court, would seem to signify a search for a stable point of ideological reference. This effort can be identified with a recoil against modernism. Bork's opponents seemed to demand a much more categorical endorsement of privacy and equality than he (or perhaps any orthodox modernist) was prepared to make. Bork's failure to make such an endorsement was the principal ground on which his opponents argued against his nomination.

For more detail on the cultural setting of the Bork nomination, see White, *Chief Justice Marshall, Justice Holmes, and the Discourse of Constitutional Adjudication,* 30 WM. & MARY L. REV. 131 (1988).

PART III

Judicial Review

Reflections on the Role of the Supreme Court: The Contemporary Debate and the "Lessons" of History*

The phrase "the role of the Supreme Court" normally has two meanings: the Court's historic role, traced through the course of its tenure, or the Court's proper contemporary role. I do not believe, however, that the two meanings can be fruitfully separated. Theories of the proper contemporary role of the Court invariably employ among their justifications an appeal from history: they argue that the Court's performing one role or another is congruent with its historic function.

The subject of this essay is the interplay between the historic and the contemporary roles of the Supreme Court. More specifically, the subject is the interplay between a contemporary debate about the proper role of the Court and historical conceptions of the Court's role. I shall be arguing, first, that recent theories of judicial review have defined the Court's historic role in a way that suits their presentist concerns. While that argument will not surprise those acquainted with commentary on the Court, I shall also be arguing, perhaps more surprisingly, that historical conceptions of the Court do support an emerging contemporary theory of judicial review, and thus that an appeal to history can serve as a proper justification for a presentist view of the Court.

I The Contemporary Debate

There are two distinguishable perspectives on the role of the Court in recent literature, which has mainly been produced by legal scholars. I will call them "intraprofessional" and "supraprofessional," respectively.[1] The use of the term "professional" in both perspectives is not unintentional. The intraprofessional perspective attempts to link the Court's proper role with commonly held assump-

*63 Judicature 162 (1979).

tions about how lawyers and judges should perform; the supraprofessional perspective questions that linkage or seeks to move beyond it.

Before discussing the central arguments of both perspectives, I want to examine an assumption about the Court that they share. The assumption is that the principal justification for the Court's power to review acts of legislatures has changed since Chief Justice Marshall's decision in *Marbury v. Madison*,[2] which established that power. Marshall's principal justification for independent judicial review was that judges did not make law, but merely "found" and "declared" it.

Marshall's argument assumed that "law" was a universal body of principles, that those principles were "discoverable" by technically skilled person, such as judges, that in "discovering," judges were merely stating "what the law was." The only power judges had, under Marshall's view, was their professional power: their technical expertise enabled them to be better "finders" of law than other persons.

Marshall tied this notion of professional power in judges to the Constitution in *Marbury v. Madison*. He suggested that while some legislators, being lawyers, might also possess the professional expertise to find and declare the law, the Constitution, by declaring itself a supreme source of law, by designating the legislature the lawmaking branch of government, and by locating powers in three separate branches of government, precluded legislative "law finding" in constitutional cases. According to Marshall, the Constitution could not be supreme over an act of Congress unless some branch other than Congress interpreted it. The ideal branch to interpret the Constitution was the judiciary, because judicial interpretation was only law finding.

Marshall thus solved the problem of unchecked lawmaking power in the judiciary by assuming that lawmaking power in the judiciary was a contradiction in terms. But that solution is no longer regarded as acceptable. Law is no longer seen as a finite body of universal principles, and judges are no longer regarded as persons who merely find and declare those principles. Twentieth-century perspectives on the Court start with two different assumptions. Law is viewed as a fluid mix of established principles and changing social values, and judges, in constitutional law and elsewhere, are seen as persons who make law by creating new principles, often in response to changes in social values.[3]

The contemporary debate between intraprofessionalist and supraprofessionalist perspectives begins with a problem raised by these new jurisprudential assumptions. Rhetorically stated, the problem, as applied to the Supreme Court's role in constitutional law cases, is this. If judges are lawmakers, and if law is an entity whose content constantly changes, what prevents the justices of the Court from making constitutional law synonymous with their own conceptions of what is currently best for society? And if nothing prevents them, how can one reconcile this role for the Court with the notion that America is a democracy?

Neither side in the debate suggests that unconstrained judicial lawmaking in the guise of constitutional interpretation is defensible. The debate is about the nature of appropriate constraints on judges. Speaking generally, those adopting an intraprofessionalist perspective toward the Court derive their notions of appropriate constraints from a conventional sense of what professionals trained in the law do and how that professional training squares with representative democracy in America. Those adopting a supraprofessionalist perspective, on the other hand, derive their notions of constraints on the Court from different, and more abstract, sources.

The intraprofessionalist argument operates at three levels. Level one asserts that constitutional lawmaking by the Court is only justified when the Court bases its decisions on the written text of the Constitution. Some intraprofessionalists rest at that point, protesting any decision grounded on less than an explicit textual basis.[4] Others, however, concede that sometimes the constitutional text did not contemplate new circumstances, and so the Court can properly engage in extrapolations of the text consistent with the discernible intentions of the framers.

The "text plus intentions" level is the resting place for additional intraprofessionalists,[5] and some proceed to a third level.[6] There, constitutional lawmaking by the Court is asserted to be proper even where the literal text or the intentions of the framers do not provide a justification for the court's decision. The Court's decision is justified, at this level, by being grounded on a proper deference to the original conception of American government.

The third level of the intraprofessionalist argument is the most novel, and requires further explanation. There are constitutional issues, of course, that the framers of the Constitution simply did not contemplate. But, according to this level of the intraprofessionalist argument, it is possible to extrapolate from the framers' conception of government a proper resolution of such issues. Take a case involving the reapportionment of voting districts in a legislature. While the framers did not address the issue of unequally apportioned districts, they tolerated specific restrictions on one's right to vote, such as those based on sex, income, race, and even occupation. But it is nonetheless possible to view the Constitution as a general affirmation of the principle of representative government. So if conceptions of what "representation" means change, it is possible to argue that an unequally apportioned legislature, whose districting process diminishes the voting power of some districts, is inconsistent with the mandate of the Constitution.

Note the shift in emphasis here between the third level and the first two levels of the intraprofessionalist argument. The first two levels link a proper role for the court to the constraints of the constitutional text or of history. Those constraints allegedly prevent judges from indiscriminate lawmaking in constitutional adjudication by limiting the range of their permissible justifications: judges can only follow the words or the intentions of the framers. The third level, however, gives judges some room to depart from specific judgments of the framers in order to preserve the broad purposes of the Constitution. In the reapportionment example, a Court affirming the one-man, one-vote principle would allegedly be affirming a basic commitment in the Constitution to representative government, even though it would be contravening some specific examples where the framers restricted the right to vote.

The third level of the intraprofessionalist argument seems necessary once one concedes that in interpreting the Constitution justices of the Supreme Court make law. Since the Constitution is primarily a general document, with limited coverage, it is inevitable that issues will arise that the framers did not contemplate.

Once one recognizes that in extrapolating the constitutional text to decide such issues the Court is making law, some justification for this elitist lawmaking power in a democracy must emerge. An argument based on the basic purposes or overall design of the Constitution provides a consistent justification. By consistent I mean a justification in keeping with the central purpose of the intraprofessionalist perspective, that of developing constraints on judges that can be evaluated and applied by persons with ordinary technical expertise. The purposes or design of the Constitution are arguably "there" to be examined and analyzed by professionals, and to provide tests for the analytical soundness of Court decisions appealing beyond the text and intentions of the framers.

At this point in the intraprofessionalist argument a crucial association is made. A professional theory of constraints on judges is associated with a political interpretation of the original meaning of the Constitution. One can see this association in stark relief in the modern voting rights cases.[7] While a professional theory of judicial review might suggest that malapportioned legislatures do not offend the Constitution (since malapportionment was not explicitly forbidden by the text nor deplored by the framers), a political interpretation of the purposes of the Constitution reveals that the principle of representativeness was purportedly implicit in the document. Protection of this principle thus justifies judicial invalidation of legislative malapportionment schemes. Note how judicial scrutiny, at this level, has a professional rationale, but the rationale itself is based on accepting a political interpretation of the Constitution as making representativeness a basic principle of American government.

Here one confronts the central dilemma for the intraprofessionalist argument. If one assumes that the Court should be constrained in the exercise of its lawmaking power and that the constraints should be "professionally" derived, and one seeks the derivation of those constraints in the text, history, and original purposes of the Constitution, how can one justify constraints that follow from a contemporary political interpretation of those purposes? In other words, what if an equally plausible or more plausible contemporary interpretation of the purposes of the Constitution can be put forth that would not justify judicial review of legislative malapportionment? Such an interpretation is, of course, relatively easy to advance. If the framers were so fundamentally dedicated to the principle of representativeness, why did they permit so many classes of persons to be denied the right to vote?

For the intraprofessionalist argument to succeed at its third and most far-reaching level, it would seem necessary that there be a decisive contemporary consensus about the original purposes of the Constitution. Otherwise the purportedly neutral, "professional" quality of the third level of argument disappears, and intraprofessionalists are forced to argue that the Court should be confined to the original intention of the Constitution in every instance except where the Court is deciding what the original intention of the Constitution was.

It is possible, however, for intraprofessionalists to evade even this difficulty. Contemporary interpretations of an eighteenth-century document are required in constitutional adjudication, and contemporary social values do not inevitably resemble those of the framers. Since few persons would commit the Court to following the framers' views of all social issues—should we, for example, follow the framers' views of indentured servitude?—why should the Court be committed to rigid applications of the framers' views about the basic purposes of the Constitution? In particular, where a later generation finds the framers' design unintelligible or inconsistent or simply wrongheaded, why should that design not be reconsidered in accordance with current values?

This intraprofessionalist response invites its perpetrators to designate some "currently held values" that are sufficiently "professional," or sufficiently widely shared, to act as effective constraints on an expansive, revisionist Court. Thus pressed, intraprofessionalist literature seems to have supplied three central values for constitutional adjudication: structure, process, and participation.[8]

"Structure" here means a commitment to the principle of separation of governmental powers and implicit checks on those powers. "Process" means a commitment to the use of fair and equal procedures in the affairs of government, and "participation" means a commitment to the principle that when someone has a claim of right denied by an institution of the state, the person having that claim denied shall have an adequate chance to take part in its denial.

The derivation of these values is as follows. The value of structure comes merely from an examination of the Constitution's own language, which provides for separate and interchecking branches of government. The value of process is derived from two sources: the traditional commitment in American civilization to the principles of fairness and equality, and the purported impossibility, in today's world, of giving those terms a universal substantive meaning that is intelligible. "Fairness" and "equality" can only mean fair and equal procedures because we cannot agree on what "fairness" and "equality" mean as substantive principles of universal application. Finally, the value of participation emerges from a reading of the constitutional design as promoting participatory democracy by vesting sovereignty in the people. Since the people are sovereign, the people must participate in their own suppression should government seek to suppress them. And since the governmental institution best designed to promote participation is the legislature, the value of participation requires a presumption that legislative constitutional lawmaking be preferred to constitutional lawmaking by the Court.

The alternative perspective expressed in the contemporary debate over the proper role of the Court I have labeled supraprofessionalist. Its central assumption is that the Constitution cannot be made into an exclusively professional document. While some of its words may have an explicit meaning, others are open-ended; while its history may be settled in some respects, it is obscure in others; while purportedly neutral professional rationales for constitutional decisions may be advanced, those rationales are necessarily grounded in inarticulate value preferences that are not confined to a community of lawyers and judges. The Constitution, in short, is a lay document as well as a professional document.

The area of constitutional law has long been regarded as peculiarly susceptible to political vicissitudes, and judges in their capacity as constitutional interpreters have long been regarded as political beings. But the lay meaning of the Constitution should not be too casually equated with contemporary politics. Recent supraprofessionalist literature on judicial review, in fact, has been more interested in political theory than in politics as currently practiced.[9] A conception of the Constitution as a lay document has been tied to a theory of reasoning in constitutional cases that stressed the importance of intuitive abstract values in American life, values such as fairness and equality and liberty and autonomy. Where professional reasoning discounts those values or converts them into professional concepts such as "process," the supraprofessionalist perspective claims that such reasoning is flawed. It is flawed not only because it discounts the degree to which the Constitution resists being reduced to a professional document, but also because converting abstract values to professional concepts diminishes the seriousness of the values.

Thus a second assumption of supraprofessionalist participants in the current debate over the Court's role is that the Constitution cannot be converted to a charter for "structure, process, and participation" because such a conversion diminishes the significance of certain values the Constitution is intended to protect. Here an example may clarify the point. Suppose that one believes that the value of sexual freedom and intimacy in a married couple is a basic foundation of American society, and consequently the couple has a presumptive right of sexual freedom and intimacy against the state. But then assume the following argument. While there may be an abstract right of sexual freedom and intimacy, the right is not enumerated in the Constitution, and therefore the structure of the Constitution operates to allow that right to be confined by the legislative branch of the government. The legislature, however, must be fair and equal in the way it confines the right: it must not deny some married couples freedom to pursue sexual relations and allow that freedom to others. The legislature must, in short, confine that right through a constitutionally permissible process. Finally, those having their rights confined by the process must have an opportunity to participate in the process and to adequately protest their being confined. If all three criteria are satisfied, the legislature may confine the right.

An assumption of the supraprofessionalist literature is that there are certain values and rights basic to American society that cannot be so confined. I have chosen the example of sexual intimacy in married couples because in this instance the source of the right is not an explicit provision of the constitutional text. It is rather an intuitive collective sense that a married couple's sexual intimacy is not the state's business, absent those instances, such as criminality, or mental or physical illness, or national defense, where the state could assert some overwhelming interest in curbing the access of one spouse to another. Since the right rests on other than an explicit textual basis, it cannot be appropriately evaluated solely by professional readings of the constitutional text. It apparently must also be evaluated by recourse to lay preferences.

Here the supraprofessionalist perspective reveals another of its assumptions: that while the text of the Constitution is an important source of legal principles in constitutional adjudication, it is not the only source. This assumption has its treacherous features. While resort beyond the body of the constitutional text to "general principles of justice" was a common practice of eighteenth- and early nineteenth-century judges such as John Marshall and Samuel Chase,[10] a jurisprudential conception of natural principles or rights outside the body of the constitutional text has undergone severe attack since the early twentieth century.[11] An influential current view of extratextual principles in constitutional law is that there are none.[12] While open-ended provisions of the Constitution may serve as potential repositories of newly perceived "rights," such as the right of privacy, some textual protection for such rights must be established. One cannot merely appeal, as Marshall did on occasion, to principles or rights in the air.

The supraprofessionalist rejoinder to the claim that the Constitution must be the only source of constitutional principles can be summarized as follows. While early judicial readings of the Constitution, such as those of Marshall, assumed that the constitutional text had a specific and permanent meaning, those readings also assumed that judges could decide constitutional cases by summoning up principles not enumerated in the text. As the notion of extratextual principles receded, a dilemma was created. If the constitutional text had a specific and permanent meaning, how could subsequent generations avoid being compelled to accept the social attitudes and values of the framers?

The framers, for example, did not prevent the government from electronic eavesdropping in the Fourth Amendment: their notion of searches and seizures assumed physical entry onto one's property. Yet the prospect of indiscriminate electronic eavesdropping by the government has seemed intolerable to twentieth-century Americans. Consequently, judicial glosses on the original language of the constitutional text have been tolerated as a substitute for the earlier appeal to sources outside the Constitution.

On reflection, however, certain of these judicial glosses appear to be more than merely "liberalized" interpretations of textual provisions. Protecting a couple's right to sexual intimacy, for example, requires a different technique of judicial interpretation from protecting persons against electronic eavesdropping. In the latter, judges merely extrapolate the original meaning of "search and seizure" to a twentieth-century technological context; in the former, judges create a constitutional right by "discovering" an unenumerated value of privacy in the design of the Constitution.

The "privacy" gloss suggests a judicial subterfuge that supraprofessionalist commentators would prefer to avoid. If the Court can adjust the Constitution to changed conditions by "inventing" constitutional rights, why should it not openly acknowledge that the source of those rights is not the constitutional text but the enhanced seriousness of certain values in American society? And are not those values analogous to the older notion of extratextual principles or rights?

Put another way, do we not acknowledge, in the abstract, certain rights against the state that are not explicitly protected by the Constitution? The Constitution says nothing about a right to eat and drink, or a right to dress as one chooses, or a right to decide how many children one wants to have. One can think of instances where the state could infringe on any of these. But surely a blanket policy of starvation by the state would be regarded as just as intolerable as a blanket policy of incarcerating persons for speaking out on political issues. The point is not that these abstract, unenumerated rights are absolutes, but that they are potentially as "fundamental" to American citizenship as enumerated rights.

Even if one shares all the foregoing supraprofessionalist assumptions, however, their implications for the proper role of the Court are not necessarily clarified. If the Constitution is a lay document as much as a professional document, if it is designed to protect rights against the state, and if rights against the state cannot be adequately protected by appeal to the structure of the Constitution, to adequate processes of government, or to the value of participation, why does it follow that the Court is the best protector of rights against the state and therefore the best institution to undertake constitutional lawmaking?

In a democracy, albeit a constitutional democracy, one assumes that elites ought not to impose their values on others unless the others have adequately consented. But the Court is unquestionably an elite branch of government, and in the name of constitutional lawmaking its members do impose values. One need only glance at history to make this point: different Courts have read phrases like "equal protection" in the area of race relations in strikingly different and even self-contradictory ways. Moreover, there is little effective political check on the elite behavior. Justices of the Court cannot be removed from office simply because one disagrees with their value orientation. Legislators, however, can: therefore why should constitutional lawmaking in a democracy not be performed by legislators?

An answer to this last question, I shall argue, can be derived from an analysis of historical conceptions of the judiciary and the Court. I thus turn to a brief discussion of the intellectual context of the Constitution, and then attempt to draw some contemporary meaning from that discussion.

II The Context of the Constitution

Recent scholarship on the intellectual context of the Constitution has produced what might be called a new historiographical synthesis.[13] In this synthesis the Constitution is seen as a revolutionary document in spite of itself. The political theory of the constitutional decade was neoclassical, essentially concerned with balances. Balances were sought between the masses of the people and elites; between visions of a homogenous, virtuous republic and fears of corruption and factionalism; between the states and the nation; between democratic and undemocratic branches of government. But the strategy adopted for achieving balance—the creation of a Constitution—subverted classical politics in that the Constitution transferred sovereignty to the people, and "the people" over time have proved not to be the predictable beings envisaged by classical political theory. In particular, the popular will in America has been conceived as less dependent on the state, and the state more dependent on it, than classical political theory assumed.

Put another way, the Constitution was one of the first "modern" philosophical documents—modern in the sense that it confronted the capacity of human experience to resist universal theories of the human condition. So far from being a manifestation of the perfect symmetry and unity of the universe, life in late eighteenth-century America was perceived as contingent and unstable. A series of institutional buffers were erected by the framers against that instability: a republic, a Constitution, the tripartite branches of government, a federal union. In erecting these buffers, the framers sought balance. But they could not justify the presence of these "aristocratic" institutions without linking them to the concept of sovereignty in the people.[14]

The debate about the Bill of Rights furnishes an example of the theoretical mood of the time. It was not part of the original Constitution, but was included as an "afterthought."[15] That afterthought surfaced when some proponents of the Declaration of Independence, many of whom had opposed the idea of a federal Constitution, insisted that rights against the state should be openly declared lest the Constitution be interpreted as not protecting those rights.[16] The response to these agitators is instructive. It did not take the form of suggestions that acts by the state that contravened the "natural" rights of citizens would automatically be void,[17] and that to single out some rights as deserving of protection would be to suggest that those rights not enumerated were not to be protected.[18]

The Bill of Rights partisans prevailed, but not on the ground that the Constitution would otherwise subvert rights. They prevailed on the ground that the American republican experiment had been distinguished by its emphasis on natural rights against the state, and that an enumeration of some such rights would link the Constitution more specifically to the Declaration of Independence.[19]

In the debate over the Bill of Rights, one can see the ambivalent intellectual context of the constitutional generation. A neoclassical theory of a republic as embodying natural rights and promoting order in society informs those who argue that there is no need for a Bill of Rights; a somewhat different theory—intuitively based, perhaps, on perceptions of the instability and contingency of experience in America—informs those who argue that there is such a need. The ambivalence comes from the design of the Constitution itself. Does its enactment foreclose any need for protection of rights against the state, since its structure automatically allows appeal to fundamental principles of republican political theory? Or does its enactment threaten rights against the state, since its institutional design allows the people's rights to be interpreted by elites?

While this ambivalence has fascinated historians of the constitutional decade, its richness tends to obscure some clear messages for contemporary scholars. Three such messages may be discerned.

First, the framers of the Constitution assumed that there were abstract natural rights against the state, that those abstract rights could not be sacrificed in a republic, and that the list of such rights was not exhausted when some were codified in the Bill of Rights. Second, both supporters and opponents of the Constitution assumed that it was an effort to erect institutional buffers against chaos, and that those buffers would be staffed and managed by elites. Third, the strategy for enactment of the Constitution was to justify elite management of the American republic by appeal to the concept of sovereignty in the people.

These three messages may be summarized and integrated in the following dictum. A decisive majority of the framers of the Constitution took rights against the state seriously, thought that the constitutional text was not the sole source of such rights, and expected that while the rights derived from the people, they were to be articulated and protected by elites. If one accepts that dictum, some issues in the contemporary debate over the proper role of the Court can be resolved, and others can be clarified.

III The Court's Contemporary Role

If my reading of the intellectual context of the constitutional decade is sound, two arguments made by intraprofessionalist scholars are arguments in the teeth of history. The framers did not intend to confine constitutionality protected rights to those enumerated in the Constitution, and thus it seems anachronistic to argue that only those rights so enumerated should receive constitutional protection. Moreover, the framers recognized, in the debate over the Bill of Rights, that enumerating certain rights could be construed as excluding protection for others, an outcome no one in the debate supported. Thus it seems equally anachronistic to argue that the framers' intent was to identify certain rights as paramount, where their intent was only to offer certain rights as exempletive of a more general theory of natural rights against the state.

Both of these anachronistic intraprofessionalist arguments can be regarded as designed to serve another purpose. The purpose is not so much to offer a historically defensible theory of the meaning of the Constitution—although that effort is part of the intraprofessionalist argument—but to devise a means of confining judicial lawmaking power. Rights against the state have been traditionally construed, in constitutional law, by the judiciary. A theory of the Constitution that confines lawmakers to the express words of the framers primarily confines lawmaking by the courts. This is because most claims of right, based on interpretations of the Constitution, are made by minorities against legislative majorities. The paradigm claim is that a legislature has usurped a constitutional right; the paradigm institution to which appeal for protection of that right has been made is the judiciary. Narrowing the scope of rights against the state to those enumerated or otherwise demonstrably supported by the framers narrows the scope of judicial power to scrutinize legislative decisions in the name of protecting rights.

Here one confronts the crucial nexus, in intraprofessionalist arguments, between a theory of limited rights against the state and a theory of limited lawmaking power in the judiciary. It is not accidental that this nexus has occurred; it is a corollary to the persistent role of the American judiciary, as exemplified by the Supreme Court, as a defender of minority rights against governmental majorities. I need not review this historical role; it is enough to note the persistent concern in late eighteenth-century constitutional theory that the people's rights be protected by elites and the artful legitimization by Marshall in *Marbury v. Madison* of the Supreme Court's role as the principal elite institution protecting the people's rights.

What has occurred since Marshall's opinion in *Marbury*, I have suggested, is a breakdown of the jurisprudential assumptions in his argument justifying elite judicial review and the consequent emergence of a fear that in a world where judges make law rather than find it, judicial protection of the people against the state can become the equivalent of judicial imposition of selective biases on the people.

Thus we reach a less obvious, but for me a more central, contemporary "lesson" of the experience of the constitutional generation. The lesson is that we cannot adequately protect rights against the state unless we suffer some elite judicial lawmaking power in the process. Moreover, we cannot adequately protect rights against the state unless we are prepared, in suffering that judicial power, also to suffer the use by the judiciary of supraprofessionalist reasoning—reasoning that goes beyond an emphasis on structure, process, and participation.

Let me begin to defend that claim by restating the jurisprudential change in the nature of law that has taken place since the years of the Constitution and *Marbury v. Madison*. Law is now generally conceived of as a repository of shifting social values rather than a set of permanent universal principles; the art of judging, where constitutional issues are at stake, is now linked not so much to a persuasive articulation of "first principles" as to a persuasive articulation of deeply felt and widely shared values. Legal principles, like the principles of privacy and autonomy, are not now regarded as immutable, if mystical axioms, but as manifestations of values currently taken with great seriousness.[20]

Some of these values, such as personal liberty and equality, have been so consistently taken seriously that they may be said to have created abstract rights against the state. But abstract rights against the state, in a jurisprudential setting where law is defined as a corpus of values, are not necessarily deserving of protection in concrete instances, since they are not regarded as inevitably and universally predominant. An abstract commitment to equality does not mean that everyone must always be treated equally, nor does an abstract commitment to liberty mean that everyone can always expect to be free. Other values—the security of the state, one's right to be different—are balanced off against equality and liberty in concrete situations.

The framers of the Constitution recognized that, even in a society that regarded the conception of abstract rights against the state as a necessary proposition of enlightened government, abstract rights needed to be confined in certain instances. But they assumed that too great a confinement of abstract rights by legislative majorities would not adequately implement the conception of rights against the state. They thus created an appeal to the Constitution as a source by which rights could be protected. Marshall in *Marbury* then supplied a compelling, if not inevitable, corollary to that appeal: constitutional protection for abstract rights against the state cannot be truly effective if the very body most inclined to usurp those rights in concrete instances—the legislature—is the principal interpreter of the Constitution.

It seems to me that Marshall's corollary, although announced in an age that defined law differently from ours, retains its vitality. We cannot allow legislative majorities to determine the scope of protection for abstract rights against the state if we truly want to protect these rights. It seems to me that what is currently bothering us about the Court's lawmaking power is not the historic role of the Court as a protection of minority rights against the state, but the contemporary role of the Court as a lawmaking, not a law-finding, institution. We somehow feel that because the Court is elitist, not being popularly checked or subject to popular reelection, it is a bad thing that it is also making law—preferring some social values to others—in the name of constitutional interpretation.

I cannot imagine that any Court whose members took seriously their historic mandate to protect minority rights would be able to avoid substituting, on a given occasion, social values that they believed to be predominantly supported by the Constitution, or a substantial number of American citizens, for social values supported by a legislative majority. If a Court did not undertake this substitution, the predominant values of American society would be deemed to be those fostered by legislative majorities. If that were the case, we would have a different type of government from the one originally established by the framers. Perhaps we should have, but that question goes well beyond a concern with discretionary power in the judiciary, and ought not to be assumed away at the outset.

I say this because it seems to me that none of the intraprofessionalist arguments adequately responds to the recurrent problem of protecting rights against the state. The level that most seriously attempts such a response is the level claiming that a proper focus on structure, process, and participation in constitutional lawmaking can secure protection for minority rights. But that level of the argument can only succeed, in my view, by elevating the values of structured balance among branches of government, fair and equal procedures, and representative democracy to a position of predominance in our society. While I am not opposed to those values, I am opposed to their predominance in every case where abstract rights against the state are being confirmed, and I have earlier offered some specific instances where I think many Americans might share my opposition.

I envisage, therefore, a role for the Court that designates it as protector of rights against the state and does not impose intraprofessional constraints on its lawmaking power. But to tolerate that sort of power in the Court I must insist that it be subject to supraprofessional constraints. That phrase may seem a contradiction in terms, since I have earlier acknowledged that judges are regarded as lawmakers and that lawmaking can be equated with value choices. Moreover, I have suggested that judges have not been and cannot be confined, in their interpretations of the Constitution, to the explicit words of the constitutional text or to the original intentions of the framers. Where, then, are the constraints?

The chief source of supraprofessionalist constraints on the Court comes, I believe, from the persistent equation, in American society, of law with abstract beliefs about morality and justice. While the content of those beliefs has changed in the course of American history, their presence has persisted. Too "immoral" or too "unjust" an interpretation of the Constitution by the Court is simply not accepted by the public. It is not, to use a term from the contemporary debate, invested with legitimacy.[21]

Dred Scott v. Sandford[22] was such an interpretation: it foundered on the immorality and injustice of black slavery. *Korematsu v. United States*,[23] upholding the incarceration of Japanese-Americans during World War II, was another: it foundered on the immorality and injustice of selecting one group of potentially dangerous Americans for incarceration when other such groups—German-Americans or Italian-Americans—were not so selected. One could give numerous additional examples, most of which have involved legislative discriminations against racial or other minorities. There has been an implicit burden on the Court to square its decisions with prevailing public perceptions of what is "right" and "wrong," "good" and "bad."

The principal place where the Court's members face this burden is in the rhetorical justifications of opinions. Why a justice decides a case in his or her "heart of hearts" is not always made public, but somewhere in the process of opinion writing at least one justice, assigned to speak for a majority of the Court, is required to offer a rhetorical justification for the decision, in "professional " language. Many segments of the public may not understand the language, but the practical consequences of the decision are easy enough for the public to discern. One knows, after *Brown v. Board of Education*[24] that racially segregated schools are "against the law," even if one is not entirely sure why.

The practical consequences of a Supreme Court decision, I submit, have a moral meaning of their own. If one violently disagrees with the morality of a given decision, one may well be motivated to examine the rhetorical justifications for it; the same may be true if one enthusiastically endorses the morality of the decision. Thus sooner or later numerous segments of the public perceive the extent to which the Court, through its rhetorical justifications for a decision, has squared that decision with current notions of morality and justice. The "squaring" analysis is made by an examination of the Court's rhetoric and an assessment of the perceived validity of its moral reasoning. Such an analysis, when undertaken by the lay public, is rarely conducted on technical, "professional" terms. But on the serious legal issues of our time and previous times it is nonetheless conducted.

If I am correct in the above suppositions, the dimension of moral reasoning of a Court opinion is its crucial source of legitimacy, and that dimension cannot be reduced to "professional" techniques of interpretation. Patently illegitimate moral reasoning in a Court opinion, regardless of how skillfully crafted, is eventually exposed. An example is the reasoning in *Plessy v. Ferguson*,[25] where the Court majority upheld racially separate but equal facilities by stating that if segregation of blacks from whites by white majorities was construed by the affected blacks as a tacit judgment that they were regarded as inferior to whites, such a construction was purely speculative. The illegitimacy of that reasoning was first made obvious by common experience. Both blacks and whites in segregated states came to realize, as racial segregation spread, that racial segregation was in fact based on the premise that blacks were inferior to whites, a premise that Justice Harlan, the lone dissenter in *Plessy,* had identified in his opinion. When public perceptions of the immorality and injustice of *Plessy*'s premise surfaced, the illegitimacy of the moral reasoning in *Plessy* was exposed.

Thus I am not as concerned as some of my contemporaries may be that active use of the Court's lawmaking power to protect rights against the state will result in Bad Judges making Bad Decisions, "Bad" being used in a moral sense. I think some Bad Decisions will occur, just as some Bad Decisions are made by legislatures. I am not particularly sanguine, after Vietnam, Watergate, and the recent incidents of influence-peddling in Congress, about the inherent capacity of elites to be moral and just. I am somewhat more sanguine about the capacity of the public to recognize immorality and injustice. And the public arguably has as much of an opportunity to scrutinize the moral dimensions of a Supreme Court opinion as it has to scrutinize the moral conduct of a legislature. The difference is a difference in the type of scrutiny, not in its extent.

I make this last observation because I believe that the American public has a meaningful device to signify its collective disapproval of the morality of a Court decision. Numerous members of the public can simply decline to abide by the decision. Decisions of the Court require implementation; they can be subverted by the implementers or those affected by the decision. Such is very regularly the case: one need only observe the discrepancy between practices concerning court-appointed representation of criminal defendants and the national rules for representation laid down in Supreme Court decisions. A judgment by segments of the public that it will not follow a Court's decision is the equivalent of a judgment by segments of the public that it will vote a legislator out of office. Only the latter practice is called a "political" check, but that seems to me simply because we have not adequately studied public noncompliance with Supreme Court decisions.

And even if one disagrees with me about the effectiveness of public checks on the Court, it seems to me that one cannot gainsay the burden on the Court to square its decisions with current standards of morality and justice. I am prepared to let the presence of that burden, coupled with the importance I assign to rights against the state and the difficulties I find in legislative protection of those rights, make my case for an "activist," lawmaking Supreme Court. I think that such a role for the Court is faithful to our history, even though the jurisprudential context has changed; faithful to our collective sense that the American government may not unduly restrict the rights of its citizens, although the citizenry will continue to change its mind about what restrictions it tolerates and what rights it protects; and faithful to a tacit assumption in American society that law, especially constitutional law, cannot be divorced from intuitive notions of morality and justice and thus can never completely become a "professional" subject.

NOTES

1. Samplings of intraprofessionalist literature include Raoul Berger, *Government by Judiciary* (1977); Robert Bork, *Neutral Principles and Some First Amendment Problems*, 47 Ind. L. J. 1 (1971); Hans Linde, *Judges, Critics, and the Realist Tradition*, 82 Yale L. J. 227 (1972); John Hart Ely, *Toward a Representation-Reinforcing Mode of Judicial Review*, 37 Md. L. Rev. 451 (1978), expanded in Ely, *Democracy and Distrust* (1980).

Samplings of supraprofessionalist literature include Ronald Dworkin, *Taking Rights Seriously* (1977), Lawrence Tribe, *American Constitutional Law* (1978); Thomas C. Grey, *Do We Have An Unwritten Constitution?*, 27 Stan. L. Rev. 703 (1975). To designate individuals as sharing a "perspective" on judicial review is not, of course to suggest that their views are identical.

2. 1 Cranch 137 (1803).

3. *See* Jerome Frank, *Law and the Modern Mind* (1930); Karl Llewellyn, *Some Realism About Realism - Responding to Dean Pound*, 44 Harv. L. Rev. 1222 (1931); Llewellyn, *A Realistic Jurisprudence-The Next Step*, 30 Colum. L. Rev. 431 (1930).

4. *See* Berger, *supra* note 1.

5. *See* Bork, *supra* note 1 and Linde, *supra* note 1.

6. *See* Ely, *supra* note 1.

7. *See, e.g., Baker v. Carr*, 369 U.S. 186 (1962); *Reynolds v. Sims*, 377 U.S. 533 (1964).

8. The most explicit statement of this view is in Ely, *Democracy and Distrust, supra* note 1.

9. *See, e.g.,* Dworkin, *supra* note 1 and Grey, *supra* note 1.

10. *See, e.g., Fletcher v. Peck,* 10 U.S. (6 Cranch) 87 (1810) (John Marshall); and *Calder v. Bull,* 3 U.S. (3 Dall.) 386 (1798) (Samuel Chase).

11. *See, e.g.,* Bork, *Neutral Principles, supra* note 1 and Ely, *Democracy and Distrust, supra* note 1.

12. This view is criticized in Grey, *supra* note 1. *See also* Robert Cover, *Justice Accused* (1975).

13. In particular, *see* Gordon Wood, *The Creation of the American Republic, 1776–1787* (1969), J.G.A. Pocock, *The Machiavellian Moment* (1975), and J. R. Pole, *Political Representation in England and the Origins of the American Republic* (1976).

14. *See* Pocock, *supra* note 13, at 515–35, Wood, *supra* note 13, at 519–36.

15. *See* Wood, *supra* note 13, at 536.

16. *See* Wood, *supra* note 13, at 536–37.

17. *See* Wood, *supra* note 13, at 538.

18. *See* Wood, *supra* note 13, at 537–40.

19. *See* discussion in Wood, *supra* note 13, at 536–43.

20. *See, e.g.,* Ronald Dworkin, *Law's Empire* (1977).

21. I have previously distinguished between an authoritative judicial decision and a legitimated judicial decision in *The Evolution of Reasoned Elaboration,* 58 Va. L. Rev. 279 (1973). *See also* Grey, *supra* note 1, and Ely, "Toward a Represention-Reinforcing Mode of Judicial Review," *supra* note 1.

22. 19 Howard 393 (1957).

23. 324 U.S. 214 (1944).

24. 347 U.S. 483 (1954).

25. 163 U.S. 537 (1896).

Judicial Activism and the Identity of the Legal Profession*

This essay reviews three books: *Death Penalties: The Supreme Court's Obstacle Course*,[1] by Raoul Berger, *Toward Increased Judicial Activism: The Political Role of the Supreme Court*,[2] by Arthur Selwyn Miller, and *The Constitution, the Courts, and Human Rights*,[3] by Michael Perry. Each book adds to the current debate over the legitimacy of Supreme Court activism in our constitutional democracy, especially in the field of individual rights. In an era where the result reached in *Brown v. Board of Education*[4] is generally understood to be the baseline from which all theories of the proper role of the Court should begin, many commentators have struggled to find a way to legitimize *Brown*, and yet retain a check on the potential ability of members of the Court to constitutionalize their own personal preferences. This potential power in judges, operating in the face of our commitment to a democratic theory of government, is often called the "counter-majoritarian difficulty."

Berger sets his argument within the framework of the debate around the constitutionality of the death penalty. Berger contends that "original intent" jurisprudence, or his version of "interpretivism," is the only means by which to check the tendency of members of the Court to turn personal predilections into law. The Court may only interpret phrases of the Constitution, such as "cruel and unusual,"[5] as would the original framers of the Constitution and its amendments. Looking to the text of the Constitution and other historical sources, Berger finds the record replete with evidence that, at the time of the framing, American society viewed the death penalty not as "cruel and unusual" punishment, but as a widely accepted mode of punishment for a broad range of crimes.

Therefore, says Berger, the Court cannot legitimately curb the power of the states to determine for themselves whether or not to have a death penalty. As a corollary, when members of the Court appeal to "evolving standards of decency,"[6] as they did in the case that was the impetus behind Berger's book[7], they overstep their constitutional bounds. Rather than allow justices to alter the meaning of the Constitution by fiat, Berger maintains that democracy demands codifi-

*67 Judicature 246 (1983).

cation of any change from the historical meaning of the text of the Constitution by formal constitutional amendment.[8]

Arthur Miller and Michael Perry, by contrast, attempt to present arguments for judicial activism. Miller urges that the Court embrace and expand its role as a policymaking body by modeling itself as a modern Council of Elders. Miller envisions the Court as an affirmative lawmaker with the authority to make pronouncements on political theory and moral philosophy. This Court would adopt and elucidate a moral principle, a "blueprint" (Miller suggests the concept of "human dignity"), with which to guide the decisionmaking process and promote the public good.

Miller is not much worried about the "countermajoritarian difficulty," for a variety of reasons. First, he sees the current Court as a policymaking body, but one that masks its result orientation in legal jargon. Miller thus believes that his vision is not so much a change, as an admission of what is already present. Further, he believes the politics of the country are more accurately characterized as anarchic pluralism than democracy. Finally, he rejects the premises of "interpretivism," maintaining that the framers meant the Constitution to be a document with a fluid rather than fixed meaning, and thus anticipated that their "original intent" would be rethought over time.

Perry also advocates judicial activism, and in his book attempts to find a "noninterpretivist" rationale for the protection of human rights. He begins with the assumption that there is no historical or textual basis for legitimizing Court rulings that interpret the Constitution as giving "rights" to the individual against the state where those "rights" were unimagined by the framers. However, he suggests that there is a functional basis for extending the scope of constitutionally protected rights: the American people conceive of their nation as one with a commitment to the moral evolution of the polity. Perry sees the United States as comprised of people who believe that their country is one that is destined to serve as a moral "beacon"[9] for the world. Therefore, he concludes, the Court performs a democratic function when it attempts to constitutionalize the "right" answers to moral human rights questions.

Perry responds to the argument that other branches of government are more appropriate vehicles of moral evolution by contending that the other branches by nature simply cannot perform the function of "institutionalization of prophecy"[10] as well as the Court. In order to counter the contention that his arguments open the door to tyranny of the judiciary, Perry claims that given Congress's constitutional ability to limit the appellate jurisdiction of the Court, the people can limit the Court's power of noninterpretive judicial review.

In considering the contributions of Berger, Miller, and Perry together, one might first wonder why "activism" on the part of judges has become a topic of such great current interest. All three books talk repeatedly about judicial activism, and each employs the term in ways that suit the respective author's purposes. None of the authors, however, would very likely seek to distinguish his definition of activism from the following "common" definition. In that definition activism is a term describing a judicial posture in which the judge exercises one of a number of options available to him or her when confronted with a case raising issues of "policy," in addition to issues of "doctrine." The option exercised by the "activist" judge is to decide the case notwithstanding the fact that it raises policy issues; to use the language of "policy" (insofar as that can be distinguished from the language of "doctrine") in justifying that decision; and to treat the case as a matter for *judicial* competence, notwithstanding the fact that another branch of government was arguably also competent to entertain and to decide the same policy issues.

If this common definition of activism is accepted, one might legitimately ask why the term has become such a lightning rod. American judges have entertained cases with policy dimensions since before their power of independent constitutional review was established. In deciding those cases they have repeatedly used the language of "policy" (calling that language by various names), and have not foresworn making decisions because of the presence of other potential institutional fora. *Marbury v. Madison*,[11] *McCulloch v. Maryland*,[12] *Dred Scott v. Sandford*,[13] the Legal Tender Cases,[14] *Plessy v. Ferguson*,[15] *Lochner v. New York*,[16] *Schenck v. United States*,[17] *Brown v. Board of Education*[18]—all the cases that repeatedly appear on commentators' "great" or "notorious" lists—were "activist" decisions.

Activism is nothing new, and it is not newly controversial. Every one of the above decisions was severely attacked, and vociferously defended, when made; the Court that made them was castigated, and applauded, not only for the outcome of the decisions but because it chose, in its judicial capacity, to make them. Why then, has a sudden urgency to reconsider activism surfaced? And why should theorists think they have anything new to say on the issue?

We may begin to fathom the sense of urgency implicit in each of these reappraisals of activism if, for purposes of argument, we label an activist stance by a judge as constitutionally unauthorized, politically dangerous, and professionally unsound. Such labels, once qualifications and disclaimers are made and the focus of inquiry restricted to the Supreme Court of the United States and probably to constitutional issues, encapsulate the "critique" of activist judging, a critique advanced regularly in the past and contained, in diverse ways, in each of the books under consideration here.

The critique has currently taken a special twist, however, and contains a powerful "hidden message." It can be explored by analyzing its separate parts, which are also the central foci of each of the books under review. Berger is concerned with the constitutional difficulties activism presents; Miller seeks to explain its political dangers; Perry confronts its implications for the stature of the judicial, and necessarily the legal, professions.

I The Constitutional Difficulties

Berger has written five books since 1969,[19] and while addressing different subjects, they advance the same philosophy of constitutional interpretation, a philosophy that is itself internally consistent. Berger's view is that judges, in "interpreting" the Constitution, are absolutely bound by the text and by history. The "text," for Berger, is the words of the document, given their usage at the time it was written: "history" is any data that helps explain the meaning of those words, provided that the data is derived from contemporaneous sources. The proper stance for the judge as constitutional interpreter is to ascertain the precise meaning of a relevant provision to its framers and to apply that meaning to the relevant case.

Death Penalties is a simple exercise in Bergerian interpretation. The relevant constitutional provision is the "cruel and unusual punishments" clause of the Eighth Amendment. The task of the Court is to determine the "meaning," of that clause: was it intended to embrace the death penalty? In determining the meaning, one looks to language (what did "cruel and unusual" mean to the framers of the Eighth Amendment) and to context (the practices with respect to penalties for death at the time of that Amendment's framing). Such an effort yields the conclusion that "cruel and unusual punishment" meant tortures and other "barbarous" acts; that putting persons to death in the absence of torture or barbarity was not thought "cruel and unusual"; and that the American public, at the time the Eighth Amendment was framed, overwhelmingly accepted the death penalty.[20] Therefore, Berger concludes, the death penalty is constitutional.

Before discussing Berger's theory itself, we should recall its relationship to activism as Berger employs that term. Activism for Berger is a catch-all term for all theories of constitutional interpretation that do not parallel his. He is willing apparently, to grant some theorists who would not endorse all of his views (Justice Black, Robert Bork, Philip Kurland are singled out) immunity from the label "activist," but nearly everyone else is identified as such. The test for Berger as to whether one can be called an activist seems to be whether one would infuse into constitutional interpretation considerations other than the "text" and "history" as he defines those terms.

Here the argument that activism is constitutionally unauthorized becomes clear. Since judges must resort only to the "text" and to "history" in interpreting provisions of the Constitution, any time they take anything else into account—contemporary conditions, perceived changes in public attitudes, unforeseen or unforeseeable developments in science or technology, newly understood meanings of language—they are being activists, and anyone who suggests that some or all of those considerations might be relevant in determining the contemporary application of the Constitution is an activist as well. "Activism" is juxtaposed against "the text or history of the Constitution."[21]

But does the Constitution require that its text and its history be the sole guides to its interpretation? The singularly eccentric feature of Berger's theory of constitutional interpretation is that there is no evidence of such a requirement. Berger has substituted the terms "text" and "history" for two conceptions of law and interpretation that the framers did hold: the conception that law is an objective body of principles, capable of being discovered but not of being subjectified,[22] and the conception that interpretation should be a process by which the first principles of republican government, necessarily embodied in law, could be restated.[23] These conceptions were part of a body of thought that denied that judges could exercise any will other than the will of law[24] and saw law as inextricably tied to politics, not distinct from it.[25] The separations of judicial lawmaking from law finding, and of law from politics, or policy, were made by later generations.

Berger's approach assumes these separations, worries about their consequences, and concludes that the way out is to have modern judges bound by the attitudes of specially favored generations—the "framers" of constitutional provisions. But the generation that did most of the framing of the Constitution did not regard either subjectivity or politicization as major problems of judicial interpretation. For this generation the text of the Constitution was neither determinative of "the law" nor capable of radical change. That dual message was the point of Chief Justice John Marshall's admonition in *McCulloch* that it is a Constitution "intended to endure for ages to come, and consequently to be adopted to the various crises of human affairs."[26]

Berger's theory thus substitutes twentieth-century conceptions of law and judging for radically different conceptions, and thereby designs a solution for a problem that the original framers did not anticipate. That might be thought to be a pardonable, even irrelevant error, since we are currently operating in Berger's jurisprudential universe, and Berger's theory is designed to give guidance in the decision of modern cases. But Berger's theory insists that the text and history of the Constitution set the limits of modern judicial interpretation because the constitutional structure of American government is predicated on fidelity to those limits. If the constitutional structure originated at a time in which fidelity to those limits was not regarded as necessary, it is hard to see why the text and history should be controlling for subsequent generations.

It appears, in fact, that Berger's theory, despite his claims, is not intended to ensure that subsequent generations honor the jurisprudential assumptions of the eighteenth century. It is intended, rather, to create "safe" points of refuge against fears identified with judging by twentieth-century jurisprudence: unchecked judicial subjectivity and nakedly political judicial "result-orientation." Fidelity to the "intended meaning" of the text forces the twentieth-century judge to transcend his or her subjective view of what a provision "should" mean; fidelity to the context of the framers' generation forces a judge to reach results they, not he or she, would have wanted to reach.

Berger's appeal is therefore not to language or to history as an intellectual historian would use those terms, but to language and history as devices to prevent modern judges from doing what the framers expected judges would do: interpret an adaptive constitution, in light of the first principles of American civilization, to the changing crises of human affairs. Berger apparently fears that if judges perform that function subjectivity and result-orientation will result. It is as if Berger is not as confident as the framers were of the capacity of legal interpretation, performed by trained lawyers and making use of established jurisprudential principles, to produce "true" and "right" decisions—that is, decisions consistent with the spirit of American government. On the contrary, he finds, once the text and history are put aside, "transparent rationalizations of judicial predelictions and barefaced manipulation of the constitutional text" result.[27]

II The Political Dangers

Berger's dark vision of the consequences of allowing the conventional techniques of legal interpretation to flourish in constitutional cases is one to which we still return. There is, however, a second part of the critique of activism that Berger implicitly endorses. In a revealing passage Berger quotes with approval a justification of constitutionalism as embodying the principle of "complete responsibility of government to the governed." [28] Fidelity to the text and to history is for Berger fidelity to a governmental structure in which those who hold public power are accountable to the public. Judicial activism threatens this principle because many judges, including Supreme Court justices, are not electorally accountable and hence free to substitute their subjective wills for law.

Arthur Miller's *Toward Increased Judicial Activism* is an effort to deflect the claim that judicial activism is politically incompatible with the philosophy of American government. Miller's argument reduces itself to three assertive propositions. First, the original constitutional design never envisaged that elite powerholders would be fully accountable to the people. Second, even if the design had envisaged such accountability, major changes in American society since the eighteenth century, such as the rise of corporatism and the replacement of an economy of abundance with one of scarcity, demand the creation of an elite-directed "corporate state" [29] to promote "social well-being." [30] Third, the "climacteric" [31] condition of the modern world and the bankruptcy of modern democratic theory, which Miller suggests is simply "pluralism as anarchy," [32] require extraordinary measures to promote "human dignity on a planetary scale." [33]

At the outset it should be said that Miller's manner of presentation seriously detracts from attention to his argument. He strings together quotations from other sources so repeatedly, and with so little commentary, that one can barely tell whether those comments are incorporated into his argument or being made to serve as substitutes for it. Having found an ostensibly apt quotation for one chapter, he repeats it in another chapter, as if the reader has not encountered it before or will appreciate its ubiquity. He adds to these quotations laundry lists of "assumptions," [34] "factors," [35] "principles" [36] that he suggests underlie his subsequent discussions, but having once made the lists apparently feels that his terms require "little discussion." [37]

Miller's argument includes summaries of the history of the Supreme Court that seemed designed for beginners in American civics, and neologisms ("Constitution of Quasi-Limitations," neofeudalism," "Counsel of State") that apparently need only to be stated to be understood. And after identifying his argument at its outset as an "unabashed proposal for greater judicial 'activism'—but only in a certain direction," [38] he makes no serious effort to suggest why that particular form of activism should be followed.

Miller's apology for activism, in short, runs the risk of being fodder for those who are inclined to suggest that activist judges receive the apologists they deserve. There are, however, two arguments of real stature in Miller's presentation, arguments that a reader, offended by other matters, might be inclined to underestimate. One is Miller's claim that since the political structure of the Constitution was never intended to be wholly consistent with democracy, arguments positing that activist judging is incompatible with the "democratic" theory of American government are flawed. The second is Miller's claim that pluralism, the "anarchistic" twentieth-century version of democratic theory, is intellectually incoherent and perhaps more threatening to political stability in American culture than excessive judicial activism.

A syllogism attacked by Miller's first argument has been so repeatedly invoked that one tends to forget that it rests on a misinterpretation of history. The syllogism runs: American government is "government of the people"; Supreme Court justices are accountable to the people; therefore any decision of the Supreme Court that frustrates the "people's will" violates democratic theory. The principal problem with this syllogism is its assumption that since the rhetorical justification for the American Constitution was popular sovereignty, the form of government the Constitution established was a "democratic" government.

Numerous historians have shown that democratic theory was not the only rationale of the Constitution; another, equally powerful rationale, was the idea of a written body of law, interpreted by some elite branch of government (probably the judiciary) as a counterweight to democratic theory.[39] The Constitution was "sold" largely on the rhetoric of majoritarianism, but the Constitution's structure was as much countermajoritarian as it was majoritarian.[40] Hence it is possible to argue that federal judges were not supposed to further democratic theory in their decisions; instead they were supposed to counter the excesses of democratic theory in the hands of politically irresponsible majorities.

The idea of the Constitution, as interpreted by judges, being a counterforce to arbitrary "democratic" power can thus be shown to have been as embedded in the original design as the idea that sovereignty ultimately resides in the people. And once this clarification of the political philosophy of American government is made, the proposition that judicial activism is "anti-democratic" loses force. Judicial scrutiny of majoritarian excesses could, in fact, be considered democratic if a goal of democracy is the preservation of individual rights against arbitrary majoritarian power. But if democracy is made synonymous with majority will, judicial scrutiny still is justifiable on the grounds that the American political structure is to an important extent countermajoritarian.

Miller's refusal to be taken in by the syllogistic fallacy described above thus deserves some credit. But many others have seen the difficulties in that syllogism and noticed the complexities in American constitutional theory. Miller's claim gains force only when added to his charge that democratic theory has evolved to a peculiarly perverse state in the late twentieth century. "The theory of pluralism," Millers writes, "is that justice will emerge from the conflicts of opposed groups; the practice is to the contrary."[41]

This statement does not quite capture the relationship of democratic theory to pluralism. Democratic theory assumes that individual interests will be in conflict, and when conflict emerges the majority (a coalition of some of those interests) will rule. The majority, then, becomes bound by its rules. Pluralism interjects into the calculus the idea that all interests are deserving of equal concern and respect. Thus when interests come into conflict the fact that one set prevails over another in a majoritarian forum does not mean that the victorious set is worth more than the other. Indeed it is incumbent on the victorious set to acknowledge that the other is equally deserving of concern and respect.

But how is the equal concern and respect principle to be implemented in a democratic society? It would seem that ultimately losers in a majoritarian forum could claim that their interests deserve to be heard, if not vindicated, notwithstanding the fact that a majority prefers not to promote them. Majoritarian policies would thus be subject to continual opposition by those whose equally important interests were not furthered by the policies. But the original rationale of democratic theory was that majorities could rule because losing minorities would consent to be ruled. Pluralism threatens that idea of consent: hence, for Miller, it leads immediately to anarchy.

From this exercise—which I have largely extrapolated from the hints Miller provides—the author moves to the startling proposition that since democracy leads to pluralism and to anarchy, anti-democratic policymaking is the answer, and the Supreme Court the ideal policymaker. The proposition is startling because it would seem that Miller could make a far more modest claim: that the American constitutional design envisaged a set of first principles, embodied in the Constitution and to be interpreted by elites, as a check against such anarchistic notions as the idea that all interests are deserving of equal concern and respect. That is, Miller could argue that the proper function of elite interpreters of the Constitution—the most obvious example being the federal judiciary—is to police the boundary between "illegal" (unconstitutional) and legal majoritarian policies, determining which politics are consistent with democratic theory and which are subversive of it. Instead Miller envisions an ideal Supreme Court as "formulat[ing] a new public philosophy," "alleviat[ing] some of the shortcomings of the pluralistic political order," "aid[ing] those not favored by fortune or inheritance," and ensuring that "equality should come in fact as well as in theory." [42]

Why does Miller forego the more modest claim for one that in its novelty and generality creates a severe analytical burden for his argument? Two answers suggest themselves. One is that Miller is not particularly interested in questions about the allocation of power among branches of American government. He lends support to his interpretation by statements such as "it is the results reached, rather than the means of attaining them, that is the crucial criterion" [43] and "Americans in general care about results . . . and not about the way those results were reached—or by whom." [44] But since the great portion of Miller's book is devoted to fashioning "a new normative posture for the Supreme Court," and to discussing the Court's "role and function" [45] it seems unlikely that he would have engaged in that undertaking if he was only seeking certain policy outcomes and was indifferent to the institutional design that fostered them.

There appears to be a deeper reason for Miller's quixotic posture, one suggested by his statement that "most present day commentary upon the Supreme Court and the Constitution" is shaped by "the dominant ideology of lawyers—legalism, the mind-set that insists that law exists separate and apart from society." [46] Legalism encourages those trained in its beliefs to construct "a heaven of legal concepts . . . from which lawyers and judges can draw appropriate and relevant principles for the resolution of human disputes.'' By casting disputes ''in legalistic verbiage,'' those trained in the law can create, Miller feels, an illusion that the disputes are best resolved in ''words and syntax familiar to lawyers.'' The result is that ''felicity in language and erudite reasoning'' become ''a substitute for justice,'' and judicial opinions ''rationaliz[ing] rather than explain[ing] reasons'' are ''considered to be good . . . without regard to what was actually decided.''[47]

It appears from these comments that Miller fears that if the judiciary were given only a modest ''interpretive'' function, even if one consistent with his view of democratic theory, ''interpretations'' would be advanced in ''legalistic verbiage,'' felicity in language would become a substitute for good results, and justice might well be subverted. The clear suggestion here is that legal language is somehow devoid of moral or ethical content; it obscures justice rather than supports it.

Miller does not trust those trained in ''the fundamental ideology of the legal profession'' to reach ''right'' results and promote ''just'' policies; he wants policymaking to be stripped of the ''interpretive'' language of the law. Rather than appointing ''mine-run lawyers'' to the Supreme Court,[48] Miller would appoint ''men and women of probity . . . courage, perception, compassion without sentimentality—men and women who . . . have the capacity to see what is right and the courage to state it.'' He would consider having ''scientists, engineers, artists, architects, [and] educators'' serve on the Court;[49] he would be particularly attracted to ''a moral philosopher . . . or even a broad-gauged political scientist.'' He suggests a few names: ''Walter Murphy of the Princeton political science faculty; philosophers John Rawls and Robert Nozick; economist Robert Heilbroner; diplomatist and historian George Kennan; physicist John Platt.''[50] The ''limitations on the Justices,'' he believes, ''come . . . from politics rather than from law.''[51]

In these last proposals one senses the crux of Miller's argument for activism, and the odd kinship that he has with Berger. Miller believes that conventional strictures on activist judging, whether derived from the constitutional text, from history, or from the political structure of American government, have the effect of converting judicial decisionmaking into an exercise in legalistic rationalization, in which truth, wisdom, and justice are obscured by ''felicity of language and erudite reasoning.'' The parallel to Berger's catalog, in the death penalty cases, of ''transparent rationalizations of judicial predilections and bare-faced manipulations of the constitutional text'' is striking. Both commentators begin their analysis from the starting point that the language, education, and ''ideology'' of the legal profession are designed to obscure and distort reality.

III The Stature of the Judicial Profession

In the last comments Berger and Miller caricature the third part of the critique of judicial activism—that it is a stance that is professionally unsound because it encourages courts to reach results that may be socially or politically expedient but are difficult to ground on "principled" reasoning that can survive professional scrutiny. Fidelity to "craftsmanship" in judging is a matter of comparative insignificance to Berger and Miller, provided their central requirements for enlightened decisionmaking are met. But in deemphasizing the idea that judges must conform to certain craft norms—the production of opinions based on sufficiently general, durable, and impartial principles and the use in opinions of a style of reasoning that disassociates a result from its immediate partisan consequences being foremost among those norms—Berger and Miller are in a distinct minority among commentators.

The jurisprudential posture of most modern commentators begins with an assumption that judging must above all be professionally sound: that is, judges must live up to the ideals, and respect the limits, of their professional role. Michael Perry's effort to carve out a limited sphere for activist judges takes that assumption seriously. The purpose of Perry's book, as he puts it, is to make "an extended inquiry into the legitimacy of constitutional policymaking by the Supreme Court" in the face of the professional critique of activism, which assumes that "the Court . . . may not legitimately engage in constitutional policy-making as opposed to constitutional interpretation."[52]

Before discussing Perry's argument, the origins and nature of the professional attitude he is addressing require brief attention. The modern professional critique of activism takes its shape from two seminal jurisprudential events of the mid-twentieth century. One was the off-hand statement, written by law clerk Louis Lusky and endorsed by Justice Harlan Fiske Stone in *United States v. Carolene Products,* that there may be occasions on which the Supreme Court might scrutinize majoritarian legislation especially carefully, such as when that legislation infringed upon free speech or the rights of "discrete and insular minorities." Another was Herbert Wechsler's 1959 lecture, "Toward Neutral Principles of Constitutional Law,"[53] in which he claimed that judicial decisions "must be genuinely principled," by which he meant based "on analysis and reasons quite transcending the immediate result that is achieved," and of "adequate neutrality and generality."

Taken together, those two events mark the emergence of a newly predominant attitude among professional commentators on the courts: the attitude that severe judicial scrutiny of majoritarian policymakers (activism) was justifiable, in limited circumstances, but only when it could be justified on "genuinely principled" grounds. The principal constraint on activism was not a constitutional or a political one, but a professional one: craft techniques justified the judiciary's substitution of its judgments for those of electorally accountable institutions.

Perry begins his analysis by maintaining that Wechsler's "professional constraint" theory is "as sound as it is classic."[54] He then identifies the constitutional and political roots of the theory in the following encapsulation:

> [I]t is . . . illegitimate for the judiciary to engage in constitutional policymaking . . . as opposed to constitutional interpretation. The question of the precise constitutional bounds that legislative policymaking and executive policy administration may not exceed must be answered . . . by reference to the value judgments

constitutionalized by the framers. When the judiciary invokes the Constitution to invalidate challenged governmental action not contrary to any of those judgments, it frustrates the will of electorally accountable officials acting within their constitutional bounds, and, moreover, exceeds its own constitutional bounds and thus acts lawlessly.[55]

In this passage we see the constitutional and political strands of the critique of activism collapsed into the professional strand. Legitimacy rests on the boundary between interpretation and policymaking. An opinion qualifies as an interpretation if the value judgments on which its starting premises rest are not those of the judge but those "constitutionalized by the framers." Such value judgments are legitimate in constitutional adjudication. But other value judgments, when invoked by the judiciary to justify the (activist) invalidation of majoritarian policies, "frustrate the will of electorally accountable officials." Professional scrutiny of judicial opinions, then, can reveal their constitutional premises (or lack thereof) and their consequent political legitimacy (or lack thereof). Activist opinions that can be shown, through professional scrutiny, not to conform to the constitutional and political requirements of the critique are given the notorious label "policymaking."

After spinning out and elaborating upon his stated version of the critique of activism for three chapters, Perry then turns to the *Carolene Products* component of modern jurisprudence: the idea that notwithstanding the rigorous requirements under which it must be undertaken, activism is sometimes justifiable. Perry seeks to expand upon that idea and to develop a justification for "constitutional policymaking" in human rights cases. He spends two chapters on that justification, concluding that "constitutional policymaking by the judiciary" can be "an agency of ongoing, insistent moral reevaluation and ultimately of moral growth."[56]

While Perry's rhetoric in those chapters is impassioned and sometimes eloquent, he begins his argument with what appears to be a most damaging concession. He states that "there is neither a textual nor a historical justification for [constitutional policymaking] in human rights cases," and that his justification is to be "functional," that is, one that "serves [to further] our system of government."[57] The "functional" justification for constitutional "interpretation" is that it facilitates the principle of electorally accountable policymaking. And, after rejecting several possibilities, Perry settles on a particular functional justification for constitutional policymaking in human rights cases, the idea that some value judgments not made by the framers are not only "right," but "discoverable" as "right."[58] By involving the principle of "ongoing moral reevaluation and moral growth" to which he regards American society as "committed,"[59] Perry finds his functional justification. Judicial scrutiny of majoritarian policies in human rights cases, even if based on value judgments not constitutionalized by the framers, is legitimate because some value judgments not made by the framers are nonetheless "demonstrably right" and moral growth is a fundamental principle of American society.

It is curious how Perry backs himself into a corner before attempting to leap to freedom in a burst of moral energy. Why does he accept, without much scrutiny, the claim that there is no textual or historical justification for constitutional policymaking (activism) in human rights cases? I have suggested that there is both a textual and a historical justification, the former based on the framers' idea that a written constitution was only a source, not the source of legal principles, and the latter based on the idea that the first principles of American government, some, but not all of which, had been catalogued in the Constitution, were not intended to change, but to be resorted to periodically in "crisis" times. Neither of those ideas implied a text, or a set of "constitutionalized values," that was to be frozen in the time of its promulgation.

Perry, apparently convinced by Berger and other advocates of interpretivism, does not probe their claims. The result is that he forces himself to make a functional argument, which, in light of his earlier concessions, appears as a desperate last resort. But it is only a last resort if one grants a greater primacy to the very narrow definitions of text and history insisted upon by Berger, definitions that I have suggested are suspect.

Perry then gets himself into a further difficulty by making an awkward analogy. He claims that the functional justification for confining judges to interpretation is that interpretation is consistent with the "extraconstitutional" principle of electorally accountable policymaking. He then summons up his own functional justification, which invokes an apparently analogous extraconstitutional principle, moral reevaluation and growth. But the analogy breaks down. Electorally accountable policymaking is a principle whose presence can be seen scattered throughout the debates on the Constitution: it is not too exalted a claim to say that it may have been the central principle of republican government for several of the debaters. The fact that the text of the Constitution does not contain the language "electorally accountable policymaking" seems insignificant in view of the fact that two of the three branches of government that the Constitution created were made directly accountable to an electorate.

The principle of moral reevaluation and growth, by contrast, played no part in the constitutional debates. To the contrary, the governing late eighteenth-century theory of human nature assumed that since human beings were inevitably susceptible to self-interest and corruption, youthful civilizations such as America would tend toward decline and decay rather than toward moral regeneration.[60]

Given his concessions, Perry is forced to make his stand on a principle whose historical and textual grounding he admits is weak and whose overriding truth seems debatable. If one disagrees with Perry that "right answers" to "moral-political problems" are "demonstrable," does that mean one has to abandon activism altogether?

The problem is that Perry has taken too seriously the mainstream mid twentieth-century blueprint for judicial performance. It does not follow, either as a matter of linguistic interpretation or of intellectual history, that judicial opinions involving values other than those constitutionalized by the framers are illegitimate. It is not necessary that judicial reasoning "quite transcend the immediate result" because one academic commentator said so and several of his contemporaries applauded. One does not have to be bound by the silence of the past just because one is self-conscious about the language of the present. All language bites the hand of its user in the end, but language is our only medium for communicating what we care about.

One does not have to honor the set of values of a prior, "favored" generation unless one is confident that one can do no better. Just as Berger and Miller seem unnecessarily afraid of the consequences of allowing contemporary judges to ground decisions in their own professional language, there seems to be an unnecessary reverence in Perry for a critique of judging that is, after all, just based on the words of those who seek to define "craft norms" for a diverse and discordant profession. I see no reason why judges should worry unduly about the former complaint or pay excessive homage to the latter stricture. The case for activism is neither as weak, nor the case against it as strong, as these books suggest.

IV The Hidden Agenda

In concluding, I want to make a final evaluative comment about the three books under review and to return to the hidden agenda that I find contained within them. Both Berger and Miller are prolific writers, undeterred and even stimulated by criticism, and I doubt that this commentary will have much effect on their respective missions. But while those authors may be senior to Perry in productivity and experience, they could profit from his example. Perry's book gives every indication of having been a learning experience for the author as well as for his audience. He grapples with his fellow commentators; he dissects their arguments; he anticipates their rejoinders; he calls for more dialogue. Berger and Miller make pretenses at "inviting" or "provoking" discussion, but their positions seem so fixed in granite, so dismissive of contrary views, or alternatively so embryonic and hastily expressed, as to forestall or deflect response.

Perry seems to read his sources; the others merely to cite them. While there is a combativeness and at times a premature closure in Perry (he regularly says someone's position is "wrong" when he means "inconsistent" or "debatable"), he gives the impression of genuinely wanting to engage others in a debate about issues that are incontestably significant. I found his book provocative, and by that term I do not mean eccentric or maddening.

But Perry seems to miss a dimension of the recent debates about judicial activism that both Berger and Miller (perhaps unconsciously) identify. When judicial activism is taken as the simple act of a modern lawyer (called a judge) setting policies for other modern Americans, it immediately raises the question of whether there is something wrong or frightening about persons with legal training making the policy decisions inherent in deciding particular cases. Berger and Miller both suggest that it is troublesome to have modern "mine-run" lawyers make policy decisions with wide consequences. Berger would confine those decisions, where constitutional issues are involved to the will of the framers; Miller would delegate them to a Council of State, packed with as many nonlawyers as possible. And even Perry, whose argument stays so closely within the current discourse of the legal profession, ultimately reaches for a justification for constitutional policymaking that has nothing to do with the Constitution or, for that matter, with law at all.

It is a sad self-indictment of a profession when the matters its representatives find most urgent—the problem of judicial activism being one—derive their urgency from the profession's lack of confidence that its members are capable of performing services they have ostensibly been trained to perform. In modern American society, no one expects lawyers to become only litigators or advisors to the private sector: countless lawyers become judges, legislators, executives, and other public officials and thereby make policy. Are we to take as a hidden message of these books a sense that becoming a lawyer in modern America is somehow incompatible with formulating wise or salutary public policies? Should we worry about judges deciding cases that involve questions of policy because they approach policy in a distinctly legal way? Do we need economists or philosophers or "even broad-gauged political scientists" to save us?

The legal profession's current doubts about its identity seem a gratuitous burden for beleaguered judges to have to bear. It is true that legal education and law practice in America suddenly seem to be missing some important elements, such as a conviction that legal advocacy is principally a means of clarifying rather than obscuring the demands of humans for justice. But the issue of whether the legal profession should begin a more thorough self-examination seems at least temporarily separable from the issue of whether judges should continue to be activists.

Unless one believes that anyone with legal training is disqualified from making sound policy decisions, one starts with the fact that judges have much better opportunities to make them than the rest of us. Having started with that fact, one next confronts the three elements of the critique of activism, each of which, I have sought to show, collapses on analysis. The case is then straightforward enough: since judges have been activists for some time, and no sufficient reasons have been advanced why they should discontinue the practice, we should expect that they will continue it, and not be unduly dismayed at the prospect.

NOTES

1. Berger, *Death Penalties: The Supreme Court's Obstacle Course* (1982).

2. Miller, *Toward Increased Judicial Activism: The Political Role of the Supreme Court* (1982).

3. Perry, *The Constitution, the Courts, and Human Rights* (1982).

4. 347 U.S. 483 (1954).

5. Eighth Amendment of the Constitution.

6. *Furman v. Georgia*, 408 U.S. 238, 269 (1972).

7. *Id.*

8. By "formal constitutional amendment" is meant in conformity with Article V of the Constitution,which outlines how the Constitution is to be amended.

9. Perry, *supra* note 3, at 98.

10. Perry, *supra* note 3, at 101.

11. 5 U.S. (1 Cranch) 137 (1803).

12. 17 U.S. (4 Wheat.) 316.

13. 60 U.S. (19 How.) 393 (1857).

14. 12 Wall. 457 (1871).

15. 163 U.S. 537 (1896).

16. 198 U.S. 45 (1905).

17. 249 U.S. 47 (1919).

18. 347 U.S. 483 (1954).

19. *Congress Versus the Supreme Court* (1969); *Impeachment: The Constitutional Problems* (1973); *Executive Privilege: A Constitutional Myth* (1974); *Government by Judiciary: The Transformation of the 14th Amendment* (1977); *Federalism: The Founders' Design* (1987).

20. Berger, *supra* note 1, at 43–53.

21. Berger, *supra* note 1, at 181.

22. *See* R. Faulkner, *The Jurisprudence of John Marshall* (1968), 58–64, 195–206, 255–60.

23. *See* G. Edward White, *The Marshall Court and Cultural Change, 1815–35*, 6–8 (1988).

24. For example, Chief Justice John Marshall posited that "[c]ourts are the mere instruments of the law, and can will nothing." *Osborn v. Bank of the United States*, 9 Wheat, 738, 866 (1824). *See also* White, *The Marshall Court and Cultural Change, supra* note 23, at 195–200.

25. *See* White, *supra* note 23, at 195–200.

26. *McCulloch v. Maryland*, 17 U.S. (4 Wheat.) 316, 415 (1819).

27. Berger, *supra* note 1, at 113.

28. Berger, *supra* note 1, at 172.

29. Miller, *supra* note 2, at 162.

30. Miller, *supra* note 2, at 171.

31. Miller, *supra* note 2, at 21.

32. Miller, *supra* note 2, at 149.

33. Miller, *supra* note 2, at 21.

34. Miller, *supra* note 2, at 19, 243.

35. Miller, *supra* note 2, at 87.

36. Miller, *supra* note 2, at 202.

37. Miller, *supra* note 2, at 234.

38. Miller, *supra* note 2, at xi.

39. *See* Leonard Levy, *Judicial Review, History and Democracy: An Introduction*, in Judicial Review and the Supreme Court, 1–8 (L. Levy ed. 1967).

40. *See generally* Wood, The Creation of the American Republic 1776–1787 (1969).

41. Miller, *supra* note 2, at 153.

42. Miller, *supra* note 2, at 300–01.

43. Miller, *supra* note 2, at 308.

44. Miller, *supra* note 2, at 309.

45. Miller, *supra* note 2, at xi.

46. Miller, *supra* note 2, at xii.

47. Miller, *supra* note 2, at 24–25.

48. Miller, *supra* note 2, at 294.

49. Miller, *supra* note 2, at 298.

50. Miller, *supra* note 2, at 286.

51. Miller, *supra* note 2, at 298.

52. Perry, *supra* note 3, at 3.

53. Reprinted in 73 Harv. L. Rev. 1 (1959).

54. Perry, *supra* note 3, at 26.

55. Perry, *supra* note 3, at 29.
56. Perry, *supra* note 3, at 163.
57. Perry, *supra* note 3, at 92.
58. Perry, *supra* note 3, at 102.
59. Perry, *supra* note 3, at 106.
60. *See* Lance Banning, *The Jeffersonian Persuasion* (1978); Gerald Stourzh, *Alexander Hamilton and the Idea of Republican Government* (1970).

Chief Justice Marshall, Justice Holmes, and the Discourse of Constitutional Adjudication*

I Introduction

This essay is precipitated by the appearance of a potentially new stage of public discourse about Justices of the United States Supreme Court. The presence of this stage is suggested by the recent nominations of Robert Bork and Anthony Kennedy, and, in particular, one feature of their confirmation proceedings. The feature to which I refer is the collapse, in both nominations, of an established justification for a President's choice of a given nominee. Established since Franklin Roosevelt's initial nominations, that justification can be stated, in lay terms, as follows. The President can name whomever he[1] wants, so long as the nominee is professionally qualified; the ideological politics of the nominee are irrelevant. After all, the justification suggests, the President himself holds partisan ideological views, why can't the nominee? I will call this justification "presidential prerogative."

An implicit corollary to the presidential prerogative justification also exists. Although the President may name ideological partisans, the nominee must disclaim his or her partisanship in the confirmation process. This corollary was in evidence in the nomination hearings of William Rehnquist and Antonin Scalia to be Associate Justices. Both men, at the time of their nominations, were known political "conservatives" and were known to be acceptable to the Presidents who nominated them in part because of those views. Nevertheless, the nominees stated repeatedly that their ideological inclinations and their partisan affiliations would be irrelevant in their interpretations of the Constitution.[2] Rehnquist and Scalia were by no means unique in these disclaimers: Thurgood Marshall made them as well in his confirmation hearings.[3]

The established justification of presidential prerogative was advanced in Bork's

*30 Wm. & Mary L. Rev. 131 (1988). An earlier version of this essay was delivered as the 1988 Wythe Lecture at the Marshall-Wythe Law School, College of William and Mary.

nomination proceedings as well. Bork, too, eventually offered a version of the nominee disclaimer corollary.[4] Yet, in Bork's confirmation proceedings, the justification collapsed. Bork abandoned the corollary and stated forthrightly his substantive views. Moreover, in Kennedy's confirmation proceedings, the presidential prerogative justification was stated in very muted terms. Kennedy did not so much disclaim his ideological orientations as intimate that his orientations were politically "moderate," that is, much less right of center than those of Bork.[5]

I am not, at this point in the essay, addressing the question of whether the apparent collapse of the presidential prerogative justification, and the attendant diminution of the significance of the nominee disclaimer corollary, mark a laudable development in the history of the process of nominating Supreme Court Justices. I am merely assuming that the Bork and Kennedy nominations may have marked the beginning of a new stage in the discourse of commentary about the proper role for Justices of the Supreme Court, and am seeking to explore the origins of that stage.

In that exploration I turn first to history, and seek to examine the discourse of commentary about the proper role for Supreme Court Justices over time. I find, in the history of that discourse, two idealized postures for Supreme Court Justices in constitutional adjudication. These postures, I will argue, have established the boundaries of discourse; they represent the polar opposites of an ongoing debate about the proper role of the Court in constitutional adjudication. The two postures are the Marshallian posture, identified with Chief Justice Marshall, and the Holmesian posture, identified with Justice Holmes. I will explore the origins and evolution of the postures and their dialectical interaction over time. I will ultimately return to the Bork and Kennedy nominations with that exploration in mind, and at that point my comments will have an explicitly normative dimension.

At this juncture a preliminary comment on what I mean by "Marshallian" and "Holmesian" postures for Supreme Court Justices seems in order. The postures are being employed as ideal types: I am not suggesting that they represent precise characterizations of the jurisprudential views of Chief Justice Marshall and Justice Holmes in every constitutional case they respectively decided. An example may clarify the distinction I have in mind. I will characterize the Holmesian posture as incorporating an attitude toward the sources of rights in American jurisprudence (either natural or constitutional) that rejects a conception of rights as having any meaningful content apart from positivistic legislation. In constitutional adjudication, rights are based, for a Holmesian, on enacted legislation or on the text of the Constitution, not on anything prior to or independent of those entities.

Yet in *Pennsylvania Coal Co. v. Mahon*[6] Holmes did not seem to hold such an attitude toward rights. The case tested the constitutionality of a state legislature's restriction on "vested" property rights. At issue were the rights of subsurface mine owners to maintain mineral rights in their land once they had conveyed the surface of that land to other private parties, expressly retaining their subsurface rights. The mine owners argued that a Pennsylvania statute[7] that forbade them from reasserting their subsurface rights was unconstitutional in several respects.[8] They asserted that it violated the Fourteenth Amendment's due process clause,[9] the Fifth Amendment's takings clause[10] as incorporated in the Fourteenth Amendment,[11] and the contracts clause,[12] which precludes states from "impairing the Obligation of Contracts."

Holmes, for the Court, held the statute unconstitutional. He argued that "the statute is admitted to destroy previously existing rights of property and contract,"[13] that "the implied limitation [of the police power of the state in eminent domain cases] must have its limits, or the contract and due process clauses are gone,"[14] and that "[t]he general rule . . . is . . . that while property may be regulated to a certain extent, if regulation goes too far it will be recognized as a taking."[15] Although Holmes may have treated all of the vested property and contract rights he protected in *Mahon* as derived from some positivistic source, a more reasonable reading of his opinion it that it is not entirely consistent with a "Holmesian" posture toward the sources of rights. That posture, therefore, is not the equivalent of Holmes' actual stance in every case he decided, although it represents a fair extrapolation of his stance in the great majority of his decisions.

II The Origins and Evolution of the Marshallian and Holmesian Postures

As employed in this essay, the Marshallian and Holmesian postures represent contrasting attitudes toward four fundamental jurisprudential issues: (1) the sources of individual rights in American jurisprudence, (2) the relationship between individual rights and the state, (3) the Constitution's role in that relationship, and (4) the respective roles of legislatures and the United States Supreme Court in that relationship. My characterization of the postures assumes not only that their respective attitudes toward these four issues are in diametrical opposition, but also that the issues themselves have remained, over time, at the core of discourse about the role of Supreme Court Justices in constitutional adjudication.

A Marshallian posture treats individual rights as natural and inalienable, existing prior to the formation of the state. Marshallians characterize the state as functioning not only to secure and preserve pre-existing rights, but also to ensure that pre-existing rights are exercised and protected through positive law. For a Marshallian, the Constitution is the paramount positive source of law in America. It is designed to preserve, promote, and defend the proper relationship between individual rights and the state and is presumptively supreme over all other positive sources of law. But the Constitution is not the exclusive source of individual rights; other extratextual natural rights retain their intelligibility and significance. Finally, for a Marshallian, the positive enactments of state or federal legislatures, when they restrict individual rights, are suspect because legislatures are potentially demagogic and corrupt. In sum, for Marshallians, the proper role of the Supreme Court in constitutional adjudication is to maintain the supremacy of the Constitution and to protect individual rights, whether they are pre-existing natural rights or "vested" rights derived from pre-existing positive law.[16]

In contrast, a Holmesian posture treats rights as solely the product of positive laws enacted by the state. Natural and inalienable rights do not exist, either in the sense of being philosophically intelligible or in the sense of being practically significant. Being the creation of the state, rights are subordinate to its dictates, which are themselves the result of majoritarian preferences. Individual rights, whatever their nature or content, must yield to the majority. The recourse of disappointed individuals whose rights are being restricted is to facilitate revolution so that they become members of a new majority. Although the Constitution is a paramount source of law, because it is a positive enactment, it has a very limited substantive meaning when it restricts majoritarian preferences. The constitutional text, for Holmesians, restricts legislative activity only when a "clear mandate" exists in the words of the text; needless to say, the text does not implicitly incorporate natural extratextual rights. Finally, Holmesians believe that Supreme Court Justices should give great weight to the positive enactments of legislatures in interpreting the Constitution, even when the positive law restricts individual rights, because legislatures are the primary institutional embodiment of the majority's will.[17]

As a shorthand summary, one could characterize the opposition between the postures as a familiar precept of constitutional commentary: the "countermajoritarian difficulty" that Alexander Bickel once claimed followed from "the essential reality that judicial review [as practiced by the Supreme Court in constitutional cases] is a deviant institution in the American democracy."[18] Marshall's Constitution is a countermajoritarian document, and the Supreme Court is a countermajoritarian force. Holmes's Constitution is one in which the Court constantly must consider the fact that the Court is not a democratic institution and that the attendant "countermajoritarian difficulty" exists.

I now turn to a brief and necessarily sketchy overview of the origins and interaction of the two postures in American constitutional history. The Marshallian posture was originally a product of a premodern jurisprudence, one in which a certain set of substantive values—protection of property, the importance of civic responsibility, a hierarchical ordering of status relationships—were taken for granted by elites as permanent features of society. Those values formed the basis for all the assumptions I have associated with Marshallians.[19] By contrast, the Holmesian posture originated in modernism; it began with the premise that any deep societal consensus on substantive values was necessarily impermanent and problematic. As modernists, Holmesians posit that humans cannot affirm reflexively the universality and permanence of substantive values. According to Holmes, all that one can affirm is that some values exist for which many individuals in a culture might die. For Holmesians, the primacy of values is determined not by their inherent rightness but by their affirmation by majorities. In other words, the best test of the truth of an idea is its power in the marketplace of ideas.[20]

The above analysis might suggest that, because none of us are now premodernists, the Holmesian view has prevailed. Furthermore, although some commentators seem bent on resurrecting a conception of property rights as absolute, inalienable, and permanent[21] and others wax enthusiastic about the virtues of republicanism,[22] the discourse of contemporary commentary remains seemingly embounded by modernist eschatological assumptions.[23] Yet at the very time that the Holmesian posture, which Holmes first articulated impressively in *Lochner v.*

New York,[24] became orthodoxy in the early 1930s,[25] a deep chasm began to emerge in modernist thought. Over the next fifty years that chasm has persisted and widened, despite impressive efforts to straddle it or to pretend it did not exist. The chasm has had a dramatic evolution in constitutional law. It began with a crack in the surface of Holmesian orthodoxy: the free speech cases in the late 1920s and 1930s.[26] It widened as modernism became linked to totalitarianism in the late 1930s and during the Second World War,[27] and the recognition of its existence precipitated the emergence of new versions of the Holmesian perspective in the 1950s.[28] The chasm deepened and widened more during the dominant years of the Warren Court,[29] and it has served as the starting point for a variety of recent efforts to resolve the "countermajoritarian difficulty."[30]

The cause of the chasm, of course, was a renewed consciousness of the potential primacy of substantive rights, even in a modernist age. But needless to say, the content of the rights elevated to prominence after the 1930s differed from the content of the rights elevated by Marshall's contemporaries. Moreover, the rights consciousness of twentieth-century jurisprudence differs from that of Marshall's time in its assumption that contemporary American culture is a far more diverse and heterogeneous configuration than that in which Marshallian jurisprudence was formulated.[31]

A few cases illustrate the history sketched above. First are the "vested rights" decisions of the Marshall Court themselves: decisions such as *Fletcher v. Peck*,[32] *Darmouth College v. Woodward*,[33] and *Ogden v. Saunders*.[34] Few contemporary commentators spend time with those cases, but they are rich illustrations of the assumptions of Marshallian jurisprudence.[35] Almost all of the Marshallian assumptions are still present as late as 1905 in the majority opinion in *Lochner v. New York*,[36] although the substantive rights being cited have shifted from "property" to "contract," and the explicit reliance on extratextual sources has been abandoned.[37] In *Lochner*, substantive rights against the state are taken for granted. The state is assumed to be in existence to protect, not to restrict, those rights, legislatures are viewed with suspicion, the judiciary is conceived as a bulwark in defense of private rights, and the Constitution remains resolutely countermajoritarian. The *Lochner* majority opinion is both the culmination and a caricature of the original Marshallian posture.

The sense in which *Lochner* is a caricature is captured vividly in Holmes's dissent. He disclaims any substantive opposition to the majority's position; he is embracing neither paternalism nor laissez-faire.[38] But his characterization of the Constitution as "made for people of fundamentally differing views"[39] is itself substantive: his Constitution is majoritarian and pluralist. The *Lochner* majority opinion is made out to be a caricature because its elevation of "liberty of contract" as a primary substantive value is jarringly out of sync with modernism. Liberty of contract is merely a "dogma";[40] dogmas have no place in the sophisticated intellectual universe of the early twentieth century. With Holmes's challenge to *Lochner*, the (now ludicrously inappropriate) strictures of premodernism become clearly exposed.

The Holmesian posture next gathers momentum, becomes orthodoxy, and begins to crack, as previously discussed. The next significant case in the history is

Brown v. Board of Education.[41] In *Brown,* as recent history has demonstrated, the Holmesian posture invites judicial abdication. Congress has not acted with respect to the question of racial segregation and the segregationist states have acted, the latter action based on majoritarian preferences emanating from a particularistic sociology. Although one can argue that segregation, like slavery, is inconsistent with the values of liberty and equality and is deeply racist, it is also a majoritarian practice. Absent the overwhelming constitutional mandate, "separate but equal" facilities satisfy the requirements of the equal protection clause and the Supreme Court should defer to legislative majorities.

It may seem incredible to us that this Holmesian argument was taken seriously at the time *Brown* was decided. Yet it was. The crucial problem for the Court in *Brown* was not, as commentators have sometimes suggested,[42] the enforcement of the *Brown* decree; the crucial problem was justifying the Court's intervention to change equal protection jurisprudence in segregation cases in the face of both southern preferences and congressional inaction. That was the problem identified both within the Court, prominently by Jackson and Frankfurter,[43] and by commentators.[44] In response, the Court in *Brown* said, in effect, that when certain rights are implicated, the Constitution insists on more than judicial deference to majority preferences. When those preferences themselves amount to the denial of substantive rights against the state, specifically rights to equal educational opportunities regardless of race or skin color, the Constitution mandates that such rights be protected. *Brown* represents, therefore, the clear emergence of what can be called a neo-Marshallian posture.[45]

The next significant case in the history is the revival of the *Lochner* majority's position in *Griswold v. Connecticut.*[46] Justice Douglas announced in *Griswold* that "[o]vertones of some arguments suggest that *Lochner v. New York* should be our guide. But we decline that invitation."[47] The "invitation" to which he referred was an argument that the Warren Court should do for privacy what the *Lochner* Court did for liberty of contract; namely, constitutionalize an extratextual right against the state. Douglas "declined," but actually accepted. Although Douglas throughout his career denied this interpretation of his *Griswold* opinion, *Griswold* elevated to constitutional stature a "liberty" of privacy, grounded in the Fourteenth Amendment's due process clause.[48] Read in that fashion, *Griswold* represents an advance from *Brown*. *Griswold* was not merely a reaffirmation of the primacy of substantive rights over majoritarianism; it also employed an openly extratextual interpretive methodology. In *Brown* the Court's reading of the equal protection clause had been doctrinally novel, but the Court was not faced with the absence of any constitutional text pertaining to equality of racial opportunity. In *Griswold* no text protecting "privacy" existed; only text protecting "liberties" existed, and Holmesian canons of interpretation suggested that substantive readings of the "liberties" text by judges was anti-majoritarian. *Griswold* was, in short, a case in which the "right" given protection was derived extratextually, from cultural attitudes that took for granted that married persons could make their own procreative decisions, and a case in which the Court merely affirmed what "everyone" already believed. It was a Marshallian opinion in a modernist setting.

The last stage in the history brings us back to the Bork and Kennedy nominations. This stage marks the establishment of the neo-Marshallian posture as a genuine alternative to the Holmesian posture, the appearance of "hard cases"[49] for each of the two postures, and commentary seeking to reconcile the postures. *Roe v. Wade*[50] has been a classic "hard case" for neo-Marshallians. It raises the problem of basing a jurisprudence on the primacy of substantive rights when "rights" in constitutional adjudication may be historically contingent, philosophically problematic, and in perceived conflict with other rights.

Conversely, a classic "hard case" for unreconstructed Holmesians is *Bowers v. Hardwick*.[51] That decision seeks to distinguish between a deeply embedded but not yet explicitly protected right—the right for adults to engage in private consensual intimate affection—and the "nonright" of adult homosexuals to engage in private consensual sex. The decision affirms a majoritarian preference, namely that the state should prohibit private consensual homosexual activity because it is thought immoral or repulsive. In *Bowers,* the Holmesian posture thus confronts the dilemma that the whims of majorities with respect to our sexual preferences affect either "all of us" or just homosexuals. If the latter view is preferable, the decision affirms that majorities can repress private consensual intimate conduct simply on the basis of their preferences. This affirmation leads Holmesians back to the problem of the close relationship between majoritarianism and totalitarianism.

In response to "hard cases" such as *Roe* or *Bowers,* constitutional commentators have produced a new outpouring of literature in the late 1970s and 1980s. I have previously alluded to some of the prominent examples of that literature,[52] but there are numerous others. As early as the late 1960s,[53] commentators had exhibited an awareness that the unreconstructed Holmesian and its neo-Holmesian versions, such as process theory, were being severely confronted by the Warren Court's neo-Marshallian tendencies. By the mid-1970s, efforts to recreate and elevate the stature of substantive rights had appeared.[54] As noted, the flood of commentary in the late 1970s and 80s has stressed the renewal of substantive rights in constitutional law, has opposed that renewal and offered up unreconstructed and neo-Holmesian perspectives, and has sought to reconcile the two positions.

III The Current State of Discourse

At this point we are in a position to revisit the jurisprudential climate in which the Bork and Kennedy nominations occurred. The history just reviewed suggests that the discourse of commentary up to the time of those nominations was an implicit dialogue between Holmesians and Marshallians about the relationship between rights, the legislature, the Constitution, and the Court. In the terms of this essay, the following questions have been at the core of the debate: Is the Court to be a protector of rights based on those substantive value judgments that, while articulated by the Justices, are deeply shared in the culture at large? Or is the Court to concede implicitly that Justices are not capable, indeed that no moderns are capable, of making a determination of which values count more than others, of which values are universal, and of which values are always to be given substantive priority?

In his confirmation hearings, Bork attempted to portray himself as something of a Holmesian. He believed in judicial "self-restraint," in following the "original intent" of the framers, and in majoritarian democracy.[55] He would not be guided by his substantive views as a Justice; he would be guided by the text of the Constitution, the original intent of its framers, and the principle of deference to majorities. Bork's self-portrait was simply not accepted as credible; it was labeled a "confirmation conversion." Bork's opponents argued that he was not only an ideologue, but that his ideological views were substantively "wrong": for example, he had been on the "wrong" side of both of the central neo-Marshallian decisions of the recent past, *Brown* and *Griswold*. Bork, his critics claimed, had come to accept *Brown*, but his previously expressed views on civil rights issues suggested that his was a belated and perhaps a convenient acceptance. He had never accepted *Griswold:* he believed that privacy was not protected by the Constitution.

Above all else, the substantive "extremism" of Bork's views was the cause of the defeat of his nomination. National politics undoubtedly played a part; the Senate that confirmed Scalia as Associate Justice and Rehnquist as Chief Justice had a different composition from the Democrat-controlled Senate that failed to confirm Bork. Yet that Senate confirmed Kennedy. Despite his impressive professional qualifications and the absence of any ethical improprieties in his career, Bork's substantive views ultimately provided the material for his defeat.

How could a person with Bork's professional credentials, who advanced Holmesian and neo-Holmesian arguments that were for the most part jurisprudential orthodoxies[56] and who was nominated in a confirmation culture in which presidential prerogative was still given great weight, fail to be confirmed? In the terms of this essay, Bork's failure principally resulted from the fact that those who passed on his confirmation believed that he was not truly a Holmesian, but rather a neo-Marshallian masquerading as a Holmesian, and found that his version of neo-Marshallianism was substantively disqualifying for a Supreme Court Justice.

Saying that one disagrees with a nominee's substantive views, and, for that matter, that one disagrees with the substantive views of the nominating president, is quite a different statement from saying that a nominee's views are so substantively wrongheaded as to disqualify him or her for the Court. Yet the latter statement is what a majority of the Senate said about Bork. The stark emergence of the orientation that a nominee's substantive views are decisive in his or her eligibility, even those of a nominee with Bork's professional qualifications, marks a new stage in the discourse of commentary on the place of Supreme Court Justices in American culture. In the Bork hearings the criterion of substantive ideology was not merely juxtaposed against other traditional criteria such as the presidential prerogative, the nominee disclaimer corollary and the nominee's professional qualifications, substantive ideology overwhelmed those criteria.

This brings me to Kennedy's successful confirmation. One might be tempted to say that Kennedy was confirmed, and Bork was not, because Kennedy successfully invoked the nominee disclaimer corollary, thereby implicitly convincing those passing on his nomination that his stance as a Justice would be that of a Holmesian. Yet that interpretation would be a misreading of the two confirmation proceedings. Kennedy and Bork both used the same orthodox language of "self-restraint" and fidelity to the Constitution,[57] but Kennedy's prior record was principally scrutinized with respect to the substantive political implications of his positions. He was ultimately deemed a "moderate"—a person with a conservative but not ultraright ideology, the sort of individual that Reagan might be expected to look favorably on but whose views were not "extreme." He was acceptable to the Senate because of the content of his ideology. The two confirmation episodes thus can be viewed as conveying the same message that the substance of a nominee's views overwhelms everything else about his or her candidacy.

IV Conclusion

The Bork and Kennedy hearings thus suggest that substantive, rights-oriented jurisprudence is not merely competing with, but encroaching upon the jurisprudence of majoritarian deference; the dialogue between Holmesians and Marshallians may no longer be in equipoise. The most fascinating aspect of this potential development is that in the face of a renewed emphasis on the substantive ideology of Supreme Court Justices, the orthodox language employed to characterize the jurisprudential stances of those Justices has apparently retained its vitality. In short, nominees and their critics continue to treat judicial "self-restraint," the catchword of Holmesian jurisprudence, as if it were a significant check on the substantive inclinations of the nominees, while at the same time treating substantive ideology as the decisive criterion in the selection of Justices.

This paradoxical situation has resulted, in my view, from a failure to distinguish two quite different features of the Holmesian posture, with its homage to judicial "self-restraint." One feature is the idea that judges can suppress their substantive views simply by deferring to "neutral" authoritative legal sources, such as the Constitution, statutes, or precedent. Thus Holmes, in deciding the *Lochner* case, suppresses his own views on labor relations because the Constitution does not embody any economic theory, whether paternalism or laissez-faire.[58] The other feature is the related but distinguishable idea that judges can suppress their substantive views by recognizing the overriding substantive commitment of the Constitution, and American culture generally, to democracy and pluralism, and by further recognizing that the only way to preserve pluralism is by accepting the primacy of institutions—primarily the legislature—that can incorporate multiple ideological perspectives.

The first feature of Holmesianism is nonsensical, and has been exposed so thoroughly as to no longer merit serious attention. Judges cannot avoid substantive choices simply by following authoritative legal sources because those sources are not themselves substantively neutral.[59] Unfortunately, the first feature and the second have been run together, to the detriment of the second. The second feature remains a significant jurisprudential message today if pluralism, the contemporary version of majoritarianism, is regarded as a significant cultural value. The strength of the second message, combined with some unreflective adherence to the first, accounts for the continued vitality of language subscribing to the canons of judicial self-restraint.

Yet even the second feature seems problematic. What if the institutional embodiments of pluralism do not preserve it? What if the legislative process functions to exclude views, rather than to include them? What if in deferring to majoritarian instructions judges are making substantive choices, namely the choice to sustain the ideology of the majority? What if, in the end, the chief restraint on judges is the content of their own substantive values, so that constitutional adjudication imposes on judges an implicit burden to convince others that the values they are affirming in a given case are the values that the rest of the culture cares deeply about? If such questions are real rather than rhetorical, then the obligation of constitutional commentators would seem to be to evaluate the Court's decisions from an unabashedly neo-Marshallian posture because substantive ideology is all that counts in those decisions.

The primacy of substantive ideology in constitutional adjudication suggests that a good deal of allegedly sophisticated modernist constitutional discourse is just rhetoric. It is rhetoric to the extent that it fails to realize that whatever institutional or doctrinal devices one enacts to prevent substantive values from being paramount in constitutional adjudication, those values will shape the devices being enacted. The Bork and Kennedy nominations may have led to the beginning of a recognition of the overarching significance of ideology in constitutional adjudications, a recognition that is by no means threatening, either to the Court or to the rest of us. We have in a sense come full circle. We are back to Marshall, but not, of course, with Marshall. Holmes is still with us as well, and perhaps we may come to understand a little better how he fits in.

NOTES

1. "She" would be misleading as applied to Presidents from Roosevelt through Reagan.

2. *Nomination of Judge Antonin Scalia to be Assoc. Justice of the Supreme Court of the United States: Hearings Before the Senate Comm. on the Judiciary,* 99th Cong., 2d Sess. 37–38, 43–44, 59, 84 (1986); *Nomination of Justice William Hubbs Rehnquist, of Arizona, to be Assoc. Justice of the Supreme Court of the United States: Hearings before the Senate Comm. on the Judiciary* 92d Cong., 1st Sess. 155, 175, 204 (1971).

3. *Nomination of Thurgood Marshall of New York, to be an Assoc. Justice of the Supreme Court of the United States: Hearings before the Senate Comm. on the Judiciary,* 90th Cong., 1st Sess. 50, 93, 158–61 (1967).

4. *See A War of Words: Nominee Denies Kennedy's Charges,* N.Y. Times, Sept. 19, 1987, at A10, col. 5.

5. *See Judge Kennedy Says Rights Are Not Always Spelled Out,* N.Y. Times, Dec. 15, 1987, at B16, col. 1.

6. 260 U.S. 393 (1922).

7. The statute at issue was the Kohler Act. *See id.*

8. *Id.* at 412.

9. U.S. CONST. amend. XIV, 1.

10. U.S. CONST. amend. V.

11. In *Chicago, Burlington & Quincy R.R. Co. v. Chicago,* 166 U.S. 226 (1897), the Supreme Court held that the Fifth Amendment's "just compensation" requirement for constitutional takings was applicable to state eminent domain statutes, of which the Kohler Act was one. *See id.* at 241.

12. U.S. CONST. art. I, 10, cl. 1.

13. 260 U.S. at 413.

14. *Id.*

15. *Id.* at 415.

16. For support for the generalizations advanced in this paragraph, see R. FAULKNER, THE JURISPRUDENCE OF JOHN MARSHALL 59–63, 69–79, 195–223, 227–68 (1968); G. E. WHITE *The Marshall Court and Cultural Change, 1815–35,* in 3–4 THE OLIVER WENDELL HOLMES DEVISE HISTORY OF THE SUPREME COURT OF THE UNITED STATES 512–35, 563–80, 595–656 (1988).

17. For support for the generalizations advanced in this paragraph, see H. L. POHLMAN, JUSTICE OLIVER WENDELL HOLMES AND UTILITARIAN JURISPRUDENCE (1984); Gordon, *Holmes' Common Law as Legal and Social Science,* 10 HOFSTRA L. REV. 719, 723–27, 734–36, 742–44 (1982); Rogat, *The Judge as Spectator* 31 U. CHI. L. REV. 213, 225–26, 249–55 (1964); White, *The Integrity of Holmes' Jurisprudence,* 10 HOFSTRA L. REV. 633, 652, 655–58, 663–71 (1982); White, *Looking at Holmes in the Mirror,* 4 LAW & HIST. REV. 439, 447–48, 451–55, 464–65 (1986). *See also* R. FAULKNER, *supra* note 16, at 227–68, for an effort to compare Marshall's and Holmes' jurisprudence.

18. A. BICKEL, THE LEAST DANGEROUS BRANCH 18 (2d ed. 1986). Bickel may have coined the phrase, but he by no means exhausted the concept. For an extensive summary of the considerable literature on the "countermajoritarian difficulty," see P. BREST AND S. LEVINSON, PROCESSES OF CONSTITUTIONAL DECISIONMAKING 889–901 (2nd ed. 1983), and sources cited therein.

19. *See* G. E. WHITE, *supra* note 16, at 595–656, and sources cited therein.

20. *Abrams v. United States,* 250 U.S. 616 (1919) (Holmes, J., dissenting). *See* H. L. POHLMAN, *supra* note 17, at 13–15, 81, 96–97, 141–43; M. G. WHITE, SOCIAL THOUGHT IN AMERICA: THE REVOLT AGAINST FORMALISM 59–75, 103–06 (2nd ed. 1957); *Special Issue: Modernist Culture in America,* 39 AM. Q. 1 (1987); White, *The Rise and Fall of Justice Holmes,* 39 U. CHI. L. REV. 51, 65–67, 75–77 (1971).

21. *See, e.g.,* B. SIEGAN, ECONOMIC LIBERTIES AND THE CONSTITUTION (1980).

22. *See* Michelman, *The Supreme Court, 1985 Term—Foreword: Traces of Self-Government,* 100 HARV. L. REV. 4 (1986); Sunstein, *Interest Groups in American Public Law,* 38 STAN. L. REV. 29 (1985).

23. *See generally* Levinson, *Law as Literature,* 60 TEX. L REV. 373 (1982). See also the exchange between Owen M. Fiss and Paul Brest in Fiss, *Objectivity and Interpretation,* 34 STAN. L. REV. 739 (1982), and Brest, *Interpretation and Interest,* 34 Stan. L Rev. 765 (1982).

24. 198 U.S. 45 (1905) (Holmes, J., dissenting). The adverb "impressively" is precipitated by Holmes's earlier opinion in *Otis v. Parker,* 187 U.S. 606 (1903), which contained the following passage:

While the courts must exercise a judgment of their own, it by no means is true that every law is void which may seem to the judges who pass upon it excessive, unsuited to its ostensible end, or based upon conceptions of morality with which they disagree. Considerable latitude must be allowed for differences of view as well as for possible peculiar conditions which this court can know but imperfectly, if at all. Otherwise a constitution, instead of embodying only relatively fundamental rules of right, as generally understood by all English-speaking communities, would become the partisan of a particular set of ethical or economical opinions. . . .

Id. at 608–09.

25. Examples of the establishment of the Holmesian perspective as orthodoxy in the early 1930s abound. *See, e.g.,* J. FRANK, LAW AND THE MODERN MIND 253 (1930) (describing Holmes as "the completely adult jurist"); F. FRANKFURTER, MR. JUSTICE HOLMES AND THE SUPREME COURT (1938); Llewellyn, *Holmes,* 35 COLUM. L. REV. 485 (1935).

26. See the "preferred position" cases, *United States v. Carolene Products,* Co., 304 U.S. 144 (1938); *Near v. Minnesota,* 283 U.S. 697 (1931); *Whitney v. California,* 274 U.S. 357 (1927).

27. The attacks on Holmes and the revival of "natural law" in the 1940s are now a familiar part of constitutional literature. *See* E. PURCELL, THE CRISIS OF DEMOCRATIC THE-ORY 167–68 (1973); L. TRIBE, AMERICAN CONSTITUTIONAL LAW 583–84, 715–16 (1978); White, *The Evolution of Reasoned Elaboration: Jurisprudential Criticism and Social Change,* 59 VA. L. REV. 279, 282–84 (1973); White, *The Rise and Fall of Justice Holmes,* 39 U. CHI. L. REV. 51, 65–68 (1971).

28. See the exchange between Mark DeWolfe Howe and Henry Hart in Howe, *The Positivism of Mr. Justice Holmes,* 64 HARV. L. REV. 529 (1951); Hart, *Holmes' Positiv-ism—An Addendum,* 64 HARV. L. REV. 929 (1951). *See* L. FULLER, THE ANATOMY OF LAW (1968); *see also* White, *The Evolution of Reasoned Elaboration, supra* note 27; *see generally* Ackerman, Book Review, 103 DAEDALUS 199 (Winter 1974) (noting the connec-tions between the 1930s Holmesians and the "Legal Process School").

29. See the exchange between Henry Hart, Thurman Arnold, and Erwin Griswold, in Hart, *The Supreme Court, 1958 Term—Foreword: The Time Chart of the Justices,* 73 HARV. L. REV. 84 (1959); Arnold, *Professor Hart's Theology,* 73 HARV. L. REV. 1298 (1960); Griswold, *The Supreme Court, 1959 Term—Foreword: Of Time and Attitudes—Professor Hart and Judge Arnold,* 74 HARV. L. REV. 81 (1960). See also the exchange precipitated by Herbert Wechsler's article, Wechsler, *Toward Neutral Principles of Consti-tutional Law,* 73 HARV. L. REV. 1 (1959). Finally, see the affirmative defense of the Warren Court's neo-Marshallian perspective in Black, *The Unfinished Business of the War-ren Court,* 46 WASH. L. REV. 3 (1970), and CHARLES L. BLACK, JR., STRUCTURE AND RELATIONSHIP IN CONSTITUTIONAL LAW (1969).

30. The efforts begin with A. BICKEL, *supra* note 18, at 16–23, and extend through Black, *supra* note 29, to L. TRIBE, *supra* note 27. *See also* P. BOBBIT, CONSTITUTIONAL FATE: THEORY OF THE CONSTITUTION (1982); J. H. CHOPER, JUDICIAL REVIEW AND THE NATIONAL POLITICAL PROCESS (1980); R. M. DWORKIN, LAW'S EMPIRE (1986); J. H. ELY, DEMOCRACY AND DISTRUST (1980); M. PERRY, THE CONSTITUTION, THE COURTS, AND HUMAN RIGHTS (1982).

31. Cross-cultural comparisons are of course treacherous, and some additional clarifi-cation of this statement seems necessary. To compare factors such as "diversity" and "heterogeneity" in any absolute fashion across time is very difficult, although social histo-rians routinely attempt to do so. Marshall's world may have in fact been far less demo-graphically and ideologically "diverse" than ours, but "diversity" is itself an ideological label that seems capable of being used only in a relative sense. It seems clear, however, that modernist commentators *perceive* contemporary American culture to be more demo-graphically and ideologically diverse than America of the late eighteenth and early nine-teenth centuries. I have argued, in G. E. WHITE, *supra* note 16, that Marshall and his contemporaries also perceived their culture as rapidly diversifying and changing, and that such a perception can be observed in the jurisprudential orientation of the Marshall Court. Indeed, the most identifiable feature of Marshall Court jurisprudence, I have argued, was the affirmation of a substantive value consensus in the face of and as a response to per-

ceived change. In short, despite the overwhelming differences between premoderns and moderns, our current debates in the area of constitutional commentary are more reminiscent of those of Marshall and his contemporaries than we might first suspect.

32. 10 U.S. (6 Cranch) 87 (1810).

33. 17 U.S. (4 Wheat.) 518 (1819).

34. 25 U.S. (12 Wheat.) 213 (1827).

35. *Fletcher,* for example, exhibits simultaneously an assumed primacy and priority for private property rights, hostility toward legislatures, an extratextual theory of constitutional interpretation, and an implicit conception of the judiciary as a countermajoritarian force.

36. 198 U.S. 45 (1905).

37. Compare *Fletcher's* reliance on "general principles which are common to our free institutions," 10 U.S. at 139, with *Lochner's* reliance on "liberty of contract as well as of person," 198 U.S. at 61. The distinction has not been regarded as insignificant, but it can be seen as one without a difference.

38. 198 U.S. at 75 (Holmes, J., dissenting) ("a constitution is not intended to embody a particular economic theory, whether of paternalism and the organic relation of the citizen to the State or of *laissez faire*").

39. *Id.* at 76.

40. *Id.* at 75.

41. 347 U.S. 483 (1954).

42. *See, e.g.,* G. GUNTHER, CONSTITUTIONAL LAW 712–14 (11th ed. 1985).

43. *See* R. KLUGER, SIMPLE JUSTICE 576–77, 596–610 (1976).

44. *See, e.g.,* Wechsler, *Toward Neutral Principles of Constitutional Law,* 73 HARV. L. REV. 1 (1959).

45. One could attempt to argue that *Brown* is not inconsistent with a Holmesian posture because that posture permits judicial reversal of a majoritarian legislative preference in the "clear constitutional mandate" situation. Yet no one regarded *Brown* as a "clear constitutional mandate" at the time it was decided. Indeed, one of the difficulties with *Brown* was that the Court had previously interpreted the equal protection clause to *permit* segregation in the public schools.

46. 381 U.S. 479 (1965).

47. *Id.* at 481–82 (citation omitted).

48. In *Roe v. Wade,* 410 U.S. 113 (1973), a majority of the Court acknowledged that the rights of privacy protected in *Griswold* and its progeny, such as *Eisenstadt v. Baird,* 405 U.S. 438, 453–54 (1972), were liberties protected by the due process clause. *Id.* at 152. In a concurring opinion in *Doe v. Bolton,* a companion case to *Roe v. Wade,* Justice Douglas continued to maintain that *Griswold* had "nothing to do with substantive due process." 410 U.S. 179, 212 n. 4 (1973) (Douglas, J., concurring).

49. By "hard cases" I mean cases conceived as such by the prevailing jurisprudential discourse of the time, not cases that are inherently difficult.

50. 410 U.S. 113 (1973).

51. 478 US. 186 (1986).

52. *See supra* note 30.

53. *See* Black, *supra* note 29.

54. A prominent effort was Grey, *Do We Have an Unwritten Constitution?,* 27 STAN. L. REV. 703 (1975), in which the terms "interpretivism" and "noninterpretivism" first appeared. Despite my admiration for Professor Grey's work, I continue to believe that the rapid acceptance of his terminology has led to an obfuscation of the language of constitutional commentary. As Grey employs the terms, "interpretivists" are those whose chief characteristic is that they disclaim the possibility of extratextual sources for constitutional

interpretation; "noninterpretivists" by contrast admit such a possibility. But because both the "interpretivist" and "noninterpretivist" postures are theories of constitutional interpretation, both groups are "interpreters." I believe that the close connection between the words "interpreter" and "interpretivist" has led to significant confusion, especially in the classroom. Although it may be too late to abandon these terms, Grey could have avoided any confusion had he used the terms "textual" and "extratextual", because the necessity for constitutional interpreters to be bound by a finite constitutional text is at the heart of the dispute between the two postures. Of course, "extratextual" may sound pejorative, which is perhaps why Grey did not use it. It only sounds pejorative, however, if one is frozen in a jurisprudential perspective that insists that the "text" control constitutional interpretation. Grey's views suggest that he is hardly "frozen" in that sense.

55. *See Bork Statement: "Philosophy of Role of Judge,"* N.Y. Times, Sept. 16, 1987, at A28, col. 1.

56. The interpretive canon of "original intent" may not qualify for the label "orthodoxy." Although the adherence to the constitutional text has been an established canon of constitutional interpretation since Marshall, *see* G. E. WHITE, *supra* note 16, at 111–56, adherence to the original intent of the framers, especially in some of its less apt contemporary versions, appears to endorse a position so limiting to modern judges as to amount to a radically new and incoherent theory of interpretation. For a sensible historical discussion, *see* Powell, *The Original Understanding of Original Intent,* 98 HARV. L. REV. 885 (1985).

57. *See Bork Statement, supra* note 55; *The Questions Begin: 'Who Is Anthony Kennedy?,'* N.Y. Times, Dec. 15, 1987, at B16, col. 3.

58. *Lochner v. New York,* 198 U.S. 45, 76 (Holmes, J., dissenting).

59. Critics of Wechsler's *Toward Neutral Principles of Constitutional Law, supra* note 44, recognized this immediately. *See* Miller and Howell, *The Myth of Neutrality in Constitutional Adjudication* 27 U. CHI. L. REV. 661 (1960).

PART IV

The Politics of Jurisprudence

The Inevitability of Critical Legal Studies*

One of the formulated purposes of this Symposium is to introduce readers of this kind of periodical to the Critical Legal Studies (CLS) movement. I don't think that CLS needs such an introduction. Since the movement's formation in 1977, it has been holding annual conferences, circulating bibliographies, and otherwise acting like a professional society. Moreover, business is booming. Attendance at the annual conference reportedly has been growing; new "converts" declare their allegiance daily; adherents increasingly occupy space in scholarly journals, citing one another's work and supporting one another's efforts. Indeed, the current danger for CLS is not that it will be overlooked or ignored, but that it will become too successful and thereby lose a piercing Critical quality that comes from a sense of marginality. A similar phenomenon occurred to the Legal Realist movement of the 1920s and 1930s. When all law professors became Realists in the sense of accepting the basic presuppositions of Realism—that legal "rules" are inherently discretionary and that "neutral" judicial decisionmaking conceals subjective value choices—suddenly no one could define what Realism was or tell where it led. If I were a member of the CLS movement, I would watch out.

I don't think, therefore, that one need devote time to recognizing the existence of CLS. It does seem worthwhile, however, to note that CLS seems to be moving into a new phase in its history. Particularly suggestive in this vein have been recent efforts on the part of Critical theorist to link their movement with Realism and to suggest that one of their goals is to reformulate the abortive program for social change that some Realists anticipated but, for a variety of reasons, never launched.[1] The self-conscious identification of Realism as a progenitor of, or an inspiration for, the CLS movement seems to be a grasp at legitimacy. Legitimation through the invocation of a historical progenitor is a common enough lawyer's trick. One could even imagine the invocation of Realism as a forerunner of Criti-

*36 Stan. L. Rev. 649 (1984). Since writing this essay I have noticed the appearance of some additional literature on Critical Legal Studies that would have been included in its coverage. *See* Unger, *The Critical Legal Studies Movement*, 96 HARV. L. REV. 561 (1983); Ball, Book Review, 51 GEO. WASH. L. REV. 309 (1983) (reviewing THE POLITICS OF LAW: A PROGRESSIVE CRITIQUE (D. Kairys ed. 1982); Levinson, Book Review, 96 HARV. L. REV. 1466 (1983) (same).

cal theory taking the form of a palliative message. "When the Realists started out," the message would go, "the established community regarded them as kooks and subversives, attacking assumptions (such as the intelligibility of legal doctrine) on which the stability and authority of the legal system seemed to rest. But as Realist arguments began to penetrate the consciousness of others, their insights came to be seen as useful rather than threatening and were eventually absorbed into the processes of legal education and professional socialization. Moreover, nothing 'subversive' occurred; arguably, the legal profession just became more self-conscious and sophisticated in its thinking. Hence, if yesterday's subversive doctrines have become today's orthodoxies, who is to say that the assumptions of Critical theory will not one day be similarly absorbed?"

I can't imagine that many Critical theorists would want to convey such a message. For one thing, a central concern of Critical legal scholarship has been to show how mainstream ideologies, such as twentieth-century liberalism, have absorbed protests against the established order and converted them to their own use. Critical scholarship on twentieth-century labor law, for example, has argued that the notion of capitalist oppression of workers was absorbed in the form of a bargaining unit for workers, and used to further other goals favored by management, such as the maintenance of industrial peace and the promotion of discipline in the labor force.[2] Given the strong tendency of prevailing ideologies to perform this function of absorption and conversion, the legitimation of Critical theory might result in the loss of its identity and the conversion (one might say perversion) of its goals.

Nonetheless, the association of Critical theory with Realism persists. And I maintain that the association is intended as a kind of legitimation for Critical theory, though surely not in the form of absorption and conversion. The summoning-up of the Realists as progenitors is primarily intended, I suggest, to lend legitimacy to two areas of CLS concern. One is the idea of tacit ideological consciousness. The other is the idea that Critical theory and transformative social change can be fused. I want to spend some time on each of these ideas and to suggest that the logic of both is threatening to, rather than supportive of, the goals of the CLS movement. I then want to consider the relationship between the Realists and the Critical theorists in another context—as part of a general theory of jurisprudential change in American culture. In the course of that last excursus, I will devote some attention to certain dimensions of the CLS critique of "liberal" thought.

I The Tacit Dimension of Legal Decisionmaking

Perhaps the most striking contribution of Realist literature was the demonstration that legal rules could be manipulated. Legal scholarship prior to Realism had been oriented toward the derivation of comprehensive rules, of reconciling principles, and of predictable guidelines for conduct. The scholar's task was that of the "expounder, systematizer, and historian;"[3] he derived general principles from a mass of cases, demonstrated the principles' potential to reconcile contradictory results, and "proved," through an evolutionary version of legal history, the endurance of the principles over time. The goal of the scholar's search, embodied in the massive treatises of the late nineteenth and early twentieth centuries, was to reduce a field of law to a series of coherent principles of general applicability.

The Realists demonstrated that such principles were always contradictory, that for every principle there existed a potential counterprinciple, and that ultimately a methodology that assumed the autonomy, permanence, or objectivity of legal rules was incoherent.[4] Having perfected that critique, Realist scholarship seemed a little at a loss as to what to do next. Some Realists rested on what they took to be the inevitably contradictory or subjective nature of legal decisionmaking and embraced nihilism.[5] Others thought that since the personal values or the power positions of decisionmakers were the prime determinants of legal rules, one could glean insights into how law "really" evolved from sociological or psychological studies of decisionmakers.[6] Still others argued that while generalizations about legal principles were hazardous, one could refine a technique of analyzing specific fact situations. The "law of the case" was always different, but the techniques for analyzing the law of the case could be replicated.[7]

Of the various "affirmative" methodological proposals of Realism, studying the underlying values of decisionmakers seems to have excited the greatest interest among advocates of Critical theory. But CLS has substantially enlarged and reoriented the Realists' concern with values. Rather than focusing on the value orientation of a particular decisionmaker, which may not tell us much about "law," given the multiplicity and diversity of "lawmakers" in American culture, Critical theory has sought to recreate the tacit value system—the shared assumptions and presuppositions—of mainstream actors in a legal culture at a point in time. That inquiry has yielded efforts to unpack the structure of Blackstone's Commentaries,[8] the ideology of twentieth-century labor law,[9] and the assumptions of "mainstream legal scholarship."[10]

This reorientation of the Realists' inquiry into values has obvious advantages for the Critical theorist. First, it frees him[11] from having to analyze values within a mainstream framework that conducts debate over marginal, unsettled questions (e.g., Shall a given approach to collective bargaining favor management or labor?) but presupposes that certain fundamental questions (e.g., Is the free market orientation of collective bargaining sound?) have been settled. By investigating the premises that mainstream opponents actually share, the Critical theorist not only penetrates to a deeper level of consciousness, but also distances himself from the objects of his analysis. He does not have to debate their value orientation; he can totally reject it.[12]

In one sense, the Critical theorists' reorientation of value analysis constitutes a methodological advance. To expose subjectivity or even prejudice in the calculus of a decisionmaker only represented a contribution when decisionmaking was assumed to be objective; once that assumption was denigrated, the fact of individual subjectivity didn't seem to lead anywhere, except perhaps to a psychological reductionism that traced judicial decisions to "what the judge ate for breakfast." The exposure of shared, often unexpressed values, by contrast, leads in two directions. First, it makes actors who tacitly share the values aware that their preference (e.g., for industrial peace or for the capitalist system) may be largely unexamined and is not unassailable. Second, it allows criticism of a legal culture to take place at a "total" rather than at a "partial" level. Saying that "Judge A consistently votes for the government in antitrust cases, which explains his antitrust opinions," and that "the government's antitrust policies consistently foster inefficiency" is arguably far less penetrating than saying that "antitrust doctrine presumes the value of 'competition,' which is a code word with false connotations, designed to provide a justification for an inhumane and inherently discriminatory economic order."

The strategy that advocates of total criticism seem to have adopted is one of penetration through distance. This is a strategy familiar to intellectual historians, who have used it to show, for example, that the formation of the American Constitution cannot be adequately understood without a recreation of the starting ideological assumptions of the framers, such as the inviolability of private property or the hierarchical nature of social organization. Such assumptions are thrown into sharp relief by the distance between the framers and contemporary students of their thought. The contemporary historian can explore the framers' intellectual universe at the deeper level because he does not share its central premises. Such a stance has resulted in some powerful recent recreations of the framers' thought and unpackings of the framers' language.[13]

But can penetration through distance be effective when the objects of the analysis are one's contemporaries? Here the logic of total criticism seems to double back on itself. The very notion that Critical analysis, if properly conducted, can expose the underlying preconceptions of mainstream scholarship is derived from a particular theory of the process of intellectual exchange. That theory assumes that intellectual discourse invariably has boundaries—the boundaries of culture, time, and place. Some intellectual options are not considered; some propositions tacitly are designated as beyond reproach, others as unthinkable. Discourse takes place within boundaries; total criticism seeks to identify the boundaries and to move beyond them. But if the theory is deterministic in the sense that it assumes that boundaries will always exist, how is it possible to penetrate the boundaries? That is, why will actors in the scholarly universe listen to those who totally criticize mainstream scholarship when the term "mainstream" is meant to signify a culturally determined set of constraints that actors "can't help" working within? It is as if a critic in late eighteenth-century America were to expose the property-consciousness of then current social theories and advocate the acquisition of all private property by the state. Given the property-consciousness of existing theories, who would listen?

Advocates of total criticism seek to evade this difficulty by arguing that their theory of intellectual exchange is not that deterministic: it allows for breakthroughs, paradigm shifts, or revolutions, in which mainstream preconceptions are exposed, found insufficiently fertile, and replaced by new preconceptions. Indeed, one could argue that total criticism is a necessary precondition for change because the primacy of mainstream scholarship at any point in time rests not on the inherent superiority of its intellectual theories but on the shared preconceptions on which those theories rest. Exposure of those preconceptions is a prerequisite for change. Developments in early twentieth-century jurisprudence serve as an illustration here. The breakdown of late nineteenth-century conceptualist methodologies in legal scholarship was made possible, one could argue, by the tacit abandonment of the idea that experience could be reduced to orderly principles. The collapse of conceptualism came not because it was an ineffective methodology—indeed, as a tool for organizing, synthesizing, and making intelligible large masses of data, it was remarkably effective—but because a widely shared assumption that data (or experience) could be organized or synthesized in a meaningful way was called into question.

But history suggests that while scholarly paradigms clearly exist and undoubtedly change, they change incrementally rather than radically. Taking twentieth-century American jurisprudence again as an example, one notes the successive emergence of antithetical paradigms of thought—conceptualism, Realism, and the "neoconceptualism" of the present age. But, on close scrutiny, one discovers that these paradigm shifts have been far from radical. The first attacks on conceptualism were launched by scholars and jurists—e.g., Roscoe Pound, John Wigmore, and Benjamin Cardozo—who shared the conceptualists' interest in maintaining order and predictability in the legal universe, but were disturbed by the capacity of doctrinal principles, once derived, to remain frozen in time and thereby incapable of accommodating change.[14] Their task had a schizoid quality, and Realism ultimately exposed its internal contradictions, laying blame on the assumption that rules were finite guides to anything. But the Realist critique, which did represent a wholesale abandonment of the starting assumptions of conceptualism, had been made possible by the earlier critics.[15]

Recent jurisprudential developments are susceptible to a similar analysis. Between Realism and contemporary neoconceptualism came the "process" jurisprudence of the 1950s and 1960s.[16] The process critics reacted to the Realist assumption that legal decisionmaking was discrete and idiosyncratic: They found this disturbingly relativistic as a philosophical statement and subversive of the idea that law could help rational actors plan their conduct. By identifying recurrent institutional functions performed by various legal decisionmakers—courts, legislatures, and agencies—this group of critics concluded that while the motivations of individual decisionmakers might be idiosyncratic and diverse, the process by which they reached their decisions had regular and predictable features. Rules of process, such as the requirements of due process or the techniques for confining the ambit of institutional discretion, were promulgated. Such rules prepared the way for the rules of substance derived by recent neoconceptualistic scholarship, which starts with asserted maxims about human conduct—e.g., rational persons maximize their own utility—and then advances legal rules that comport with those maxims—e.g., efficient breaches of contracts are permissible.[17]

Thus it has not been the case that paradigm shifts in American legal history have resulted from total criticism of an orthodoxy. Such shifts have resulted, rather, from criticism that had retained the starting assumptions of an entrenched paradigm but then interpreted them in ways that expose their contradictions. In accommodating doctrinal rules to changed social conditions, the sociological jurisprudes raised the possibility, seized upon by the Realists, that doctrinal rules were unintelligible without reference to the context of this application. In arguing that the discrete behavior of decisionmakers could be generalized into rules of process, the process jurisprudes raised the possibility, seized upon by neoconceptualists, that legal rules were, after all, intelligible as general propositions. That sort of incremental change is not, I take it, what is proposed by advocates of Critical theory. Indeed, retaining any of the starting preconceptions of mainstream scholarship seems incompatible with the CLS approach. History suggests, however, that incremental, rather than total, criticism precipitates legal change.

In sum, I believe that exposure of the tacit dimension of prevailing legal scholarship facilitates change only when the premises that constitute that dimension are significantly retained by critics of the established orthodoxy. Yet is seems to be a sine qua non of Critical theory that established assumptions be abandoned wholly before any reconstitutive work is begun. I suspect that if this commitment to total criticism is retained, it will only retard the effectiveness of the CLS movement. It is as if a labor union were debating whether to retain its present system of worker representation or move to a system in which individual workers had greater direct input into bargaining, and, in the course of the debate, a critic called for the complete dissolution of the union form of representation because it exploited workers. Such a result might eventually emerge if individual workers, gradually given more autonomy over bargaining, came to realize that they had little need for a union structure. But that result would have emerged through incremental, not total, criticism.

The CLSers have an additional justification for total criticism. It is illusory, they maintain, to engage in academic criticism as a nonideological exercise. Mainstream thought is necessarily ideological: its starting premises have distinct ideological consequences. Thus the critic should not only attack the intellectual incoherence of established thought: he also should attack its ideological ramifications and propose alternatives. Criticism of academic discourse is to be accompanied by exhortatory political discourse directed at the "real world"; theory and practice are to be fused.

II The Fusion of Theory and Practice

At the end of numerous recent CLS articles, one finds varied calls for "the transformation of social, political, and economic processes."[18] The specific steps of this transformation are rarely set forth in any detail. References are made to "a genuine reconstitution of society" based on "citizen participation in the community's public discourse,"[19] or to "a basic rethinking of liberalism and then a restructuring of our society itself,"[20] or to a radical expansion of the economic power of workers,[21] or to "the utopian project of experiencing . . . in social life the radical disintegration of the intellectual and institutional constraints of capitalist society."[22] One of these references calls for "a radical scholarship of practice," that would "enmesh legal scholars . . . in endeavors that, beginning with a transformative objective, would explore the capacity of social structure to respond to efforts towards fundamental change."[23] Such "endeavors" could include the creation by scholars of "situations that would blur the boundary between political and legal discourse by setting up conflict-resolution mechanisms in which community members served as arbitrators of neighborhood disputes."[24]

Even the above response is notable for its vagueness; indeed, I think the utopian proposals made at the conclusion of Critical articles are deliberately vague, since most Critical theorists concede that their concrete thinking about utopia has not yet crystallized. But where concrete proposals have been advanced, they appear to have a surrealistic quality. Consider the idea of establishing conflict-resolution mechanisms in "total environments," such as prisons, hospitals, or workplaces. Does this mean that scholars and students with a background in Critical theory would go into prisons or hospitals and encourage the resident population to decide for itself whether to punish an inmate or patient who had been unruly or a guard or nurse who had been uncooperative? Or does it mean that disputes over living conditions in mental institutions would be submitted to a panel of properly "Critical" scholars, students, and community members? Why is there any reason to think that in even the most blatantly exploitative environments oppressed persons would welcome the help and planning of Critical theorists, even if the oppressors suddenly did decide to abdicate authority?

Or take a recent proposal that Harvard Law School be transformed into a "counterhegemonic enclave." Among the suggestions advanced in that proposal were that staff member salaries be equalized, including secretaries and janitors; that "every person . . . spend one month per year performing a job in a different part of the hierarchy from his or her normal job"; that admission to the school be achieved through a lottery, with "quotas within the lottery for women, minorities, and working-class students" (the last group presumably being identifiable); and that disparities in students' educational attainment be "reduce[d] through . . . investment of large sums of money and resources in students at the bottom of the academic hierarchy."[25]

What is one to make of these last suggestions? They appear to be made seriously, but strategically—that is, not with any expectation that they will be adopted or even given other than cursory consideration, but rather with a view towards articulating a set of practices so radical that merely suggesting them broadens the range of discourse and thereby makes other proposals, equally transformative but less stunning, appear within the range of conceivable options. One is reminded of the strategy of protest groups in the 1960s, who would engage in anarchic or disruptive behavior—e.g., leaving water faucets on for 24 hours or lying down in front of toll booths on bridges—in order to expand public debate to include their claims and proposals. Perhaps a fusion of theory and practice is to come about only after enough surrealistic practices have been proposed that people begin to pay attention to the theory.

Here one finds a sense of deja vu. In the middle and late 1960s, we heard similar calls for the transformation of American society, although not in the stylized language of today's Critical theorists. When researching the backgrounds of CLS members, one finds that many of them were undergraduates or law students in the late 1960s. This sense of generational solidarity has been made explicit by some CLSers, who see the political experiences of the 1960s as crucial to the group's formation.[26] One analyst of the CLS movement describes the "intellectual biography" of its prototypical adherent as including "liberal (civil rights and anti-war) political involvements in the 1960s and 1970s" or "radical activi[sm] of the 1960s."[27] And there is a striking congruence between one central lesson of the 1960s—distrust the rhetoric of the establishment in power—and one analytical strategy of the CLS movement—exposing the ideological presuppositions of main-stream thought. In both instances, a cynicism about the motives of those in power, especially when their rhetoric purportedly is designed to promote ends other than the preservation of the status quo, yields transformative proposals, for example, the assertion of "power to the people" or the creation of "a radical left world view."[28]

There may yet be some important differences between the radical activism of the 1960s and that of the Critical theorists. With some exceptions, Critical theory does not seem oriented toward influencing the masses, as evidenced by its use of a vocabulary that would be incomprehensible to the nonspecialist. Moreover, some recent contributions to Critical legal scholarship seem to reject a conspirato-rial view of legal change—that economic or political elites impose their views on the populace by hiring lawyer elites to ground particularistic results in appeals to common values—in favor of a view that change is the product of ideological premises which, while historically contingent, are deeply and widely held.[29] Thus, to portray Critical theorists as simply protesting the sinister machinations of the Establishment may be inaccurate. But there are echoes of the 1960s in CLS none-theless: a marked sensitivity to relationships or arrangements that are hierarchical in character; a sense that "trashing" (a 1960s term) or "delegitimation" is liberat-ing rather than corrosive; a concern for the oppressed segments of society; and, above all, a sense that the university experience, for both faculty and students, quite properly ought to arouse awareness of the political character of society and help one develop techniques for responding to that fact.

The experience of the 1960s suggests, however, that universities are ill-cast as breeding grounds for political organization. Academic communities are notable for their lack of structure, for the precarious commitment on the part of their members to collective activity, and for their marginal status as sources of leader-ship for the public at large. Many Critical theorists, even those whose social vi-sions are radically transformative, have sensed that what academics do best is exposit and criticize ideas. The chief impact of the CLS movement, as its name implies, promises to be in its exposure of the underlying presuppositions of main-stream legal scholarship. The more Critical scholarship insists on a fusion of the-ory and practice, the more Critical articles insist on preaching utopian, "counter-hegemonic" solutions, the less likely it is to attract new converts, especially ones outside the university.

Even if one rejects the above assertions about the nature of academic commu-nities, one needs to confront the historical inhospitability of American culture to efforts to achieve a fusion of radical theory and practice. The promise of such a fusion rests on a certain model of the relationship of intellectual elites to the culture at large. The model assumes that intellectual elites can have their greatest impact on the rest of the culture when they play the role of political activists. But such has not been the case in twentieth-century America. While one can see ample evidence that ideas originally generated by intellectuals—the idea that skin color is not a reliable or even a relevant index of human ability being perhaps the most prominent—have penetrated the public consciousness, often with momentous consequences, there is very little indication that intellectuals, especially those espousing radical ideas, have been effective public leaders. Cultural change has come about when originally radical ideas, such as affirmative action, have been converted into effective political slogans by experienced politicians. The radical theories of late nineteenth-century Progressives became the popular slogans of twentieth-century economists; the quasi-socialistic statism of turn-of-the-century political theorists became the all-purpose liberalism of the New Deal. Yet part of the Progressives' appeal was as a response to socialism; part of the New Deal's was as an alternative to communism. What seems necessary to implement the insights of Critical theory is not a fusion of theory and practice, but a conversion of controversial theories into more palatable ones. I suspect that the Critical theorists themselves are neither well-suited nor inclined to make such a conversion.

III Critical Theory and the Disintegration of Liberalism: Three Liberal Presuppositions

Under the view of cultural change advanced in this essay, the CLS movement cannot "win"—that is, have its theoretical insights transformed into influential practical policies—without "losing"—that is, having its contributions absorbed and converted into policies that are more compatible with mainstream thought. In the language of CLS, this process is one of co-optation. Indeed, it is no overstatement to say that Critical theory views the relationship between American radicalism and American liberalism, at least since the First World War, as one of co-optation. In that view, the goals of radical thought—a mature, affirmative state, a degree of autonomy for the individual worker, a class-consciousness in labor relations, a realization of the inherent capacity of majorities to oppress minorities—have been converted into the milder policies of liberalism.

Thus, when radical theory has exposed a flaw in existing social relations—e.g., that the "freedom" of workers to bargain for their services with their employers is a fiction—liberal theory has moved to absorb and convert the insight—e.g., the legitimation of labor unions as bargaining agents, but the retention of the freedom-to-bargain assumption. While this relationship between radical theory and liberalism appears to annoy contemporary Critical theorists, I believe that it is likely either to continue or, at most, to be replaced by a comparable relationship between radical theory and some other mainstream ideology. That being so, I think it worthwhile to explore the CLS critique of liberalism in an attempt to determine whether the ideology of liberalism is capable of yet another round of absorption and conversion. Put another way, can liberalism co-opt radical theory one more time, or have the contributions of Critical theory and other ideologies unfriendly to liberalism exposed contradictions in liberal theory that are so deep as to be irremediable?

In my earlier discussion of paradigm shifts in American jurisprudence, I referred to the modifications of Realism made by the process theorists of the 1950s and 1960s. I find that in those decades three such modifications evolved into central presuppositions of process jurisprudence: the idea that process leads to justice, the idea that advocacy leads to truth, and the idea that expertise leads to wisdom. Each presupposition, while originally based on an insight of the Realists, can be seen as a strategy to deflect the corrosive implications of that insight; to absorb and convert it. These presuppositions of process theory form a central dimension of the ideology that Critical theorists call liberalism.[30] I take the emergence of Critical theory to be a testament to the current inability of the central presuppositions of process theory to command widespread allegiance. Moreover, the current interaction of liberalism and Critical theory, when seen as part of a general pattern of jurisprudential change in American culture, may foreshadow the future course of the CLS movement.

All three of the central presuppositions of process jurisprudence have been exposed and attacked by the CLS movement. Attacks on the presupposition that process leads to justice[31] may be seen as the Critical scholars' way of chastising their precursors, the Realists, for failing to heed one of their own axioms. Realism asserted that nothing could be learned from a discrete legal decision other than that a decision had been made; one could not read the rule accompanying the decision as a principle of general applicability. This assertion, when coupled with the Realists' skepticism about the validity of moral absolutes, yielded the notion that justice was individualized and subjective. It was this notion that eventually came to plague Realism. Subjective decisionmaking was equated with the ideas that power, rather than wisdom or goodness, was the basis of law, and that legal decisions were idiosyncratic. Under pressure, the Realists retreated, disclaiming relativism and endorsing the idea that a methodology of analyzing legal decisions, which was all that some self-styled Realists claimed their movement was, could be generalized.[32] Legal decisions were discrete, but the process by which they were reached was recurrent.

It was not an extreme step from this concession to the proposition, advanced by scholars after the Second World War, that the regularity and integrity of the process by which discrete decisions were made had an "inner morality" of its own.[33] In other words, procedural requirements, such a publication, intelligibility, the presence of an adequate record, sufficient representation and advocacy, and the presence of articulate criticism, could prevent subjective decisionmaking from becoming arbitrary. And, by an intellectual sleight of hand, reason, as opposed to fiat, became one of the procedural requirements.[34] Thus, a phenomenon—legal decisionmaking—that had been conceded to be subjective and discretionary was suddenly seen as capable of being regularized, constrained by procedural requirements, and limited, at least in the case of judges, by the obligation to produce reasoned justifications for results. Moreover, reason was not an entirely malleable concept: some proffered justifications of results would be rejected as too nakedly subjective or idiosyncratic. So, when all was said and done, judicial subjectivity appeared to be constrained by an objective requirement of reasoned elaboration. The objectivity of doctrine had been discredited, only to be replaced by the objectivity of process. And due process or reasoned elaboration was a necessary condition for the achievement of justice. It was what made law moral.[35]

One of CLS's contributions has been to debunk this equation of reason, process, and justice. With this debunking I wholly concur. Consider the following example. A candidate for tenure at a law school has offended a majority of the faculty by his lifestyle. He wears the "wrong" clothes, he openly engages in unconventional social practices, his interchanges with other faculty and with students are often uncomfortably abrasive. On the other hand, the candidate has met the conventional requirements for tenure at a law school: He has written books and articles, served on committees, and taught the average number of courses.

Suppose that the candidate is first evaluated by a faculty subcommittee whose members, for their own political and personal reasons, have resolved to deny him tenure. Indeed the committee members are quite explicit about this decision: they openly discuss how best to accomplish their aim. They resolve to critique his scholarship and teaching in such a way as to suggest that he falls below acceptable standards for tenure "on the merits." Their evaluation of the candidate is tainted by their a priori decision to recommend against tenure: they manipulate evidence about his teaching, supply criticism of the candidate's scholarship that gives it no credit for its positive contributions, dismiss favorable outside commentary as flawed or corrupt, and collect numerous comments on the candidate from other faculty members that are not comments on his teaching and scholarship, but comments on his personality and lifestyle. They then solemnly announce that, after a full evaluation of the candidate's scholarship, teaching, and service to the institution, they have concluded that the candidate fails to meet tenure standards.

If the motivations of the subcommittee members are never revealed publicly, the decision to deny the candidate tenure, assuming it is upheld after nominal further review by the entire faculty, appears to satisfy procedural requirements, even though it is substantively corrupt. The liberal equation of process with justice would seem to suggest either that mere compliance with proper procedures is all that justice requires or that such compliance will reveal substantive injustice by demanding the articulation of "good" reasons for a course of action. Indeed, the liberal theory of process seems to suggest that if one can find good reasons to justify a result, the covert motivations of those elaborating the reasons become irrelevant. Thus, if committee member A attacks candidate D's scholarship because he deplores D's lifestyle, A's attack is proper, despite its motivation, if D's scholarship is indeed lousy.

Surely there is something wrong here. If Hitler decides that all Jews, just because of their religion, shall be executed as traitors to the state, and one member of the Jewish community has actually stolen and communicated state secrets, does that legitimize his execution for treason? Or, if all those indicted for treason are allowed representation, given a formal hearing and a statement of reasons, and executed as violators of a duly promulgated law, can one call their execution just? The very idea that procedure leads to justice presupposes that procedural and substantive justice can be separated, so that a substantively unfair result will be legitimized if it results from fair procedures. Somehow the promulgation of fair procedures is supposed to result in the articulation of good reasons for decisions, thereby endowing the system with an inner morality and an inherent justness. But of course "fair," "good," and "moral" are substantive terms. Procedures do not make particular results fair; rather, current conceptions of justice dictate what are fair procedures. And even the fairest of procedures can be manipulated, corrupted, and perverted. Substance rules procedure in negative as well as positive ways.

So the Critical theorists seem to have exposed and devastated one presupposition of liberalism. The original Realists were right after all: process, like doctrine, is there for the manipulating, and it is the values of the manipulators, not the rules or procedures they employ, that count. That is not to say that the manipulators are not constrained: their values cannot be too much out of sync with the values of those affected by their decisions. But how much is too much cannot be answered in advance, and the manipulators have the advantage of power and, often, the wherewithal to summon up reasons that have a persuasive common appeal. Indeed, a willful, energetic set of decisionmakers, such as the late Warren Court, can successfully justify even unpopular results to its constituents by grounding them in deeply held common values. In such cases, it is hard to say that the decisionmakers are the ones constrained; rather, it is the constituents who, by reasons of power and of a commitment to common values, are constrained to accept unpopular decisions. Round one goes to the Critical theorists.

Round two involves the claim of liberal theory that advocacy leads to truth. This claim is closely related to the first—that process leads to justice—in that it assumes a basic integrity in a procedural system, here the system of adversarial representation. The claim presupposes that the effective working of the adversarial system will produce a full airing of both sides of a dispute, and thereby a true sense of what the dispute was all about, which is necessary for a fair resolution.[36] Here, again, the corrosive implications of a Realist insight were deflected by process theory. As noted earlier, the Realist critique of the objectivity of legal doctrine demonstrated that for every principle of law there was a counterprinciple: one could not merely extract principles from cases and convert them into rules of general applicability. The existence of counterprinciples threatened the image of law as an impartial mediator of disputes. How was one to choose from the mass of competing principles? The process theorists supplied an answer: the adversarial system itself would do the choosing. Truth was to emerge from the clash of competing arguments. Because the adversarial system was itself based on analytical reason, the best arguments were sure to prevail.[37]

We might start here by clearing away some objections to the advocacy-truth correlation that its supporters would dismiss as trivial. One is that the system makes errors. Persons are convicted of crimes that they did not in fact commit; spouses receive alimony payments by successfully concealing the adultery that should have disqualified them. Such errors, however, seem unavoidable because of human fallibility. They are not intrinsically related to advocacy: errors are made and truth is concealed in nonadversarial settings as well. A second, assertedly trivial, objection to the advocacy-truth correlation is that the system is skewed because advocates have disproportionate skills. The response is that while a more competent advocate may prevail even when his client's cause seems on its face to be weaker, the appropriate conclusion to draw is that adversaries need to be relatively equally matched, not that truth is ill-served by advocacy.

Ultimately, however, the disproportionate skills example illustrates the vulnerability of the advocacy-truth correlation. Part of the reason the skilled advocate is able to subvert the truth is that his overarching concern is winning disputes, not discovering truth. But the skilled advocate is not the only one uninterested in discovering truth; no one playing a central role in the adjudication of legal disputes—litigant, lawyer, or judge—has that as his primary concern. The litigants are interested primarily in winning their dispute, the lawyers in helping them do so, and the judge in finding a basis to resolve the dispute. That basis may not be the "truth"; indeed, given the primary motivations of the other principal actors, it is not likely to be the truth. The advocacy system is really designed to further not truth, but dispute resolution—winning and losing. In fact, as anyone familiar with litigation knows, truth often can be an impediment to winning, and is sometimes best suppressed if one wants to win. The best test of the truth of an idea may be its power to get itself accepted in the competition of the market, as Holmes once said,[38] but the best test of the truth of a legal argument surely is not the fact that it prevailed in court. Round two goes as well to the Critical theorists.

CLS has also attacked the third presupposition of liberal thought—that expertise leads to wisdom.[39] On this issue, one sees a significant difference between the Critical theorists and their predecessors, the Realists. While Realist literature emphasized the idiosyncratic and subjective character of judicial decisionmaking,[40] the Realists were not thereby led to view human relations either as essentially irrational or as dominated by factors, such as power or status, that bore no obvious relationship to rationality. Instead, the Realist literature that considered the question, "What does one do with the reality of subjectivity?" seems to have answered, "One becomes more self-conscious about one's own prejudices and more scientific in one's thinking." That is, the scientifically trained judge would be more effective than his untrained counterpart; although both would be susceptible to bias, one would be more aware of it than the other.[41]

The relationship between subjectivity, empiricism, and the social sciences was a central concern of Realism. And the Realist formulation of that relationship doubled back on itself. Realists took seriously the idea that studies of human behavior could be conducted scientifically. In fact, their discovery that judging was biased was made possible by their belief that certain psychological theories had been validated empirically. In other words, one demonstrated the idiosyncratic nature of human behavior with the aid of an explanatory theory of human idiosyncrasy that one took to be other than idiosyncratic. While decisionmaking was subjective, the theories that revealed its subjectivity were objective, in the sense that they were empirically verifiable. There was, then, a curious dichotomy in Realism. Legal rules and doctrines were exposed for their false objectivity, but the techniques that exposed them were taken to have been validated objectively. Thus, the Realists' vision of social science was hardly Kuhnian:[42] they did not take the step from seeing decisionmaking as controlled by cultural bias to seeing theories that explained decisionmaking as similarly controlled.

Scientific analysis thus did not merely reveal the existence of an explanatory paradigm for Realists; it led to expertise. And expertise led to wisdom. The Realists trusted properly trained elites, such as administrative agencies, a "managerial" executive, and a scientifically minded judiciary. That faith perfectly complemented the policies of the New Deal, which emphasized the operation of government by expert commission, the infiltration of federal institutions by academic and professional elites, and the idea of tinkering and experimenting with government, the way one would tinker with materials in a laboratory. For the Realists, an ideal state would have to be staffed and managed by technicians.[43]

Process jurisprudence absorbed and converted the idea of government experts as social engineers by positing a corollary. Expertise led to wisdom, to be sure, but wise leaders recognized the limits of their own expertise. Thus judges needed to be more self-conscious about their biases in order to subsume them in reasoned elaboration. Legislatures, courts, and agencies ought to be given freedom to make law and articulate policy, but only within the limits of their institutional competence. Judicial maturity came not only from knowing how to do well what judges should do—articulate good reasons for results—but also from knowing what judges should not do at all—invade the province of other branches of government.

It has taken a long time for the association of expertise and wisdom to break down. In foreign policy, for example, the association survived the Second World War because the arbitrary decisions made by "experts" about who was to kill and be killed, whose pockets were to be lined, and which minorities were to be oppressed were justified by the "war effort," a mystical entity originating out of the American public's revulsion against totalitarianism, genocide, and the threat of an invasion by alien forces. Indeed, the significance of the war effort construct became clear in the decades in which the expertise-wisdom association was first challenged, the decades of the Vietnam War. There was no comparable war effort mentality buttressing that war, despite attempts on the part of the Kennedy and Johnson Administrations to manufacture one. It was painfully clear, almost from the start, that the heavy-handed involvement of the United States in an Asian nation's civil war bore little resemblance to efforts to resist the spread of the Axis. Vietnam was neither a war to make the world safe for democracy nor a war to save Asia from Communist aggression; it was an attempt to buttress a corrupt, pro-Western regime that was being threatened by a corrupt, anti-Western one.

Whether Vietnam was perceived as a different war because it was different, being a land war in Asia against an elusive enemy that was not an "aggressor" in the Nazi sense, or whether it was so perceived because a cold war model of foreign affairs had begun to show signs of strain, thereby debilitating the reflexive "us-they" mentality of World War II, are not questions that concern me here. The fact is that Vietnam was regarded as different, and as less justifiable, almost from the beginning; consequently, the war effort justifications uttered by those making arbitrary decisions came under more searching scrutiny. In particular, the ultimately arbitrary feature of all wars—that some people get to designate others to do the actual fighting—was starkly revealed. Put simply, thousands of young Americans, because of the accident of being born in a certain year, were confronted by the risk of death on the battlefield. And they were not being asked to fight, they were being told. In asking the logical question, "Why us?," members of this generation were told, "Because of the war effort." But that justification simply didn't wash. The values summoned up to buttress it were not the values of World War II: democracy, freedom, equality, survival. None of those values was truly at stake in Vietnam, and when the "established" generation attempted to act as if they were at stake, its credibility was destroyed.

With the loss of credibility came another loss—the loss of the illusion that expertise begets wisdom. For the people escalating the war, expanding the armed services, ordering others into combat, and justifying those actions by summoning up the war effort concept were the experts of the generation then in power. They were the "best and brightest" of their time. But they seemed, at least to those immediately affected by their decisions, to have gotten things all wrong. They used doublespeak; they lied; they covered up; and they apparently fooled themselves by subscribing to a model of the world that simply did not apply to a civil war in southeast Asia. By the conventional standards of their time they had expertise, but where was their wisdom?

It is no accident that the established generation that escalated the war in Vietnam was first perceived as being trapped in its own Cold War logic at the same time that the more general theory of paradigmatic thinking first came into prominence.[44] Vietnam was a lesson in the confining orthodoxy of "normal science." No one charged with making decisions in the early stages of that war was able to step out of the cold war model, the assumptions of which were being used to guide the war effort. The lesson of Vietnam was thus a powerful one: what shapes the decisions of human actors is not so much their talent, training, or status, as their consciousness. And consciousness has its greatest impact not at the overt level, where alternatives are weighed and priorities are ranked, but at the covert level, where some options are dismissed as unthinkable and others are not even conceived. It is the tacit presuppositions of a culture's leaders, shaped by their generational experiences and those who have gone before, that dictate their decisions, not their expertise. If they are wise, it is solely within the limits of their permissible thought; few ever escape those limits.

There is no guarantee, then, that expertise will lead to wisdom. Indeed, there is a sort of guarantee that the reverse will happen if one assumes that professional communities have strong incentives to retain and refine the normal science in which they engage. The trained person becomes the socialized person; he becomes accustomed to speaking in jargon, reacting to a small, select group of people, having a clear notion of his own status and power within the professional community, and acting accordingly. In this context, one of the functions of the expert's wisdom is the justification and preservation of power for those with expertise. No wonder that the assumptions of whole generations are rarely dismissed outright by their successors. There is a powerful incentive to hold on to assumptions, whether or not life bears them out.

IV Conclusion: Some Inevitabilities

The Critical theorists, to a large extent members of the generation most directly affected by Vietnam and nurtured on Kuhn, have decisively parted company with Realism on the association of expertise and wisdom. And here they appear to have won the third round over liberal theory, but, in doing so, they have raised an issue that is not helpful to their cause. If we shouldn't believe in the wisdom of elites just because they are impeccably trained, why should we believe in the wisdom of Critical legal scholars? Let there be no mistake about it: participants in the CLS movement are members of an elite. They are impeccably trained; they earn comfortable salaries; they are associated with academic institutions of high status; their names have a certain visibility and prestige. Moreover, part of their elite status comes from their being designated as the trainers of future generations of lawyers. At the individual level, when one thinks about how few students one has actually "trained," this last point seems trivial. In a Kuhnian sense, however, generational educational experiences are decisive elements of the way one thinks, and therefore the issues deemed central to one's education are issues that may well remain central in later life.

The Critical theorists therefore cannot have it both ways. In calling for the transformation of social institutions, they are calling for the transformation of a world in which they have been comfortable and prominent. Few of the designated beneficiaries of their calls for change share their close identification with a hierarchical educational system in which the most prestigious members of the hierarchy get the fewest apparent demands made on their time. How many members of the oppressed classes would applaud a world in which persons designated as law professors got paid rather well for teaching five hours a week, or perhaps not at all? How many would be inclined to think that persons living that kind of life have any idea what it means to be oppressed? And while some Critical theorists might willingly work one month out of a year as janitors or secretaries, others might not like to have their salaries equalized even with other law professors, let alone with maintenance workers. There are powerful forces of self-preservation operating to retard the impact of transformative proposals, and when one adds to those forces a newly emergent skepticism about the wisdom of elites, one can readily imagine a scenario in which Critical legal scholars preach their transformative proposals to audiences wearing headsets.

The model of jurisprudential change set forth in this essay assumes that change is deterministic in two respects. First, one generation's presuppositions inevitably replace those of another, so that orthodox legal doctrine is fated eventually to become obsolete. Liberal thought may be on its way to obsolescence; the emergence of CLS may be indicative of liberalism's decline, and the contributions of Critical theorists may hasten that decline. As we have seen, the CLS critique of liberalism's presuppositions is a powerful one: I even sense a certain inevitability that liberalism, at least in its pure "process" form, will lose the fight.

But the model I have presented is deterministic in another respect. Change will take place only incrementally—that is, only when those in power perceive they will be advantaged by the change. While the ideologies of elites may differ, their membership, at least in terms of recruitment, training, and advancement, has tended to remain constant throughout twentieth-century American professional life. The kinds of people who become lawyers and law professors may change, but their professional roles will remain relatively constant. The Critical theorist of the 1980s is not likely to be very different, in terms of what he does, how much he gets paid relative to other highly qualified persons in his profession, or how he increases his prestige and visibility, from a Realist of the 1930s. And despite "counterhegemonic proposals," he has powerful incentives not to abandon his elite status. Law professors then, as now, started off writing impassioned critiques of the established order and ended up becoming deans or federal judges. Absorption and conversion is as inevitable as the passing of orthodoxy.

For that reason, the Critical theorists' pleas for social transformations appear incongruous. The most dedicated "rebel from principle"[45] is unlikely to elicit successfully a social transformation that threatens the very things that made it possible for him to propose that transformation—the freedom, leisure, and prestige of his vocation. The very audience to which his transformative proposals seems directed—elite law professors and students from prestigious universities—is the one least likely to benefit from them.

But when one divorces the utopian proposals of Critical theorists from Critical theory itself, a powerful attack on mainstream liberal thought remains. What will be the effect of that critique? If history is any guide, liberalism will absorb and convert Critical theory, thus producing a new synthesis. Or, possibly, liberalism may collapse from the weight of its internal contradictions and, and over time, a new orthodoxy may emerge, perhaps containing some of the presuppositions of CLS. But, either way, very little will have changed, and nothing will have progressed, let alone have been transformed. Change is neither transformation nor progress; it is just a series of inevitabilities.

NOTES

1. *See* Freeman, *Truth and Mystification in Legal Scholarship,* 90 YALE L. J. 1229 (1981); Tushnet, *Post-Realist Legal Scholarship,* 15 J. SOC'Y PUB. TCHRS. L. 20, 21 (1980); Note, *'Round and 'Round the Bramble Bush: From Legal Realism to Critical Legal Scholarship,* 95 HARV. L. REV. 1669 (1982).

2. *See,* Klare, *Labor Law as Ideology: Toward a New Historiography of Collective Bargaining Laws,* 4 INDUS. REL. L. J. 450 (1981); Lynd, *Government Without Rights: The Labor Law Vision of Archibald Cox,* 4 INDUS. REL. L. J. 483 (1981).

3. THE HARVARD LAW SCHOOL ASS'N, THE CENTENNIAL HISTORY OF THE HARVARD LAW SCHOOL; 1817–1917, at 31 (1918) (quoting Charles Elliot).

4. *See, e.g.,* Cook, *The Logical and Legal Bases of the Conflict of Laws,* 33 YALE L. J. 457 (1924); Llewellyn, *The Rule of Law in Our Case Law of Contract,* 47 YALE L. J. 1243 (1938); Llewellyn, *On Warranty of Quality, and Society,* 36 COLUM. L. REV. 699 (1936).

5. *See, e.g.,* W. STURGES, CASES AND MATERIALS ON THE LAW OF CREDIT TRANSACTIONS (1930); Sturges and Clark, *Legal Theory and Real Property Mortgages,* 37 YALE L.

J. 691 (1928). On Sturges' nihilism, see G. GILMORE, THE AGES OF AMERICAN LAW 70–81 (1977).

6. *See, e.g.,* J. FRANK, LAW AND THE MODERN MIND (1930); Haines, *General Observations on the Effects of Personal, Political and Economic Influences in the Decisions of Judges,* 17 ILL. L. REV. 96 (1922); Moore, *Rational Basis of Legal Institutions,* 23 COLUM. L. REV. 609 (1923).

7. The evolution of Karl Llewellyn's thought is relevant here. *Compare* Llewellyn, *Some Realism About Realism—Responding to Dean Pound,* 44 HARV. L. REV. 1222 (1931), *with* K. LLEWELLYN, THE COMMON LAW TRADITION: DECIDING APPEALS (1960).

8. Kennedy, *The Structure of Blackstone's Commentaries,* 28 BUFFALO L. REV. 205 (1979).

9. *See* Klare, *supra* note 2.

10. Gordon, *Historicism in Legal Scholarship,* 90 YALE L. J. 1017 (1981).

11. The CLS movement of course includes women as well as men. I have arbitrarily chosen to use male pronouns throughout this essay.

12. *Cf.* R. UNGER, KNOWLEDGE AND POLITICS (1975) (discusses need for, and practice of, total criticism).

13. *E.g.,* W. ADAMS, THE FIRST AMERICAN CONSTITUTIONS (1980); J. POCOCK, THE MACHIAVELLIAN MOMENT (1975); G. WOOD, THE CREATION OF THE AMERICAN REPUBLIC, 1776–1787 (1969).

14. *See* G. WHITE, PATTERNS OF AMERICAN LEGAL THOUGHT 105–115 (1978) [hereinafter cited as G. WHITE, PATTERNS]; G. WHITE, TORT LAW IN AMERICA 58–62, 118–24 (1980).

15. *See* G. WHITE, PATTERNS, *supra* note 14, at 99–132; G. WHITE, TORT LAW IN AMERICA, *supra* note 14, at 65–83.

16. For discussions of the process school, see G. WHITE, PATTERNS, *supra* note 14, at 136–163; Peller, *In Defense of Federal Habeas Corpus Relitigation* 16 HARV. C.R.-C.L. L. REV. 579, 670–75 (1982); Ackerman, Book Review, 103 DAEDALUS 119 (1974).

17. For examples of neoconceptualistic scholarship of the law and economics variety, see R. POSNER, THE ECONOMICS OF JUSTICE (1981); Goetz and Scott, *Principles of Relational Contracts,* 67 VA. L. REV. 1089 (1981).

18. Note, *supra* note 1, at 1682.

19. Brest, *The Fundamental Rights Controversy: The Essential Contradictions of Normative Constitutional Scholarship,* 90 YALE L.J. 1063, 1109 (1981).

20. Frug, *The City as a Legal Concept,* 93 HARV. L. REV. 1057, 1151 (1980).

21. *See* Lynd, *supra* note 2, at 494.

22. Klare, *supra* note 2, at 482.

23. Note, *supra* note 1, at 1687.

24. *Id.*

25. D. Kennedy, Utopian Proposal or Law School as a Counter-hegemonic Enclave (Apr. 1, 1980) (unpublished manuscript prepared as a dissent to the Report of the Committee on Educational Planning and Development [The Michelman Report], Harvard Law School, May 1982, on file with the *Stanford Law Review*).

26. *See, e.g.,* Parker, *The Past of Constitutional Theory—And Its Future,* 42 OHIO ST. L. J. 223 (1981).

27. Gordon, *New Developments in Legal Theory,* in THE POLITICS OF LAW: A PROGRESSIVE CRITIQUE 281, 282 (D. Kairys ed. 1982) [hereinafter cited as THE POLITICS OF LAW].

28. Kennedy, *Critical Labor Law Theory: A Comment,* 4 INDUS. REL. L. J. 503, 506 (1981).

29. *Compare* M. HORWITZ, THE TRANSFORMATION OF AMERICAN LAW (1977) *with* Gordon, *supra* note 27, *and* Mensch, *The History of Mainstream Legal Thought,* in THE POLITICS OF LAW, *supra* note 27, at 18.

30. In singling out these presuppositions for analysis, I mean to suggest only that they are significant features of liberalism which the Critical theorists have attacked, not that they *define* liberalism or that they have been the *principal* features of liberalism against which Critical theorists have reacted.

31. *See, e.g.,* Brest, *The Substance of Process,* 42 OHIO ST. L. J. 131 (1981); Parker, *supra* note 26, at 232–35; Peller, *supra* note 16, at 669–90.

32. *See* E. PURCELL, THE CRISIS OF DEMOCRATIC THEORY 159–79 (1973); G. WHITE, PATTERNS, at 141–50.

33. *See, e.g.,* L. FULLER, THE MORALITY OF LAW (1964); H. HART AND A. SACKS, THE LEGAL PROCESS: BASIC PROBLEMS IN THE MAKING AND APPLICATION OF LAW (1958).

34. *See, e.g.,* Fuller, *Reason and Fiat in Case Law,* 59 HARV. L. REV. 376 (1946).

35. *See* L. FULLER, THE PROBLEMS OF JURISPRUDENCE. 705–08, 727–29 (1949); H. HART AND A. SACKS, *supra* note 33, at 168–70.

36. For criticism of this presupposition, see Simon, *The Ideology of Advocacy: Procedural Justice and Professional Ethics,* 1978 WIS. L. REV. 29; Simon, *Homo Psychologicus: Notes on a New Legal Formalism,* 32 STAN L. REV. 487 (1980).

37. The swan song of Karl Llewellyn provides an example of scholarship employing this strategy. *See* K. LLEWELLYN, The Common Law Tradition, *supra* note 7.

38. *Abrams v. United States,* 250 U.S. 616, 630 (1919) (Holmes, J., dissenting).

39. For criticism of this presupposition, see J. AUERBACH, UNEQUAL JUSTICE: LAWYERS AND SOCIAL CHANGE IN MODERN AMERICA (1976); W. CHASE, THE AMERICAN LAW SCHOOL AND THE RISE OF ADMINISTRATIVE GOVERNMENT (1982).

40. One Realist judge wrote a celebrated article revealing that he decided cases on the basis of "hunches." *See* Hutcheson, *The Judgment Intuitive: The Function of the Hunch in Judicial Decision,* 14 CORNELL L. Q. 274 (1929).

41. *See* J. FRANK, COURTS ON TRIAL: MYTH AND REALITY IN AMERICAN JUSTICE (1950); Frank, *Realism in Jurisprudence,* 7 AM. L. SCH. REV. 1063 (1934).

42. *See* T. KUHN, THE STRUCTURE OF SCIENTIFIC REVOLUTIONS (2d ed. 1970).

43. On the connections between Realism and the New Deal, see generally Frank, *supra* note 41; Purcell, *American Jurisprudence between the Wars: Legal Realism and the Crisis of Democratic Theory,* 75 AM HIST. REV. 424 (1969).

44. The first edition of Thomas Kuhn's *The Structure of Scientific Revolutions* appeared, to almost no comment, in 1962. Reviews and comments began to pick up the mid-1960s and were widespread by the end of the decade.

45. *See* Kennedy, *Rebels From Principle: Changing the Corporate Law Firm From Within,* 33 HARV. L. SCH. BULL. 36 (1981).

From Realism to Critical Legal Studies: A Truncated Intellectual History*

Introduction: Reassessing Influence

In the 1930s a school of literary criticism surfaced that emphasized the influence certain writers had on later writers. Shakespeare, it was claimed, influenced Melville; Hawthorne influenced the early writings of Henry James, and so on. The image furthered by this critical attitude was that of a writer reading passages from previous writers and incorporating their language, their tone, their sentence structure, or their metaphors into his or her own writing. Living writers to whom the theory was applied resolutely denied being so influenced, but their denials were not taken seriously, either because of the maxim that no writer likes to admit not being wholly original and unique or because the influence could be recharacterized as unconscious.[1]

Influence is now perceived to be a more complex and subtle phenomenon than the 1930s scholars assumed. In particular, influence is perceived as revealing more about the persons being influenced than those doing the influencing. The world of ideas has come to be seen as in some respects a remarkably closed world, bound in by time, place, politics, economics, institutional structures, and above all the tacit presuppositions of mainstream thought in a give era. Extant ideas are received and filtered through a series of ideological structures that refashion their content and especially their implications.[2] From this perspective, Shakespeare does not so much influence Melville as Melville influences Shakespeare: that is, Melville, and others sharing his starting assumptions about the nature of existence and social organization, tacitly emphasize certain features of Shakespeare and de-emphasize others. An image of Shakespeare is created for Melville and like readers; it is this image that may be said to be influential. The process of influence, from this perspective, can be most clearly observed in writers that are not read by some subsequent generations and then "discovered" by others. What has

*40 Southwestern L. J. 819 (1986). A previous version of this essay was delivered as the 1986 Ray Lecture, Southern Methodist University.

changed, of course, is not the content or style of the original writer but the values and tastes of the successive readers; what has changed is the image.[3]

With this in mind, it is interesting to find, in a recent symposium on the Critical Legal Studies (CLS) movement, explicit statements that CLS has been influenced by the Realist movement of the 1930s. Both supporters and critics of CLS have posited a linkage between the two movements. David Trubek describes the Critical Legal Studies movement as "an outgrowth of American Legal Realism";[4] Mark Tushnet calls CLS "the direct descendant of Realism."[5] Philip Johnson states that one of the parents of CLS is "the American Legal Realism of 50 years ago";[6] Louis Schwartz claims that "the 'Realist' school of jurisprudence that flourished in the 1930s must be counted as an important earlier model for CLS."[7] While the obvious implication of the linkage is that the Realists have somehow influenced Critical Legal Studies scholars, the question raised in this article is who has really influenced whom. In an essay in the same symposium[8] I suggested that the "self-conscious identification of Realism as a progenitor of, or an inspiration for, the CLS movement" seemed to be "a grasp at legitimacy" and was "a common enough lawyer's trick."[9] Those phrases sounded all right when I wrote them, but flippancy tends to cut off intellectual inquiry, and I want to take a further look at the relationship of Realism to Critical Legal Studies.

The exploration of that relationship has produced a complex intellectual history that will have to be severely truncated and oversimplified here. While I shall spend a little time sketching out that history, my primary purpose is not to add to the lore of those who regard themselves as "aficionados of the thirties and forties."[10] My main concern is rather to ask why, if Realism is widely perceived as something that "ran itself into the sand" as "a coherent intellectual force in American legal thought,"[11] the Critical Legal Studies movement, which seeks intellectual prominence, if certainly not respectability, would claim Realism as an influence; why Realism has come to be perceived as an intellectual dead end; and whether the same fate may await Critical Legal Studies. The exploration of those questions is necessarily historical, but history here is in the service of contemporary philosophy and politics.

There is a missing link in the evolution from Realism to Critical Legal Studies. The link is not so much missing in the sense of unrecognized, but rather in the sense of ignored or unexplained. That link is the Law and Society movement, which began in the 1960s and still exists. The link turns out to be, in my view, important for understanding the relationship of Realism to Critical Legal Studies and important to any prognostication of the future of CLS. An explanation of the importance of the Law and Society movement to the history sketched here requires some laying of groundwork.

I The Internal Contradictions of Realism

I have previously argued that the emergence of Realism in the 1920s and 1930s can be traced to the simultaneous convergence of two phenomena: the acceptance of social science theory as legitimate academic discourse and the apparent collapse of a late nineteenth-century individualist ethos in the face of the ostensibly interdependent nature of twentieth-century American society.[12] Legal scholars who came to call themselves Realists began with the perception that many early twentieth-century judicial decisions were "wrong." They were wrong as matters of policy in that they promoted antiquated concepts and values and ignored changed social conditions. They were wrong as exercises in logic in that they began with unexamined premises and reasoned syllogistically and artificially to conclusions. They were wrong as efforts in governance in that they refused to include relevant information, such as data about the effects of legal rules on those subject to them, and insisted upon a conception of law as an autonomous entity isolated from nonlegal phenomena. Finally, they were wrong in that they perpetuated a status quo that fostered rank inequalities of wealth, status, and condition and was out of touch with the modern world.

This perception may have been the source of Realism, but it was not what made Realism distinctive.[13] The distinctive feature of Realism came in the methodologies its adherents employed to demonstrate the validity of their perception. The Realists employed two quite separate methodological approaches; the distinctiveness of the movement springs from the perception of its adherents that the approaches were complementary rather than contradictory. One approach, termed "debunking" by those employing it and revived as "deconstruction" by Critical Legal Studies scholars, subjected "wrong" opinions to a logical analysis that exposed their inconsistencies, their unsubstantiated premises, and their tendency to pass off contingent judgments as inexorable. The analytical basis for debunking, for most Realists, was Wesley Hohfeld's series of articles in the years prior to the First World War,[14] in which he demonstrated the capacity of legal propositions to be "flipped": that is, the sense in which every legal doctrine can be seen as a suppressed version of an alternative doctrine.[15] Karl Llewellyn once summarized debunking as the process of demonstrating that "in any case doubtful enough to make litigation respectable the available authoritative premises . . . are at least two, and . . . the two are mutually contradictory as applied to the case in hand."[16]

Much of Realist scholarship was thus devoted to exposing the incoherence of established patterns of reasoning in judicial decisions. By undermining the inexorability of such logic, the Realists hoped to reveal the "real" question in judicial decisions: why "the court select[ed] . . . one available premise rather than the other."[17] This was the point in Realist analysis where social science entered. The answer to the question of premise selection was, in most cases, that a given premise rested on unexamined value judgments that were simply assumed by the court to be controlling. For example, in cases raising the question whether state hours and wages legislation violated a liberty to contract embodied in the Fourteenth Amendment's due process clause, two authoritative premises were present. One premise was that employers and employees had rights to define the terms of employment, and that statutory prescriptions of those terms unduly curtailed those rights. The alternative premise was that the balance of power between employers and employees in the industrial marketplace was sufficiently unequal that no such rights in employees could be said to exist: the contracts were simply coercive.

Nothing in the nature of contract or liberty compelled the choice of one or the other premise: the premises were social judgments about the desirability or undesirability of protecting workers who had little bargaining power.

The "real" question in liberty of contract cases was, therefore, not "is there a liberty to contract in the due process clause?" but "do industrial workers in fact have no bargaining power to choose the terms of their employment?" [18] This question was, the Realists believed, susceptible of empirical analysis. One could, as Robert Hutchins said in 1927, ascertain "how the rules of law are working" through "practicable investigation" into their operation.[19] In sum, the Realists assumed that techniques existed for determining and analyzing human behavior, that meaningful generalizations could be derived from those techniques, and that the generalizations could then be reflected in policy proposals. Once one found "how the judicial system actually works [and] how it is affecting the community," Hutchins argued, one could learn how that system "may be altered to attain more readily the objects for which it has been developed."[20] Much later, Karl Llewellyn generalized this perceived connection between empirical investigation and law reform: "Every fact-pattern of common life . . . carries within itself its appropriate, natural rules, its right law. . . . The highest task of lawgiving consists in uncovering and implementing this immanent law."[21]

Recognizing that the Realist impulse was basically political in that it originated with a judgment that many early twentieth-century judicial decisions represented examples of bad social policy helps to explain the simultaneous attachment of Realists to debunking and empirical research. Critiques of the logic of opinions would reveal the outmoded character of their premises; empirical research would demonstrate why the premises were outmoded. But while the fusion of debunking and social science is explicable in one sense,[22] it remains puzzling in another. Why didn't the Realists apply the logic of their criticism to social science research itself? Why did they assume that while arguments based on legal doctrines were necessarily value laden, arguments based on empirical observation could be value free? Why did Llewellyn, to take an example, define his concern to be with "law as a social science, a science of observation," and then assert that "one's fighting convictions [should] never [be] allowed to interfere with accurate observations?"[23]

To criticize the Realists for not emphasizing that "scientific" inquiry has its own ideological presuppositions is, in a sense, to impose the received wisdom of one generation on another. The social sciences, in the early twentieth century, were widely perceived of as antidotes to the soft epistemology of traditional disciplines: they were exploring facts and revealing the world as it really was. It is too much to say that no one recognized that social science, or even "pure" science, was susceptible to being organized ideologically. As traditionalist a legal scholar as Roscoe Pound argued, in 1931, that "preconceptions will creep in and will determine the choice of pure fact of fact as they determined the pure fact of law. . . ."[24] Nevertheless the freshness of empirical social science, for Realists, principally came from its assumed freedom from the conceptualist web of value-laden doctrine.

Thus the common explanations for why Realism ran into the sand as an influential intellectual movement do not take an additional, and perhaps obvious, explanatory step. Realism is typically said to have declined in influence because its debunking ultimately led to moral relativism and nihilism, and suddenly, in the shadow of the Second World War, no one wanted to endorse either of those positions; or because the empirical research called for by the Realists was either not done or resulted in trivial findings. Neither explanation is inaccurate, but the two can be combined. If one recalls that Realism started with a political perception, and that its energies were thus ultimately directed at the formation of "good" or "right" policy, the combination of deconstructionist logic and empirical research may have had a devastating effect. With the revelation that all legal doctrine was based on value premises, "objective" methodologies became necessary. But the end purpose of those methodologies was to conform doctrine to "real" life, that is, to produce "better" legal decisions. Facts (the observation that something really existed) were thus inseparable from values (the judgment that doctrines should facilitate what did exist). Discovering what was there was also discovering what was good.

It may be that those Realist legal scholars who set out to do empirical research with the idea that "better" policies would emerge from it confronted, somewhere along the way, the realization that they had skewed their observations at the outset. It may be, in other words, that such Realists sensed a fundamental contradiction between debunking and empirical social science: what I will term the fact-value dichotomy.[25] This might explain the remarkable collective inability of Realist empiricists to complete their research projects and the tendency of legal scholars initially enthused with social science to abandon it for other work or for silence. Of the Realist enthusiasts for empirical research that clustered at Yale and Columbia law schools in the 1920s and 1930s, only one, Underhill Moore, was still identified with social science by 1940, and Moore's work was widely regarded as ludicrous.[26] William O. Douglas, Walton Hamilton, Walter Dodd, Charles Clark, Wesley Sturges, and Llewellyn had each abandoned social science research, abandoned scholarship altogether, or abandoned law teaching. Their abandonment cannot be attributed to the demise of social science research generally, for it continued to flourish in other departments of universities. Social science research did not assume, however, an explicit policy orientation in the fields of economics, statistics, sociology, anthropology, and psychology. Scholars in those fields were perceived as neutral, objective experts. Law professors had never been so perceived and apparently could not think of themselves in such terms.

II Postwar Closure: The First Post-Realist Movements

The uneasy interaction of deconstructionist logic and objective social science can also be seen as background to the growth of two movements in the 1940s whose emergence severely pinched, and ultimately co-opted, the vitality of Realism. One was the Law, Science, and Policy movement, ushered into existence by Harold Lasswell's and Myres McDougal's 1942 article, Legal Education and Public Policy.[27] Lasswell and McDougal identified law as a social science, called for "scientific thinking," which meant a "familar[ity] with the procedures by which facts are established by planned observation," and even advocated "realism," which they defined as "access to a body of fact" through a process that "protect[s] the integrity of thought by excluding or nullifying the non-relevant." [28] Most of the scholarly efforts that formed the inspiration for their article were by Realists, [29] but Lasswell and McDougal made clear that they were not going to become bogged down in distinctions between "is" and "ought," facts and values. They urged that legal education be reoriented so that empirical research was placed in the service of democratic values:

> What is needed now is to . . . [reorient] . . . every phase of law school curricula and skill training toward the achievement of clearly defined democratic values. . . .
>
> The student needs to clarify his moral values . . . he needs to orient himself in past trends and future probabilities; finally, he needs to acquire the scientific knowledge and skills necessary to implement objectives. [30]

Lasswell and McDougal were equally clear about the reason for their reorientation of the relationship between value orientation and empirical research:

> It should need no re-emphasis here that . . . democratic values have been on the wane in recent years. The dominant trends of world politics have been away from the symbols and practices of a free society and toward the slogans, doctrines and structures of despotism. . . .
>
> [A] legitimate aim of education is to seek to promote the major values of a democratic society and to reduce the number of moral mavericks who do not share democratic preferences. [31]

A "clarification of values" [32] was thus the first step in Lasswell's and McDougal's program for training policymakers. One clarified and identified one's value preferences before doing any empirical research; one then sought to implement values through what Lasswell and McDougal called "trend-thinking" and "scientific thinking." [33] Those terms turned out to be fancy ways of suggesting that before one implemented one's values one should try to identify "the shape of things to come regardless of preference" and to "guide . . . judgment by what is scientifically known and knowable about the causal variables that condition the democratic variables." [34]

Lasswell's and McDougal's move evaded two difficulties in which the Realists had found themselves. First, no one could accuse Law, Science, and Policy advocates of being moral relativists or soft on totalitarianism. Lasswell, who was identified in the article as the Director of War Communications Research for the Library of Congress, and McDougal, who informed his public that he had taken leave from the Yale faculty "to become General Counsel of the Office of Foreign Relief and Rehabilitation Operations in the State Department," [35] identified their proposals as part of the war effort. "The war period," they announced, "is a propitious moment to retool our system of legal education. . . . War is the time to retool our educational processes in the hope of making them fit instruments for their future job." [36] It was "self-congratulatory falsehood to [claim] that recent catastrophes have come upon us like bolts from the blue'';[37] the program of Law, Science, and Policy would be ready for the next totalitarian cycle.[38]

Second, Lasswell and McDougal refused to linger over the dialectics of the fact-value dichotomy. They did not consider the possibility that the dogmatism of antiquated rules might also be reflected in newer rules derived from contemporaneous empirical observation. The question of whether facts overwhelmed values or values overwhelmed facts they resolved summarily. Their advice to law students at the value "clarification stage" is instructive:

> Clarification of values . . . must for effective training be distinguished from the traditional, logical, derivation of values by philosophers. Such derivation . . . is a notorious blind alley. Divorced from operational rules, it quickly becomes a futile quest for a meaningless why perpetually culminating in "some inevitably circular and infinitely regressive logical justification" for ambiguous preferences. From any relatively specific statements of social goal . . . can be elaborated an infinite series of normative propositions of ever increasing generality; conversely, normative statements of high-level abstraction can be manipulated to support any specific social goal. Prospective lawyers should be exposed, by way of warning . . . to the work of representative specialists in derivation; relatively little time should be required, however, to teach them how to handle, and how to achieve emotional freedom from, [it].[39]

The solution to the fact-value dichotomy, then, was to ignore it. One dismissed infinite logical regressions and took a stand. Having taken a stand, one implemented one's values by empirical research that confirmed them.

Law, Science, and Policy, despite the prolificity and mutual supportiveness of its adherents, has never gained widespread support in legal academic culture,[40] partly, as one observer has noted, because "it seems to be wearisome, or too pretentious, or unpalatable,"[41] and partly because its adherents' repeated cataloguing of "values" and "goals" relevant to policymaking have appeared to some observers as assertions or laundry lists. Nevertheless the arrival of the movement, with all its fanfare, was a clear signal that the Realists' belief in the coexistence of value premise deconstruction and objective empirical research had backed them into a corner.

The other movement pinching Realism in the 1940s was more subtle, more effective, and gained a far wider acceptability. This movement was Process Jurisprudence, which began with Lon Fuller's critique of Realism in the 1930s and 1940s,[42] expanded to become a fullblown political science theory in the 1950s, prescribing carefully defined roles for courts, legislatures, and administrative agencies,[43] survived attacks by substantive rights theorists in the 1960s, and is still very much a part of mainstream academic thought, notwithstanding the problematic nature of its normative assumptions. I will not attempt a detailed sketch of Process Jurisprudence here, having done that in other places[44] and not wanting to sidetrack the progression of this history unduly. I merely want to point out the basic strategy of confession and avoidance that Process Jurisprudence theorists adopted toward Realism.

Despite the Realists' difficulties, they had made two contributions to American jurisprudence that by the 1940s had come to be regarded as settled propositions. The first was that judges, in declaring legal rules, made law in the sense that the rules were not logically necessary and reflected policy judgments; the second was that law could not be a static entity, and that its progressive development rested on its rules being responsive to current social conditions. By the 1940s it was no longer possible for judges to ground decisions on appeals to law as a disembodied entity or as a bundle of settled precedents. Universal or static conceptions of law were thus no longer perceived as genuine constraints on judges.

Advocates of Process Jurisprudence took the above propositions as a given and sought to fashion new sets of constraints on judicial lawmaking. One set focused on the nature of judicial reasoning: process theorists insisted that judges engaged in "reasoned elaboration" of the results they reached by invoking legal principles of sufficient neutrality and generality to "transcend" immediate results. In constitutional adjudication judges should invoke and articulate "neutral principles"; in statutory interpretation they should identify and follow the purposes of the relevant statutes; in common law decisionmaking they should articulate the principles and policies embodied in common law rules. These exercises would insure that judicial decisionmaking would be subject to intellectual constraints. Failure to engage in appropriately "principled" adjudication would result in opinions being subject to academic criticism and a consequent loss of stature.[45]

The other set of constraints was institutional. Process theorists developed a model of political science in which the leading lawmaking institutions in American society were assigned functional roles. Administrative agencies "found facts" and developed "expertise" in specific areas of the economy; legislatures made policy by weighing the competing demands of interests and reaching compromise solutions through the process of democratic politics; courts identified and articulated legal principles, some of which justified judicial lawmaking, others of which envisaged judicial deference to more expert or more democratic lawmaking bodies. So defined, the legal process insured responsiveness to changing social conditions through the democracy of legislatures and the expertise of agencies and erected safeguards against irresponsible or insular judicial rulemaking. The process could even be said to have an "inner morality," since the requirements of reasoned elaboration and institutional competence insured that lawmaking would be fair, democratic, and accountable.[46] The model thus solved, for its adherents, the problems of judicial unresponsiveness and unchecked judicial power, and had the added attraction of being faithful to democratic values.

Law, Science, and Policy and Process Jurisprudence were jurisprudential movements predicated on the existence of a deep consensus among Americans about values and institutional roles. They were in that sense products of a period in American history in which the "end of ideology"[47] was announced, conformity and solidarity were regarded as virtues, and social ferment was assumed to have receded. No sooner was this assumed consensus in place than the civil rights movement began to erode it. That movement suggested that a group of Americans had been existing well outside the majoritarian democratic mainstream; that the rights of those Americans to be treated fairly and equally overrode institutional considerations such as deference to legislative policy; that renewed attention to the civil rights of minorities had not come through democratic processes, but through the recognition of the substantive validity of minority claims; that judicial deference to administrative expertise or to legislative representativeness would have retarded the recognition of minority rights; and that neutral principles of constitutional adjudication were not much help in protecting minorities against discrimination. The interaction of Process Jurisprudence with the civil rights movement of the 1960s, and the emergence of the Warren Court as a visible defender of minority rights, sparked an intellectual debate about the meaning and efficacy of reasoned elaboration and principled adjudication.[48]

My interest here is not with that debate, however, but with another, lesser known development in the 1960s. Recall the two principal features of Realism: deconstruction of judicial opinions and calls for empirical research. Process Jurisprudence and the Law, Science, and Policy movement had sought to fuse those efforts in a reconstructed theory of law and legal institutions. Under the Law, Science, and Policy version of that theory, deconstruction would begin with open statements of value orientation, and empirical research would be enlisted in the reformulation of doctrine that followed from such statements. Under the Process Jurisprudence version, deconstruction became subsumed in the ideals of reasoned elaboration and principled adjudication, in which normative assumptions were rounded in appeals to principles or policies extrinsic to the court invoking the appeal; empirical research became subsumed in the theory of institutional competence and the idea of deference to administrative rules or policies based on expertise.

The result was to produce two closed jurisprudential systems: one system in which the proper functioning of legal institutions guaranteed progressive and democratic results and another system in which that functioning guaranteed responsive and enlightened policies. The attacks on neutral principles theory generated by the civil rights movement were a protest against the first closed system. A protest against the second closed system was less visible and influential in legal academic life in the 1960s, but it emerged with the Law and Society movement. The governing assumption of the Law and Society movement can be said to have been that Law, Science, and Policy or Process Jurisprudence had obfuscated a central inquiry of the Realists: whether the "law on the books" was the equivalent of the "law in action." Was the implementation of democratic values prescribed by Law, Science, and Policy actually taking place? Were the expert judgments of agencies truly based on the detached empirical observation of social conditions? Was there a gap between the claims of lawmakers that they were responsive to social needs and their actual responses to those needs?

III The Missing Link: From Law and Society to Critical Legal Studies

The formation of the Law and Society Association in 1964 and the appearance two years later of the *Law and Society Review* marked the official emergence of the Law and Society movement. The movement was initially originated by sociologists as well as law professors, and its first endeavors reflected that fact. The aims of the movement were described exclusively in neutral, academic terms: no political dimension was suggested. The first president of the Law and Society Association called for "more rigorous and formal interdisciplinary training" in law and sociology,[49] and the initial edition of the *Law and Society Review* described its appearance as a response to "a growing need on the part of social scientists and lawyers for a forum in which to carry on an interdisciplinary dialogue."[50] The Review sought, its editor suggested, to create "a professional cadre who are able to move freely from their original disciplinary base into the related fields."[51]

This tone was typical of academic discourse throughout the 1950s and most of the 1960s: rarely were intellectual movements described in ideological terms. The orientation of the movement becomes clear, however, on a further perusal of the first volume of the *Law and Society Review*. In the second issue Richard Schwartz, the editor, in referring to a recently published book by sociologist Jerome Skolnick, described the work as "enlighten[ing] us on the process by which law on the books is transformed (or distorted) into law in action."[52] The key word in that sentence was "distorted." Schwartz went on to describe examples of unanticipated consequences of legal policies, such as "drug addiction increasing because of efforts at enforcement, public defender systems enhancing conviction rates, [and] Draconian divorce codes generating perjury."[53] Schwartz's point was that empirical research often revealed the dysfunctional effects of legal rules and policies or the hidden purposes of a rule or policy that had been justified on different grounds. The first article to appear in the *Law and Society Review* had, in fact, taken Schwartz's logic one step further. In a report in "Civil Justice and the Poor"[54] three sociologists based at Berkeley had argued that "the law is not a neutral instrument, but rather that it is oriented in favor of those groups or classes in society having the power to bend the legal order to their advantage."[55] "[T]oday as in the past," the authors maintained, "the law primarily serves to protect and enhance the rights and interests of property holders and those in positions of wealth and authority."[56]

If one views the emergence of the Law and Society movement in the context of both Realism and the efforts to co-opt Realist insights in the 1940s and 1950s, the movement's initial emphasis appears as an effort to return to a "purer" strand of Realist research. The Realists had, of course, sounded a call for studies of the transformation of law on the books to law in action, and they had suggested that such studies would reveal a gap between "paper rules" and the realities of implementative practice. Both the Law, Science, and Policy movement and Process Jurisprudence had, however, suggested that if such a gap existed, it could be corrected either by an adjustment of value orientation (such as "caring more" above the rights of the poor) or by an adjustment of the processes through which law was made (to make those processes more consistent with the purposes of the rules themselves). The Law and Society movement's return to "pure" Realism suggested that these adjustments were naive or unworkable. Its suggestion that law was not neutral but rather facilitative of the interests of the wealthy and powerful flew directly in the face of claims that the reconstituted postwar legal order of processes and policies was democratic, egalitarian, and dispassionate.

The Law and Society movement, aided by foundation support,[57] made significant inroads in some academic institutions in the 1960s and 1970s. Notable were Berkeley, where a Center for the Study of Law and Society was established; Wisconsin, which began a program in sociology and law and funded a Law and Society section in the Wisconsin Law Review; Northwestern, which had instituted a joint Ph.D.-J.D. program in law and the social sciences in 1964; and Denver, which in the same year began a program in the administration of justice. All these programs benefitted from the perceived crisis brought about by the apparently dramatic rise in criminal behavior and violence in the early 1960s. The programs may be said to represent the first concentration of interdisciplinary research at American law schools since the 1930s. Social scientists had joined the Columbia and Yale faculties at that time, but in the years after the Second World War interdisciplinary work had almost disappeared, notwithstanding the Law, Science, and Policy movement's program. With the infusion of sociologists and psychologists into law faculties in the 1960s, however, a new pattern of interdisciplinary emphasis was established that has not yet abated.

Of the various institutional centers of the Law and Society movement, Wisconsin, for a variety of reasons, has turned out to be the most influential. Wisconsin had to its advantage a long state tradition of assumed compatibility between empirical research and progressive policymaking, stretching back to the early days of the twentieth century. It also, partly because of that tradition, had closer interdisciplinary cooperation than many other universities, and by the late 1960s had assembled a cluster of persons such as Stewart Macaulay, Jack Ladinsky, Lawrence Friedman, and Robert Rabin, to name only some, who had an abiding interest in the relationship of law to other disciplines. By the end of the 1960s this group of persons had begun to produce a body of scholarship whose emphasis could fairly be described as that reflected in the initial volume of the Law and Society Review. Friedman and Macaulay, in particular, had universalized the theory that legal rules reflected the needs and interests of powerful elites.[58] As Friedman put it in A History of American Law, which appeared in 1973:

> This is a social history of American law. I have tried to fight free of jargon, legal and sociological; but I have surrendered myself wholeheartedly to some of the central insights of social science. . . .
>
> The laws of China, the United States, Nazi Germany, France, and the Union of South Africa reflect the goals and policies of those who call the tune in those societies. Often, when we call law "archaic," we mean that the power system of its society is morally out of tune. But change the power system, and the law too will change. The basic premise of this book is that . . . the strongest ingredient in American law, at any given time, is the present: current emotions, real economic interests, concrete political groups.[59]

In the preface to his History Friedman acknowledged the contributions of Wisconsin, where, he said, "[t]here was an atmosphere of ferment that centered about studies in legal history and in law and the social sciences."[60] But Wisconsin is as important, in this history, for what happened there shortly after the publication of Friedman's book, at the very moment, one might have thought, when the core ideas of the Law and Society movement were about to expand beyond a relatively narrow base of empirically minded law professors and social scientists to the legal academic profession at large. Friedman's book was in a sense an effort in that vein; it presented history as the continuous playing out of a thesis about law and power. In 1977, however, as Friedman's work was settling into the general consciousness of law professors and historians, three events occurred, each of them associated with Wisconsin, that signified an alteration in the intellectual atmosphere of elite legal academic culture, an alteration that was to have negative effects on the influence of the Law and Society movement.

The first two events took place in scholarly literature, and represented efforts on the part of younger scholars who had been part of the Law and Society circle to distinguish themselves from the movement. In a book review of Friedman's *A History of American Law* in the *Wisconsin Law Review,* Mark Tushnet called Friedman's approach "the last great work of the 1950s."[61] Friedman's perspective, Tushnet claimed, ignored "the influence of autonomy on the legal order" and "the ideological functions of the legal order . . . [in] persuading both oppressor and oppressed that their conditions or existence are just."[62] Tushnet's point was that the Law and Society tradition from which Friedman's *History* had emerged had too reflexively treated law as molded by society and had thus wrongly characterized gaps between law on the books and law in action as indications of archaic or unresponsive legal rules. Rules often functioned, Tushnet maintained, to legitimate a calculated unresponsiveness on the part of the legal order. "Material benefits," Tushnet asserted, "have never been equally distributed in American society, and the law serves as a partial explanation, to those who receive less, of why they do."[63] Friedman's *History,* in short, "ignore[d] the ideological functions of law."[64]

Tushnet's review was accompanied by an article in the *Law and Society Review* by David Trubek, another Wisconsin law professor, that called for a "new realism" in the study of law in society.[65] The new realism, for Trubek, consisted of a combination of empirical research and "critical social thought."[66] Trubek outlined an "agenda of critical social inquiry":

> Our program must be concerned with an analysis of the tension between ideals and reality in the legal order, and of the relations between law and society. . . .
> It must be concerned with the gap between the ideals of the law and its reality, between law in the books and law in action, without falling into the belief either that all such gaps are inevitable or that any is merely accidental.[67]

Two features of Trubek's formulation deserve comment. The first is his effort to stress continuity between critical social thought, the Law and Society movement, and Realism by wrapping his agenda in certain evocative phrases. Critical social thought was a "new realism"; its focus was the traditional Realist and Law and Society inquiry into "the gap between . . . law in the books and law in ac-

tion'';[68] it was a perspective in "the basic tradition of the law and society movement,"[69] there was "nothing 'new' about the realism [he was] describ[ing]";[70]
critical social thought was what Realists and Law and Society people "have been
doing all along."[71] Trubek's evocation of continuity can be said to represent the
first effort of Critical Legal Studies to identify itself with the Realist movement.

The second striking feature of Trubek's proposal was its flipping of the normative consequences of discovery of a gap between legal rules as articulated and as
implemented. Friedman had suggested that while such a gap had regularly existed,
it was reparable in either of two ways: through a closer analysis of what purposes
the rules "really" served, in which case the rules could be shown to be doing
quite a good job of furthering the interests of powerful elites; or through a kind
of benign resignation, reflected in Friedman's comment that if the legal system
was not working in one sector, another sector would emerge in which the gap
between ideals and practice was narrower.[72] Trubek suggested, to the contrary,
that gaps were never reparable in those terms because the gaps were never accidental or inevitable, and that merely documenting the existence of gaps in an
"objective" manner was not enough;[73] the scholar had to recognize "the necessity of normative inquiry"[74] and the responsibility for "transcending" legal structures whose purpose was to perpetuate gaps.[75]

The latter emphasis of Trubek's proposal signified an abandonment of the Realist assumption, shared by the Law and Society movement, that empirical research could be conducted from an objective perspective. While Trubek wished to
retain the empirical emphasis of earlier movements, he was quick to equate objective empiricism with "positivism" and to suggest that to rest on a finding that
gaps existed was to legitimate the gaps.[76] The association of empirical research
with positivism thus made two implicit suggestions, which later work in Critical
Legal Studies was to make explicit. The first suggestion was that empirical research legitimated the status quo by implying that the "facts" of the research
were somehow inevitably "there" as part of the permanent "reality" of American
culture. The second, related suggestion was that a scholar could not separate ideology from methodology in empirical, or any, research: to be politically reformist
and methodologically neutral was a contradiction in terms. In making the second
suggestion Trubek had resurrected the fact-value dichotomy again, this time communicating it in the evocative word "positivism."

Of all the issues that were to demarcate Critical Legal Studies from the Law
and Society movement, the association of objective empiricism with positivism
was the most explosive and the most clearly joined. As Critical theorists came to
suggest that by ignoring ideology and autonomy and by not conducting research
from an openly normative and critical perspective, reformist scholars were reinforcing the status quo, some members of the Law and Society movement balked,
refusing to accept such a characterization of their work. The eventual result was
a fragmentation of the Law and Society movement.[77]

In 1977 another development also facilitated the fragmentation of Law and
Society. By that year elite law schools had tenured four persons whose ideological
stance was leftist but whose scholarship had not been empirically oriented in the

Law and Society tradition. The individuals were Morton Horwitz, Duncan Kennedy, and Roberto Unger, all on the Harvard faculty, and Tushnet, who had gained tenure at Wisconsin. The scholarly emphasis of the four had been historical and philosophical, and their methodology had been qualitative and even doctrinal, though not in a traditional sense. While Horwitz's *Transformation of American Law*[78] identified powerful elites whose interests, he argued, had been furthered by changing common law rules, he neither made an empirical effort to particularize the members of those elites nor suggested that their presence was inevitable or accidental. Moreover, his methodology focused on the normative assumptions and content of doctrine, seeking thereby to identify a consciousness embodied in legal rules. Kennedy's, Unger's, and Tushnet's work, although diverse, was similarly interested in legal doctrine, legal consciousness, and the ideological structures in which legal rules were embedded.[79]

The tenuring of those individuals was itself an implicit recognition of the worth of their scholarship by elite law schools, but it had other consequences as well. The presence of Horwitz, Kennedy, Tushnet, and Unger as "accepted" law professors, when coupled with the existence of other tenured academics who were politically left and sympathetic to the Law and Society movement, stimulated an effort to create, as one CLS insider has termed it, "an alliance" between "senior law and society teachers" and "a newly tenured group of Harvard people."[80] The intermediaries facilitating this alliance were Trubek and Tushnet of the Wisconsin faculty and Richard Abel, who had been a law student at Yale with Kennedy and Tushnet in the late sixties and early seventies. The initial vehicle for the alliance was a conference, held at Madison in May 1977, to which selected Law and Society and critical scholars were invited. The organizing committee for that conference included Trubek, Kennedy, Horwitz, Unger, Tushnet, Abel, two additional Wisconsin faculty members, Macaulay and Tom Heller, and Rand Rosenblatt, a member of the faculty of Rutgers Law School at Camden. The list of invitees included such Law and Society types as Marc Galanter, from Wisconsin, and Phillipe Nonet and Jerome Selznick, both from Berkeley. The list also included a group of "ex-students of the Harvard profs," such as Robert Gordon, Karl Klare, William Simon, Mark Kelman, and Peter Gabel, who "were either already in or about to enter law teaching."[81]

As histories of the Critical Legal Studies movement have suggested, the alliance between Law and Society scholars and the newer critical theorists failed to come off. According to one version, "the senior law and society types either didn't show up or left in dismay at the politically radical rhetoric of most participants";[82] according to another, "the attack on social science at the first meeting . . . was so strong that it [engendered a] bitter, fifties-like denunciation" and a resigned estrangement from two Law and Society scholars.[83] The result has been that to the extent there are wings in the current Critical Legal Studies movement, they are represented by other than senior Law and Society scholars. Only Abel and Trubek currently retain a foothold in both CLS and the Law and Society movement, and the latter movement includes members committed to "positivist" empirical research and unsympathetic to Critical theory.[84]

IV The Emergence of Critical Legal Studies

The separation of Critical Legal Studies from the Law and Society movement invites a further look at the intellectual origins of critical theory, for it is clear, notwithstanding the linkage between Law and Society and Critical Legal Studies, that other factors played a part in generating the attack on "positivist" social science that fostered the split. Important among those factors were the critical Marxist scholarship of continental academics[85] and the New Left ideas[86] that had gained currency in American academic circles in the 1960s. The contributions of continentalist theorists have been catalogued as "the indeterminacy of social circumstances . . . the impossibility of deriving intelligible laws of historical change, economic or otherwise," and the significance of "alienation, ideology, historical contingency, and the role of human agency in history."[87] In particular, the continentalists seem to have convinced many critical theorists that systems of ideology and structures of language and discourse, including law, play a significant role in making contingent and indeterminate value judgments appear to be universal and fundamental propositions. They have directed attention to the tacit presuppositions of ideological systems and structures, and suggested that those presuppositions be "unpacked" to reveal their contingent nature.

The memory of 1960s New Left politics, for this same group of scholars, appears to have been recast as historical evidence of a protest against the attempted legitimation of a contingent set of assumptions. As the memory goes, the leadership community that escalated and justified the Vietnam War conceived that war in terms that reflected historically contingent assumptions: while the Vietnam leadership "knew" that the struggle in Southeast Asia was between the free world and the Communist bloc, that division was wholly their creation. The ideology of the war effort, however, functioned to legitimate that conceptualization and to justify committing American soldiers to fight against the Vietcong and the North Vietnamese. The ideology also served to rationalize the deaths of those Americans killed in the fighting as having died fighting for their country. To protest groups in the 1960s, many of whose members were directly affected by the war effort, the leadership's assumptions seemed wrongheaded and their power to conscript unwilling draftees seemed morally dubious.[88] While New Left politics were not limited to protests against the war effort, the apparently naked use of an alien ideological system to determine whether young people lived or died had a galvanizing effect. Both commentators on Critical Legal Studies and members of the movement have noted that most of its principals "came to maturity during the late sixties or early seventies," and "[m]ost began teaching during those years . . . often after a stint in legal services or some other reform-oriented post, as well as participating in the antiwar movement."[89]

One might push the 1960s antiwar experience one step further in explaining the excitement generated by continental critical theory for several members of CLS. The continental theorists suggested that the material conditions in a society, while not unimportant factors in any causal explanations of human conduct, could not be separated from the total ideological gestalt of a culture. Data, in their perspective, were inevitably filtered and given significance by ideological structures. The recast memory of Vietnam may well appear relevant to this insight. One of the dominant characteristics of the Vietnam War leadership was its continual skewing and even falsification of relevant data about the war: statistics were used to demonstrate the validity of the leadership's assumptions and to convey a finite sense that the war effort was succeeding when that conclusion required a rather perverse definition of success. The Vietnam War effort was, in short, an ideological exercise in which empirical data was regularly enlisted in the service of the dominant ideology.

Conclusion: The Future Influence of Critical Legal Studies

Thus a combination of factors internal to and external to American academic life in the 1970s helped define an environment favorable to the emergence of the Critical Legal Studies movement: in that sense CLS is not simply a reincarnation of Realism or the Law and Society movement. But if CLS is unique, it is also part of a continuing intellectual history, the history of twentieth-century American legal scholarship. Where does Critical Legal Studies fit in that history? What place will the movement be occupying (or have occupied) in the year 2000?

If we look at the ideological map of current legal scholarship, it is clear that we have come very far from the consensus of the 1950s, when Law, Science, and Policy and Process Jurisprudence closed ranks to produce broad agreement on what "good" scholarship was and what ideological purposes it served. We now find on the map, reading from right to left, the Law and Economics movement; reconstructed substantive rights theory, with its emphasis on "principles" and, depending on one's political point of view, libertarian or contractarian "rights";[90] so-called mainstream scholarship, a blend of an older analytical tradition, emphasizing doctrinal exegesis and the assumptions of unreconstructed Law, Science, and Policy or Process Jurisprudence; the unreconstructed Law and Society movement, whose practitioners, with a handful of exceptions, now distinguish themselves from Critical Legal Studies as well as from mainstream scholarship;[91] and Critical Legal Studies. No one of these groups can be said to be dominant, but the intellectual energy of elite law schools seems concentrated more in Law and Economics and in Critical Legal Studies than in the other movements. It seems fair to say, in fact, that mainstream scholarship and the Law and Society movement are currently on the defensive and that substantive rights theory is still in the gestation stage.

Critical Legal Studies thus can be said to be currently in a position of visibility and perhaps even prominence, but at the same time to occupy an extreme and perhaps a marginal position on the ideological spectrum. Here the historical links to the Law and Society movement and to Realism are suggestive. The Realists began as academic rebels whose claims were perceived by mainstream scholars as anywhere from infuriating to lunatic, but, despite attacks by previous reformers such as Pound, the Realists penetrated the consciousness of academics, so that by the 1940s only the relativist and nihilist underpinnings of Realism had to be sloughed off, and those under the perhaps unique pressure of a war against Nazis.

Domesticated Realism, in the form of process theory and Law, Science, and Policy, may have betrayed the original Realist impulse, but it was hardly anything like the early twentieth-century conceptualism the Realists sought to dismantle.

Similarly, the Law and Society movement, initially a collection of voices crying in a wilderness, has had its own form of domestication. Interdisciplinary research is now the norm at elite schools; "law and" continues to be the rage. Not only do law faculties have their more than token social scientist faculty members, "traditionalist" scholars regularly do work that involves exploration into other disciplines. One of the ironies of the domestication of the Law and Society movement, in fact, is the great success of a discipline not originally included in the cluster of social sciences identified by the Law and Society Association at its formation: economics. It is ironic that the economists were left out originally; it is also ironic that their stock has dramatically risen as the Law and Society movement has been placed on the defensive. The explanation of the ironies is easy enough: Law and Economics has been, from its modern renaissance in 1960, both ideological and right wing.[92] It has staked its prominence on welfare models of a free-market kind, and those models have become politically resonant. It has also not gotten bogged down in the fact-value dialectic: when its practitioners encounter thorny complexities in the process of designing their models, they label them externalities and put them aside. Contemporary normative Law and Economics is an almost perfect mirror of Langdellian conceptualism: when an outcome is inefficient, just as when a case did not fit a principle, it is rejected as "wrong."

I have suggested elsewhere that domestication is a possible fate of Critical Legal Studies.[93] But what is the feature of the movement most likely to be absorbed into mainstream consciousness and thus domesticated? Here a recapitulation of the linear progression form Realism to Critical Legal Studies is appropriate. The distinctive feature of Realism, I have argued, was the Realists' disinclination to regard the simultaneous pursuit of debunking and empirical social science research as a contradictory enterprise. Empirical research, in their view, was somehow objective and thus immune from deconstructionist analysis. The Law and Society movement, while not deconstructionist, may be said to have held at its origins the deconstructionists' view that empirical inquiry was an objective enterprise: empirical data contained their own inherent truth, which could then be used as a corrective to subjectivist rules and policies.

This very issue—whether empirical research was somehow exempt from the fact-value complexities that invade other areas of intellectual discourse—prompted the split between unreconstructed Law and Society theorists and advocates of Critical Legal Studies. The critique of empirical research as "positivist" has been a technique by which critical theorists have suggested that no immunity can exist: all research is necessarily value laden and political, and to pretend that some is not is to advance claims of neutrality that serve to reinforce the status quo.

At this point the linear relationship between Realism, the Law and Society movement, and Critical Legal Studies becomes severed, and Critical Legal Studies appears as the heir to only one phase of the Realist movement, its deconstructionist phase. The insight of critical theorists that all research is value laden, especially in the less overt sense of being shaped by tacit agreements about its "proper" agenda and direction, is both the single most radical feature of the Critical Legal Studies movement and, because of its radical implications, the feature others will be most anxious to domesticate.

Nonempiricist Critical Legal Studies scholarship has up to this point channeled its energy into two modes. One mode had been deconstruction: the exposure of fundamental contradictions in mainstream doctrines and policies. The other mode has been "transformative" political appeals, beginning with the claim that since the very premises on which mainstream rules and policies have been erected are contingent and self-contradictory, "things could be otherwise." I think that the first mode has made a genuine contribution to twentieth-century intellectual discourse; that it has been wrongly characterized by both supporters and opponents as "trashing"; that it may well be domesticated as "hermeneutics" or some other "fancy" methodological approach; and that it is likely to endure for some time. I think that the second mode cannot be domesticated and may therefore be at once the least vulnerable and the least potentially influential strand of contemporary critical theory. Finally, I think that the question of whether the two modes can be separated is fundamental to an assessment of the future influence of CLS. The remainder of this essay elaborates on those thoughts.

The first mode raises a series of scholarly inquiries that need not be undertaken with the purpose of demonstrating that mainstream scholarship is a self-contradictory enterprise. The idea that ideology takes several forms, from the more explicit forms of policy and principles to the less explicit forms of boundary theory and paradigmatic research designs, is a liberating one. It helps us understand not only why balancing in the first amendment can be seen as contingent or flawed, but why cultural conditions and academic structures define certain questions as relevant and others as marginal or beyond dispute at certain times. Above all, it exposes all scholarship, policymaking, or rule declaration as imprisoned by time and place and thus incapable of being universalized. It prevents any discipline from a claim of either being value free or of searching for truth. It makes history, linguistic analysis, and philosophy more than mere esoterica, and it strips the hardness from the hard and even the harder sciences. It has the potential to transform scholarly inquiry and even conceptions of what knowledge and education are.

But one need not believe in political revolution to endorse the perhaps revolutionary intellectual contribution described above. That is the problem advocates of critical theory face in summoning up the Realists as their progenitor. Critical theorists are not merely carrying out the Realists' unfinished programs. They have gone well beyond Realism, but in ways that do not necessarily require the political radicalism they espouse. Just as we were once "all Realists," in the domesticated sense, we may at some point become "all crits." Then, by definition, radicalism and transformative politics of the kind envisaged by critical theorists will not be possible.

But any total domestication of the Critical Legal Studies movement seems to rest on an assumption that the political messages of the movement are capable of being separated from the methodological messages. My experience up to this point, and my intuitions about the future, incline me to suggest that such a separation is not easy and may not be possible. A movement whose first premise is that law is inseparable from politics is hardly likely to cooperate in any such separation, and the politicization of one segment of a law school may have a ripple effect. Efforts on the part of faculty or students to agree with CLS theory but disagree with CLS politics may come to appear, both to those making such efforts and to others, as schizoid. By asking other faculty and students to take stands on issues, critical theorists may be contributing to the emergence of an attitude among most persons engaged in academic law that scholarship (or teaching) is politics, and politics is scholarship.

If one assumes that separation of the two modes of critical theory is difficult at best, critical theory can be seen as a profoundly destabilizing force in American legal education and, eventually, in American legal culture. In a number of respects critical theory undermines the basic argument implicitly made by law professors to justify their stature: that they "know the law." If law is inseparable from politics and knowledge contingent and culturally determined, "knowing the law" becomes close to synonymous with having current political power. Even if one does not want to transform legal education by throwing out all the reactionary guardians of the hierarchy and replacing them with persons with the proper political consciousness and experience,[94] one may have to concede that political transformations have become possible when the basic grounds justifying deference to statured persons in a profession have been shaken. In a universe populated by students as well as faculty, with a certain degree of intragenerational conflict, attacks on the legitimacy of the elders are necessarily destabilizing.

If the threat of destabilization is taken seriously, a backlash against critical theory may occur. The paradox of the backlash may be that the same tactics employed by opponents of Critical Legal Studies—politicization of scholarship and teaching, agendas and strategies in appointments and other internal matters, and attribution of "lunatic fringe" views to one's political enemies—are those allegedly employed by the critical theorists themselves. If this scenario comes to pass, the "crits" will in a sense have won even if they lose individual battles: they will have transformed the discourse of legal academic life. Furthermore, if a generation of law students experiences that transformed discourse, it requires little imagination to anticipate their entering the profession with a view that law is indeed inseparable from politics.

The nightmarish vision embedded in this scenario, to those in legal academics who deeply believe that law is above or beyond or outside politics, may precipitate efforts to domesticate the critical theory movement. Such efforts have already surfaced. One such effort might be represented in the claim that critical theory provides "an interesting angle on my work"; another by efforts to merge the more "civil" or "acceptable" critical theorists into traditionalist academic power roles, such as chairs of significant committees; another by the simple act of purging the less acceptable members of CLS by tenure denials so that others will "get the message." All these domestication strategies may result in the harnessing of critical theory in ways comparable to the harnessing of the Realists.

But so long as the dramatic dissolution of the fact-value dichotomy, first perpetrated in legal scholarship by the CLS movement, takes hold, I venture to suggest that twentieth-century American legal theory will not likely be the same again. The tacit alliance between empiricism and neutrality will be shattered; the contradiction between value orientation and objective research will be exposed. With the breakup of the fact-value dichotomy, ideology may come to be seen as the dominant force in academic life, and claims to neutrality in scholarship or teaching put decisively on the defensive. If that scenario comes to pass, the 1970s may one day appear to be as important an intellectual watershed for American law and legal thought as Langdell's 1870s.

NOTES

1. *See* LITERARY HISTORY OF THE UNITED STATES xvii-xxiv (R. Spiller ed. 3d ed. 1963).

2. The seminal work here is T. KUHN, THE STRUCTURE OF SCIENTIFIC REVOLUTIONS (2d ed. 1970).

3. *Cf.* White, *The Rise and Fall of Justice Holmes,* 39 U. CHI. L. REV. 51 (1971) (chronicling various images of Justice Holmes).

4. Trubek, *Where the Action Is: Critical Legal Studies and Empiricism,* 36 STAN. L. REV. 575, 577 (1984).

5. Tushnet, *Critical Legal Studies and Constitutional Law: An Essay in Deconstruction,* 36 STAN. L. REV. 623, 626 (1984).

6. Johnson, *Do You Sincerely Want To Be Radical,* 36 STAN. L. REV. 247, 252 (1984).

7. Schwartz, *With Gun and Camera Through Darkest CLS-Land,* 36 STAN. L. REV. 413, 415 (1984).

8. White, *The Inevitability of Critical Legal Studies,* 36 STAN. L. REV. 649 (1984).

9. *Id.* at 650.

10. Schlegel, *Notes Towards an Intimate, Opinionated, and Affectionate History of the Conference on Critical Legal Studies,* 36 STAN. L. REV. 391, 405 (1984).

11. Schlegel, *American Legal Realism and Empirical Social Science: From the Yale Experience,* 28 BUFFALO L. REV. 459, 459 (1979).

12. White, *From Sociological Jurisprudence to Realism: Jurisprudence and Social Change in Early Twentieth-Century America,* 58 VA. L. REV. 999, 1013-27 (1972).

13. The same perception characterized the writings of Roscoe Pound, Joseph Bingham, Arthur Corbin, and other early twentieth-century advocates of sociological jurisprudence. *See id.* at 1000–12.

14. Hohfeld, *Some Fundamental Legal Conceptions as Applied in Judicial Reasoning,* 23 YALE L. J. 16 (1913) was the best known of Hohfeld's works. For a collection of Hohfeld's published and unpublished materials, including *A Vital School of Jurisprudence and Law,* Hohfeld's 1914 model of a "scientific" law school, see W. HOHFELD, FUNDAMENTAL LEGAL CONCEPTIONS (W. Cook ed. 1923).

15. *See* Schlegel, *supra* note 10, at 405 (analyzing Hohfeld). A frequently cited example of Realist scholarship employing the "Hohfeldian flip" is the work of Robert Hale. In three articles in the 1920s Hale argued that certain legal rights taken by established orthodoxy to be natural or absolute, such as freedom of contract or private property, could be seen as the products of a public policy that tacitly allowed some free bargainers to be coerced and some propertied persons to prevail over other nonpropertied persons. Legal rights in some, Hale concluded, produced the absence of rights in others; the tacit policy

choice to prefer entrenched rights could not be seen as a simple deference to the natural order of things. Hale, *Value and Vested Rights*, 27 COLUM. L. REV. 523, 523 (1927); Hale, *Coercion and Distribution in a Supposedly Non-Coercive State*, 38 POL. SCI. Q. 470 (1923); Hale, *Rate Making and the Revision of the Property Concept*, 22 COLUM. L. REV. 209, 212–14 (1922). A trenchant discussion of Hale appears in Peller, *The Metaphysics of American Law*, 73 CALIF. L. REV. 1151, 1232–39 (1985).

16. Llewellyn, *Some Realism About Realism—Responding to Dean Pound*, 44 HARV. L. REV. 1222, 1239 (1931).

17. *Id.*

18. *Cf.* Hale, *Coercion and Distribution in a Supposedly Non-Coercive State, supra* note 15.

19. Hutchins, Report of Acting Dean, 1926–27, Yale Law School Achieves 118–19, *quoted in* Schlegel, *supra* note 11, at 493, 496.

20. Hutchins, Report of Dean, 1927–28, Yale Law School Archives 118, *quoted in* Schlegel, *supra* note 11, at 493.

21. K. LLEWELLYN, THE COMMON LAW TRADITION 122 (1960) (quoting L. Goldschmidt, *preface* to Kritik des Entwurfs eines Handelsgesetzbuchs, Kirit, Zeitschr. f.d. ges. Rechtswissenschaft, Vol. 4, No. 4).

22. The fusion is explicable, that is, if one assumes that social science research was an apolitical, neutral activity. Treating social science as apolitical may have had its own political ramifications: reformist academics in the 1920s may have wanted to avoid too close an identification with collectivist left movements such as Bolshevism. *See generally* D. FELIX, PROTEST: SACCO-VANZETTI AND THE INTELLECTUALS (1965).

23. Llewellyn, *Legal Tradition and Social Science Method*, in ESSAYS ON RESEARCH IN THE SOCIAL SCIENCES 89, 90 (1931) (emphasis in original); *see* Llewellyn, *On the Good, the True, the Beautiful in Law*, 9 U. CHI. L. REV. 224, 250–64 (1942).

24. Pound, *The Call for a Realist Jurisprudence*, 44 HARV. L. REV. 697, 700 (1931).

25. The "fact-value dichotomy" is a shorthand phrase for conveying the simultaneous need, in early and mid-twentieth-century reformist American elite thought, to separate value judgments from empirical observation, lest the observation be biased, and to base value judgments on empirical observations, since objective fact-finding revealed the "realities" of American culture.

26. On Moore see Schlegel, *American Legal Realism and Empirical Social Science: The Singular Case of Underhill Moore*, 29 BUFFALO L. REV. 195 (1980).

27. Lasswell and McDougal, *Legal Education and Public Policy: Professional Training in the Public Interest*, 52 YALE L. J. 203 (1942).

28. *Id.* at 204, 212, 214, 229, 231.

29. Lasswell and McDougal cited works by Hohfeld, Clark, Douglas, Jerome Frank, Herman, Oliphant, and Llewellyn as inspiration for their article. *See id.* at 203–04 nn. 1 & 2.

30. *Id.* at 207, 212.

31. *Id.*

32. *Id.* at 212.

33. *Id.* at 213, 214.

34. *Id.*

35. *Id.* at 203.

36. *Id.* at 211.

37. *Id.*

38. *Id.*

39. *Id.* at 213.

40. Bruce Ackerman, in his recent work RECONSTRUCTING AMERICAN LAW (1984),

called Lasswell and McDougal "brave scholars," and their efforts "heroic," but noted that "the [Law, Science, and Policy] school utterly failed to establish itself as a conversational presence in ongoing professional interchange." *Id.* at 40, 41. Although Ackerman's comments seem largely accurate, the influence of Law, Science, and Policy on public international law has been considerable. For one reaction from a public international law scholar see Moore, *Prolegomenon to the Jurisprudence of Myres McDougal and Harold Lasswell,* 54 VA. L. REV. 662, 663–64 (1968). Moore's point of view has been recently reinforced in Tipson, *The Lasswell-McDougal Public Enterprise,* 14 VA. J. INT'L. L. 535, 535–37 (1974). Nonetheless, it seems fair to say that the Law, Science, and Policy movement's initial goal, to replace Realism as the dominant domestic jurisprudence of American law schools, has not come to fruition.

41. W. TWINING, KARL LLEWELLYN AND THE REALIST MOVEMENT 386 (1973).

42. L. FULLER, THE LAW IN QUEST OF ITSELF (1940); Fuller, *Reason and Fiat in Case Law,* 59 HARV. L. REV. 376, 381–95 (1946).

43. H. HART AND A. SACKS, THE LEGAL PROCESS (1958).

44. *See* G. WHITE, THE AMERICAN JUDICIAL TRADITION 230–96 (1978); White, *The Evolution of Reasoned Elaboration: Jurisprudential Criticism and Social Change,* 59 VA. L. REV. 279, 279–94 (1973).

45. For contemporary examples see Hart, *The Time Chart of the Justices,* 73 HARV. L. REV. 84, 98–99 (1959); Wechsler, *Toward Neutral Principles of Constitutional Law,* 73 HARV. L. REV. 1, 10–20 (1959).

46. The most representative statement of institutional competence theory is H. HART AND A. SACKS, *supra* note 43. For a claim that properly functioning processes had an "inner morality" see L. FULLER, THE MORALITY OF LAW 33–91 (1963).

47. *Cf.* D. BELL, THE END OF IDEOLOGY (1960).

48. For the details see White, *The Evolution of Reasoned Elaboration, supra* note 44, at 294–98.

49. Yegge, *The Law and Society Association to Date,* L. & SOC'Y REV., Nov. 1966, at 3, 4.

50. Schwartz, *From the Editor . . . ,* L. & SOC'Y REV., Nov. 1966, AT 6.

51. *Id.* at 7.

52. Schwartz, *Personnel and Progress in Sociological Research,* L. & SOC'Y REV., June 1967, at 4.

53. *Id.* at 6.

54. Carlin, Howard & Messinger, *Civil Justice and the Poor: Issues for Sociological Research,* L. & SOC'Y REV., Nov. 1966, at 9.

55. *Id.* at 12 (footnotes omitted).

56. *Id.*

57. The Russell Sage Foundation and the Walter E. Meyer Research Institute of Law supported early Law and Society research projects. *See* Yegge, *President's Report,* L. & SOC'Y REV., June 1967, at 7.

58. *See, e.g.,* S. MACAULAY, LAW AND THE BALANCE OF POWER: AUTOMOBILE MANUFACTURERS AND THEIR DEALERS (1966); Friedman, *Legal Culture and Social Development,* L. & SOC'Y REV., Aug. 1969, at 29; Friedman, *Legal Rules and the Process of Social Change,* 19 STAN. L. REV. 786 (1967); Macaulay, *Non-Contractual Relations in Business: A Preliminary Study,* 28 AM. SOC. REV. 55 (1963).

59. L. FRIEDMAN, A HISTORY OF AMERICAN LAW 10, 14 (1973).

60. *Id.* at 11.

61. Tushnet, *Perspectives on the Development of American Law: A Critical Review of Friedman's "A History of American Law,"* 1977 WIS. L. REV. 81, 82.

62. *Id.* at 83.

63. *Id.* at 94.

64. *Id.*

65. Trubek, *Complexity and Contradiction in the Legal Order: Balbus and the Challenge of Critical Social Thought About Law,* 11 L. & Soc'y Rev. 529, 540–45 (1977).

66. *Id.* at 566.

67. *Id.* at 566–67.

68. *Id.* at 567.

69. *Id.* at 568.

70. *Id.*

71. *Id.*

72. "The legal system always 'works'; it always functions. . . . If the courts, for example, are hidebound and ineffective, that merely means some other agency has taken over what courts might otherwise do." L. Friedman, *supra* note 59, at 14.

73. Trubek, *supra* note 65, at 567.

74. *Id.*

75. *Id.*

76. *Id.*

77. *See infra* note 84.

78. M. Horwitz, The Transformation of American Law, 1780–1860, at 253–54 (1977).

79. *See, e.g.,* R. Unger, Knowledge and Politics (1975); Kennedy, *Form and Substance in Private Law Adjudication,* 89 Harv. L. Rev. 1685 (1976); Tushnet, *The American Law of Slavery, 1810–1860,* 10 L. & Soc'y Rev. 119 (1975).

80. 2 Lizard 3 (1985). The *Lizard* is a mimeographed newsletter occasionally distributed around the time of the annual meeting of the Association of American Law Schools. Its contributors are anonymous. The *Lizard's* staff has described itself as "an emanation of a small faction within the critical legal studies movement, sometimes referred to as the True Left." 1 Lizard 3 (1984). The editors of *Lizard* claim that it "does not conform to the general attitude of the membership [of the Conference on Critical Legal Studies], which is far more responsible and boring." *Id.* My claim that the remarks quoted in this sentence are those of an insider should thus be taken in context, although Johnson, *supra* note 6, at 286 n.103, has identified Duncan Kennedy as one of the *Lizard's* editors. The *Lizard* also has a tendency to delight in the vivid overstatement; its characterizations of the meaning of events may reflect that tendency.

81. 2 Lizard 3 (1985); Schlegel, *supra* note 10, at 394–96.

82. 2 Lizard 3 (1985).

83. Schlegel, *supra* note 10, at 408.

84. A recent issue of the *Law and Society Review* provides a starting point for analysis of the current condition of the Law and Society movement. In his presidential address to the Law and Society Association in June 1984, Marc Galanter sought to characterize "[t]he law and society enterprise." Galanter, *The Legal Malaise; or, Justice Observed,* 19 L & Soc'y Rev. 537, 537 (1985). The synopsis of Galanter's remarks was as follows:

During the twenty years since the founding of the Law and Society Association, a distinctive "law and society" discourse has emerged and been instrumental in producing a tremendous increase in systematic knowledge about the law in action. The growth of law and society research has accompanied other changes in the distribution of information about the legal process, including a new legal journalism and greater media coverage that make the law in action more visible to a wider audience. Current distress of legal elites about the hypertrophy of legal institutions is viewed as a reaction to the increased currency of information that discredits the perceived picture of the legal world. The coincidence of structural changes in law with changes in the social institutions of knowledge about law creates the possibility of a more responsive and inquiring legal process.

Id. The vocabulary employed in this synopsis is strikingly evocative. The Law and Society movement is characterized as employing a "distinctive . . . discourse." That discourse has been "institutionalized" and spread to a "multidisciplinary scholarly community." The consequence of the discourse's spreading is a "tremendous increase in systematic knowledge," and the knowledge is about that familiar Realist topic, "the law in action." Law and Society research can be viewed as part of an information explosion that has had the effect of "mak[ing] the law in action more visible."

The "[c]urrent distress of legal elites" about the dysfunctional character of legal institutions can be traced to that information explosion. The information has served to "discredit . . . the received picture of the legal world." The consequence has been changes in both the structure of law and "the social institutions of knowledge about law." The changes augur the promise of a new and "inquiring legal process."

In this vision of the history of the twenty years of Law and Society movement, Law-and-Society-style research is pictured as an important causative factor in fomenting distress about law and legal institutions and in increasing the hope of a more responsive legal process.

The original goals of the movement remain intact and to some extent have been achieved. The vehicle for this achievement, "systematic knowledge," has taken on an objective quality: it is a currency of information, tangible and real like other currencies. This development is so even though the knowledge emerged with the institutionalization of a discourse. A theoretical approach to research has thus evolved, in the vision, into something real: knowledge about how the "law in action" "works." The paragraph thus appears to be an archetypal example of the positivization of an academic theory. In this view, it is no accident that eight pages later in the article Galanter notes that Law and Society discourse "is a discourse with a rich and sometimes uneasy mix of positivist and interpretivist ingredients" exemplified, as "several readers have pointed out," by his own essay. *Id.* at 543 and n. 17.

The invitation Galanter makes in his article, written for a group of peers, is to close ranks around the positivistic vision of the Law and Society movement. Yet at the same time Galanter is well aware that the relationship between scholarly interpretation and positivism is uneasy. I believe that uneasiness to be the central source of potential fragmentation in the current Law and Society movement.

85. Examples would be Theodor Adorno, Jurgen Habermas, Max Horkheimer, and Herbert Marcuse, who were associated with the Frankfurt Institute for Social Research from the 1950s through the 1970s, and, more recently, Michael Foucault and Jacques Derrida, French linguistic philosophers. On the Frankfurt school theorists see G. FRIEDMAN, THE POLITICAL PHILOSOPHY OF THE FRANKFURT SCHOOL (1981). On Derrida and Foucault see Heller, *Structuralism and Critique,* 36 STAN. L. REV. 127 (1984); Peller, *supra* note 15.

86. The phrase "New Left ideas" is difficult to particularize much further. Here it refers to the revived interest in the views of radical theorists such as Antonio Gramsci, George Lukacs, and Jean-Paul Sartre, that took place in the 1960s, an interest that was reinforced by the political examples of Fidel Castro's Cuba and Mao Tse-Tung's China. Two sources with widely different perspectives on the New Left are A. GOULDNER, THE TWO MARXISMS (1980) and W. O'NEILL, COMING APART: AN INFORMAL HISTORY OF AMERICA IN THE 1960's (1971).

87. Schlegel, *supra* note 10, at 393–94 n. 9.

88. This is, of course, a bare-bones summary of a complicated process. For more detail see White, *supra* note 8, at 668–70.

89. Schlegel, *supra* note 10, at 406; *see also* Parker, *The Past of Constitutional Theory—And Its Future,* 42 OHIO ST. L. J. 223, 257 (1981).

90. Thus certain substantive rights theorists, such as Bruce Ackerman, SOCIAL JUSTICE IN THE LIBERAL STATE (1980), Ronald Dworkin, TAKING RIGHTS SERIOUSLY (1977), and John Rawls, A THEORY OF JUSTICE (1971), would be contractarian, and others, such as Robert Nozick, ANARCHY, STATE, AND UTOPIA (1974), Richard Epstein, and David A. J. Richards would be libertarian. The distinction reflects an emphasis on the primacy of deep beliefs in equality (the contractarians) or autonomy (the libertarians).

91. *See supra* note 84.

92. Of course Law and Economics, while it cannot avoid being ideological, could be left wing or centrist as well, as has economic theory in past generations. Since 1960, however, the Law and Economics movement in American law schools has been dominated by welfare economics and public choice theorists who tend to be opposed to governmental distributions of economic benefits and burdens when the capitalist market offers an alternative distribution. Given the commitment of centrist and leftist policies to governmental intervention in the market since the 1930s, this stance among Law and Economics theorists can fairly be characterized as New Right or reactionary, depending on how one feels about it.

93. White, *supra* note 8, at 650–51. My phrase "absorption and conversion" in that article is the equivalent of "domestication" here.

94. *Cf.* D. KENNEDY, LEGAL EDUCATION AND THE REPRODUCTION OF HIERARCHY (1983).

Conclusion

The theme of the concluding section of *Patterns of American Legal Thought*, written about fifteen years ago, was the role of professional constraints on scholarly exploration. When I wrote that section American legal history was in a period of growth, excitement, and conflict. While scholars in the field had a sense that its boundaries were expanding, at the same time distinctive methodological and political perspectives were emerging and to an extent competing with one another for primacy. Two older models of legal history, the model caricatured as "lawyer's legal history" and a model that implicitly trivialized the field by treating the history of the law as the province of the antiquarian, were in the process of disintegration. Legal history was no longer regarded as a "prologue" to contemporary concerns or as a curiosity shop for the scholarly equivalent of antique hunters. It was becoming a discipline capable of attracting scholars of the first rank and of producing scholarship that garnered respect from historians and legal scholars at large. The risks to the field, as I saw them, were that this promise might be squandered by too strident an insistence among practitioners that certain "approved" perspectives and orientations be displayed in any work that was to be taken seriously.

This concern of mine turned out to be misplaced, and in the meantime another, potentially graver, set of risks surfaced. Intimations in the 1970s suggested that the politically correct stance for the legal historian coveting stature would be one or another variety of neo-Marxism, with the methodology of social history and the politics of the 1960s Left figuring prominently. While I would hazard a guess that most American legal historians in the 1990s continue to regard their politics as placing them on the Left, the anticipated monolith of instrumentalist Marxist methodology has not occurred. Instead the leftist methodological tradition has split into two distinct modes, "irrationalist" as well as instrumentalist, and the irrationalist mode, reinforced from an exposure to continental structuralist scholarship, has revived a focus on the history of ideas. This development has "freed up" the field, legitimizing a number of diverse methodological foci, ranging from quantitative studies of the behavior of some legal actors to analyses of the language and rhetorical assumptions of other actors. The field is consequently more diverse and tolerant of alternative methodological perspectives than I would have anticipated. It is for that reason a rich and exciting scholarly community.

At the same time the forces of postmodernism, which doubtless had a hand in the emergence of structuralist methodologies in American legal history in the first place, have precipitated a potential crisis for those who seek to define themselves primarily as people who engage in scholarship. In a world in which the tacit presuppositions of interpretive communities are granted significant power to affect scholarship, in which the idea of universalistic canons of scholarly performance is regarded as problematic, and in which no can say, with any authority, where the constraints that shape the scholarship of a particular age originate, a genuine crisis in scholarly evaluation has occurred, and some have suggested that in a world in which "merit" is an illusion and other evaluative criteria are indeterminate, one might as well abandon the effort to do more than simply write up one's own personal and political prejudices.

That argument is particularly troublesome for those concerned with the "shelf life" of their scholarship. The concept of "shelf life" presumes that some scholarship has qualities that endure over time, making it less easy to ground within the particularistic concerns of a point in history and thus of greater potential significance to future scholars. It may be difficult to define qualities that give a work "shelf life," but the phenomenon is widely recognized among scholars. The argument that evaluative criteria are indeterminate and essentially political and personal might seem to suggest that there is no basis for determining shelf life other than a given scholar's intuitions. If this is so, the concept of scholarship communicating over time seems problematic and fortuitous, a form of preaching to the already converted.

At one level it seems true that scholarship is inescapably personal and political, and at another level it seems true that all writing, scholarly or otherwise, is eventually frozen in time. But the assumption of this collection—indeed the assumption behind any effort to "collect" and publish scholarly work—is that between those two "truths" lies a lot of space for the concept of shelf life to take root. Whether postmodernists or not, scholars continue to distinguish between enduring and ephemeral work, indeed between "distinguished" and "ordinary" work. An ambition of scholars is to penetrate the canons of one's own time and produce work that resonates to subsequent generations.

In his old age Justice Holmes became concerned with professional recognition, which prompted him to form a coterie of new friends, who thought of themselves as "progressive" intellectuals and helped perpetuate his work. Part of Holmes' attraction for this group was that they mistakenly took him for a "progressive." While Holmes' young friends played a part in the growth of his reputation very late in his life and after his death, he has continued to be a figure of scholarly interest well beyond the time when his lack of affinity with early twentieth-century "progressive" ideology was exposed. The continuing interest in Holmes cannot fully be explained on ideological grounds. Nor can the continuing interest in Shakespeare, or Darwin, or Montesquieu, or Plato. That interest has a good deal to do with the shelf life of their work. It has to do with the tacit recognition that despite the inevitabilities of culture, ideology, and change, there are features of a scholarly product that enable it to endure.

In a scholarly world seemingly hemmed in by contingency and impermanency,

I think that the focus of scholarship should be all the more on the goal of shelf life. If one tries to imagine one's work communicating beyond a circle of contemporary readers who are looking for this or that ideological spin to some imagined readership not concerned with the politics of contemporary scholarship, one may be inclined to focus on scholarly messages that could be revisited when their contemporary significance has been lost. Such messages principally have to do with the subject matter dimensions, as distinguished from the authorial dimensions, of scholarly work. It is easy enough to predict that this particular author's ideas will not be of great concern for future generations; my expectations, however, is that subjects such as Holmes or the New Deal or the nature of historical interpretation or judicial review or Critical Legal Studies may be. As such I have tried to write about those subjects so that their continued accessibility over time will not be unduly affected by the potential inaccessibility of my interpretations of them. That effort is what I like to think of as the principal challenge of scholarship.

And so I end this collection holding a perspective not very different from that with which I began it. In a late twentieth-century epistemological universe whose prior stabilizing principles—empiricism and objectivity—have been wisely taken to be foundationless or illusory, one wonders how one can make contributions to historical or jurisprudential scholarship that are more than evanescent. The concern at one level is a valid one: individual constructions of scholarly work become obsolescent with time. At another level, however, the dilemmas of a postmodernist condition are liberating. A recognition that the scholar cannot escape the forces of contingency and contructedness and even obsolescence can prevent one from taking refuge in scholarly perspectives, such as objectivity or ''the search for truth,'' that serve as barriers to an understanding of the nature of scholarly inquiry. The same recognition can serve to focus one's scholarly energy on the achievement of a provisional, modest shelf life for one's work. One would like to catch a glimpse of the eternal; to be touched with fire; to possess the gift of imparting ferment. If one is not granted those blessings, there is nonetheless a good deal left over: a great many subjects to write about; the perennial challenges of excellence and influence.

Index

Abrams v. United States, 93, 121–22

Acheson, Dean, 162, 163, 179

Activism, judicial, 10, 96–97, 107, 220, 223–24, 225, 227, 230, 231, 234–35
  constitutional constraints on, 224–26
  political constraints on, 227–30
  professional constraints on, 231–34

Adair v. United States, 89

Adams, Henry, *History of the United States of America During the Administrations of Thomas Jefferson and James Madison 1801-1816,* 54

Adams, John, 65

Adkins v. Children's Hospital, 89

Agger, Carol, 138

Agricultural Adjustment Administration (AAA), 137–38, 144, 151, 163, 182

Albert Parvin Foundation, 140

Ames, James Barr, 112, 154, 155, 156

Anti-Semitism, 152, 164

Arnold, Fortas, and Porter, 138, 183

Atiyah, Patrick, "The Legacy of Holmes Through English Eyes," 106, 113, 114, 127

Austin, John, 111

Baltimore and Ohio Railroad v. Goodman. See Goodman case

Beale, Joseph, 156

Beard, Charles, 56
  An Economic Interpretation of the Constitution, 54, 55, 57–58

Bentham, Jeremy, 111

Berger, Raoul, 233, 234
  Death Penalties: The Supreme Court's Obstacle Course, 222–23, 224–27, 230, 234

Beveridge, Albert, 60
  The Life of John Marshall, 60–62, 65

Bickel, Alexander, 241, 248*n*.18

Bigelow, Melville, 81

Black, Hugo, 140–41, 225

Bork, Robert, 186, 203*n*.72, 225, 238, 239, 243, 245–46, 247

Bowers v. Hardwick, 9–10, 244

"Brains Trust," the, 178–79

Brandeis, Louis D., 117, 152, 185, 190
  extrajudicial activities of, 144, 182, 185, 186–87
  and Frankfurter, 144, 156, 157, 158, 159, 179, 183
  and his clerks, 138, 162

Brant, Irving, 64

Brennan, William, 140–41

Britt case, 90, 91–92, 94, 95

Brown v. Board of Education, 9, 219, 222, 224, 243, 245

Bryce, James, 79

Burt v. Advertiser Newspaper Co., 83

Capitalism,
  as economic ideology, 133
  identified with Republican party, 133, 136

Cardozo, Benjamin N., 158, 190, 259

Carnegie Endowment for International Peace, 138

Carolene Products case, 231, 232

Chambers, Whittaker, 138, 142, 144

Chase, Samuel, 212

Civil Aeronautics Board, 139, 164

Civil rights movement, 281

Clark, Charles, 278

Clarke, John, 123

Cohen, Benjamin, 177, 178, 180, 188, 190, 194
  ethnic origins, 189, 196*n*.16
  and Frankfurter, 179

Cohen, Morris Raphael, 153

Columbia Law School, 139, 114, 278, 284
  as elite law school, 134
  and its placement network, 135, 163, 164

Communist Party, 138, 144

Conceptualism, 112, 259, 290
Consensus history, 63, 64–65
Constitution, U.S., intellectual context of,
214–15
Constitutional adjudication. *See also* Supreme
Court
as dialectical process, 98–99
Marshallian and Holmesian postures in, 239,
240–45, 246–47
Constitutional text
as constraint on legislature, 241
its role in constitutional interpretation, 37–38,
224, 226
Cooley, Thomas, 81
Corcoran, Thomas C., 145, 164, 178, 180, 188,
194–95
ethnic origins, 134, 189–90, 196n.16
and placement network, 135, 136, 162–63
and Court-packing plan, 140
career of, 140, 173n.86
ethical difficulties of, 140–41, 142
and Frankfurter, 179
Countermajoritarian difficulty, 8, 222, 223,
241–42, 248n.18
Court-packing plan, 140, 144, 185, 192–93
Cowley v. Pulsifer, 81
Critical Legal Studies movement, 11, 14n.9,
107, 117, 127
critique of liberalism, 256, 263–69, 270, 271
and elite legal education, 12–13
and Holmes, Oliver Wendell, Jr., 117, 118,
127
and Law and Society movement, 275, 286–88,
289, 290
and Law, Science, and Policy movement, 289
and Legal Realism, 12, 255–56, 257, 264,
266, 267, 271, 275, 289, 290–91
and postmodernism, 12–13
and Process Jurisprudence, 264–69, 289
and social transformation, 260–63, 270–71,
291
Croly, Herbert, 157

Dartmouth College v. Woodward, 242
Death penalty, constitutionality of, 222, 225
"Debunking," as Realist methodology, 276, 290
Deconstruction, as Critical Legal Studies
methodology, 276, 291
Deference, judicial, 96–97. *See also* Holmes,
Oliver Wendell, Jr.
Derrida, Jacques, 12
Dietrich v. Northhampton, 82
Diggins, John, "Power and Authority in
American History: The Case of Charles A.
Beard and His Critics," 55, 56, 58
Dorfman, Charles, 63, 64

Douglas, William O., 142
and Columbia placement network, 138,
163–64
ethical difficulties, 140, 141
extrajudicial activities of, 140, 185
and Frankfurter, 173–74n.95
Points of Rebellion, 140
pre-Court career, 139–40, 182, 278
as Supreme Court Justice, 140, 243
Dred Scott v. Sandford, 9, 10, 218, 224
Drury, Allen, 183, 184
Advise and Consent, 183

Einstein, Lewis, 87
Eliot, Charles W., 154
Elites, 133, 188
and Critical Legal Studies, 270–71
in academic life, 47–48
and Legal Realism, 268
role of in Framers' conception of the
Constitution, 214–15, 227, 229
Emerson, Ralph Waldo, 75
Engels, Friedrich, 28
Epistemology, 6, 175, 176, 201n.54
Expertise
as ideal among New Dealers, 192
and scholars, 10–11
and twentieth-century jurisprudence, 268

Fact-value dichotomy, 278, 280, 290, 292–93,
294n.25
Faulkner, Robert, *The Jurisprudence of John
Marshall,* 65, 66
Fetus, legal rights of, 82
Fish, Stanley, 41–43, 46, 47
Is There a Text in This Class?, 36–38, 39,
40, 43–44
"Working on the Chain Gang: Interpretation in
Law and Literature," 36, 39, 40–41
Fletcher v. Peck, 242
Formalism, 108
Fortas, Abe, 145, 164, 202n.68
ethical difficulties of, 139, 140, 141, 142,
194, 198n.30
ethnic origins, 138, 189–90, 199n.41
extrajudicial activities of, 182, 187–88,
200n.45
pre-Court career, 138, 163, 173n.95, 182–83,
197–98n.25–26
resignation from the Court, 183–87, 198n.27
as Supreme Court Justice, 138, 176, 183,
199n.35
Frank, Jerome, 125, 163, 164, 190
Law and the Modern Mind, 114
Frankfurter, Felix, 134, 137, 138, 139, 140, 144,
170n.11, 173–74n.95, 190, 243

as advisor to FDR, 178–80, 185
and anti-semitism, 152
and Brandeis, 144, 156, 157, 158, 159, 179,
    183
early career, 151–52, 153–60
extrajudicial activities of, 182, 185, 186–87
at Harvard, 153–56, 158
and Holmes, 87, 110, 123, 156, 157, 158
and House of Truth, 157–58
and idea of meritocracy, 153, 154–56, 165,
    191–92
identifies liberalism with progressivism, 157,
    172*n*.56
involvement with public issues, 159–60
Jewish heritage, 153
and Legal Realism, 166
and placement network, 135, 149, 150–51,
    160–63, 168
and sponsorship, 155–56, 160
appointed to Supreme Court, 158, 169*n*.5
"The Young Men Go to Washington," 151
Freund, Paul, 162, 164
Friedman, Lawrence, 284
    A History of American Law, 18–19, 284–85,
    286
Fuller, Lon, 280

Gabel, Peter, 287
Galanter, Marc, 287
Gellhorn, Walter, 164
Gesell, Gerhard, 163, 164
Gilmore, Grant, 110–11, 112, 125, 129*n*.26
Gitlow v. United States, 93
Goodman case, 90–91, 92, 94, 109, 113
Gordon, Robert, 287
Graham, Philip, 162, 164
Gray, John Chipman, 87, 154, 155, 156
Griswold, Erwin, 162, 163, 164
Griswold v. Connecticut, 243, 245

Haines, Charles Grove, *The Role of the Supreme
    Court in American Government and
    Politics*, 62–63
Hamilton, Walton, 278
Hart, Henry, 109, 162, 164
Harvard Law School, 154, 261
    as elite law school, 134, 150
    and its placement network, 135, 160, 161–63
    as meritocratic institution, 154–55, 191
Harvard University, 154
    attempts to limit number of Jewish students,
    155
Hermeneutics, 291
Hiss, Alger, 145, 177, 194
    career of, 137–38, 164

legal difficulties, 142, 144
and placement network, 162
History. *See also* Legal History
    and bias, 19–21, 25–26, 27, 29
    canon of detachment (objectivity), 3–4, 5, 10,
    18–22
    consensus, 63, 64–65
    as constraint on constitutional interpretation,
    224–25, 226
    criteria for "successful" historical scholarship,
    20–22, 24, 26, 32, 56–57
    generations in, 132
    interpretations in, 51, 52
    interpretations vs. facts, 51–52, 56, 58, 68
    interpretive detachment, 19, 21–22, 29, 31
    levels of communication in, 18–19, 22, 26
    Marxist approaches to, 17, 27–31, 299
    methodology in, 3–6, 17–32, 132
    and presentism, 3, 5, 53
    and the "record," 21, 22–23, 31, 51–53
    revisionist, 50–59, 68–69
    role of professional communities in, 24–26,
    31, 32
    truth detachment, 19, 21–22
    and "truth in history," 17, 21–22, 26, 31–32
Historiography, 50, 53, 57–59
Hofstadter, Richard, *The Progressive Historians:
    Turner, Beard, Parrington*, 56, 64
Hohfeld, Wesley, 276, 293*n*.14–15
Holcombe, Arthur, 63, 64
Holmes, Fanny Dixwell, 88
Holmes, Oliver Wendell, Jr., 75, 154
    as alleged progenitor of Law and Economics,
    117, 127
    as alleged progenitor of Critical Legal Studies,
    117, 118, 127
    as ancestor of Legal Realism, 107, 114–19
    aphorisms and epigrams, 76, 88, 95–96, 106,
    113, 119, 123
    on certainty and predictability as goals in the
    law, 78, 96, 110
    changing reputation, 75, 95–97, 99, 107,
    124–25, 300
    as civil libertarian, 109, 123–24
    and conceptualism, 109, 110, 113, 116, 119,
    126, 127
    and formalism, 108
    Harvard professorship, 79
    as intellectual radical, 108, 126
    on John Marshall and the Marshall Court,
    59–61
    as judge on Supreme Judicial Court of
    Massachusetts, 76, 79–80, 80–87, 94, 110,
    115, 119; torts cases, 80, 81–84
    and juries, 78, 86, 90–91, 92, 109
    marriage, 88

Holmes, Oliver Wendell, Jr., (*continued*)
   as positivist, 109, 118, 239–40
   posture of resignation, 75, 76, 107, 116
   and pragmatism, 111, 112, 113
   as "progressive," 300
   role in private law cases, 107–14, 127
   scholarship, 76–77, 77–78, 79, 80, 85,
      107–14: *The Common Law,* 76, 77, 78, 79,
      80, 81, 88, 90, 107, 112, 113, 114, 115,
      117; on Contracts, 109, 110; *Kent's
      Commentaries,* 108, 109; "Law in Science
      and Science in Law," 85, 115; legal science
      and classification, 77, 111, 127; on
      Property, 110; "The Path of the Law," 85,
      99, 112, 114, 115, 116, 118, 125; "The
      Theory of Torts," 81, 85; on Torts, 77, 78,
      81, 90, 108, 109, 110 (and the negligence
      principle, 77, 78, 81, 109, 112); "Trespass
      and Negligence," 81; use of history in,
      77–78, 111, 112–13
   as Supreme Court Justice, 76, 87–95: and
      attitude of detachment, 88, 109, 125; and
      his clerks, 87, 134, 137, 140, 162; and job
      mentality, 87, 88, 94–95, 97, 99, 127;
      style, 95, 119–23, 124, 127 (facts vs. rules
      in, 119–21); torts cases, 90–93
   theories of judging, 76: activist, 76, 78, 80,
      90–94; affected by experience as state
      judge, 76, 84–86, 118, 127; deferential, 76,
      85, 87, 88–90, 94, 95–97, 109, 125; as an
      exercise in arbitrary linedrawing, 81,
      84–87, 89, 94, 95, 97; role of rights in,
      239–40, 240–44; and "sovereign
      prerogative of choice," 86, 116, 127
   and theory of evolution, 111–13, 113–14,
      116, 119, 125, 127
Hoover, Herbert, 159, 161
Horwitz, Morton J., 287
   Transformation of American Law, 34*n.*28–29,
      287
"House of Truth," 157–58, 172*n.*57, 174*n.*98
House Un-American Activities Committee, 138,
   142, 144
Howe, Mark De Wolfe, 76, 78, 109–10, 115,
   162
Hoyt v. Florida, 9, 10
Hutchins, Robert, 277

Indeterminacy, in modern legal scholarship, 127
Interior Department, 138, 162, 182
Internal Revenue Service, 140, 144
Interpretivism, 222, 233, 250–51*n.*54

Jackson, Robert 95, 243
James, William, 88, 113, 154

Jefferson, Thomas, 60, 65
Jews
   and anti-semitism, 152
   and ethno-cultural assimilation, 152
   "German-Russian" division, 152
   and negative stereotyping, 152
   quotas for at elite institutions, 190
Johnson, Lyndon Baines, 138, 182, 184, 186
Johnson, Philip, 275
Johnson, William, 60
Judicial activism. *See* Activism, judicial
Judicial self-restraint, 246–47
Judicial review. *See also* Supreme Court
   and constraints on judges, 7–9, 208–9, 210,
      218–20
   intraprofessional perspective, 207–11,
      216–17, 217–18; role of text in, 209
   law making vs law finding, 7–8, 208, 216,
      217
   supraprofessional perspective, 207–9, 211,
      218–20; role of text in, 212
Justice Department, 138, 139, 160, 163, 164,
   177

Kaplan, Benjamin, "Encounters with O. W.
   Holmes, Jr.," 106, 113, 114, 119, 121,
   122, 125–26, 127
Katz, Milton, 177, 181
Kellogg, Frederic Rogers, *The Formative Essays
   of Justice Holmes,* 106, 111–13, 114, 117,
   127
Kelman, Mark, 287
Kennan, George, 230
Kennedy, Anthony, 238, 239, 243, 245–46, 247
Kennedy, Duncan, 287
   "Legal Education and the Reproduction of
      Hierarchy," 117
Kennedy, Joseph P., 139
Klare, Karl, 287
Korematsu v. United States, 218
Kuhn, Thomas, S., 22, 23–24, 25, 31–32, 35,
   42, 47, 267, 270
   The Structure of Scientific Revolutions, 12
Kuhnian logic, 35–36, 40
Kurland, Philip, 225

La Follette, Robert, 159
Landis, James M., 162
   career, 138–39, 163, 164, 173*n.*79
   ethical difficulties of, 142, 144–45, 194
   and Frankfurter, 138, 179
   The Administrative Process, 139
Langdell, Christopher Columbus, 110, 111, 112,
   154, 293

Lash, Joseph, 176, 177, 178, 179, 180
  *Dealers and Dreamers: A New Look at the
    New Deal,* 176, 177–81, 188, 189, 194–95
Laski, Harold, 63, 79, 110, 123
Lasswell, Harold, 278–79. *See also* Law,
    Science, and Policy movement
Law
  as objective body of principles, 225, 281
  and politics, 14*n*.9, 225–26, 292
Law and Economics, 11, 107, 289, 290, 298*n*.92
  and Holmes, Oliver Wendell, Jr., 117, 127
Law and Society movement, 290, 296–97*n*.84
  and Critical Legal Studies, 275, 286–88, 289,
    290
  and Law, Science, and Policy movement,
    282, 283
  and Legal Realism, 275, 282, 283, 285–86
  and Process Jurisprudence, 282, 283
  role of Wisconsin Law School in, 284–85
Law schools, elite, 133, 150, 166, 286, 287
Law, Science, and Policy movement, 278,
    294–95*n*.40
  and Critical Legal Studies, 289
  identification of law as social science, 278–79
  and Law and Society movement, 282, 283
  and Legal Realism, 279–80, 282, 290
  and Process Jurisprudence, 281
  role of values in, 279–80
Lawyers, elite, 133, 145, 169*n*.1
Lawyers, New Deal, 133, 169*n*.2
  career patterns of, 134–37
  characteristics of, 136–37
  implicit rules of conduct of, 186
  legal and ethical difficulties of, 137–41, 142,
    143
  and placement networks, 135
  social and ethnic origins of, 133, 134,
    189–90, 200–201*n*.48–53
  symbolic meaning of careers of, 141, 143–46
Legal History, American, 18, 44, 46
  competing models in, 299
  and Critical Legal Studies, 11
  critical standards in. *See* Scholarship, role of
    critical standards in
  emphasis on private law subjects in 76, 107
  evolutionary version of, 257
  methodology in. *See* History, methodology in
  paradigm shifts in, 259
  postmodernism and, 300
  and social history, 284–85, 299
Legalism, 229–30
Legal Realism, 107, 112, 114, 116, 165–66,
    191, 289–90
  and Critical Legal Studies, 12, 255–56, 257,
    264, 266, 267, 271, 275, 276, 285–86

and expertise, 268
and Holmes, Oliver Wendell, Jr., 107, 114–19
and Law, Science, and Policy movement,
    279–80, 282, 290
and law making vs law finding distinction, 281
and Law and Society movement, 275, 282,
    283, 285–86
and the New Deal, 268
and Process Jurisprudence, 264, 266, 268,
    280, 282, 290
and social science, 267–68, 275–78, 282,
    286, 290; and debunking, 276–78, 282,
    294*n*.22. *See also* Fact-value dichotomy
tacit dimension of legal decisionmaking,
    256–57
Legal Tender cases, 224
Lerner, Max, "John Marshall and the Campaign
    of History," 62
Levinson, Sanford, "Law as Literature," 36,
    37–44, 46
Liberalism, 107, 175–76
  Critical Legal Studies critique of, 256,
    263–69, 270, 271
"Liberty of contract," 242, 276–77
Lippmann, Walter, 47, 153, 157, 158, 180
Llewellyn, Karl N., 114, 276, 277, 278
Lochner v. New York, 89, 90, 95, 108, 118, 119,
    224, 241–42, 243
Lowell, A. Lawrence, 160, 173*n*.79
Louchheim, Katie, 134, 136, 177
  *The Making of the New Deal: The Insiders
    Speak,* 134, 136, 177, 181
Lusky, Louis, 231

Macaulay, Stewart, 284, 287
Mahon case, 90, 93, 94, 239–40
Marbury v. Madison, 208, 216, 217, 224
Margold, Nathan, 162, 173*n*.79
Marshall Court, the
  use of labels to describe, 59–64, 65–66
  and "Republicanism," 65–68
Marshall, John, 48*n*.13, 62, 65, 137, 208, 212,
    213
  Holmes on, 59–61
  Life of George Washington, 65
  theory of judging, 239–40, 240–44
Marshall, Thurgood, 238
Marx, Karl, 27–28
Marxism, approaches to history, 17, 27–31, 299
McCulloch v. Maryland, 224, 226
McDougal, Myres, 278–79. *See also* Law,
    Science, and Policy movement
McReynolds, James, 185
Melting pot, theory of ethnic acculturation, 152,
    162

Meritocracy, 135, 143, 153, 154–56, 160, 161,
    165–68, 191
  aristocratic vs. democratic versions, 154, 161
Metaphysical Club, 109, 111
Miller, Arthur Selwyn, 234
  *Toward Increased Judicial Activism: The
    Political Role of the Supreme Court,* 222,
    223, 224, 227–30, 231
Modernism
  and constitutional discourse, 247
  contrast with postmodernism, 193–94,
    202–3*n*.65–66
  contrast with premodernism, 241–42
  as epistemology, 13*n*.2, 176, 188–89, 195,
    201–2*n*.65–66
  and the New Deal, 7, 188–95
Moore, Underhill, 118, 278
Morgan, Donald, 63–64
Murphy, Bruce Alan, 176
  *Fortas: The Rise and Ruin of a Supreme Court
    Justice,* 176, 181–88, 189, 194
  The Brandeis/Frankfurter Connection, 183
Murphy, Walter, 230

Natural rights, as jurisprudential conception, 212,
    215, 239, 240–41
Nelson, William E., "Standards of Criticism,"
    36, 44–46
Neoconceptualism, 259, 260
New Deal, 7, 132, 133, 168, 263
  historiography of, approaches to 175–76,
    177–78, 180–81, 188–95, 202*n*.71
  lawyers in the. *See* Lawyers, New Deal
  and Legal Realism, 118, 268
  and modernism, 7, 188–95
New Republic, The, 159
Nixon, Richard M., 184
Nixon v. Herndon, 93, 94
Nonet, Phillipe, 287
Nozick, Robert, 230

Ogden v. Saunders, 242
Original intent, jurisprudence of. *See*
    Interpretivism
Osborn v. Bank of the United States, 7

Parrington, Vernon, 56, 60
  Main Currents in American Thought, 56,
    61–62
*Patnoude v. New York, New Haven, and
    Hartford Railway,* 84–85, 86, 91
Patsone v. Pennsylvania, 94, 99, 113
Pennsylvania Coal Co. v. Mahon. See Mahon
    case
Perry, Michael, *The Constitution, the Courts,*

    and Human Rights, 222, 223, 224,
    231–34, 234
Pierce, Charles S., 111
Placement networks, 135, 150
  intellectual legacy of, 164–69
  as meritocratic institutions, 166
  as "old boy" network, 160, 164, 168–69
Plessy v. *Ferguson,* 9, 10, 219, 224
Pluralism, 45, 46–47, 228–29, 246
Pollock, Sir Frederick, 83, 87
Popper, Karl, 21–22, 23–24, 31, 51–52
Posner, Richard, 117
Postmodernism, 7, 12–13, 13*n*.2, 14*n*.11, 193,
    202*n*.70, 300
Pound, Roscoe, 155, 160, 173*n*.79, 259, 277,
    289
Pragmatism, Oliver Wendell Holmes, Jr., and,
    111, 112, 113
Prichard, Edward, 139, 142, 145, 162, 164, 194
Process jurisprudence, 117, 123, 259–60,
    281–82
  and Critical Legal Studies, 264–69, 289
  and Law, Society, and Policy, 281
  and Law and Society movement, 282, 283
  and Legal Realism, 264, 266, 268, 280, 282,
    290
  and Liberalism, 264
Progressivism, 157, 201*n*.55

Rauh, Joseph, 162, 164
Rawls, John, 230
Realism. *See* Legal Realism
Reasoned elaboration. *See* Process jurisprudence
Reconstruction Finance Corporation (RFC), 140,
    163, 177
Rehnquist, William, 238, 245
Revisionism. *See* History, revisionist
Riesman, David, 162
Roe v. Wade, 98, 244
Rogat, Yosal, 87, 107, 109, 111, 123–24
Roosevelt, Eleanor, 178
Roosevelt, Franklin Delano, 132, 133, 136, 159,
    161, 162, 177–78, 180, 182, 192, 200*n*.48,
    238; and Frankfurter, 151, 158, 163,
    179–80, 182
Roosevelt, Theodore, 59, 60, 157

Sacco-Vanzetti trial, 159
Scalia, Antonin, 238, 245
Schenck v. United States, 120–22, 224
Scholarship
  "approved," 10–11, 299
  and Critical Legal Studies, 11–12, 13
  elitism v. pluralism in, 47–48
  and history, 10

interpretive (scholarly) communities in, 37,
    39–41, 45–46, 47, 300
role of critical standards in, 36, 43, 44–46,
    46, 48
role of interpretation in, 36, 39–44, 48
role of text in, 36–39; relationship to meaning,
    36, 37–39, 48
Schwimmer case, 93
Securities and Exchange Commission (SEC),
    134, 138, 139, 140, 163, 164, 177, 182
Smith, Al, 159, 190
Sociological jurisprudence, 259
Solicitor General's Office, 138, 164
Sponsorship, role in New Deal placement
    networks, 155–56, 160
Sturges, Wesley, 278
Stimson, Henry, 157
Stone, Harlan Fiske, 139, 164, 231
Story, Joseph, 48*n*.13
Supreme Court of the United States, 140–41. *See
    also* Constitutional adjudication
    and Court-packing plan, 140, 144, 185,
        192–93
    and judicial activism, 220, 224–35
    and judicial review. *See* Judicial review
    nominations to, role of partisan ideology in,
        238–39, 245–46
    as policymaking body, 223, 231
Sutherland, George, 185
Swisher, Carl, 63–64

Taft, William Howard, 157
Taylor, Telford, 162, 164
Thayer, James Bradley, 79, 88, 155, 156
    "The Origin and Scope of the American
        Doctrine of Constitutional Law," 156
Trubek, David, 275, 285–86, 287
Turner, Frederick Jackson, 56
    The Frontier in American History, 54
Tushnet, Mark, 275, 285, 287
Truman, Harry S, 139

Unger, Roberto, 287
*United States v. Carolene Products. See
    Carolene Products* case
United States v. Schwimmer, 93
United Zinc & Chemical Co. v. Britt. See Britt
    case

Valentine, Robert Grosvenor, 157
Van Devanter, Willis, 185
Vetter, Jan, "The Evolution of Holmes: Holmes
    and Evolution," 106, 113, 114, 123–24,
    127
Vietnam, role of war in, 132, 166–67, 268–69,
    288–89
Vinson, Fred, 185

War Labor Policies Board, 152, 158, 160
Warren, Charles, *The Supreme Court in United
    States History,* 60–61
Warren, Earl, 144
Warren, Edward H., 156
Warren Court, 9, 96, 244, 266, 282
Wechsler, Herbert, 164
    "Toward Neutral Principles of Constitutional
        Law," 231–32
White, James Boyd, 36, 37
White, Morton, *Social Thought in America: The
    Revolt Against Formalism,* 108
Wigmore, John, 81, 259
Williston, Samuel, 156
Wilson, Edmund, 47, 179
Wolfson Foundation, 138, 140
Wolfson, Louis, 138, 140
World War I, 158, 160, 189
Wyzanski, Charles, 162, 163, 164, 179

Yale Law School, 138, 139, 163, 182, 278,
    279, 284
    as elite law school, 134
    and its placement network, 135, 163